Dumfries and Galloway
a literary guide

To Ehrich, for use on his trips

Dumfries and Galloway
a literary guide

Julia Muir Watt

Dumfries and Galloway
Libraries, Information and Archives
2000

First published 2000
© publication copyright Dumfries and Galloway Council
© text copyright Julia Muir Watt

The right of Julia Muir Watt to be identified as the author of this work has been asserted by her in accordance with the Copyright, Designs and Patents Act, 1988.

All rights reserved. No part of this work may be reproduced, stored in a retrieval system, or transmitted, in any form or by any means, electronic, mechanical, optical, photocopying, recording or otherwise, without the written permission of Dumfries and Galloway Libraries, Information and Archives.

Design, set and print by Solway Offset Services Limited, Dumfries for the publisher, Dumfries and Galloway Libraries, Information and Archives

ISBN   0 946280 46 0

Dumfries and Galloway Libraries, Information and Archives
Central Support Unit, Catherine Street
Dumfries DG1 1JB

We also publish -

Dumfries and Galloway : *Through the Lens*

Wigtownshire	ISBN 0 946280 21 5	Machars Farm Life	ISBN 0 946280 28 2
Dalbeattie+District	ISBN 0 946280 25 8	Whithorn	ISBN 0 946280 23 1
Thornhill+District	ISBN 0 946280 25 8	South Machars	ISBN 0 946280 24 X
Queen of the South	ISBN 0 946280 27 4	Sanquhar+District	ISBN 0 946280 29 0
South Rhinns	ISBN 0 946280 32 0	Langholm+District	ISBN 0 946280 30 4
Stranraer F C	ISBN 0 946280 37 1	Characters of D+G	ISBN 0 946280 36 3
Dalbeattie Words	ISBN 0 946280 34 7	Maxwelltown	ISBN 0 946280 40 1
Creetown	ISBN 0 946280 41 X	Whithorn+Glasserton	ISBN 0 946280 42 8
		Ruthwell, Cummertrees+Mouswald	ISBN 0 946280 45 2

The titles above are available through local libraries or any good bookshop, priced £2.50 or £3.50 per title including postage+packing from the above address.

Other titles available include-
Ross's Story: 20th Century farming in South West Scotland   ISBN 0 946280 31
Sang o the Nith: a poetic journey through Dumfries and Galloway   ISBN 0 946280 19
From the Serchio to the Solway   ISBN 0 946280 33
The Sound of our Voices, Dumfries and Galloway poetry, prose and photography   ISBN 0 946280 39
Chinese Spare Ribs, young poets of Dumfries and Galloway   ISBN 0 946280 35

A complete list of our publications is available from the above address or on our website at www.dumgal.gov.uk/lia

A Literary Guide

INTRODUCTION

"A suppose ye ken yt Gallowa's hotchin' wi' poets; a wasp-bike's naething till't! gude-for-little doylocks, maist o' them, fond o' onything but wark. Some o' them haes nae objection tae drink, though."

So wrote Robert de Bruce Trotter in his *"Galloway Gossip"* (1901). Though one might dispute Trotter's conclusions, this book has certainly been written in the conviction that both Dumfriesshire and Galloway are indeed "hotchin'" with writers, both known and little known, and that the time is overdue for a new survey. Thomas Murray's *"Literary History of Galloway"* was published in 1822; Malcolm McL Harper and Alexander Trotter, indefatigable preservers of literary tradition in the province, to whom all literary historians owe an inextinguishable debt, wrote either at the end of the nineteenth century or at the very beginning of the twentieth; and Frank Miller wrote his *"Poets of Dumfriesshire"* in 1910. At the beginning of the twenty-first century therefore, and at a time when these books are themselves becoming rarities, there is perhaps a new need for for an assessment of literary achievement in Dumfries and Galloway.

It will be as well to define at the outset what this book is, and what it is not : it contains a survey of one hundred authors, with sufficient details of their lives and works – it is hoped – that would enable the interested reader to embark on a quest of his or her own. The authors are listed not chronologically, or by subject, but geographically, from east to west, so that the guide can be used to travel through the region, either in imagination or on the roads. For use with either method, a map is provided inside the back cover, with indications of the whereabouts of sites with literary associations. The guide is therefore not encyclopaedic; a much larger book would be required to give details of all the authors listed in the catalogues, and no doubt any number of different selections of a hundred authors might have been made, using different principles of selection.

The book is also essentially a guide to the literary *heritage* of Dumfries and Galloway; it does not include details of authors still actively at work in the region, and whose corpus of work is still in process of formation. Some apology may be thought necessary for what may seem a reactionary, or unduly nostalgic exclusion. The first reason is the lame, but compelling one, that simply on grounds of space alone and in order to produce a guide which was not too unwieldy, contemporary authors had to be set on one side. The second relates to the fact that this book was in part conceived as a rescue for authors, some of whom at least are at risk of falling into oblivion, whose works are becoming difficult, if not almost impossible, to find, at least for the average reader with an interest in the region's literature. Many of us will have passed by, perhaps sometimes with vague curiosity, plaques and obelisks placed in frequently obscure and surprising areas of Dumfries and Galloway, which often prove to have been erected by devotees of the time to famous sons of the parish. Anyone who has looked further into the matter will testify that it takes time and energy to search out biographical details, copies of works and information about dates, which are often scattered in obscure periodicals, old newspapers, or in collections of rare books. For this reason, dates and biographies, sometimes garnered with difficulty, have been included for each author listed, along with a photograph, engraving or portrait where at all possible. Lastly, and perhaps most contentiously, it is possible to question whether contemporary authors stand in quite the same relationship to their locality as those did, who wrote in the last centuries; not because of some defect, lower standard, or lack of care on the part of these writers, but because, in virtue of mobility, technologies, the pace and extent of cultural interchanges, and sheer secular doubt, none of us stand in relation to locality as we once might have done.

That contention brings us to the difficult question as to how a "Dumfries and Galloway author" may be defined, and is defined for the purposes of this book. I have taken the conscious decision – once again, a choice which might have been otherwise – to select those authors who have some organic connection with the region: that is to say, those who have been born, or lived, or been educated here, and not those who have written, however expertly and excellently, about it, without that intimacy. To justify this choice by postulating some essence or spirit of place would

A Literary Guide

be to burden oneself with much unattractive metaphysical baggage; even to explain how writers are influenced by their heredity is a matter of great difficulty and controversy. Reading through this selection, however, one may be struck by the extent to which many, if not all, kept up an affectionate and umbilical connection with their place of origin, and many, indeed, chose to make its landscape, characters and – perhaps most significantly – its language, the subject, if not the obsession, of their works. There is little doubt that, during the centuries when the bulk of authors here listed were writing, and for all sorts of social and economic reasons, Scotland was a country of intense localisms. It is even significant that, until now, the histories written of the literature in the region have always kept Dumfriesshire and Galloway rigidly distinct, as the defined, consciously and historically, separate counties they were (and are) perceived to be. One thinks, in this context, of the welcome Edward Irving gave to Thomas Carlyle, when both were teaching in far-away Kirkcaldy, when he said: "Two Annandale men cannot be strangers in Fife": there was no question about the immediate self-identification and mutual recognition of each as an "Annandale" - not Dumfriesshire - man. Or one can consider that, when Allan Cunningham saw the distressed state of William Nicholson in London, he directed him, as a matter of course, to an expatriate community of Dumfriesshire men and Gallovidians, who helped him find a passage home. Apart from the web of personal relationships, assistance with finding career opportunities and mutual financial aid, which already account for complex links between many authors, many consciously shared the speaking and recording of local dialect; and there was the awareness of the literary history of the region, which involved both literary debts acquired by reading and imitation, and the deliberate re-publishing of old texts: all of these, one may argue, begin to amount to the density of a regional literary tradition. It is for this reason, that a deliberate attempt has been made here to mention personal and literary acquaintances, and, in recognition of this complexity, cross-references within the articles to other authors within the book have been highlighted.

The range of subject-matter and the types of authorship have been chosen to represent as broad a spectrum as possible: not only the "high literature" of imaginative prose and poetry, but legal and religious treatises, medical works, natural history, journalism, science and exploration all receive their mention here, in the belief that it is not one mode of literary production which goes to make up a living literary culture. Likewise, as far as quality and productivity are concerned, the book is concerned not only with those in the highest rank, whose works went to enrich the general stream of world literature: we are also interested in those who published perhaps only one book, never reprinted; those who were in the middle rank of literature or published works only with local reference; or those who, like Stewart Lewis and Susannah Hawkins, sold their poetry from a pack and represented, perhaps, the strand of literature which was the most popular and widely distributed at the time.

That question of literary standing brings us to what touches local loyalties to the quick, even today when we are less prone to celebratory banquets and the pieties of dedicatory plaques: how should we assess the contribution of Dumfries and Galloway to Scottish literary effort and writing as a whole? It is not difficult to pick out the names of those who stand here as the great innovators in their fields: Burns, Carlyle, MacDiarmid, Clerk Maxwell and Stair. It is interesting that we feel the constant need to assess ourselves in these terms, and that we pay this often unwitting tribute to literature and the achievements of the mind, that we feel somehow better for the recitation of such roll-calls of the famous. But one may perhaps avoid an undue concentration on literary heroes and hero-worship by looking at the broad sweep of movements in Scottish literature and the way in which writers from the area have participated in these.

With a broad and unscholarly brush, we can outline nine main phases, which are relevant to the literature of the region: the last gasp of late mediaeval Scots poetry under James VI and I; religious and controversial literature in the times of the Covenant; political and legal literature emerging out of the Union; popular ballads, including Jacobite material; the period of the "Edinburgh Reviewers" and the Enlightenment; Burns, Scott and the revival of the ideal of Scotland; the emergence of the "Kailyard" and of historical romance; and the rejection of these by the Scottish renaissance movement. There are representatives of all of these phases in the following pages: sometimes, these are the chief protagonists,

A Literary Guide

like SR Crockett in the Kailyard school, or Rutherford in the seventeenth century literature of religious protest. For other periods, we have only echoes and hints of an impact from a movement whose main players lived and worked elsewhere: we are constantly aware, for example, of the influence of Scott, from his correspondents and informants in Galloway, from those who were helped by his characteristic generosity, or from the number of idealistic young men, who walked to Edinburgh to buy *"Marmion"* on scanty wages, or to catch a glimpse of the Great Unknown. It is not surprising, either, to find that numbers of students who went from Dumfries and Galloway to Edinburgh at the height of the Enlightenment were caught up in the influences of the circle surrounding the *"Edinburgh Review"*, but it may give one pause to think that a notable cluster of these came from the area between Minnigaff and Kirkmabreck parishes and the remote and hardly populous Glenkens; Thomas Brown, Rev. William Gillespie, and Alexander Murray. At least by lengthening the chronology from which we take our selection, by broadening the geography and by selecting the disciplines and modes of writing with broad-mindedness, we may hope to arrive at a more balanced and less anxious view of the region's achievement than that which may be reached by focussing simply on its "great men".

There are other social and economic conclusions which can be drawn from the selection: not surprisingly, in days when the ministry was the aim of the talented pupil and the study of divinity was the summit of a university career, local ministers have contributed their fair share to the literature of the counties. They and local doctors must have acted as the nucleus of educated society in the parishes, sometimes in contact with the owners of estates, who themselves often had the learning, wealth and leisure for writing: one thinks here of the medical and literary dynasty of the Trotter family, and of the two significant writers produced by the family of the Maxwells of Monreith. At the opposite end of the spectrum, there is no doubting the virility and regional uniqueness of the spoken language, and of the tradition of song, story-telling and superstition belonging to the wider population: when representatives of the oral tradition did publish, the results could be classic literature, as in the case of William Nicholson. In other cases, the nuances of local language and poetry were recorded by those who were not themselves directly part of

Dumfries and Galloway

the tradition: those who documented, transmuted, borrowed or even faked, popular language and culture included writers as various as Burns, Allan Cunningham, Denniston and Barbour, Crockett and the Trotters, each with his own intention and degree of success.

Having attempted to justify the concept of a literary guide to Dumfries and Galloway, and the particular selection chosen herein, it remains for me to say that much of the research for this book was carried out at the library of Broughton House, Kirkcudbright. The origins of the library date to the purchase of a book collection belonging to the important publisher and printer, Thomas Fraser of Dalbeattie, by the artist, EA Hornel, whose home was at Broughton House. From 1919 onwards, Hornel began an intensive campaign of collecting: he spared no means to acquire any book by a writer with connections in Dumfries and Galloway, or who had written about it. The value of this archive to the cultural history and life of the area cannot be overstated. The library, which is now owned by the National Trust for Scotland, amounts to some 25,000 books.

Jim Allan, librarian, and Frances Scott, property manager, afforded generous access to the Broughton House collection , and Jim Allan made suggestions, researched, advised, read, checked, provided bibliographical information and illustrations, and, in short, contributed much to the book, saving its errors. My colleagues and friends, Lesley Murray and Joseph Whiteford, helped produce illustrations and provided me with pleasant memories of many trips of literary discovery and other wild goose chases, across the countryside of Dumfries and Galloway, during the summer of 1999. My thanks also go to Ian Barr, of the Wigtown Book Town Company, for believing in this project at its inception; and to Jack Hunter, who first – and perhaps unwittingly – persuaded me, as he has done many others, that there was a real fascination in the literature of Dumfries and Galloway.

Julia H Muir Watt, April 2000

A Literary Guide

CONTENTS

Introduction   v

Dumfriesshire

Neill, A S	1
Macdiarmid, Hugh (Grieve, C M)	5
Mickle, W J	12
Malcolm, Sir John	16
Telford, Thomas	22
Irving, Edward	28
Blacklock, Thomas	32
Clapperton, Hugh	36
Miller, Frank	40
Dick, Reverend C H, and Buchan, John	43
Jardine, Sir William	48
Carlyle, Thomas	50
Lewis, Stewart	58
Sharpe, Charles Kirkpatrick	61
Duncan, Reverend Henry	64
Hawkins, Susannah	70
Neilson, George	72
Burns, Robert	75
Barrie, J M	81
Riddell, Maria	84
Bell, Benjamin	88
Richardson, Sir John	91
MacKenna, R W	95
McDowall, William	98
Aird, Thomas	102
McDiarmid, John	105
Mayne, John	108
Wood, John Maxwell	111
Cunningham, Allan	114
Service, Robert	119
Paterson, William	122
Beattie, William	127

Dumfries and Galloway

Morrison, John	131
Gerrond, John	134
Currie, James	137
Thomson, Joseph	143
Gladstone, Hugh S	149
Hewison, J K	152
Waugh, Joseph Laing	155
Wilson, Tom and Wilson, William	158
Simpson, Reverend Robert	161
Hyslop, James	164
Anderson, Alexander	168
Rae, Peter	172

Stewartry of Kirkcudbright

Trotter, Robert de Bruce	176
Trotter, Dr James	180
Heughan, Joseph	183
Muirhead, Dr James	185
Kerr, Robert	188
Maxwell, James Clerk	191
Wilson, John and Wilson, Samuel	196
Harper, Malcolm M	199
Crockett, Samuel R	202
Reid, Professor H M B	208
Heron, Robert	211
Gillespie, Reverend W	216
Lowe, John	219
Barbour, John Gordon	221
Landsborough, Reverend David	224
Trotter, Robert	227
Trotter, Isabella	230
Trotter, Alexander	232
Clark-Kennedy, Captain A W M	235
Macadam, John Loudon	237
Sayers, Dorothy Leigh	242
Mackenzie, W	245
Nicholson, John	249
Douglas, Thomas, 5th Earl of Selkirk	252

A Literary Guide

Montgomerie, Alexander	258
Mactaggart, John	260
Nicholson, William	264
Murray, Thomas	268
Denniston, Captain J M	271
Rutherford, Reverend Samuel	274
Brown, Thomas	279
Hannay, Patrick	283

Wigtownshire

Train, Joseph	286
McCormick, Andrew	292
Murray, Alexander	295
McNeillie, John	301
Ruskin, John	306
McKerlie, P H	309
Fraser, Gordon	312
Lauderdale, John	315
Robinson, Samuel	318
Symson, Andrew	320
McCulloch, J R	324
Latinus Stone	329
Donnan, Jeanie	332
Cannon, J F	334
Maxwell, Sir Herbert	336
Maxwell, Gavin	340
Patrick, John, 3rd Marquess of Bute	348
Vaus, Patrick	353
Dalrymple, James, 1st Viscount Stair	355
Ross, Sir James Clerk and Ross, Sir John	361
Agnew, Sir Andrew	370
Barke, James	373
Todd, William	376

Index

Index to Authors	381

Dumfries and Galloway

A Literary Guide

Alexander Sutherland Neill
1883-1973
Gretna

AS Neill, alternately regarded as apostle of educational reform or as dangerous crank, was one of the first, and the most prominent of British theorists to break away from the Victorian model of schooling and to develop a theory of child development and education which drew on the thinking of Freud, and later of Wilhelm Reich and Homer Lane. The radicalisation of his thinking about teaching and the child began while he was a headmaster at Gretna, and resulted in his eventual establishment of the famous "Summerhill School", the first school in the world to be based on "self-governing" principles.

Neill at twenty-five.

AS Neill was born at Forfar in Angus in 1883. His parents were both teachers and had met during their years of training; his father was the schoolmaster at Kingsmuir. He gives a detailed account of his country childhood in his autobiography *Neill, Neill, Orange Peel!* where the sternness of his father, who communicated little with his children, the Calvinistic religious background and the social aspirations of his mother, proved a crippling mixture for young Neill, who failed to thrive at school. Unlike his brothers, he did not go to Forfar Academy, and had little taste for the learning which was expected of the Neill boys. Neill was ultimately sent to be a junior clerk in the office of W&B Cowan, gas meter manufacturers in Edinburgh. When he suffered a crisis of homesickness, he was entered into the drapery business closer to home, as an apprentice, but the long hours of standing and walking to work affected his feet. His mother suggested a career in teaching, as assistant to his father, who unsmilingly commented that he was fit for nothing else. For four years, he was Student

1

Teacher in Kingsmuir, learnt mathematics from a talented teacher at the Academy in Forfar, and was inspired by **JM Barrie's** stories and novels, whose home town was only seven miles away. When he was qualified, he obtained a teaching post at Bonnyrigg near Edinburgh, and then at Kingskettle in Fife, where he saw the bad effects of discipline rigorously and unthinkingly enforced: everyone was "insincere, inhuman, fearful". His next job at Newport, Dundee, was at a school with a more relaxed regime, and he looked back with enjoyment at his time there. He began studying for university entrance, and left Newport in 1908 to lodge with his brother, who was also a student at Edinburgh. He began by studying chemistry and natural philosophy, but then switched to Honours English and his first literary efforts were as editor of *The Student*, and providing some comic sketches for the *Glasgow Herald*. Since he regarded teaching as a last resort, he applied for a job editing an encyclopaedia with an Edinburgh publisher, was transferred to London, and just as he had acquired a post as art editor for a magazine, the 1914 war cut short his career in journalism. Since he was deemed unfit, after experiencing a dangerous blood clot to the leg, he took a job with Gretna Green school, where he was left in effective charge of the school. It was here that he began recording his thoughts about education in what was later published as *A Dominie's Log*. He began to move leftwards in politics, and to develop alternatives to traditional discipline and teaching methods: in Gretna, the changes were noticed, not always favourably. Neill was eventually passed fit for military service in 1917 at Dumfries, and joined the Royal Scots Fusiliers. In the army, as at his father's school, he suffered from a feeling of absolute powerlessness, which shaped his ideas about authority and fear. His mathematical knowledge was an advantage, when he was called upon to study and teach map-making and lines of fire, but, while awaiting his call to the front, he collapsed with neurasthenia and was recommended to give up his commission. By this time, Neill had already made contact with Homer Lane's "Little Commonwealth" for young delinquents, but, since it had been closed by the time his army service was over, he obtained a post at the King Alfred's School, in North London. The school was considered advanced for its day, but Neill, under the impact of being analysed by Homer Lane, began to feel that its freedom existed in name only. When he had tried and failed in an experiment in "self-government" at the King Alfred's, he resigned. He found work

A Literary Guide

editing *The New Era* journal. In 1921, he was invited to travel abroad, and joined a group which founded the Internationalschule at Hellerau; it was there he met Frau Doktor Neustadter, who was to become his first wife. Neill's own part of the school moved to the Tyrol, because of a revolution in Saxony in 1923, but after the Austrian government made the teaching of religion compulsory, Neill left for Britain, and in 1924, he rented a house in Lyme Regis, Dorset, called Summerhill. The school, which struggled for its existence in its early years, moved to Leiston, Suffolk, and during World War II moved temporarily to Ffestiniog in Wales. Neill's wife died in 1944, and, after experiencing problems with the building in Wales, the Welsh weather and Welsh religion, he returned with relief to Leiston in 1945. Neill continued his European contacts, meeting Wilhelm Stekel and being analysed by him in Vienna, but he moved away from conventional analysis, when he concluded that, under a free regime, both those children who came to analysis and those who did not were "cured", so that "freedom, not analysis, was the active agent". He was more impressed by the societal analysis of Wilhelm Reich, who gave Neill sessions of "vegetotherapy" in Oslo. By the 1930's, Summerhill had become well-known, having its greatest impact in the US, Germany and Japan, where his books were best-sellers. Initially, the school specialised in "problem children", but the emphasis changed, as Neill developed a slightly less optimistic view as to what factors in a child's psychology could be changed, and as he perceived that "normal" children could benefit from his therapy of freedom. Many schools sprang up in imitation of Summerhill principles, and Kilquhanity School in Galloway was influenced by Neill's theories, but Neill did not franchise his idea. He died in 1973 at Aldeburgh, Sussex, and the school was continued by his second wife, Ena, and his daughter, Zoe Readhead.

* * *

Neill published over twenty books and *Summerhill: a Radical Approach to Child-Rearing* provided a theoretical underpinning for the generation bringing up children in the liberal climate of the 1960's; it remains on the prescribed reading list in American colleges of education. The most important of Neill's writings, from the point of view of this book, is *A Dominie's Log*, which he wrote at Gretna, because the Scottish educational code forbade the entry of personal notes in the official teacher's log-book. (Its sequel *A Dominie Dismissed*, composed during his army service, is fictional). Neill's unofficial record, which charts the progressive radicalisation of his thinking, was published in 1915. From his first despair, engendered by the apparent hopelessness of educating children destined, without appeal, to be farm-labourers, Neill develops a commitment to bring out the self-reliance and honesty of his "bairns", over and above all formal education. The log records the inventive ways in which Neill experimented with stretching the boundaries of what the children could understand, his doubts and introspections, his use of humour to make "a bairn think all the time", his innovations with discipline and his battles with the establishment and the parents. The log shows that the main elements of Neill's thinking on education, formulated in reaction to his own early and negative experience, were in place during his Gretna days, and that it only required the stimulus of seeing Homer Lane's experimental community to develop into the fully-fledged theory of "self-regulation". This notion influenced Neill in developing his regime of non-compulsory lessons at Summerhill, for which it became famous, and of governing the community through the "Meeting", where pupils and teachers have equal rights. Although Neill remained agnostic about theories of psychology and preferred to be regarded as a practitioner rather than a theorist, the notion of a child's radical goodness and ability to develop through freedom can be fruitfully compared with the ideas of the Enlightenment, and particularly with Jean-Jacques Rousseau's *Emile*. Neill's prose may claim to be unvarnished – "the important thing is <u>what</u> is said, not <u>how</u>" – but the honesty with which the oppressiveness of his Forfarshire childhood and his reactions to his family are described, make his autobiography *Neill, Neill, Orange Peel!* a classic of confessional literature.

BIBLIOGRAPHY:
A Dominie's Log (1915); A Dominie Dismissed (1917); Summerhill: a Radical Approach to Child-Rearing (1960); *Neill, Neill, Orange Peel!* (1972)

A Literary Guide

Hugh MacDiarmid
(pseudonym of Christopher Murray Grieve)
1892-1978
Langholm

Christopher Murray Grieve, who later took the pseudonym of "Hugh MacDiarmid", born at Langholm, is the principal Scottish poet of the twentieth century, ranking with James Joyce for his experimentation with modernist forms and with language. MacDiarmid's impact on the use of Scots language was as innovative and as seminal as that of Burns in the eighteenth century. His aim was to overcome much of the mediocrity of the Scots prose and poetry of the nineteenth century, particularly that which represented the worst of the sentimentalism of the "Kailyard" school, and to develop Scots as a vehicle for a highly intellectual form of meditation. His connection with Langholm, though often ambivalently expressed, was never abandoned and his works are besprinkled with references to his childhood home.

Hugh MacDiarmid

Christopher Murray Grieve was born at what is now 17 Arkinholm Terrace, Langholm; he had family at Wauchope, Eskdalemuir, Middlebie, Dalbeattie and Tundergarth. The geographical locations of his childhood in and around Langholm were to become vehicles for metaphysical speculation in his later work and his autobiography *Lucky Poet* returns constantly to its scenes. He wrote: "After journeying over most of Scotland, England and central, southern and eastern Europe, as well as America, Siberia and China, I am of the opinion that my 'native place' – the Muckle Toon of Langholm, in Dumfriesshire – is the bonniest place I know.." He was also to claim that several previous authors and famous sons of Dumfriesshire and Galloway influenced him: **Thomas Telford**

5

endowed Langholm Library, where he was to become an avid reader; Grieve supported **William Mickle's** claims to be the author of *There's Nae Luck aboot the Hoose*; and in *In Memoriam James Joyce*, he claims to be related to the linguist **Alexander Murray**, whose remarkable linguistic abilities would no doubt have appealed to Grieve. His father became a postman in Langholm, and the family moved to Henry Street; Grieve attended the infant school at Langholm, and thereafter the primary school at Langholm Academy. They moved to the Library Buildings in Langholm, where the ceremony of the Common Riding is centred, and where Grieve, whose mother had the keys to the library, was able to read voraciously, filling a "big washing-basket" with books. The Grieves were devoutly religious, and notions of self-sacrifice and salvation appear in MacDiarmid's later poetry. Their minister, TS Cairncross, was a poet and wrote a satirical book *Blawearie*, about the small Langholm community. Grieve was also fortunate in his English teacher, FG Scott, who became a talented composer and was later to set MacDiarmid lyrics to music, and to receive a dedication in MacDiarmid's masterpiece, *A Drunk Man Looks at the Thistle*, 1926. At 16, Grieve joined the Independent Labour Party, at the beginning of a turbulent and often bewildering political career, which was to lead him to Scottish Nationalism and to Communism, and signed up for the territorial Army. Leaving for Edinburgh, where he was to attend Broughton Junior Student Centre, to train as a teacher, he published *Memories of Langholm*, under a pseudonym. At Broughton, he acquired a literary reputation through the school magazine, fell under the Nietzschean and evangelical Christian influences of his teacher, George Ogilvie, and joined the university Fabian Society. After a scandal, which involved the apparent theft of some books, Grieve left Broughton, and turned to journalism. His father, who appears in *Fatherless in Boyhood* and *At My Father's Grave*, died in 1910. Grieve's post at the *Edinburgh Evening Dispatch* was also to end in ignominious dismissal, and he left for Wales. There, the turbulent politics of Ebbw Vale suited him, and Grieve met Keir Hardie, whose joint inspirations of Burns and the Bible appealed to him. Once again, however, he argued with the editorial committee of his newspaper, and, after a spell in Langholm, began a series of jobs in newspapers in Clydebank, Cupar, and Forfar, where he began to drink heavily. From 1915-1919 he was engaged in war service with the RAMC, and travelled to Thessalonica, where he was sergeant-caterer for the mess. During these years, he had been inspired by the Easter Rising in Ireland, 1916, and by the Bolshevik Revolution, and was also taking an interest in Scottish Neo-Catholicism. He began work on essays which were to become part of the *Annals of the Five Senses*. He arrived home in 1918 as a pronounced Anglophobe. On arrival, he proposed to Margaret "Peggy" Skinner, whom he had met in Cupar. At this time too, he had his first taste of literary approval from an authority, when John Buchan (see entry under **CH Dick**) expressed appreciation of his wartime *Voice from Macedonia*; later Buchan was to write a perceptive preface to *Sangschaw*. In 1919, he was at work on *Northern Numbers*, which was to include work by established poets such as John Buchan and Neil Munro, and to provide a stepping stone towards fame for the unknown Christopher Grieve. What did attract attention at the time was Grieve's rather exaggerated editorial assertion that the book was the concerted work of a group, which he boldly claimed represented a new force in Scottish literature. By 1920, Grieve and his wife had moved to a remote shooting lodge in Ross and Cromarty, owned by Mr Perrins of Worcester Sauce fame and fortune, where Grieve occupied the rather unlikely post of caretaker for shooting parties, and also taught at an estate school. At this point in his literary career, Grieve had little time for those proposing the revival of Scots as a literary language, and had a much greater regard for literary English as a vehicle for poetic expression. When he moved to Montrose, where he worked on the *Montrose Review*, a new volume of *Northern Numbers* brought him into contact with Lewis Spence, a mythologist and folklorist, who was gradually moving to a pro-independence stance in Scottish Nationalism. 1922 was a momentous year for Grieve and for literature: Spence entered into a public defence of the Scots of Henryson, Douglas and Dunbar, and the two definitive works of modernism appeared – James Joyce published *Ulysses* and TS Eliot, *The Wasteland*. By the time of the publication of Grieve's *The Scottish Chapbook*, Grieve was articulating support for the development of Scots verse and theatre, and published in it his first pseudonymous work under the Gaelic name, "MacDiarmid". His first Scots verse, such as *The Watergaw*, which meditates his father's death, marked the start of a rapid development, during which Grieve studied Jamieson's Scots Dictionary and classic Scots poets, such as Gavin Douglas. His political development was also rapid, and he became active in the Scottish Home Rule Association, and in his *Scottish Nation* occasionally went as far as advocating a "Scottish Fascism". The *Annals of the Five Senses* was published in 1923, dedicated to John Buchan, and consisted of poems and sketches. It was Buchan, who in the preface to *Sangschaw*, noted the watershed marked by MacDiarmid's revolt against sentimentalism in Scots verse: he is "at once reactionary and revolutionary. He would treat Scots as a living language and apply it to matters which have been foreign to it since the sixteenth century. Since there is no canon of the vernacular, he makes his own, as Burns did, and borrows words and idioms from the old masters". By the mid-1920's, the concept of a Scottish Renaissance was well under way, with MacDiarmid using the war-cry "Dunbar, not Burns!" to deflate uncritical Burns worship. He also attempted to introduce a certain internationalism to Scottish literature, including his own masters, Dostoevskii and Nietszche, and to promote the work of other radical Scots thinkers, such as the educational theorist, **AS Neill**. 1926 saw the culmination of MacDiarmid's growing literary self-assurance, with the publication of *A Drunk Man looks at the Thistle*, a poem of 2685 lines, which charts a metaphysical progression of Scotland's fall and spiritual regeneration. The importance of the poem was grasped by few, except for Joyce's friend, Oliver St John Gogarty, and Edwin Muir. His growing contact with other authors of note, however, did obtain for him, in 1929, thanks to Compton MacKenzie's influence, a job on a new radio magazine in London. Despite financial and personal uncertainty (his family stayed in London, when he left for Liverpool to find work), he was completing work on *To Circumjack Cencrastus*, which shows MacDiarmid's ambivalent attitude to Scotland and his frustration with the cultural shackles created by its own self-image and the heritage of the "Whistle-Binkie bards". It is a measure of the rapidity of MacDiarmid's literary development that, by 1931 and the publication of the *First Hymn to Lenin*, he was already moving away from the concept of "Synthetic Scots", to which critics had barely become accustomed, and was writing again in English. The poems of this period, despite overtly political content, were also, and perhaps more essentially, meditations on his own artistic mission and gift, and on the inspiration of his Langholm past. Despite his literary productivity at this period, he was on the verge of bankruptcy, when Valda Trevelyan, his second wife, was delivered of their first son. They moved to a new life on Whalsay, in the Shetlands, where MacDiarmid was assistant to a local doctor from 1933-41. It was in this unlikely setting, in a Highland croft, that MacDiarmid began to develop the notion of "Synthetic English", which was amplified by large borrowings from technical and scientific vocabulary, used for their acoustic and aesthetic effect, and sometimes later, by voluminous extracts from the writings of others, using a technique reminiscent of Joyce's experimentation in *Finnegan's Wake*. MacDiarmid's political path continued to be extreme and highly idiosyncratic, justifying his own much-quoted words (later inscribed on his tomb-stone): " I'll ha'e nae hauf-way hoose, but aye be whaur/ Extremes meet". He was expelled from the Scottish National Party for Communist sympathies, and, after joining the Communist Party in 1934, was investigated for "national deviation". The truth was that MacDiarmid was too much of a poet and had too great a dedication to his own artistic mission to be comfortable in any group. Despite his isolation in the Shetlands, his contacts at this time included most of the important writers of his generation: Sorley MacLean, Lewis Grassic Gibbon (whose *Grey Granite* is dedicated to MacDiarmid), Eric Linklater, Edwin Muir and **AS Neill** (with whom he worked on *Meanings for Scotland*). In his *In Memoriam James Joyce*, he turns to one of his acknowledged masters, and sees Joyce as representing Ireland, himself Scotland, and Dylan Thomas, Wales. His epic *Cornish Heroic Song for Valda Trevelyan* moves to a new stage of linguistic internationalism, with a Joycean celebration of "language as the central mystery / Of the intellectual life". Prose works of this period include *Scottish Eccentrics* and his serialised autobiography, which scandalised Langholm because of its inclusion of some material regarded as "delicate" locally, but which in fact celebrated MacDiarmid's debt to its literary and linguistic heritage and to its landscape. MacDiarmid eventually left Whalsay, suffering from a nervous breakdown, but then engaged in demanding war service on Clydeside in the Engineering Department. After the war, he received a Civil List pension, and moved to Brownsbank Cottage, a few miles from Biggar, and forty miles north-east of Langholm. With age, his gift for controversy did not cool and he followed his own prescription from *Lucky Poet*, "to keep up perpetually a sort of Berserker rage .. in the way of the old heroes". He spoke against nuclear armaments, listed his hobby in *Who's Who* as "anglophobia", in *Burns and Tomorrow* characterised **Burns** as a good songwriter and a poor poet, in 1970 met that other great controversial figure of modernism, Ezra Pound, and refused the Freedom of Langholm. He was buried at Langholm on 13th September 1978; even after his death, the monument erected to him on Whita Hill was the subject of a planning controversy.

* * *

An assessment of a corpus of poetic work as significant and extensive as MacDiarmid's is out of place in this book, but a brief description of his masterpiece *A Drunk Man Looks at the Thistle* will serve as an introduction to MacDiarmid's essential and recurrent themes. MacDiarmid's old master, FG Scott, apparently suggested the theme, and later helped prune it of inessentials. The structure, based on the visions of a native of Langholm, who has been drinking with cronies, and whose (physical) fall and (spiritual) rise comes to represent that of Scotland itself, obviously harks back to Joyce's *Ulysses*. In an alcoholic stupor, the drunk man sees a thistle by moonlight, whose symbolism startles a whole train of thought about his country. Many characteristic MacDiarmid themes emerge: there is, for example, the hatred of the Burnsian cult and a sense of the need to fight the inevitable threat of mediocrity – "To dodge the curst conceit o' being richt/ That damns the vast majority o' men". But there is also the more optimistic sense that victory over drawbacks – physical and geographical – can be achieved through culture, and that Scotland's problem, which has a universal significance, is to be addressed by attending to the Nietzschean and human task – "To be yersel's - / and to mak' that worth bein' / Nae harder job to mortals has been gi'en". MacDiarmid's achievement was quite simply unheard of : after at least two centuries of self-imposed provincialism, to make Scots verse capable of handling a metaphysical vision (with reminiscences of both Plotinus and Dante) and, at the same time, to contain the abstract thought so as to allow images of real visual and poetic power – "The michty trunk o' Space that spreids/ Ramel o' licht that ha'e nae end". It was little wonder that the critics were slow to absorb its novelty. No mention of MacDiarmid's oeuvre would be complete without a reference to what might be called his gift for vituperation, and his ability to produce vigorous prose, which seems at bursting point under the conflicting demands of his hopes for Scotland's

A Literary Guide

possibility and his frustration with its reality. His *Scottish Eccentrics* includes some splendid displays of MacDiarmid prejudices, and whether one agrees with him or not, it is impossible not to enjoy some of his more rumbustious passages. Who else, but "Scotland's Public Enemy Number One", would have begun an article on Christopher North with: "It is well known today that exceedingly few people think; that only an infinitesimal proportion of humanity have ever accomplished that exceedingly painful and unnatural feat.."? MacDiarmid then goes on to demolish Scotland's well-respected tradition in moral philosophy, including the work of Dugald Stewart, **Thomas Brown,** and North himself. The collection also includes articles on Elspeth Buchan, leader of the sect which settled at Crocketford, on James Hogg, and on the *Caledonian Antisyzygy*, a mixing of extremes, which he argues belongs to Scotland as a country, and which is certainly a technique of MacDiarmid's own poetry, and an expression of his turbulent life.

BIBLIOGRAPHY:
Northern Numbers (1920-1922); *The Scottish Chapbook* (vol. 1, no.3, October 1922); *Annals of the Five Senses* (1923); *Sangschaw* (1925); *A Drunk Man Looks at the Thistle* (1926); *To Circumjack Cencrastus, or the Curly Snake* (1930); *First Hymn to Lenin and Other Poems* (1931); *Scottish Eccentrics* (1936); *Lucky Poet* (1943); *In Memoriam James Joyce* (1955); *Burns Today and Tomorrow* (1959)

PLACES TO VISIT:
The MacDiarmid memorial stands on a hill above Langholm, close to the obelisk to the **Malcolm** brothers. Many places immortalised in his poems can be identified in and around Langholm.

William Julius Mickle
1734-1788
Langholm

William Julius Mickle (originally Meikle; the "Julius" was also added) was born in Langholm, where his father became minister in 1716. His lasting achievement was a translation of the "Lusiads" of Luis de Camoens from the Portuguese, which, in the manner of Pope's Homer, was a poetic interpretation, as much as a translation. It set the standard for translation of this work for a century and continues to receive respectful mention in Camoens scholarship.

Mickle's father was minister of Langholm from 1716-1744 and was himself a talented translator: he had been one of those chosen to translate Bayle's *Dictionary*. Mickle attended Langholm Grammar School until his father returned to Edinburgh owing to ill health, when he became a pupil at Edinburgh High School. The principal intellectual influence on him at school was a reading of Spenser's *Faerie Queen*, and later he was to produce a moral tale *The Concubine* or *Sir Martyn* in Spenserian stanzas. At 18, he was apprenticed to an uncle with a successful brewing business in Edinburgh, but since he had already begun publishing – some pieces appearing in the *Edinburgh Review* – this proved uncongenial and unsuccessful, and he moved to London in 1763. There he began a lengthy correspondence about his poetry and his literary prospects with Lord Lyttelton, who had a reputation as a patron of literature. Like Mickle's other involvements with potential patrons, it appeared to bring him little benefit and he pondered a career abroad to gain his financial independence. The

A Literary Guide

Clarendon Press, however, offered him a situation as corrector and this enabled him to earn a living while devoting time to composing poetry and publishing it. In 1762, he wrote *Pollio*, an elegiac ode on the death of his brother, which was published in 1766, followed by *The Concubine*, *Mary Queen of Scots*, and *Knowledge – an Ode*. In 1770, he wrote *Voltaire in the Shades*, the first salvo in a controversy with the great thinkers of the Enlightenment which Mickle was to continue throughout his life: in the dialogue, all the important figures in the then current deistical controversy – Hume, Voltaire, Rousseau – appear as souls after death, to discuss their views on religion and eternal life. Voltaire remained a target for heated criticism in the introduction to his next and greatest venture, the translation of Camoens, since he had commented adversely on the poem's epic structure in his *Essay on Epic Poetry*. Mickle had read a French translation of the *Lusiads* by Castara and resolved to learn Portuguese in order to create an English version; there had been none since a translation by Sir Richard Fanshawe in 1655. The translation was completed over five years, from 1770 to 1775, and its first volume met with immediate literary applause. Mickle was never far from controversy, however, and the dedication of the book to the Duke of Buccleuch, who was expected to provide patronage in return for the dedication, resulted in another – perhaps one-sided – disagreement with the leading figures of the Scottish Enlightenment. He blamed the Duke's failure to respond to the dedication on the intervention of Adam Smith and Hume and later inserted some Spenserian lines on the *Neglect of Poetry* into his introduction: "And is it thus the gross-fed lordling's pride / And hind's base tongue the gentle bard upbraid?" Clearly, he saw parallels to his own career in the biography of Camoens himself, who , interpreted by Mickle, comments in *Lusiad V*: "Unheard, in vain their native poet sings, / And cold neglect weighs down the Muse's wings". The introduction and footnotes to the translation bore many marks of other controversies into which Mickle fell with his great contemporaries: angry notes were inserted after a tragedy was refused by David Garrick and Mickle was only narrowly dissuaded by James Boswell from publishing a *Dunciad* denouncing Garrick. Despite his complaints, the translation was financially highly successful and none less than Dr Johnson himself favourably commended it to Oliver Goldsmith, commenting that he had once cherished the ambition of translating it himself. Nonetheless, Mickle was still seeking means of supporting himself and took a position as Purser on a man-of-war, the "Romney", commanded by Commodore Johnstone, another Dumfriesshire man. On this journey, Mickle finally reached Lisbon, where he was feted as translator of the national epic, was made member of the Royal Academy of Lisbon, and composed the poem *Almada Hill*, intended as a supplement to the translation. It was the disposal of the prizes won at sea on this trip which finally gained him the long-sought financial independence. He married a Miss Tomkins and retired to Forest Hill, in Oxfordshire, to devote himself to writing and editing. A slight piece, *Eskdale Braes*, written on request to compose something on his native county, was his last work, shortly before his death in 1788.

* * *

The reasons which determined Mickle's apparently surprising choice of subject for his magnum opus, the translation of the *Lusiads*, written in a language little cultivated at the time, are clear from his introduction, where he describes it as the "epic poem of the birth of commerce". There is little doubt that he intended to hold up the Portuguese maritime empire, its strengths and weaknesses, as a mirror to the emerging British empire of his own time, and considered it an epic richer in meaning for the eighteenth century than the martial epics of Virgil and Homer. The translation was prefixed by a lengthy argument as to the civilising benefits of commerce and discovery to mankind, but this was tempered by a consciousness of the lessons of history and the risk of decline. The moral becomes explicit in *Almada Hill* where he writes of the decline of Portuguese fortunes "And shall the Briton view that downward race / With eye unmoved, and no sad likeness traced?". He comments that Camoens wrote at a time of decadence among the Portuguese nobility and it is likely that the prevailing theme, throughout his poetry, of the risks of dissipation and the threat to virtue posed by Enlightenment values, were dictated by a concern with the need to safeguard and foster the strengths required by a nation with the responsibility of ruling a maritime empire. Mickle's other works, however, show that he was capable of working in several registers. His *Prophecy of Queen Emma*, 1782, includes a satirical essay on the contemporary literary storm over the genuineness of James MacPherson's "discovery" of texts by "Ossian".

A Literary Guide

His *Cumnor Hall*, contributed to Evans's *Old Ballads, Historical and Narrative* is a piece of pure lyrical beauty, whose haunting quality fascinated Sir Walter Scott, who considered adopting it as a title for what became *Kenilworth*. The controversy is not resolved as to whether Mickle or Jean Adam wrote the popular piece *There's nae luck about the house* about the preparations of a sailor's wife for her husband's return from the sea. If Mickle composed it – and his wife insisted the poem was found corrected among his posthumous papers and that he had explained Scots words to her – he had a rare talent for composition in the Scots vernacular. The accumulation of detail in the description of the welcome the wife hurriedly plans for her returning husband adds to the sense of anticipation, as she arranges the children's clothing, becomes irritable with delay (" Is this a time to think o' wark? / Ye jauds, fling by your wheel") and sets forth the best food she can supply: for "His very foot has music in't/ As he comes up the stair".

BIBLIOGRAPHY:
Pollio: an Elegiac Ode (1766); *The Concubine* (1767); *Voltaire in the Shades* (1770); *The Lusiad: or, the Discovery of India* (1775); *Sir Martyn* (1777); *Almada Hill* (1781); *The Prophecy of Queen Emma* (1782)

Sir John Malcolm
1769-1833
Burnfoot, in Westerkirk

Sir John Malcolm, born at Burnfoot in the parish of Westerkirk, Dumfriesshire, became one of the most eminent Indian diplomatists and specialists in Indian and Persian affairs, in an era when the eastern empire was attracting many men of talent and energy. His "History of Persia", based on an acquaintance with original sources, remained for long a standard authority on the subject, and his "Political History of India" was an eye-witness account of the great Indian diplomatists and soldiers of his own era, such as the Duke of Wellington, Lord Cornwallis and Lord Clive, with whom he was personally acquainted. In 1824, Wellington wrote that: "I can answer for it that from the year 1796, no great transaction has taken place in the East in which you have not played a principle (sic), most useful, conspicuous and honourable part".

John Malcolm was part of a large family of ten sons and seven daughters, born to George Malcolm, son of a farmer and clergyman, who farmed in the parish of Westerkirk. His mother was Margaret, daughter of James Pasley, also of Dumfriesshire. John was considered the most unruly of this tribe of children, and left Westerkirk Parish School aged twelve. His father, who had made unfortunate speculations, had to place his sons in public service to make their livings: his elder brothers, two of whom were also to be knighted for military and marine service, were already either in the East India Company or in the Marines. John Malcolm was taken to

London by a maternal uncle in 1781, and was procured an interview with the East India Company, at the unlikely age of thirteen. The Directors patronised the boy, asking what he would do if he met the notorious Hyder Ali; without hesitation, the boy replied that he would "cut aff his heid". He was instantly passed into the service. He sailed for India in 1782 and was appointed, on arrival, to duty with a regiment at Vellore. The "Boy Malcolm", a nickname which remained with him for years to come, was a good shot, reckless and often penniless. By the age of 19, he was adjutant to a wing of his native infantry regiment. Seeing that diplomatic service offered a means of ascent for ambitious and penniless young men, he studied Persian and speedily mastered it. In 1792, he was appointed Persian interpreter at Lord Cornwallis's camp. When poor health induced him to take leave in England, he wrote a paper on the grievances of East Indian Company officers. By 1795, he was appointed to the staff of the commander in chief, Sir Alured Clarke, who was about to proceed to Madras. He visited his parents at Burnfoot, for what was to be his last interview with them. Though, on his return to India, he held the position of secretary and then town–major of Fort St George, his mind was fixed on the diplomatic service, for which he continued to prepare himself. From early on, he had taken notes on the state of India, and in 1798 he was in a position to present Lord Wellesley (later the Duke of Wellington) with a survey of the native state of India. He was appointed assistant to the Resident of Hyderabad and during a dangerous mutiny of troops under the Nizam of the Deccan, he found his own life in danger; he was eventually able, during the scrimmage, to take command of 1500 British cavalry and reduce the mutineers to obedience. He made the acquaintance of the Governor General of Calcutta and set sail for Southern India. By 1799, he had become involved in the war with the sultan of Mysore, commanded a troop of infantry, and, in co-operation with Wellesley, marched on Seringapatam. His diplomatic activity began when he was appointed to settle the government of Mysore. Wellesley, now a political ally and close friend, chose Malcolm as an envoy to Persia, where there were concerns about the Afghan menace, French influence and the promotion of British trade. Malcolm sailed for Persia in 1799, but became entangled in complex negotiations relating to royal protocol in Teheran, which must have given him ample material for his future works on Persia. He was eventually presented to the Shah, to whom he made extravagant offers of gifts, a gesture for which he was later criticised. It was in fact Malcolm's view that this was the way to achieve British foreign policy aims, and he did negotiate two treaties favourable to British trade, the interests of the East India Company, and aimed at hampering French intervention in Persia. On his return from Persia, he became secretary to the Governor General of Calcutta. Wellesley, himself delighted with the outcome of the Persian mission, went with him on a fact-finding mission up the Ganges. It was at this time that he was referred to as "Lord Wellesley's factotum and the greatest man in Calcutta". His diplomatic skills were put to the test by the murder in Bombay of the Persian ambassador, but he successfully overcame Persian outrage by means of tact and gifts. In the war with the Mahrattas, he assisted General Wellesley and he was an active diplomatist in the peace which followed. In spite of a brief contretemps with Wellesley, who wished to see a more vigorous stance in the peace negotiations with the Mahrattas, he remained involved in the duties of settlement following upon the war until 1807. By this time, both his health and his finances had been affected by his long and costly missions. He married Charlotte, daughter of Colonel Alexander Campbell and became involved in the peaceful administration of Mysore. This was not to last, since he was selected for another mission to Teheran, to guard against French influence, especially in so far as it threatened Western India. By this time, he had a reputation for extravagance on his missions and his Wellesley connection was viewed, by some, with mistrust. As a result, he had a junior role in the mission, and his mission of 1808, divided in its command, was not wholly successful. Back in India, he was despatched to deal with the Madras mutiny, where he successfully negotiated with the garrison, but his policy was once again criticised for its lack of severity. Once again, he was despatched on a diplomatic mission to Persia, but, because of a conflict of responsibility with the king's ambassador, his main achievements were the beginning of his *Political History of India*, his cordial reception by the Shah (who created for him the Order of the Lion and the Sun) and his introduction of potatoes to Persia. On his return to Bombay, he received government encouragement for his literary work on Persia, but censure for his mission's expenses. He also wrote a pamphlet justifying his conduct in the Madras rebellion. In 1812, he was back in England and at this point, made the acquaintance of Sir

Walter Scott (later, in 1825, he stayed at Abbotsford) and was given a knighthood, a KCB and an honorary doctorate of laws at Oxford. Parliament consulted him on Indian topics and he eventually received some recompense for his Indian services, much needed at this time, since his finances were in disarray. In 1815, he was on the Continent and toured the battlefield of Waterloo, which he discussed with Wellington. In Paris and in Germany, he found that his eastern scholarship and his works were in demand, owing to the growing taste for Orientalism at this time; in Russia, his *History of Persia* was consulted for more immediate political gain. His literary acquaintances here included Mme. De Stael and the geographer and scientist, Baron von Humboldt. At this time too, he and his two elder brothers, now both also knighted for public service, were hosted to a public dinner in Langholm, where the toast was to "Our own three knights of Eskdale". Despite his reception at home and abroad, he failed to obtain office, and realising that prospects awaited him in India, rather than at home, he sailed for India in 1816. There, he was appointed brigadier in the Deccan army and went on a tour of native courts. Once again, however, minor skirmishes broke out into a Mahrattan war, and it was the reckless courage of Malcolm himself, riding at the front of his men, which broke up the enemy cavalry. It was for his role in the rout, that Canning, the British Prime Minister, said of him that "the name of this gallant officer will be remembered in India as long as the British flag is hoisted in that country". In 1818, he concluded a treaty of peace, but only secured the surrender of the peishwah by means of an extravagant pension, which cost the Indian exchequer £2 million by the time of the prince's death. Further outbreaks of violence were crushed by Malcolm. Despite his success, he failed to obtain other prominent appointments, such as the governorship of Bombay. His literary output continued unabated, with a vast *Report on Malwah* in 1820. After spending his leave in London, from 1822 he tried again for the governorship of Madras, and eventually obtained the governorship of Bombay. On his voyage over to India, he is seen, with characteristic energy, composing the *Life of Robert, Lord Clive* on board ship, with metrical versions of the Psalms to occupy him on a Sunday. His governorship was marred by an acrimonious dispute with the supreme court of Bombay over their respective jurisdictions; the dispute was only resolved by the appointment from London of new judges, but not before the scandal had erupted in the press. His administration was marked by his attempt to retrench government services, the construction of roads and his encouragement of forward-looking ventures, such as steam communication with Egypt. His popularity with different sections of the community was evident at the end of his term. When a marble statue of him by Chantrey was erected in Bombay Town Hall, the Asiatic Society requested a bust for their library, and "a group of native gentlemen" ordered a portrait. In 1831, he returned to England and on the eve of Parliamentary Reform, he was elected to Parliament for the pocket borough of Launceston, in Cornwall. He vigorously opposed the cause of reform, but when his seat was lost in the reforms, he tried to canvass for a seat in the Dumfries burghs: he sent a copy of his parting address to the Dumfries electors to his friend **Allan Cunningham**, amanuensis to Chantrey, stating that he would campaign without promises or favours. When his campaign showed no likelihood of success, he retired to his new estate in Berkshire to effect improvements in the mansion and grounds, and worked on the *Life of Robert, Lord Clive* (eventually completed posthumously by another hand) and the *Administration of British India*. His last political act was to assist India House against the attempted revision of its charter by the government. His last address to the public, while his health was failing, was to appeal for a subscription to purchase Abbotsford for the Scott family. After his death, a statue by Chantrey was placed in Westminster Abbey and a huge obelisk erected on Whita Hill, Langholm, to his memory.

* * *

Malcolm's most readable work is the *Sketches of Persia*, which purport to be by "The Traveller", who mocks at "Malcolm's ponderous quartos". It is an example of humorous and elegant travel-writing and contains fascinating insight into what at the time was a largely closed world, including his experience of the protocol of Teheran and his personal interview with the Shah. In his *Sketch of the Sikhs*, in which he was helped by the eminent linguist Dr Leyden, he collates information on the history, institutions and religious belief of a people who were at the time the object of much curiosity, and about whom such information was regarded as being of political importance. His *Political History of India* for the period of 1784-1823 is written from the standpoint of one who

A Literary Guide

was in a unique position to know the events which he describes and had personal acquaintance with the great empire-builders of the era. It is in effect a handbook for maintaining the empire, but is written with an awareness of the anomaly of the East India Company's role in government, and with the insight that there should be "the most unceasing attention to the religious prejudices and civil rights of our Indian subjects". This moderation, which earned him some censure, was the foundation for what was called the "Malcolm school" of Indian diplomacy. His poems, published in Bombay, in 1829, include a long poem on *Persia*, which was much inspired by contemporary European thinking on the nature of the despot, by contrast with the nature of the constitutional ruler presiding over free subjects: "Wrapt in himself, the Despot sits alone, / Dreaded by all, and yet of all afraid". The other pieces are slight, but his translations from the Persian are pleasing, and his prologues composed for plays acted on ships to and from India give an interesting insight into shipboard entertainments.

BIBLIOGRAPHY:
Sketch of the Sikhs (1812); *The History of Persia* (1815); *The Political History of India* (1826); *Sketches of Persia, from the Journal of a Traveller in the East* (1827); *Miscellaneous Poems* (1829); *The Administration of British India* (1833); *The Life of Robert, Lord Clive* (1836)

PLACES TO VISIT: The Malcolm Obelisk on Whita Hill, Langholm, overlooking the monument to **Hugh MacDiarmid**, has magnificent views over Langholm and the surrounding hills.

Dumfries and Galloway

Thomas Telford
1757-1834
Glendinning, Westerkirk

Thomas Telford, born at the tiny settlement of Glendinning, and later educated at the village school at Westerkirk, became one of the engineering giants of the era of the industrial revolution. His bridge over the Menai Straits employed revolutionary principles and new use of materials; his road system opened up the Highlands of Scotland; and there was almost no aspect of civil engineering to which he did not contribute substantively. His achievement was recognised in his being chosen to be the first President of the Institute of Civil Engineers.

Thomas Telford was born in a cottage by the Meggat Water, the son of John and Janet Telford. His father died in the year of Thomas's birth, and his mother moved in 1758 to a one-room cottage further down the valley. His mother stayed there until 1794. Her brother helped her to fund the education of her son at the village school. There, Telford was the school-fellow of Pulteney Malcolm, the elder brother of **John Malcolm**, both of whom were to be knighted for military and diplomatic service. Telford worked on the farms in his spare time, but was thought to have the best opportunity of improving his lot by becoming apprenticed to a stone-mason. His first master at Lochmaben mistreated him, but he fared better when he became apprenticed to Andrew Thomson at Langholm. At this time, the Duke of Buccleuch, the most important landowner in the Langholm area was carrying out improvements to his properties, and in 1778, this included the construction across the Esk at Langholm, the first bridge project in which Telford was to be involved. At Langholm,

A Literary Guide

his apprenticeship involved all branches of the trade, a fact on which he was later to comment: "I ever congratulate myself upon the circumstances which compelled me to begin by working with my own hands, and thus to acquire early experience of the habits and feelings of workmen". Before he left Langholm, he was to apply his new-found stone-craft to sculpting an inscription on his father's unmarked stone, describing him as an "unblameable shepherd". At Langholm too, Telford had not neglected the educational opportunities which offered – particularly, the use of the Pasley family library, where he read Milton and Cowper. Southey, the poet, later become a friend and chronicled Telford's successes. By this time, he had gained sufficiently in confidence to write and to publish some verse. In 1780, he set off for Edinburgh, where he was introduced to "the Art of delineating Architecture upon Paper" and closely observed the style of the New Town. In 1782, he left for London, where Elizabeth Pasley's brother introduced him to two of the most eminent architects of his day: Robert Adam and Robert Chambers. Through these means, he immediately was set to work upon the construction of Somerset House, where there was plentiful work for stonemasons. The first commission in which he was to work directly with clients upon his own account was in his native Eskdale, when he was invited to improve Westerhall for the Johnstone family, another contact which was to prove useful in his future career. He found work on the improvement of the Portsmouth dockyards and was able to witness engineering works on a vast scale at first hand. In 1786, Sir William Pulteney, a relative of the Johnstones, invited him to take on the renovation of Shrewsbury Castle, since he had just been elected MP for Shrewsbury. Telford, while working hard at his professional career, continued to improve his mind and at one point, even essayed a correspondence with **Burns**, putting to him the rather unlikely request that he "preserve the virtuous character of the young". At Shrewsbury, he was appointed County Surveyor and for the first time he had public projects under his control. He met Howard, the reformer of jails, and he followed his suggestions in designing a jail and infirmary, and employed prisoners on his works, including the excavation of some Roman remains at Wroxeter. His first bridge was built over the Severn, to the west of Shrewsbury, and its design took into account Telford's experience of the practicalities of construction. In the early 1790's, Britain was entering a great era of canal-building, and Telford, who had little experience in the field, was chosen over the head of the supervising engineer, William Jessop, by the committee in charge, to face the huge civil engineering problems of joining three rivers and making accessible the ironworks of North Wales. The result – the Ellesmere canal – more than justified the Committee's choice and Telford's innovative cast-iron acqueduct at Pontcysyllte attracted national attention. Telford's advice was now in demand for assessing works and judging the plans of other engineers; he was in touch with James Watt, to pump water for the Liverpool Water Works, and he designed an iron bridge for London. Despite his extraordinarily busy schedule, Telford continued to take a broader interest in culture, particularly in the achievements of his fellow Scots, and at this time took under his wing the poet Thomas Campbell, who was also to receive help from **James Currie** and **William Beattie**; Campbell was later to show his gratitude by calling his son Thomas Telford Campbell. The engineering project which was to appeal most to Telford's undoubted patriotism was the development of a system of communications for the Highlands, where there was grave concern about depopulation. By 1801, Telford was in charge of a survey which included suggesting improvements to the fishing industry, the construction of a canal from Inverness to Fort William, and the consideration of a new route for the Lowlands from Carlisle to Portpatrick. What Telford reported were little less than crisis conditions, but, adopting a view diametrically opposed to that of the 5th **Earl of Selkirk**, the other major theorist of Highland emigration, Telford believed that the solution was in the provision of a roads and canal system, which would not only open up markets, but would also provide direct employment for the Highlanders. The construction of the Caledonian Canal was to take from between 1803 until 1822 to complete, and encompassed a scale of operations which was hitherto unknown. Telford's scheme suffered from government bureaucracy, the idiosyncrasies of an untrained Highland workforce, and landowners' intransigence. The canal opened with great pomp in October 1822; while its naval use was by then obsolete with the ending of the war, and while it could not accommodate the greater hull size of steam-ships, it did a great deal to revitalise the Highlands and to bring benefits to remote communities. Telford was also engineer to the Commission for roads and bridges and it is barely possible to grasp the scale of his achievement in this capacity: he constructed 1,000 miles of

A Literary Guide

new roads (using a technique of solid foundations differing from McAdam's method), perhaps a thousand bridges, forty harbours, and innumerable churches and manses. Within Dumfries and Galloway, he constructed the Tongland bridge, where he experimented with flood arches in the Gothic style, with twin semicircular towers with arrow slits to flank the arch and a crenellated parapet. In 1806, he was consulted on the problem of the silting up of the Clyde and the success he had in creating a deeper channel had a substantive impact on the future success of Clydebank as a major shipping and ship-building river. The success of the Caledonian Canal inspired the Swedish Count von Platen to invite Telford to design a ship canal – the Gotha Canal – which would cross Sweden between the North Sea and the Baltic. Telford was necessarily often distant from the project, but thanks to the amiable persistence of von Platen, the canal was opened in 1822. After Waterloo, Telford was occupied by a new challenge at home: access to Ireland, now part of the Union, could be facilitated by better roads to Holyhead and bridges over the dangerous Menai Straits and over the Conwy. The bridge which Telford built over the Conwy has emblazoned upon it the emblems symbolising the Act of Union – the thistle, the rose, the shamrock and the leek; his bridge over the Menai Straits, for which he introduced a revolutionary use of suspension chains, was his greatest bridge, opened in 1826, and is still standing. Other substantial projects of the time were the draining of the Fens and the construction of the massive St. Katherine's Dock, London. Telford's existence had been so entirely committed to work that for twenty-one years, he had only lived at rooms at the Salopian Coffee House. There he held court and was besieged by visitors, not least by impecunious Scotsmen. Telford acquired a house in Westminster and there provided rooms for young engineers. He was the natural choice, therefore, of a group of young Turks who founded the Institution of Civil Engineers in 1818, and invited him to be their first President. Telford set the aims of the Institution in his inaugural address: they were to increase the confidence of the public by constituting a trained body of engineers, and to share knowledge (which involved the establishment of an archive). Telford did not share the coming enthusiasm for railways, believing always that they were supplementary to the canal system and that tramways, rather than steam railways, were appropriate where terrain forbade the successful building of a canal. Perhaps it was the sign of a new era, when George Stephenson, despite Telford's predictions, successfully completed the Liverpool to Manchester railway, and the young Isambard Kingdom Brunel, having carefully studied Telford's Menai Straits bridge, won a competition against Telford, for a bridge at Bristol. By 1832, his health was failing, and his relentless work-schedule was beginning to tell. He began work on his autobiography. He was still engaged on official work, site visits and reports, when he died in 1834. Despite his own request, he was buried at Westminster Abbey. Among those to benefit from his will, which included Southey and other old friends, was the town of Langholm, to which he left £1000 to start a library. This had an unforeseen consequence for Scottish literature more than half a century later, when **Hugh MacDiarmid** became one of its most avid readers, and justified Telford's own prediction in his poem: "Nor pass the tentie curious lad/ Who o'er the ingle hangs his head/ And begs of neighbours books to read".

* * *

Apart from his early attempts at poetry (some of it in praise of his native Eskdale: "Where the flowery meadows down their margins spread / And the brown hamlet lifts its humble head / There, round his little fields, the peasant strays / And sees his flock along the mountain graze") Telford's prose is workmanlike and gives little of his personality away. Even in his autobiography, *The Life of Thomas Telford, Civil Engineer, Written by Himself* (edited by his executor, John Rickman, in 1838), there is the briefest of introductions to his life in Eskdale, some indication of his interest in architecture and its traditions, before he plunges into the detail of his work – invaluable record though this may be. Perhaps it is fortunate that in Robert Southey, by then Poet Laureate, we have a witness whose enthusiasm makes up for Telford's taciturnity, and who documented their tour of the Caledonian canal works in 1819. The sheer scale of the works was bound to impress: "here we see the power of nature brought to act upon a great scale, in subservience to the purposes of man". Southey also composed a celebratory poem on the canal and its creator. Telford's own characteristic method of communication – the official reports into any project on which he was then engaged – show that he always appreciated the wider social and economic impact of the purely technical works. In a report on the "proposed cast iron railway from Glasgow to

Berwick", he summed up the impact of the communications system in the era of industrial development: "the prosperity of a country is most essentially promoted, by introducing perfect modes of intercourse in its several districts". He knew, in his report on "the coasts and central Highlands of Scotland" (1803) that the roads system would "furnish Employment for the industrious and valuable Part of the People in their own Country, (and) they would by this means be accustomed to Labour". Aware of the vast intervention of which his engineering feats were capable in promoting social and economic good, perhaps Telford felt that literature was for others to cultivate; his generosity, particularly to essays in the field of Scottish literature, including a subscription to an edition of Burns' poetry, shows that he was far from insensible to its importance.

BIBLIOGRAPHY:
Eskdale: a poem (1781); *A Survey and Report on the Coasts and Central Highlands of Scotland* (1803); *Report and Estimates relative to a Proposed Road in Scotland ...in Perthshire by Rannoch Moor* (1810); *Report relative to the Proposed Railway from Glasgow to Berwick-upon-Tweed* (1810); John Rickman, ed., *The Life of Thomas Telford, Civil Engineer, Written by Himself* (1838); Robert Southey, *Journal of a Tour in Scotland in 1819* (1929); Anthony Burton, *Thomas Telford* (1999)

PLACES TO VISIT: Telford's bridge over the Dee at Tongland is still used by traffic today. A monument to him has been erected outside Westerkirk Library. Outside Langholm Library, endowed by Telford, stands an arch, a sample of his original work as a stone-mason.

Edward Irving
1792-1834
Annan

Edward Irving, who was born in Annan and was the contemporary and friend of **Thomas Carlyle**, *became the founder of the church which later was to become known as the "Catholic Apostolic Church". His charismatic preaching style had a huge impact on contemporary London, but the later apparitions, approved by Irving, of the pentecostal gift of "speaking in tongues" alienated many followers and caused his excommunication and the decline of his church to a marginal sect.*

Irving was born in 1792 in Butts Street, Annan, the son of a tanner and one of eight children. His mother was the daughter of a small landed proprietor in the parish of Dornock. He was the neighbour, contemporary, and friend of the explorer, **Hugh Clapperton**, with whom he maintained contact throughout his life; Clapperton's last message, before his death, was addressed to Irving. He first attended "Peggie Payne's School", and later a private school run by the master, Adam Hope, who was later to teach both Irving and **Carlyle** at Annan Academy, and of whom Carlyle leaves a formidable portrait. Adam Hope was a "Burgher Seceder" from the Church of Scotland, and Irving would often join him when he walked to Ecclefechan to join the secession church congregation there, where Carlyle also worshipped. At age 13, Irving left the Academy, and went to Edinburgh, where he was destined for the ministry. There he lodged with relatives of Clapperton. By the age of seventeen, he was studying divinity, but supporting himself by teaching mathematics at Haddington Mathematical School. Carlyle describes one of Irving's visits home when he was "fresh from Edinburgh with college prizes, high character and promise". In his spare hours at Haddington, he became tutor to the talented and fascinating daughter of Dr Welsh, who was later to become Carlyle's wife, Jane Welsh. Irving actually married Isabella Martin, to whom he became engaged in 1812. He was promoted to become master of the new Academy at Kirkcaldy and in 1815, was licensed to preach by the Presbytery of Kirkcaldy. He continued to teach and became acquainted with the routine of ministry, of which he clearly found the conventionalities oppressive. In 1818, he left for Edinburgh, where he began delving into older theology and inaugurated a style of preaching which was to electrify audiences in London a few years later. It attracted notice by one famous churchman, Dr. Chalmers, who was looking for an assistant to help with his evangelical work in the poor quarters of Glasgow. Irving remained with Chalmers for two years, but eventually accepted a call to the Caledonian Chapel, London in 1822. It was here that his peculiarities of thought and diction began to create a stir in the fashionable world and his celebrity began. Not only expatriate Scotsmen, like David Wilkie and **Allan Cunningham** attended the small church in Hatton Garden, but the Prime Minister, Canning, referred to Irving's sermons in the House of Commons, and the fashionable world followed the hint. Irving was coming under the increasing influence of millenarian thinking and writings on prophecy, which were being promoted by a group which included Samuel Taylor Coleridge and centred around Henry Drummond, a wealthy promoter, who organised summer sessions for discussion at his home at Albury. By 1827, a new church, with a thousand sittings had been built, but Irving's heterodoxy was beginning to make the authorities within the Church of Scotland uneasy. Despite the length of his sermons, the power of his oratory seems to have been mesmeric; but, as his apocalyptic speculations grew more extreme and less clear, his support in the fashionable world diminished and his friends quailed. Carlyle, who left a lengthy account of Irving in his *Reminiscences* wrote: "Could he but rid himself of apocalyptic and prophetic chimaeras, and see the world as it is, then we might fight together for God's <u>true</u> cause, even to the death". Mrs Carlyle said, more succinctly: "If Irving had married me, there would have been no Tongues". By this time, indeed,

Irving's church had attracted a large number of millenarians and believers in Charismata, who had little or nothing to do with the Presbyterian church, of which he was an ordained minister. Irving himself was by this time convinced that, if there was going to be a speedy advent of the Lord, the Charismata, the signs and wonders of the Apostolic church, would also revive, and the order of the ancient church should be reconstructed. In 1830, in the parish of Rosneath, Mary Campbell burst out into unintelligible vociferation, a display which Irving accepted as the display of a Pentecostal gift. Needless to say, by 1831, the "Gift of Tongues" had appeared in Regent's Square Church and Irving, who put the speakers to the test only of his private judgement, allowed these outbursts as part of the service. Carlyle exclaimed against "Bedlam and Chaos!" and the Trustees of the Church protested that he must confine himself to the ritual of the Church of Scotland. The Presbytery of London, despite an eloquent four-hour defence of himself by Irving, backed the Trustees, and the gates of the church were locked against Irving and his followers. In actual fact, the grounds on which Irving was excommunicated were not the most telling claims which could have been made against him: the Church found him guilty of heresy on the question of Christ's human nature, whereas examination of his texts shows that he seemed to maintain the ultimately orthodox position that Christ was wholly human and exposed to sinfulness, but kept free of sin by God's will. Of greater concern might have been his vulnerability to being gulled by manipulative or hysterical subjects, and his tendency to condemn those who attempted to reason on matters of his conviction as lacking in faith: "Keep your conscience", he wrote, "unfettered by your understanding". The Presbytery of Annan, which had ordained him, called upon him to defend himself, the **Rev Dr Henry Duncan** being among his accusers. Irving meanwhile inflamed the situation in Scotland by calling the General Assembly a "Synagogue of Satan". Despite the opposition, and despite the effect the heresy trial had had on Irving's health, his faith in his apostolic mission remained unshaken and his church reconstituted itself at Newman Street in London, this time with the full panoply of Catholic Apostolic order and ritual. Irving himself was ordained "Angel" of the Church and his influence was by now limited to the confines of the sect. Carlyle gives a touching description of his friend, who he believed was ultimately a disappointed and broken man. It was while travelling

A Literary Guide

in Scotland, for the purposes of establishing a Scottish branch church, but also to recuperate his own health, that he died in Glasgow in 1834. A statue to Irving was unveiled, perhaps rather incongruously, by the Moderator of the Church of Scotland, to celebrate the centenary of his birth, in 1892.

* * *

Irving's works are written, as his sermons were spoken, in an outpouring of religious language which had perhaps not been paralleled since the time of the Covenanters: the prose is weighted with a sense of prophetic burden, and larded with Biblical language, reference and metaphor. Added to this specifically Scots inheritance, the influence of Coleridge, to whom he inscribed a discourse, inspired reflections on the godlessness and degeneracy of the age. The very content of Irving's *Orations* and *For Judgement to Come, an Argument* enabled him to dismiss his critics, as manifestations of the spirit which he wished to oppose: "I pray for their unregenerate souls, and for this nation, which harboureth such fountains of poison". Hatley Frere, who in 1813, had written a *Combined View of the Christian Prophecies*, initiated him into the chronological interpretations of the Bible and it was after meeting Frere that Irving wrote *Babylon and Infidelity Foredoomed of God*. Irving was also deeply impressed by the millenarian ideas expressed in the writings of the Spanish Jesuit, Lacunza, and the application of prophecy to current events; he translated Lacunza's work under the title *The Second Coming of the Messiah in Glory and Majesty* (1827). What we can only reconstruct from contemporary accounts is the magnetic effect which Irving's spoken word and his personal presence seem without doubt to have had on his audiences and friends.

BIBLIOGRAPHY:
Babylon and Infidelity Foredoomed of God (1826); *Collected Writings of Edward Irving* (1864-1865); Mrs Oliphant, *Life of Edward Irving* (1862); Thomas Carlyle, *Reminiscences* (1881)

Dumfries and Galloway

Thomas Blacklock
1721-1791
Annan

Thomas Blacklock, who was blind from infancy, was something of a phenomenon in his day, being referred to with respect by Samuel Johnson, Edmund Burke and David Hume, although his poems today are not thought to be deeply original. He is perhaps best remembered for his kindly encouragement of other authors, most famously of Robert Burns, who decided against emigration to Jamaica upon reading Blacklock's generous appreciation of his "Poems, Chiefly in the Scottish Dialect".

Thomas Blacklock was born in 1721 at Annan, the son of parents of Cumbrian origin. His father was a bricklayer in Dumfries, but was clearly an enlightened and educated man: when his son was blinded by smallpox at the age of six months, he endeavoured to cheer his spirits by reading him Spenser, Milton, Pope, Thomson, Prior and Allan Ramsay. At the age of twelve, the boy began to write poetry himself and these were circulated in manuscript form. His father was killed when he was 19 after falling into a malt-kiln and he later wrote an elegy on his father's death. Fortunately, his verses came to the attention of Dr. Stevenson, an eminent Edinburgh physician, who was on a professional visit to Dumfries; he paid for him to come to Edinburgh in 1741 and to be educated at the grammar school for four years. He returned to Dumfries during the 1745 rebellion (during which he wrote a poem against the rebel army) and published a volume of poems in 1746. He returned to the University at Edinburgh and studied a further six years; remarkably, he acquired a knowledge of Greek, Latin and

A Literary Guide

French. During this time, he became acquainted with the philosopher, David Hume, who did his best to get him tutorships and employment. In 1754, Hume had a dispute with the Faculty of Advocates, by whom he had been appointed librarian in 1752. He showed his indignation by giving Blacklock a bond of annuity of £40 per year for the salary, whilst retaining the office himself. To aid Blacklock's career further, Hume wrote an account of Blacklock to Joseph Spence, a friend of Pope's and Professor of Poetry at Oxford, who brought out an edition of Blacklock's poems, prefaced with an account of the life and character of the author. Spence also endeavoured to persuade Blacklock to write a play for David Garrick, but nothing came of this proposal. Hume dissuaded Blacklock from making a living by lecturing on oratory, and instead, he began the study of divinity. He was licensed as a preacher in 1759. In 1762, he married Sara Johnston, daughter of a surgeon in Dumfries, who was the "Melissa" of his poetry. Through the intervention of the Earl of Selkirk, he was presented to the ministry of Kirkcudbright. Unfortunately, his parishioners considered him unsuitable for the duties of the ministry on account of his blindness and the dispute which arose between the Town Council and Blacklock makes painful reading. After a legal dispute and when Blacklock had actually received threats from a weaver of Kirkcudbright (who was duly punished), he demitted office on the payment of a small annuity. He took his revenge on the councillors of Kirkcudbright in a savage unpublished satirical poem *Pistapolis* (first edited and published by **Frank Miller**), with full notes on the personalities of the town. He returned to Edinburgh in 1764 and took in pupils as boarders, including the nephew of David Hume. It seems that later the friendship with Hume deteriorated and Blacklock, in 1770, published a defence of the principles of Hume's rival, Dr. Beattie. In 1767, he received the degree of Doctor of Divinity from Marischal College, Aberdeen on Beattie's recommendation. It was in 1786 that he wrote the momentous letter, on receiving a copy of Burns's poems, stating to a friend that "I shall never open the book without feeling my astonishment renewed and increased". **Burns**, who received the letter from Blacklock's original correspondent via Gavin Hamilton, and whose trunk was already on its way to Greenock prior to his intended embarkation for Jamaica as an assistant to a plantation overseer, immediately visited Blacklock in Edinburgh. Burns wrote later: "The Doctor belonged to a class of critics for whose applause I had not even dared to hope. His idea that I would meet with every encouragement for a second edition fired me so much that I posted to Edinburgh without a single acquaintance, or a single letter of recommendation in my pocket". Blacklock, though reserved on the subject of Burns's boldly expressed views ("With joy to praise, with freedom blame...To speak his mind, but fear or shame .."), received him kindly and introduced him to many influential people. Some complimentary poems later passed between the two men. He also received Walter Scott as a boy, who remembered his generously opening up his library and recommending the reading of Ossian and Spenser. Blacklock died in 1791 of a fever, and was buried at St Cuthbert's Churchyard, Edinburgh, his tombstone being inscribed with a Latin motto by Dr. Beattie.

* * *

In the philosophical climate of the late eighteenth century, the ability of a blind man to describe visible objects, complete with descriptions of colours, was a question of great interest. In the introduction to Blacklock's poems, Joseph Spence tried to establish an explanation as to how he had developed a vocabulary by associating words for visible objects with metaphorical meanings. Dr. Johnson was probably closer to the truth when he wrote that the poems were mere echoes of the poetical language of his time and that this accounted for the extraordinary fluency and rapidity of his composition, noted by his amanuenses. His paraphrase of Ecclesiastes, Chapter XII, verse 1 "In life's gay dawn, when sprightly youth / With vital ardour glows.." became, in a slightly altered version, a popular Presbyterian hymn. His debt to Pope, evident in his poems, he acknowledged in his *On the Death of Mr. Pope*: " Tho' deep involv'd in adamantine night / Ask'd I again to view heavn's chearful light? / Pope's love I sought.." His references throughout his poetry to his blindness and his consciousness of continuing the tradition of Milton and Homer, both blind themselves, are interesting: " The Muse with Pity view'd his Doom, / And darting thro' th' eternal Gloom / An intellectual Ray, / Bade him with Music's Voice inspire / The plaintive Flute, the sprightly lyre, / And tune th' Impassion'd Lay". His soliloquy on escaping a fall into a well, and his verses on his father's death, which removed his chief support in life, are touching, without leaving the bounds of conventionally expressed emotion. He also wrote the article on blindness for the

Encyclopaedia Britannica and translated, though did not publish, the treatise on the education of the blind by the Abbe Hauy: in both cases, he argued for allowing the blind as much independence as possible. Perhaps more surprising are his *Ode on the Present Rebellion* of 1745, in which he referred to "The spurious exile" and his *The Graham*, which is an heroic ballad celebrating the Union of Scotland and England. His other writings are religious and philosophical, and include an *Essay on Universal Etymology*.

BIBLIOGRAPHY:
Poems on Several Occasions (1746); *An Essay on Universal Etymology* (1756); *The Graham: an Heroic Ballad* (1774); J. Spence, ed., *Poems: to which is prefixed an Account of the Life, Character, and Writings, of the Author* (1754)

Hugh Clapperton
1788-1827
Annan

Hugh Clapperton, born at Annan, was the first European to cross the region of Central Africa from the Bight of Benin to the Mediterranean. The journals of his travels testify to the extraordinary bravery and resilience required on these pioneering explorations.

Clapperton's grandfather was in medical practice at Lochmaben; his eldest son was a surgeon of some skill and reputation, and married to the daughter of John Johnstone, proprietor of lands at Thorniethwaite and Lochmaben Castle. George Clapperton, Hugh's father, actually married twice and had twenty-one children in all, Hugh being the youngest son of his first wife. At Annan, they were neighbours to the family of **Edward Irving**, and Clapperton was also taught mathematics, and particularly trigonometry and navigation by Bryce Downie, who also inspired Irving with an interest in the subject. At the age of thirteen, he requested to be apprenticed as a cabin boy on a ship, presumably engaged in the slave trade, between Liverpool and America. He had already made several Atlantic crossings when he was caught smuggling rock-salt ashore in his handkerchief, for his landlady, and given the alternative of imprisonment or service in the British navy. After embarking at Plymouth, when he became ship's mate, he was pressed on board the frigate "Renommee" at Gibraltar. After an attempt to escape by swimming ashore, he was recaptured, and, through the influence of relatives, he was promoted to midshipman. He saw active service on the

A Literary Guide

coast of Spain, during the Peninsular War. In 1808, he obtained the influence of friends to join the frigate "Clorinde", which was to serve in the East Indies. His bravery was shown during his years in the East, when he was first in the breach during the storming of Port Louis, Isle of France, and hauled down the French colours. In 1813, he was one of those selected to learn an exercise with the cutlass, taught by the famous swordsman, Angelo, and then became drill-master aboard the "Asia" at Spithead. He volunteered for service on the Canadian Lakes, where Britain was expecting to have to defend her interests against American military activity, and, on the lakes, was promoted to the command of the "Confiance" schooner. Here, too, he was noted for his outstanding bravery, defending his blockhouse against American attack and later leading his men to safety at the nearest British fort, seventy miles away across the ice. During this trip, he carried a boy, dying from frostbite, on his back, and partially lost the use of his hand as a result of his compassionate action. He hunted with the Huron Indians, came near to marrying a Huron princess, and considered a life in the Canadian woods, when his commission aboard the "Confiance" failed to be confirmed. In 1817, the British flotilla on the lakes was dismantled, and Clapperton returned to settle at Lochmaben, with an elderly aunt. This period of rest was unlikely to satisfy him for long, and in 1820, he went to Edinburgh, where he met Walter Oudney, who turned his thoughts to African exploration. When Oudney was appointed to be British consul of Bornu, Clapperton was chosen to accompany him to Central Africa. Major Dixon Denham accompanied the expedition, which moved south from the Mediterranean in 1822. They reached Lake Chad, where Denham went his own way, while Oudney and Clapperton reached Sokota. They failed to ascertain the source and termination of the Niger, but contributed largely to the mapping of the kingdoms of Mandara, Bornu and Houssa. In 1824, Oudney died at Murmur, and Clapperton proceeded alone, reaching Tripoli in 1825. Back in Britain, Clapperton's contact with the Sultan of the Fellans was thought to represent a favourable opportunity to open up British contact with the interior of Africa, and a second expedition was planned in 1825. In the meantime, Denham was to publish the *Narrative of Travels and Discoveries in Northern and Central Africa in the Years 1822, 1823, and 1824, by Major Denham, Captain Clapperton and the Late Dr. Oudney,* to which

Clapperton's contribution was chiefly on the excursion from Kuka to Sokota. The new expedition consisted of himself, and Pearce, Dickson and Morrison, variously qualified to help on the journey, and Clapperton's servant, Richard Lander. The original leaders died shortly after the expedition quitted the Bight of Benin, and Clapperton himself suffered from fever. Despite great hardship, and the illness of Lander, whom Clapperton at times carried across rivers which he was unable to swim, the depleted expedition reached the capital of Yoruba and crossed the Niger, at the point where Mungo Park died. It was in fact Clapperton who obtained accurate testimonies as to the circumstances of Park's death. They rejoined the route of Clapperton's first expedition, and were hoping to present gifts to rival sultans, by then engaged in a civil war, but the gifts intended for the sultan of Bornu were intercepted by the sultan of Sokota, and they were prevented from going any further. After this set-back, Clapperton, broken in health, felt that his expedition was a failure, and, according to his faithful servant, Lander, "after this act of duplicity on the part of Belo, to the hour of his death, I never observed him to smile". Tended by Lander, Clapperton failed under renewed attacks of dysentery, and was eventually buried at Chungary, near Sokota, in April 1827. Lander, with difficulty, managed to return to the coast, following detailed instructions given him by Clapperton on his death-bed, and bringing away safely his master's journals and papers. Lander was eventually able to publish *Records of Captain Clapperton's Last Expedition to Africa*, and returned for a second time to the region, finally being able to confirm the point of termination of the Niger by sailing down it, with his brother.

* * *

Several editions of Clapperton's journal exist, the best being that of 1829, with a magnificent frontispiece portrait of Clapperton, which includes some fascinating engravings based on Clapperton's and Denham's drawings. The continuation of the journal, after Clapperton's death, is by Richard Lander: the *Journal of a Second Expedition into the Interior of Africa from the Bight of Benin to Soccatoo*, which includes a humorous account of the penchant of the widow Zuma for white explorers, and of "the elopement of that most bulky individual". The aim of the journal, it states, is to give an account of the "recreations and songs of the people,

A Literary Guide

as well as their wars, laws, religion and government". There is also an edition of 1831, *Travels and Discoveries.. in 1822-4, with a Short Account of Clapperton and Lander's Second Journey in 1825-7* including an impressive engraving of Lander, wearing a turban, in the frontispiece. Clapperton's prose has no literary frills, but he was capable of lively observation of customs around him, of the detailed negotiations required to present gifts to dignitaries, and of the houses and dress of the people at Sokota. Perhaps the most moving part of the journal is the record of Clapperton's brave death and solitary burial, when Lander describes how he took his master's lifeless body, loaded it onto a camel, draped it in the Union Jack, and read the burial service over his master's corpse. He had a wooden house built over the remote grave.

BIBLIOGRAPHY :

Major Denham, Hugh Clapperton & Dr Oudney, *Narrative of Travels and Discoveries in Northern and Central Africa in the Years 1822, 1823, and 1824* (1826); *Journal of a Second Expedition into the Interior of Africa, from the Bight of Benin to Soccatoo* (1829); *Travels and Discoveries in Northern and Central Africa, in 1822, 1823, and 1824, with a Short Account of Clapperton's and Lander's Second Journey in 1825, 1826, and 1827* (1831); Richard Lander, *Records of Captain Clapperton's Last Expedition to Africa* (1830)

Frank Miller
1854-1944
Annan

Frank Miller was a resident of Annan and devoted himself to the study of the literature of Dumfriesshire: his work on the poets and writers of the area is marked by a scholarly attention to sources and a meticulous investigation of original manuscripts. Along with William Macmath, and Dr. George Neilson, he was one of those whose collections of Dumfries and Galloway literature laid the foundations of the modern collections at the Ewart Library and Broughton House, Kirkcudbright. He was particularly expert on the Border and Dumfriesshire ballads.

Frank Miller's father, George Miller, was a woollen manufacturer in Tillicoultry. His mother was the daughter of WS Lindsay, MP. When his father died, he was four years old and the family moved to Helensburgh. After attending Larchfield Academy, Helensburgh, he had originally intended to enter the ministry, but as a result of a long illness, he abandoned the idea and entered service with the Bank of Scotland. He held a post at the Annan branch from the late 1870's. In 1879 he recalled looking out from the Bank's windows and seeing **Thomas Carlyle** walking across Annan High Street, on what must have been his last visit to the town; Miller was later to document the connections of **Carlyle, Irving** and **Clapperton** with Annan. Shortly after arriving in Annan, he joined the Dumfriesshire and Galloway Natural History and Antiquarian Society, to whose *Transactions* he made numerous contributions, largely on the subject of the Border ballads. Ultimately, he became President of the Society in 1929/30 and bequeathed his library and a legacy to it. He assisted Professor Child with his definitive work on Ballad literature and thereby came into contact with the small Dumfries and Galloway group of scholars, including William Macmath and **George Neilson**, who were devoting scholarly attention to manuscript sources. He was for 50 years Secretary of the Annan Literary Society, which commemorated his retirement with a public dinner. He was also a committed member of the Church of Scotland and his *Poems from the Carlyle Country* include

A Literary Guide

some religious poetry, and articles on **Edward Irving** and **Carlyle**'s missionary friend, Dr. Glen. He died in his ninetieth year on 16th January 1944.

* * *

Frank Miller's *The Poets of Dumfriesshire*, published in 1910, remains the only systematic and scholarly discussion of the whole context of development of Dumfriesshire song and poetry. The book gives biographical details of each author, critical discussions of the provenance of the poems where this is complex, and substantial extracts from the originals. The historical development of poetry in the county is divided into its main stages, from the early ballads, Covenanting and Jacobite verse, Classical poets, Burns and poets writing in the vernacular, to Georgian balladists, the circle surrounding Thomas Carlyle, and poets nearly contemporary with Miller, such as **Alexander Anderson.** The discussion of early poetry is particularly worthwhile: among others, Miller's account of James, or "The Admirable", Crichton, so called because of his acquaintance with many languages and the learned public disputation he conducted in Italy, shortly before his early death, is interesting. He reminds us that ballads like *Lads of Wamphray* or *Lord Maxwell's Good-Night* show that eastern Dumfriesshire formed part of the Western Marches. *Fair Helen of Kirkconnel* is probably one of the most famous early poems of the region, inspiring poems by **John Mayne, Stewart Lewis,** Carlyle's cousin Dr. Waugh, and Wordsworth's *Ellen Irwin.* It concerns the tragic love story of the daughter of the laird of Kirkconnel, north of Annan, who was ardently loved by Adam Fleming, heir to what is now Mossknowe, and by Bell, the proprietor of Blackethouse. When she met her lover, Adam Fleming, on the banks of the Kirtle, Bell suddenly appeared on the banks opposite and levelled his carabine at his rival. Helen sprang in front of Fleming, to protect him, and died in his arms. The murderer was cut to pieces by Fleming, who then had to flee the country; it was said that he constantly heard a voice calling him and returned eventually to die on Helen's grave at Kirkconnel churchyard. The lines: "I wish I were where Helen lies/Where night and day she on me cries / I wish I were where Helen lies / On fair Kirkconnel Lea" touchingly embody this story and will be familiar to many. Another ballad *Annie Laurie*, which was based on the story of Anna Laurie, daughter of

Robert Laurie of Maxwelton, is said to have been composed by the unsuccessful lover, William Douglas. It was revised and set to music by Lady John Scott in 1848 and it is this version which became widely known. Any literary historian writing on such authors as **Allan Cunningham** (whose various literary "forgeries" Miller was particularly well fitted to trace), **Stewart Lewis, Edward Irving, William McDowall, Henry Duncan,** who all appear under separate notices in this volume, will be indebted to Miller's careful analyses. Another of Miller's services to local history and literature was his extensive *Bibliography of the Parish of Annan*, which originated in his own researches, and which includes biographical sketches of authors connected with Annan, or writing about its life and history.

BIBLIOGRAPHY:

The Poets of Dumfriesshire (1910); *A Bibliography of the Parish of Annan* (1925); *Poems from the Carlyle Country* (1937); Articles in *Transactions of the Dumfriesshire and Galloway Natural History and Antiquarian Society*

A Literary Guide

Rev C(harles) H(ill) Dick and John Buchan 1875-1939
Moffat

CH Dick was minister of St Mary's United Free Church at Moffat from 1910-1919, having also briefly been assistant minister at Stranraer St Ninian's in 1904-1905, in the absence of the resident minister. Perhaps surprisingly, given his long residence in Annandale, his celebrated work "Highways and Byways of Galloway and Carrick" shows an intimate knowledge of the west of the region and remains the best introduction to the history and topography of the area. He was also, from his schooldays, a close friend of John Buchan, who himself came to set four novels or stories in Galloway.

Charles Hill Dick was born in Glasgow on 27th December 1875, the son of a clerical family: his father was Rev. George Hill Dick, minister of Eglinton Street United Presbyterian Church, and his mother, Jessie Imbrie Mearns, was the daughter of Rev. Peter Mearns, minister of Coldstream West United Presbyterian Church. After attending Glasgow Albert Road Primary School, he went to Hutcheson's Grammar School, where he was a classmate of the charismatic and ambitious John Buchan. According to Buchan's recent biographer, Andrew Lownie, Dick and a small group of other boys were entranced by Buchan's personality, a devotion which was to last into the years they shared at Glasgow University, when the editor of the university magazine had to edit Dick's review of one of Buchan's novels, after he had described his style as being bettered only "by Shakespeare and the better parts of the Bible". At Glasgow University, Dick, Buchan and another Hutchesonian, John Edgar, set up a society, "The Nameless Club", whose honorary presidents were RL Stevenson, Walter Pater, and Prince Charles Edward Stuart, and whose rules required that the members descended to "nothing that is common or unclean". The friendship, however extravagantly admiring on Dick's part at this time, appears to have had deep roots on both sides, since the record of Buchan's extensive correspondence shows that he wrote to Dick constantly throughout his life, confiding to him all its major events, literary, personal and political; indeed, such was the closeness between Dick and Buchan, who characteristically formed strong male friendships, that their correspondence is one of the most important sources of insight into John Buchan's life and thought. During their university years at Glasgow, the long summer vacations were spent on walking and on fishing tours, sometimes by bicycle, mainly in Buchan's home territory of the Borders. Even after Buchan left Glasgow for Oxford, he was back in Scotland and, in 1897, in Galloway, typically covering 65 miles of challenging Galloway hill country in under 24 hours: it was the countryside he was later to use as the setting for *The Thirty-Nine Steps* and his short story *No-Man's Land*. During Buchan's time at Oxford, he had further opportunity of becoming acquainted with the Galloway countryside, since he cemented a friendship with another Scot, Johnnie Jameson, whose family occupied an ancestral estate at Ardwall, outside Gatehouse of Fleet. In 1898, Buchan visited the Jamesons' home at Ardwall and found the mixture of sociability with vigorous outdoor pursuits much to his taste. Crowds of young guests were hospitably entertained by Jameson's father, who was then Sheriff of Perth, but who was to become Lord Ardwall in 1904. Buchan was later to pay affectionate tribute to this larger than life character, who might have stepped out "from a Raeburn picture", in his *Andrew Jameson, Lord Ardwall*, written at the family's request after his death. During his visit, Buchan climbed to the top of the Dungeon of Buchan and drank burgundy there, and raced horses across the sands of Fleet. It was during this time that Dick, who shared Buchan's tastes for the outdoors and for fishing, edited *The Compleat Angler* of Isaak Walton and Charles Cotton (1895), a book which is known to have interested Buchan and which he considered editing himself. In 1898, Dick received his MA from Glasgow, his BD and his licence for the ministry in 1901. Thereafter, he held several positions as *locum* in churches in different parts of the country, his first permanent appointment being in Hamilton at Bellshill McDonald Memorial Church in 1906. He was translated to Moffat St Mary's in 1910, and there began work consolidating into book-form some of his previously published articles on walking, fishing and antiquities of Galloway, written originally for the *Glasgow Herald, Chambers's Journal,* the *Scottish Field* and the *Scottish Review*. The book was to appear in the *Highways and Byways* series published by Messrs. MacMillan. By 1914, at the height of the national fever about German spies, Hugh Thomson was at work on the illustrations, sketching scenery and buildings in Dumfries and Galloway: he was arrested at Maxwellton and detained for questioning at Auchencairn, prompting Dick to write to the *Wigtown Free Press* to inform a nervous public that any artist seen sketching might simply be preparing the illustrations for his forthcoming book. In *Highways and Byways...* he comments wryly on the atmosphere of suspicion at the outset of the war, which prompted fears of an enemy base in the Minnigaff hills and which also permeated the novels of Buchan at this time: "Schoolboys neglected the works of Mr. Henty and Captain Brereton for more immediate thrills, and Mr. Buchan wrote *The Thirty-Nine Steps*. Dick himself, however, had his own sense of adventure, and in 1913 paid a visit to the steppes of Russia; his illustrated lectures on this and on his local walking trips, which raised funds in aid of the war effort, acquired him a reputation as a photographer and speaker. By 1918, Dick had volunteered for war service "in one of the Scottish Churches' tents" on the line in France. On his return, he married Catriona MacRae and both left for Port of Spain, Trinidad, where he was minister at Greyfriars until 1924. Thereafter, he became minister on one of Shetland's most northerly islands, Unst, where Buchan and his family visited him in 1926, Buchan giving an address in Dick's church at Uyeasound. In 1933 and again in 1934, when Dick had moved again from the Shetlands to Cunningsburgh and after the United Free Church had become united with the Church of Scotland, he and Buchan met again: Dick acted as his chaplain and was one of many friends and family in Buchan's entourage when Buchan had been chosen as Lord High Commissioner to the General Assembly of the Church of Scotland. After Buchan had been ennobled as Lord Tweedsmuir and his career reached its apogee, when he had taken up his appointment as Governor-General of Canada in 1935, Dick visited him a year later, keeping up a friendship which had now lasted half a century. CH Dick died in 1936, while Buchan lived on, in increasingly indifferent health, until 1940.

* * *

Dick's *Highways and Byways of Galloway and Carrick* was written, as he declares and as its patient understanding of the country shows, from the perspective of a bicyclist and walker; but it far exceeds – both in the excellence of its writing and the depth and range of its references – the scope of any walking tour guide. His references range from geology, archaeology – with copious quotations from what was then the newly published *Inventory of Ancient Monuments* for Wigtownshire – Covenanting and smuggling lore, literary links and place-name analysis, to the merits of a river or loch for fishing, and lively historical description of local battles. In the best tradition of travel literature, the reader is left with a sense of the unique fusion of place and history, which goes to make up the essence of Galloway and the Gallovidian. What is still striking at the distance of over eighty years is the accuracy of Dick's descriptions; one thinks of his account of the traditional story of the Murder Hole at the Rowantree toll, which was borrowed and transported by **SR Crockett** to the "Murder Hole" at Loch Neldricken; and his "infallible" instructions for reaching Walter Scott's "Dirk Hatteraick's Cave" may still be followed, despite the intervention of the modern A75. Despite their lifetime friendship, Dick's references to Buchan and to his Galloway connections in the book are laconic; in fact, whether under the influence of his walking tours with Charles Dick or his sojourns at Ardwall with Johnnie Jameson, Buchan set four important works in Galloway and, more particularly, the Galloway hills, which seem to have symbolised for him a certain, possibly menacing, potential for the primitive to resurface in the midst of apparent civilisation. His most famous story or "shocker" as he called it, *The Thirty-Nine Steps*, where he first introduces the characteristic Buchan hero, Richard Hannay, is set in the country round Cairnsmore of Fleet, where his pursuit over the moors by a by-plane brings the story's sense of tension to its height. Perhaps sadly, none of the three screen versions of the novel have been filmed in Galloway: Hitchcock's most famous version of the story transposes the action to the Highlands and introduces humour to the story by handcuffing the hero, played by Robert Donat, to an unwilling heroine, played by Madeleine Carroll. A 1950's version starred Kenneth More and one in 1978, Robert Powell. Buchan's *No-Man's Land* is a powerful short story of the supernatural, about an expert on Celtic languages who ventures into the Scottish hills in defiance of the local advice and native intuition of the shepherd, only to find himself captured by a remnant of the tribes of Pictish aborigines. The countryside described is unmistakably that round the Dungeon of Buchan. Two novels out of the three forming Buchan's Dickson McCunn trilogy, *Huntingtower* and *Castle Gay* are also set in Galloway and south Ayrshire, and in *Castle Gay* many Galloway towns appear under code names: "Portaway" is Newton Stewart, "Gledmouth" is Dumfries, "Castle Gay" itself is the Castle of Old Risk, and "Fallatown" is Wigtown. Buchan's only non-fictionalised references to Galloway, with an atmospheric portrait of Lord Ardwall's almost eighteenth century household regime, occur in his affectionate portrait, *Andrew Jameson, Lord Ardwall.*

BIBLIOGRAPHY:
CH Dick - (CH Dick, Ed.) Isaac Walton & Charles Cotton, *The Compleat Angler* (1895); *Highways and Byways of Galloway and Carrick* (1916)

John Buchan - *Andrew Jameson, Lord Ardwall* (1913); *The Thirty-Nine Steps* (1915); *Huntingtower* (1922); *Castle Gay* (1930)

Sir William Jardine
1800-1894
Applegarth, Lockerbie

Sir William Jardine, one of the largest landed proprietors in the county of Annandale, was what might be described as the "grand old man" of ornithology and zoology in the area, and was nationally recognised for his achievements and extensive publications on the subject. His books are highly prized for their lavish illustrations.

William Jardine was born in 1800 in Edinburgh, and was later sent to York to "learn English". He went on to Edinburgh and Paris to study medicine. In 1821, he succeeded to his father's baronetcy and became an important landed proprietor in the county, by succeeding to the estate at Jardine Hall, Applegarth. His publications were prolific: from 1826-43, he collaborated with PJ Selby on *Illustrations of Ornithology* and from 1833-43, he was in charge of the *Naturalist's Library*, which ran to 40 volumes. His account of the birds of Applegarth and Sibbaldbie in the *New Statistical Account of Scotland* in 1845 was regarded as authoritative. His magnificently illustrated *Ichnology of Annandale* on the subject of the recently discovered fossil footprints, appeared in 1853. He also annotated editions of White's *History of Selborne*, and provided a biography of Alexander Wilson, a native of Paisley, for Wilson's *American Ornithology*, and jointly – with PJ Selby and Dr. Johnston – edited the *Magazine of Zoology and Botany*. His public responsibilities included his appointment as Deputy Lieutenant for Dumfries in 1841, acting as one of the Royal Commissioners on Salmon Fisheries in 1860, and was inaugural President of the Dumfries and Galloway Natural History and Antiquarian Society in 1862. He died at Sandown on the Isle of Wight, and was interred at Applegarth

A Literary Guide

Parish Kirk. Some of his very extensive collection of birds and eggs went to the Royal Scottish Museum, Edinburgh.

* * *

Sir William Jardine's contribution to zoology and ornithology truly warrants the description of "encyclopaedic". It was an era of great scholarly activity in the natural sciences and in the classification of natural phenomena, and Jardine's *The Naturalist's Library* appealed to a popular appetite for information on the subject. His introduction makes it clear what the editors' aims were: "It is with the view .. of enabling all classes to procure information regarding the <u>Great Works of Creation</u>, at a moderate price, in a convenient shape, and in the most accurate manner, that the proprietors of the <u>Naturalist's Library</u> have embarked in the undertaking." Each major zoological class was dealt with in a separate volume, and these were fully illustrated with coloured plates; the lives of famous naturalists, from Aristotle to Linnaeus, von Humboldt and Bewick, were appended to each. There were several editions in a variety of formats. Jardine's *Illustrations of Ornithology* is likewise a collector's item, with both coloured and black and white plates illustrating for each bird listed. His *Ichnology of Annandale*, a folio volume, includes remarkable and sometimes life-size plates of the fossil footprints first discovered on Corncockle Muir, near Lochmaben, by **Dr. Henry Duncan,** and includes illustrations of the *Chelichnus Duncani* first identified by him. His other venture into geology was his edition of the *Memoirs* of Hugh Edwin Strickland, reader in geology at Oxford. It is perhaps the best measure of Jardine's standing that he provided additions and notes for a much-republished edition of the famous classic of natural history, Gilbert White's *Selborne*. In addition to books published under his own name, Jardine also contributed widely to periodicals without signing his works.

BIBLIOGRAPHY:
Life of Alexander Wilson (Preface to Wilson's *American Ornithology)* (1832); *Naturalist's Library* (1833-1843); *The Ichnology of Annandale* (1853); *Memoirs of Hugh Edwin Strickland* (1858); With P.J. Selby, *Illustrations of Ornithology* (1826-1843)

Thomas Carlyle
1795-1881
Ecclefechan

Thomas Carlyle, born at Ecclefechan, was one of the most original and influential social critics and philosophical thinkers of the nineteenth century. To his contemporaries, he was the "Sage of Chelsea", a great man to be glimpsed by curious visitors to his house at Cheyne Row, and for whom, in his last illness, Queen Victoria ordered the streets to be covered in straw to deafen the noise of carriages. His long life spanned the period from the early Romantic movement (when he introduced much German thought and writing to Britain) to the High Victorian period, when he became increasingly isolated, extreme and embittered about the prospects of a mechanised society. His well-known style, "Carlylese", a combination of pulpit oratory and Germanicisms, is unmistakeable.

There can be no under-estimating the influence of Carlyle's childhood at Ecclefechan: his admiration for his father is one of the most touching and revealing of his testimonies in *Reminiscences* and he wrote home for 50 years, returning there regularly when he was able. His father, a self-respecting member of the New Licht Burgher Secession Church at Ecclefechan (also attended by **Edward Irving**), was a stone-mason, along with his brothers, and built the arched house at Ecclefechan with his own hands. His second wife was Margaret Aitken, and Thomas Carlyle was their eldest son. By 1800, his father was teaching him arithmetic; then he attended "Tom Donaldson's School" and later the village school. The deficiencies of teaching there were supplied by the Minister of the Secession church, who taught Carlyle Latin. As a result, he was qualified to go to Annan Academy, which he did not enjoy, but benefited from instruction by Adam Hope, **Irving's** old master, and by an able teacher of mathematics, a subject

A Literary Guide

in which Carlyle excelled. At home, there was little encouragement to read beyond sacred texts, but the Carlyles were vivid and copious conversationalists, whose tongues could be a dreaded weapon in controversies. Carlyle went to Edinburgh University in 1809 and en route, met **Thomas Murray**, his closest student friend. It was there that he began a concentrated course of private reading, which enabled him, in later writings, to draw upon a vast stock of allusions. Thomas Murray described him at the time, in his *Autobiography*, as indulging in "sarcasm, irony, extravagance of sentiment, and a strong tendency to undervalue others, combined, however, with great kindness of heart and great simplicity of manner". The later Carlyle is already recognisable in this picture of his student days. Carlyle found the mathematics taught by John Leslie stimulating (and was given credit for a new solution to a problem in Leslie's *Elements of Geometry*), but abhorred the logic classes, and found **Thomas Brown's** literary approach to moral philosophy affected, later referring to him contemptuously as "missy Brown, that used to spout poetry". Carlyle's Arts course was finished by 1813, and, amid growing religious doubts, probably opted for the part-time divinity course not only for financial reasons, but also because his conscience and his intellect revolted at the training of Divinity Hall. His parents were grieved at his losing the opportunity the ministry offered, as well as at his loss of faith, when he left the course in 1817. He began on an unsettled period, teaching, without enthusiasm or conviction, at Annan, and then at Kirkcaldy, at a school rival to that at which **Irving** taught. The company Irving offered ("two Annandale people must not be strangers in Fife", wrote Irving) as well as the intellectual stimulation of his vivid conversation, was essential to Carlyle at this time. In 1818, he moved back to Edinburgh, where there was some prospect of literary work, but he suffered from a lack of purpose and both nervous and physical complaints during this time : this period of intellectual self-doubt is charted in the descent to the "Everlasting No" in *Sartor Resartus*. The thread, which was to enable him to find an intellectual solution to his intense and religious need for purpose, in the event came from his reading of German writers, and in the 1820's, he began writing on German thought , working on a life of Schiller and translating Goethe's *Wilhelm Meister*. Thanks to Irving, he also had some financial security through his appointment as tutor to the Buller family, and had become acquainted with Irving's talented and witty young pupil, Jane Welsh, whom he tutored in European literature and who was to become his wife. He visited London at this time, quickly summing up the literary scene and its lions, like Coleridge, meeting **Irving**, whose notoriety was just beginning, and viewing the industrial landscapes of the Midlands. He lived, undecided for a year about his future direction, at Hoddam Hill, just above Ecclefechan, but Jane Welsh's mother, reconciled to the idea of Carlyle as a suitor, rented a house outside Edinburgh in 1826 and they were married in October of that year. Carlyle's Edinburgh period was a stimulating one and the Carlyles' sparkling literary evenings, which included John Wilson and Francis Jeffrey, were anticipations of the court they were to hold at Cheyne Row in London. Jeffrey was able to give Carlyle access to the pages of the *Edinburgh Review* and, though he tried to tone down the famous *Essay on Burns*, Carlyle obstinately refused any alterations and it became one of the *Review*'s best known articles. Still under financial pressure, they moved in 1828 to the remote farm of Craigenputtock in Dumfriesshire, part of Jane's father's estate, to cut down on the expense of living in Edinburgh. After the social existence of Edinburgh, Craigenputtock was a lonely and often uncomfortable place, especially for Jane Welsh, but Carlyle concentrated on the composition *of Sartor Resartus*, turned his thoughts to questions of social reform, and received guests, such as Emerson, one of his early American admirers. There were occasionally trips outside Dumfriesshire, to relieve the long winters, and in London in 1831, Carlyle engaged with gusto in the debates about Reform, finally quarrelled with **Irving** (though he was to pay him tribute in the *Death of Edward Irving*), whose belief in the manifestations of "speaking in tongues" Carlyle's incisive intellect found it impossible to accept, and entered into an influential intellectual group, including Mill, Hunt, Lamb, Lockhart and Hogg. Edinburgh, by contrast with the new challenges and influences, seemed provincial; more probably, Carlyle's demanding temperament meant that he had become intolerant of it: "My utterances fall like red-hot aerolithes or bursting bombs into the peaceful tea-garden of their existence, and they look upon me with astonishment, and an incipient shudder". In spring of 1834, after a Craigenputtock winter, they chose London as their future home, and selected an economical house in unfashionable Chelsea, where they were to stay for fifty years. There they were to create a circle of great brilliance,

A Literary Guide

where Carlyle's and Jane Welsh's flood of conversation, brilliant imagery, and blazing satire, were the wonder of visitors. Here, Carlyle began work on *The French Revolution*, a subject which enabled him to bring together his concerns with the need for reform, his horror of disorder, and the potential cataclysm awaiting societies which failed to heed warning signs. The loss of the painfully corrected manuscript of volume 1, when John Stuart Mill lent it to Harriet Taylor, whose maid used the blotted copy to light the fire, is one of the celebrated disasters of literary history. It was, despite its vicissitudes, published in 1837. He also earned publicity and some income from public lectures, of which the most famous was *On Heroes, Hero-Worship and the Heroic in History* (1841), and from the interest shown in his work in America, where Emerson worked to popularise his writings. His *Chartism* marks a change of tone, perhaps a growing exasperation, which led him to address himself directly to the reader, drawing the lessons of the French revolution for Britain, if it failed to overhaul its sick society. The seeds of what some see as the growing authoritarianism of Carlyle are here: he develops the idea of a man who will come forward to answer the needs of the time, and to whom it is one's duty to submit. *Past and Present* (1843) further elaborates the arguments of the shorter piece, and not surprisingly, Carlyle was already turning his attention to the work of Oliver Cromwell, a man who might answer to the definition of a Carlylean hero. *Oliver Cromwell's Letters and Speeches*, (1845), is the principal work of the decade. Carlyle travelled ceaselessly to amass original documents, although the characteristic Carlylean interjections and apostrophisings of the principal actor make it far from an orthodox piece of historical research. By the end of the decade, Carlyle's views were hardening, and those who were beginning to feel alienated from his increasing dogmatism were horrified by his *Occasional Discourse on the Negro Question* and his eight *Latter Day Pamphlets*. Here, he argued that the unrest among Jamaican sugar workers should be, if necessary, forcibly suppressed, because, as he saw it, work was a divine duty and the only bulwark against disorder, the Carlylean Hell. In the *Pamphlets*, his rhetoric was certainly violent, and the subtlety of his position on the question of "Model Prisons", which involved a questioning of a hypocritically indulgent regime for prisoners amidst the squalor of the London poor, was often missed amidst the sadism of its utterance. His interest in authoritarian figures reached its peak in his researches – including trips to Germany – into the life of Frederick the Great, whose military government and strong monarchy had an obvious appeal to the seeker after inspired leaders. The painful five years of research and re-writing of *Frederick* (1853-1858) coincided with a period of illness for Jane, who respectfully kept in the background during the creative ferment of her husband's writings. The work was only finished in 1865, and its reception was muted both because of their overwhelming bulk, and also because of the militaristic overtones and perhaps a certain palling of the Carlylean style. While Carlyle was away in Scotland, having accepted the Lord Rectorship of Edinburgh University, Jane Welsh died after a slight accident while out in her carriage. Despite the often tense relationship which had existed between this extremely demanding pair, there was no doubting Carlyle's wholehearted devotion to and his dependence on Jane. At the suggestion of a friend of Jane's, he began sorting her papers, and the *Reminiscences*, an intensely personal document not originally intended for publication, emerged from this therapeutic process. In 1868, he turned to editing her voluminous correspondence, which has proved an invaluable and fascinating document for the biographers of the Carlyles. Carlyle was by now reaching legendary status, was almost a tourist attraction in London, and in 1869, as the seal of approval for this standing, he met Queen Victoria. Ironically, it was at that time that his publications, such as *Shooting Niagara – And After?* were alienating even devoted friends like Mill : in this controversy over the Jamaican riots, in which **Ruskin** and Tennyson were on his side, he adopted the view that the West Indians should be made to work, if they were disrupting commerce, and, if necessary, and if applied with the right intention, force could be applied. Nonetheless, he still had many contacts, including Charles Eliot Norton, responsible for producing his works in America, and in the 1870's, he received a gold medal signed by a glittering array of the era's great men: the Darwins, Browning, Tennyson, George Eliot, and Trollope, among others. His last publication, which shows signs of a loss of vigour, was *The Early Kings of Norway*, one of his least known and least regarded works. Having outlived many contemporaries, such as Dickens, he grew progressively weaker in health, and in 1881, made his last trip outside Cheyne Row. The streets were hushed for the man who had obsessively detested the noise of London, but, when he died, despite the offer of

A Literary Guide

burial at London's Westminster Abbey, he had ordered that his coffin be taken to Ecclefechan. The controversies caused by Carlyle were not over, however, since he had left his literary papers to Froude, including the private papers he had edited after his wife's death but never finally destined for publication. When Froude decided to publish them, and when, in his pictures of the Carlyles at home, perhaps allowed Carlyle to appear in a less than flattering light in his conduct towards Jane (to whom Froude had been devoted), Froude was attacked, both for failings in editorship (which were undeniable) but also for his publication of sensitive material relating to their marriage. The entire controversy resulted in a ransacking of the Carlyle material for proof or disproof of biographical theories, and accounts in part for the huge bulk of work on the Carlyles' life together. This celebrity, or notoriety, was not, however, underpinned by a more scholarly consideration of his work, and his inaccessible style perhaps contributed to a strangely rapid decline in his literary reputation. That decline has begun to be redressed in the late twentieth century, when new editions of the letters, an appreciation of the innovativeness of his style, and a distance from the events which caused Carlyle to be interpreted as a proto-Fascist, have restored him to his position as one of the seminal thinkers of the nineteenth century.

* * *

Like those of many cultural prophets, Carlyle's works lend themselves to misinterpretation : his first work *Sartor Resartus* is perhaps one of his least accessible, though most influential books, which had a role in shaping literature not only in Britain, but also in America and elsewhere. Not only is there the difficulty of the style, a mingling of quasi-prophetic exhortation and German transcendentalism, but there are the narratological games (the presence of an editor, giving an account of the absurdly named Teufelsdröckh), and the literary form in which the thinking about spiritual ills (later addressed more directly) is enveloped. As biographers have realised, the progress of Teufelsdröckh through the "Everlasting No", through the "Centre of Indifference" to the "Everlasting Yea" reflects some of Carlyle's own battle with doubt. The description of the "Everlasting No" chronicles spiritual emptiness in terms which slightly recall Blake, but in a rhetoric which is uniquely Carlylean: "To me the Universe was all void of Life, of Purpose, of Volition, even of

Hostility: it was one huge, dead, immeasurable Steam-engine, rolling on, in its dead indifference, to grind me limb from limb. O, the vast gloomy solitary Golgotha, and Mill of Death! Why was the Living banished thither, companionless, conscious?" It is perhaps not surprising that the pilgrimage through the book betrays a deep religious need, which has to be satisfied without recourse to the theological God. *On Heroes, Hero-Worship and the Heroic in History* represents Carlyle at his most accessible: here too, there is the preoccupation with decadence (the types of heroes succeed each other, answering the call of progressively more decadent ages), the interpretation of mechanism as the cause of the absence of spiritual certainty, of the advent of nothingness in man: "You shall not measure them [i.e. right and wrong]; they are incommensurable: the one is death eternal to a man, the other is life eternal. Benthamee Utility, virtue by Profit and Loss; reducing this God's world to a dead brute Steam-engine, the infinite celestial Soul of Man to a kind of Hay-balance for weighing hay and thistles on, pleasures and pains on.." One can detect here the impatience of an impassioned and strong-willed man for the compromises of the less than heroic life which surrounded him. Here too, is the possibility of misinterpretation, which the violence of the rhetoric fosters : it is easy to miss the fact that for Carlyle, the hero is strong not because of physical force, but because he is right – the force is that of reason. The wise man, or hero's , communion with reason, with – as it were – the soul and substance of the universe, enables him to expect obedience as of right from those who are not similarly inspired. The only right of the non-reasonable man is "the right of the ignorant man to be guided by the wiser, to be, gently or forcibly, held in the true course by him!" and this compulsion is something for which he may be expected to beg, as if his soul were at stake. Indeed, for Carlyle, that is exactly the case : the difference is precisely that between the saved and the damned, and if the destined man is not allowed to prevail, then we have the Carlylean hell, the upsurge of non-entity, of non-right. It is the absolute Carlylean division between the sheep and goats which can shock and offend modern taste: in language reminiscent of Nietzsche (who is equally subject to over-simplified interpretation), he writes "Whom Heaven has made a slave, no parliament of men, nor power that exists on Earth can render free. No; he is chained by fetters which parliaments with their millions cannot reach. You can label him free; yes, and it is but a labelling him a solecism". While Carlyle may be regarded from political, historical or literary points of view, it is the understanding of his metaphysical position which is the critical element in making sense of these aspects of his works. Whatever one concludes on the questions of his militarism, sadism, politics, sexuality and so on, one can hardly deny that he has provided the best portrait of his own intellectual passion in his description of Abbot Samson in *Past and Present*: " There exists in him a heart-abhorrence of whatever is incoherent, pusillanimous, unveracious, that is to say, chaotic, ungoverned; of the Devil, not of God".

BIBLIOGRAPHY:
Wilhelm Meister's Apprenticeship (1824); *Essay on Burns* (1828); *Death of Edward Irving* (1835); *Sartor Resartus* (1836); *The French Revolution* (1837); *Chartism* (1839); *On Heroes, Hero-Worship and the Heroic in History* (1841); *Past and Present* (1843); *Oliver Cromwell's Letters and Speeches* (1845); *Occasional Discourse on the Negro Question* (1849); *Latter-Day Pamphlets* (1850); *History of Friedrich II of Prussia, called Frederick the Great* (1858-1865); *Shooting Niagara - And After?* (1867); *The Early Kings of Norway* (1875); James Anthony Froude, ed., *Reminiscences* (1881); there are numerous collected editions of Carlyle's works, the standard one being the Centenary Edition (1896-1899)

PLACES TO VISIT : The "Arched House", Ecclefechan, is open to the public and is run by the National Trust for Scotland. A statue of Carlyle dominates the head of the village of Ecclefechan.

Stewart Lewis
1756-1818
Ecclefechan

*Stewart Lewis was born in Ecclefechan and is best remembered for his versions of the ballad "Fair Helen of Kirkconnel" and pastoral "O'er the Moor amang the Heather". Like **William Nicholson**, he became a pedlar and ultimately depended entirely on selling his songs and begging food. His lyrics express egalitarian sentiments on slavery, poverty, and include some lively Scots verse, particularly his "The Muse in a Passion".*

Stewart Lewis was born in 1756, the son of an innkeeper and farmer, who left the family destitute when he died bankrupt. Lewis was taught at Ecclefechan by William Irving, who wrote the vigorous Covenanting song *Lag's Elegy*, picturing the persecutor's torments in hell. At 13, Lewis went to Manchester to help his brother in business, and then became a clothier at Chester. After ten years in England, his partner absconded with the proceeds and left him with the debts; he returned penniless to Ecclefechan to set up business as a tailor, and married a local girl. He was active in setting up a village library and a debating club. At this point, he wrote a version of the well-known tragic story of *Fair Helen of Kirkconnel* (see entry under **Frank Miller**), which was published along with the fragments of the traditional poem, said to be written by the unhappy lover of Helen. In 1793, after some time as an itinerant seller of cloth, he became a private sentinel in the Hopetoun Fencibles and made some income by composing madrigals and acrostics for the officers. While stationed at Aberdeen, he published a collection of poetry, including one on the discomfort of encampment on the "links of Don". When the Fencibles were disbanded in 1799, he became a pedlar in the west of England, but was robbed while drunk. He became an umbrella-maker in Manchester, and his wife took on jobs in manufacturing. At the age of 50, he became a wandering poet, entirely dependent on selling his poems, often exchanging them for food or whisky; he and his wife, with five or six children, roamed the whole extent of the Lowlands, and even went as far as the Highlands. He was much affected by his wife's death in the

A Literary Guide

Cowgate, Edinburgh in 1817, and his life became yet more precarious, especially when he began to drink heavily. In 1818, he visited **Thomas Carlyle,** a fellow native of Ecclefechan, who did his best to help him. He returned to Dumfriesshire, by this time an incorrigible drunk, and died after falling into the Nith and catching a fever, at a lodging house at Ruthwell on 22nd September 1818.

* * *

Lewis was one of many to take up the tragic story of *Fair Helen*, a story recounted in the Statistical Account of the parish of Kirkpatrick Fleming. In Lewis's version, he pictures a fight between two rivals for Helen's affections, Fleming, heir to Mossknowe, and the vengeful Bell, heir to Blackwood-house. Lewis's historical introduction dates the story to the reign of Mary Tudor or James VI. Bell takes his revenge on his successful rival by attempting to assassinate him, but ends by killing his love. The description is atmospheric: "Low in a vale by Kirtle's stream, /An ancient church-yard stands, / Where solemn silence sits enthron'd / And sacred awe commands". His pastoral description in his *O'er the moor amang the heather* is equally happy, where the maid answers his inquiry with "I go, kind sir, to seek my father, / Whose fleecy charge, he tends at large,/ On yon green hills, beyond the heather". His other themes are more autobiographical, such as the ode on Annan, *In praise of Scotch whisky,* and his thoughts on poverty, which is the constant companion of the poet ("Who long has lived beneath thy sway"), but also has its purpose as "virtue's fiery test". That his humanitarian sentiments extended to all is testified to by his early plea for *The African Slave,* a long narrative poem ending in praise of Wilberforce. He gives a description of the pre-lapsarian paradise of the slave's African homeland, followed by the horrors of the slave-ships : "Numbers crammed in narrow compass, / Chained in rows, like beasts of prey". Perhaps one of his most successful, but little known, essays in Scots verse, is the comic poem addressed to one James MacGill in Wigtown, entitled *The Muse in a Passion,* where the poet receives an unexpected visit from his Muse, whom he at first fails to recognise, until she begins a scolding reproof: "..thou senseless, sakeless snool, / Thou poor hen-hearted worthless tool, / I am thy Muse, thou hair-brain'd fool, / And no a ghost; Wi' thee I ha'e dreed muckle dool / And labour lost". She ends , prophetically, reflecting Lewis's insight into his own ultimate fate: "Adieu ! thou worthless peddlin' dog, / Gae trot thy ways o'er moss and bog.. / May thou be ever curs'd , thou rogue, / Wi' chapman's drouth!"

BIBLIOGRAPHY:
Fair Helen of Kirkconnel (1796); *A Collection of Poems and Songs* (1802); *The African Slave* (1815)

A Literary Guide

Charles Kirkpatrick Sharpe
1781-1851
Closeburn, Hoddam

Charles Kirkpatrick Sharpe, man of letters and dilettante antiquarian, was a friend of Sir Walter Scott's and published some important collections of ballads. He also edited some antiquarian literary curiosities and published some etchings, some of which were prized possessions of Scott.

Charles Kirkpatrick Sharpe was descended from the noble families of Eglinton and Cassilis on his mother's side and from the family of Closeburn on his father's. He was born at Hoddam Castle in 1781. He was educated with a view to taking episcopal orders and for a time attended Christ Church College, Oxford, where he was an accomplished classicist. He was, however, too much a leisured man of letters to pursue a career in the church, and, on his return to Scotland, devoted himself to the collection of antiquarian objects and some poetic composition. He was notable for his Jacobite beliefs and for dressing in the fashions of a bygone generation, carrying a green umbrella with a long brass point and a crozier-shaped horn handle, which made him a kenspeckle figure in Edinburgh. Perhaps not surprisingly, since he had been inspired by traditional songs he had heard from his father's servants, he became a correspondent of Sir Walter Scott's, after the first two volumes of the *Minstrelsy of the Scottish Border* were published. In 1803, he contributed two old ballads *The Twa Corbies* and *The Douglas Tragedy* and two of his own composition *The Murder of Caerlaveroc* and *The Lord Herries - his complaint*. His later *Metrical Legends* were again favourably noticed by Scott, who would have recruited him as a writer for the *Quarterly Review*, had Sharpe's dilettantism not proved an obstacle. From 1813, Sharpe was living in Edinburgh, in Princes Street,

61

with his widowed mother. His *Ballad Book* collection was also indebted to Scott. Kirkpatrick Sharpe's sketches were put on display at Abbotsford: one was a humorous etching entitled "Queen Elizabeth Dancing High and Disposedly", showing the Queen demonstrating to the Scottish envoy, Sir James Melville, that she could out-dance Mary Stuart. Another sketch illustrated a border legend, the subject of a ballad by James Hogg, *The Marriage of Muckle-mou'd Meg* and a collection of his etchings appeared as *Portraits by an Amateur* in 1833. He was a prolific, and often quixotic, editor of obscure histories and letters; Scott reviewed his edition of Kirkton's *The Secret and True History of the Church of Scotland* at length in 1818, which was notable for its piquant footnotes and introduction. Kirkpatrick Sharpe was a mine of information on genealogies, often contributing information to other authors and editors; Scott wrote in his diary: "Strange that a man should be so curious after scandal of centuries old! Not but that Charles loves it fresh and fresh also.." Scott also described Kirkpatrick Sharpe's artistic talent as "a mixture between Hogarth and some of those foreign masters who painted temptations of St. Anthony, and such grotesque subjects". His collection of rare manuscripts and antiquities was considerable, and he was able to contribute some of Hume's letters to another Scott publication, *The Annual Register*, from his family archive at Hoddam. In 1841, he had succeeded to the Hoddam estate, after his father's death, but continued living much of the time in Edinburgh, engaging in his favourite literary and artistic pursuits. He died a bachelor in 1851 and his collections were auctioned. He is buried in the family vault at Hoddam.

* * *

Of Sharpe's original work, his contribution to Scott's *Minstrelsy* of his *Lord Herries* is the best, relating to Repentance Tower, which stood on his father's estate at Hoddam. Sharpe's ballad explains the name of the tower by the action of Lord Herries, who ruthlessly drowned some English soldiers in the Solway to prevent his boat from sinking in a storm. George Neilson later traced the name to another Lord Herries, prominent at the battle of Langside on Queen Mary's side, who caused the death of fourteen hostages at Carlisle, who were executed in retaliation for Herries' treacherous attack on the English. Whatever the history, Sharpe's ballad achieves a dark mood of regret: "Bright shone the moon on Hoddam's

A Literary Guide

wall, / Bright on Repentance Tower; / Mirk was the Lord of Hoddam's saul, / That chief sae sad and sour". His preservation of traditional ballads was equally important; *The Twa Corbies* contains an unforgettable and chilling picture of a fresh slain corpse, through the crow's eye view: "Ye'll sit on his white hause-bane, / And I'll pike out his twa blue e'en; / Wi' ae lock o' his yellow hair / We'll theek our nest when it grows bare". His *Ballad Book* of 1823, inscribed to Walter Scott, included the well-known song *Annie Laurie* and he also conserved versions of others, like *Fair Janet*; others are coarse and humorous tales, popular in the country. Of the unusual historical works Kirkpatrick Sharpe edited, most have become rare editions, since they were issued in small impressions. Most betray his taste for the bizarre, or the quaintly exotic: in 1827, he edited *A Memorial of the Conversion of Jean Livingston, Lady Waristoun, with an Account of her Carriage at her Execution, July 1600*, being an account of the trial of a lady executed for the murder of her husband. His introduction to *Memorialls, or the Memorable Things that Fell Out within this Island of Brittain from 1638 to 1684* contains a classic account of witchcraft. He also brought out *Surgundo, or the Valiant Christian*, a celebration of the victory of Roman Catholic forces at Glenlivet in 1594.

BIBLIOGRAPHY:
Metrical Legends and Other Poems (1807); *Memorialls, or, the Memorable Things that fell out within this Island of Brittain from 1638 to 1684* (1818); *A Ballad Book* (1823); *A Memorial of the Conversion of Jean Livingston, Lady Waristoun, with an Account of her Carriage at her Execution, July 1600* (1827); *Portraits by an Amateur* (1833); *Surgundo, or the Valiant Christian* (1837); James Kirkton, *The Secret and True History of the Church of Scotland* (1817); Walter Scott, *Minstrelsy of the Scottish Border* (1802-1803)

PLACES TO VISIT: A rare collection of Charles Kirkpatrick Sharpe manuscripts and sketches is held at Broughton House, Kirkcudbright.

Henry Duncan
1774-1846
Ruthwell

Henry Duncan, minister of Ruthwell for 47 years, was distinguished in an extraordinary variety of fields: he rescued from obscurity and decay the world-famous Ruthwell cross, the finest survival from Anglo-Saxon Britain and probably one of the finest monuments of early Mediaeval Europe; he founded the first Savings Bank on business principles; he engaged in popular education; he founded two newspapers and discovered fossil footprints at Corncockle Muir quarry.

Henry Duncan's father, George Duncan, was minister of Lochrutton in the Stewartry of Kirkcudbright; his mother was the daughter of William McMurdo, burgess and magistrate of Dumfries. At first, the children were educated at home by a tutor, and then Henry Duncan was sent to the Academy at Dumfries. In 1788, he went to St. Andrew's University, where he largely concentrated on languages. In his son's *Memoir* of 1848, it is recorded that at this time, Henry built a mausoleum for a pet nightingale, complete with a figure weeping real tears and decorated with a Latin motto: both the construction and the Latin composition were his own work. **James Currie**, a cousin to the family, proposed to George Duncan that Henry should follow his brothers to Liverpool, where he could obtain a post with the bankers, Messrs. Heywood. Henry Duncan arrived in Liverpool in 1790, where he found in Currie's house the hub of intellectual and social life of the city. At age 16, Duncan took part in the Socinian controversy then raging in the church, and earned Currie's disapprobation

A Literary Guide

for his stance, as well as for an apparent inattention to business. George Duncan allowed Henry to return home after three years, and he joined Dugald Stewart's moral philosophy class in Edinburgh in 1793. He spent the next four years studying with the aim of entering the Church, and attended classes at both Glasgow and Edinburgh. He composed satires, epigrams and some poetry, and was a companion of the **Rev William Gillespie** of Kells. In 1798, he returned to Lochrutton, and was taken on trial for licence by the Presbytery of Dumfries. Before obtaining a charge, he became tutor for some time to the sons of Colonel Erskine of Mar and made a name for himself by rallying the Highlanders against the threat of French invasion. In 1799, both Lochmaben and Ruthwell parishes fell vacant, and Duncan took the less prestigious charge at Ruthwell. He began his career of practical philanthropy almost immediately, finding great distress in the parish, whose minister had been ineffective during an illness lasting thirteen years, and which had been devastated by the consecutive bad harvests of the late 1790's. Duncan arranged through his brothers in Liverpool to ship a cargo of Indian corn to the parish, which he retailed in Ruthwell through a reliable agent, also allowing credit to the needy. He rallied the parish against French invasion, publishing newspaper articles and captaining the "Ruthwell Volunteers". Anxious about the habit of dependence on the "poor box", he re-established a Friendly Society, established a parish library, and ran conversational lectures on a Sunday, encouraged by his friend, Sir David Brewster. In 1804, he married the daughter of his predecessor in the parish, Miss Agnes Craig, who is famed for entertaining **Burns**, during his last visit to the Brow Well; Duncan had himself seen the great man, when Burns was on friendly terms with his father at Lochrutton, and he was later to help sponsor the Mausoleum at Dumfries. Duncan's campaign for popular education and, particularly, the instilling of the virtue of independence, was pursued through a series of publications under the title of *The Scotch Cheap Repository Tracts*, a pioneer of the popular monthly magazine, and to which he himself contributed *The Cottage Fireside* and *The Honest Farmer*. Sir David Brewster asked him for contributions to the *Edinburgh Encyclopaedia*, to which he contributed an article on **Thomas Blacklock**, and Thomson pressed him for articles for the *Christian Instructor*. Duncan next turned his attention to the press, as a means for his schemes to promote social reform, and, with financial aid from his brothers in Liverpool, he began publishing the *Dumfries and Galloway Courier* in 1809 : **Carlyle**, who was among the visitors to the Ruthwell manse, made some early contributions to the newspaper, and was introduced to Brewster through Duncan's help. In 1810, Duncan was among the many concerned about a proposed introduction of poor rates, and, having read with excitement a proposal by John Bone to establish an "economical bank" for savings, which would depend for its success on prudent habits among the poor themselves, he wrote a paper promoting the idea of a Bank for Savings. The first trial was made at Ruthwell, with its own draconian rules enforcing the required level of savings for each depositor, and the example rapidly spread. In 1815, Duncan published his *On the Nature and Advantages of Parish Banks; Together with a Corrected Copy of the Rules and Regulations of the Parent Institution in Ruthwell*. The success of the idea involved Duncan not only in voluminous correspondence with potential organisers of such banks, but also in government legislation designed to provide legal protection, and in some controversy, when the claim of Ruthwell to be the first of its kind was challenged. In 1823, Duncan received the degree of Doctor of Divinity from his old university of St Andrew's. The number of schemes in which he was involved was truly astonishing : he promoted the Mechanics' Institute at Dumfries, employed the poor on his own glebe and on road repairs, wrote *The Young South Country Weaver* to counter disaffection among workers in manufactures, and wrote a voluminous novel *William Douglas, or the Scottish Exiles* (1826), inspired by Scott and set in Covenanting times. The greatest of his contributions, however, was undoubtedly his re-discovery of the Ruthwell Cross, which had been demolished by decree of the General Assembly in 1642 under the terms of the "Act anent the demolishing of Idolatrous Monuments". Despite orders to chip and splinter the cross, the minister of the time, the Rev. Gavin Young, had preserved large sections of the cross in the clay floor of the parish church, where they remained until alterations to the floor carried out in 1790. Duncan was fascinated by the fragments, some of which had already attracted the attention of antiquarians over the preceding 150 years, and set about piecing them together, in a crusade which would last 25 years. In 1802, he re-erected the main shaft of the cross, and finally in 1832, he completed it by an imaginative reconstruction of the missing cross-head, which he had

A Literary Guide

decorated with Masonic symbols. A model was constructed for the Society of Antiquaries, and he created another out of beeswax, which is still on display in Ruthwell, at the Savings Bank Museum. He delivered a paper on the subject to the Society of Antiquaries in 1832, and wrote an account of his discovery for the *New Statistical Account of Scotland*. Perhaps equally epoch-making was his discovery, at Corncockle Muir, near Lochmaben, in 1827, of the fossil footprints of a four-footed animal. He corresponded with Dr. Buckland at Oxford, thus becoming the first man to attempt a scientific analysis of the traces, and the animal was tentatively identified as a reptile, probably a tortoise. He also published his most substantial poetical work, *The Sacred Philosophy of the Seasons*, beginning with *Winter*, published in the winter of 1835. In 1836, Duncan remarried – his first wife, Agnes, had died in 1832; his second wife was Mary Grey Lundie, herself a widow of a minister at Kelso. Duncan meanwhile continued to plunge into other controversies, where he consistently adopted a Liberal position : he supported the Roman Catholic Relief Bill, 1829, wrote his *Presbyter's Letters on the West India Question* on the subject of the slave trade, tried to promote a University at Dumfries, and was Moderator of the General Assembly in the momentous years leading up to the Disruption. By 1842, he was being slowly drawn into the controversy over patronage in the church, and published his *Letter from the Minister of Ruthwell to his Flock on the Spiritual Independence of the Church* and left the church in the Disruption of 1843. He was one of those who launched the newspaper, the *Dumfries Standard* on the basis of "Non-Intrusion" principles, and, suffering some personal hardship, began the building of a Free Church, often preaching in the open air to congregations which no longer had a church building. His health was already deteriorating as he travelled to Liverpool to raise money for a new Free Church manse at Mount Kedar, near Mouswald, and it was on his return, while preaching, that he became ill and was taken to his brother-in-law's home at Comlongon, where he died. He is buried in the parish churchyard at Ruthwell, and an obelisk was erected to his memory at Mount Kedar.

* * *

The Ruthwell Cross, whose preservation was largely due to Henry Duncan's intervention, deserves a mention in its own right as a work of literature, belonging to the era round 700 AD, in which Dumfriesshire formed part of the Anglo-Saxon kingdom of Northumbria. The runes incised on its margins had puzzled and fascinated visiting antiquarians, and Duncan contacted Danish and Icelandic scholars, principally TG Repp, Librarian of the Advocates' Library, Edinburgh, who was able to transliterate the characters but was baffled in their translation. His unsuccessful attempt at translation was appended to Henry Duncan's essay on the Cross, but the notion that the inscription was actually written in Anglo-Saxon did not dawn until John Mitchell Kemble, friend of Lord Tennyson and an early editor of *Beowulf*, correctly published the translation in 1840, in his *Runes of the Anglo-Saxons*. Further and dramatic enlightenment came when Kemble found in the Vercelli Codex, preserved at Piedmont in Italy, a prosopopoeic work in which the Cross itself speaks movingly to the poet of its own experience of the crucifixion: he recognised that lines from this work of Anglo-Saxon literature were those he had seen carved on the Cross at Ruthwell. Since Kemble's discovery, no aspect of the Cross has failed to generate scholarly heat : interpretations of the inscription and the ascription of its craftsmanship have been used for and against claims for native British standards in art and literature; Dr Duncan's words and those of his successors, who moved the cross to a specially constructed apse in the Ruthwell Church, have been pored over for clues as to the correctness, or otherwise, of the reconstruction. There is little doubting, however, that it was Duncan's descriptive essay which paved the way for Kemble's decipherment, and for the re-discovery of one of Northern Europe's most magnificent early art-works and of the most moving poem in the Anglo-Saxon canon. Duncan's second major find, that of reptilian footprints at Corncockle Muir, involved him in the discovery of what was then the almost unthinkably remote geological eras of prehistory : these traces lead "the mind into the remotest antiquity, and perplexes it in a maze of interminable conjectures as to the state of the earth's materials when these living creatures walked on its surface, and bathed in other waters, and browsed on other pastures; and not less as to the extraordinary changes and convulsions of nature which have since then taken place, and which have broken up, overturned, and remodelled all things". Amongst his works of popular education, his *Sacred Philosophy of the Seasons* is an interesting attempt to combine religious edification with

A Literary Guide

education on subjects as diverse as astronomy, the Eddystone lighthouse, Brunel's Thames tunnel, and the Esquimaux. The books were composed so as to provide a reading for every day of the year, with secular information being provided during the week and a moral being pointed for the Sabbath. At the other end of the spectrum from Duncan's technical papers on geology and economics is his lively *Curling Song*: it is quoted in the *Memorabilia Curliana Mabenensia*, 1830, as "perhaps the best curling song ever composed". It is written in a spirited vernacular and with an insider's knowledge: "Up Curler ! frae your bed sae warm,/ And leave your coaxing wife, man; / Gae get your besom, tramps, and stane, / And join the friendly strife, man : -". It concludes with a moral, couched humorously in curling terms : "May Curlers on life's slippery rink, / Frae cruel rubs be free, man. / Or should a treacherous bias lead, / Their erring course ajee, man / Some friendly in-ring may they meet/ To guide them to the tee, man". Interestingly, Duncan's second wife, Mary Lundie, was a prolific author in her own right, producing a memoir of Rev. M Bruen, and of her daughter, Mary Lundie Duncan, a life of her son, George Archibald Lundie who was a missionary in Samoa, and *America as I Found it*, the text of which is now in possession of the University of Michigan.

BIBLIOGRAPHY:
On the Nature and Advantages of Parish Banks (1815); *The Scotch Cheap Repository Tracts* (1815); *The Cottage Fireside* (1815); *The Young South Country Weaver* (1820-1821); *William Douglas, or the Scottish Exiles* (1826); *Presbyter's Letters on the West India Question* (1830); *Curling Song* in *Memorabilia Curliana Mabenensia* (1830); *The Sacred Philosophy of the Seasons* (1835-1836); *Parish of Ruthwell* in *New Statistical Account of Scotland* (1837); George John C. Duncan, *Memoir of the Rev. Henry Duncan* (1848)

PLACES TO VISIT: The Ruthwell Savings Bank Museum contains a full display on the life and work of Henry Duncan. Ruthwell Church houses the famous Ruthwell Cross. There is a statue to Henry Duncan at Dumfries and an obelisk to his memory at Mount Kedar, Mouswald.

Susannah Hawkins
1787-1868
Burnswark

Susannah Hawkins' verse cannot be classed as literature, but it may well be a specimen - unusual in having survived at all - of a popular class of verse, which must have been much more extensive than we can now know: it was sold as pamphlets from house to house by travelling packmen. In this case, Susannah Hawkins was both author and seller. She was a well-known figure on the roads in Galloway, and travelled as far as central Scotland and northern England.

Susannah Hawkins was born near Burnswark Hill, daughter of a blacksmith. As soon as she had learnt to read, she was engaged to tend cattle, and it was then that "the Muse first inspired her to sing the praises of the great God". The muse was quite particular in her views, since she also "whispered in my ear to keep by the Protestant faith – the Established religion of the kingdom – to look around me, and Nature would tell me I had but one God to serve, and one faith to believe". When she was employed, probably dairying, or as a farm servant, an employer wrote to **John McDiarmid**, editor of the *Courier* on her behalf. He was interested in her aspirations to literature, and in 1829, *The Poetical Works of Susannah Hawkins* appeared. All subsequent editions, up to her death in 1868 were published by the McDiarmids. When she was taken on as a servant by a Mr. Halliday, schoolmaster of Mouswald, he gave her lessons, and she may have acquired the rudiments of French. Her anonymous obituarist wrote that, since she had a warm admiration for Burns, she visited the monument when in Ayrshire and exclaimed: "Hech, sirs, an' this is what they do wi' us whan we are dead". Her labours, hawking her new editions year by year, must have borne fruit, since she was able to build herself a cottage, near Burnswark, which she called "Relief Cottage"; as her obituary commented, she had pursued the muse with "industry and perseverance". She died there, after accidentally falling, and is buried at Ecclefechan.

* * *

A Literary Guide

Susannah Hawkins's verses are marked by a simple religious faith in the workings of providence, obvious morals, and a disarmingly frank avowal that her poetry may lack polish : "Sir, These few lines that I do write, / Do shew my merit's small, / For my dull muse does seldom give / Me any help at all". Often, poems are addressed to the local nobility, whose homes, one suspects, were frequent ports of call in her travels. In the 1861 edition, she gave a brief account of her life, and adopted a motto which expressed her satisfaction in writing : "Tis pleasant sure to see one's name in print - / A book's a book, although there's nothing in't". It is hard not to be moved by the picture this conjures up of Susannah Hawkins, whose artistic aspirations were never dampened by the prospect of trudging the roads, even well into her eighties.

BIBLIOGRAPHY:
The Poetical Works of Susannah Hawkins (1829); *The Poems and Songs of Susannah Hawkins* (1832-1867)

George Neilson
1858-1923
Horseclose, near Ruthwell

George Neilson, born at the farm of Horseclose in the eastern part of Ruthwell, was a historian of meticulous scholarship, with a particular interest in the Scottish history and poetry of the twelfth to the fifteenth centuries. He wrote extensively on the history of Annandale, commenting that local history "after all ceases to be local when, as it scarcely ever fails to do, it illustrates the particular working of general principles".

George Neilson's father, Captain Edward Neilson, who had married Janet Paterson, daughter of the tenant of Horseclose farm, died on a passage to Buenos Aires, and his son was brought up by his mother and her family. It was an enlightened and educated household, the nearest neighbours with whom they were on visiting terms being **Thomas Carlyle's** sister and brother in law, the Austins of the Gill. Neilson attended the parish school of Cummertrees, but later, at his maternal uncle's recommendation, was transferred to King William's College on the Isle of Man. He was then apprenticed to the law at the prominent law firm of Adamson and Symons in Dumfries. At Glasgow University, he came first in his class in law and later dedicated his legal study *Trial by Combat* to his friend and mentor, Professor Berry. By 1881, he had completed his legal training and in 1884, entered practice on his own account. He became Procurator Fiscal in Glasgow and was noted for his wit and judgement in court. Later he was the obvious choice for Stipendiary Magistrate for Glasgow. His earliest literary and historical work appeared in the *Dumfries and Galloway Standard*, and later he was a prolific contributor to the *Scottish Historical Review*. He was

A Literary Guide

married in 1892 to a daughter of Mr. Thomas Richardson of Hexham. In 1902, he was invited to give university lectures on *Early Scottish Literature and History* and was rewarded by the University of Glasgow with the degree of LL.D; he also gave the Rhind Lectures on *Scottish Feudal Traits*. He retired from the magistrate's bench through ill-health and died in 1923.

* * *

Even Neilson's earliest work *Annandale under the Bruces* is distinguished by a meticulous attention to chronicles, charters and archaeological evidence. Frequently, a shrewd wit is interspersed with the scholarly detail: speaking of social conditions and religious belief in Annandale, he writes that "(t)he gallows tree .. is an indispensable adjunct of civilisation. Placed under due control, a deil is an equally indispensable adjunct of true religion". His most substantial work was both legal and antiquarian, on the obsolete legal remedy of "trial by combat", whereby a plea would be staked on the issue of a duel. In it, he gives an historical account of the clan fight on the North Inch of Perth, of which Sir Walter Scott gives a romanticised picture in the *Fair Maid of Perth*. His later works were shorter pieces, often dedicated to Border antiquities and are distinguished by a learned attention to etymologies (eg. In *Peel: its Meaning and Derivation*, where he derives the word from "palus", a stake, by attending to the originally wooden construction of these fortified structures), by tense logical argument and by their literary quality. In "*Per Lineam Valli*" on the nature and dating of the defensive mounds at Hadrian's Wall, he concludes: "A new theory has pitched its camp .. it has completed its entrenchment of fact and argument for winter quarters, not without apprehension of attack, but ready, and hopeful afterwards to rest secure." Romantic traditions of the area, such as that of Repentance Tower and other Solway legends (*Annals of the Solway*) are also well described, and false provenances analysed and discarded. He applied the techniques of detailed comparative literary analysis which he had first employed on the works of Barbour to the poetry of Huchown of Awle Ryale, to prove that he was identical with Sir Hew of Eglinton, and author of a considerable body of mediaeval poetry. He edited the quarter-centenary volume on George Buchanan and his latest work was on the history of the Scottish Parliament - an edition of the *Acts of the Lords of Council in Civil Cases*.

Dumfries and Galloway

BIBLIOGRAPHY :
Annandale under the Bruces (1887); *Trial by Combat* (1890); *Per Lineam Valli* (1891); *Peel: its Meaning and Derivation* (1893); *Repentance Tower and its Tradition* (1895); *Annals of the Solway* (1899); *George Buchanan* (1906); *Acts of the Lords of Council in Civil Cases* (1918)

PLACES TO VISIT : Repentance Tower, near Hoddam, may be visited.

A Literary Guide

Robert Burns
1759-1796
Ellisland and Dumfries

The figure of Robert Burns towers like a colossus over Scottish culture and letters: for any writer since, and, perhaps, for any Scot, whether attracted or repelled by Burns's antithetical qualities, a reaction of some kind has been inevitable. Each generation has reshaped Burns's image to suit its own requirements and preoccupations : the mythological figures of the divinely inspired "ploughman poet" or the drunken debaucher are now being replaced by a more balanced view of Burns's acquaintance with early Scots poetry and Enlightenment thinking. His fame rests largely on the 34 carefully chosen poems of the "Kilmarnock Edition" (1786), but the work he did after moving to Dumfriesshire in 1788 includes his lengthiest and most masterly work "Tam O' Shanter" and the important work he did to rescue Scottish folk song, both by his own original contributions and re-worked versions of traditional compositions.

Robert Burns, eldest son of seven children born to William Burnes and Agnes Brown, was born at Alloway, Ayrshire in 1759. William Burnes was setting up a market garden at Alloway and was also a gardener at Doonholm. His father took a much greater interest in his children's education than most men of his class and means : at the age of six, Robert and Gilbert Burns attended John Murdoch's school, where Robert read a modernised version of Blind Harry's *William Wallace* and an anthology of verse. At home, his father took charge of the children's religious education, but his mother and her cousin's widow, Betty Davidson, influenced Robert through their stock of traditional songs and stories, particularly of the supernatural. William Burnes' employer owned the farm of Mount Oliphant, and Burnes was offered a 12 year tenancy in 1765; in 1768, Burns's education with John Murdoch ended. Mount Oliphant was not a successful venture, but the period was a formative one for Burns : he wrote a love-song "O, once I lov'd a bonnie lass" for Nelly Kirkpatrick and, as he writes : "Thus with me began Love and Poesy". He was sent to Kirkoswald to study surveying and there met some of the characters – John Davidson and Douglas Graham – who were much later to feature in *Tam O' Shanter*. After the death of the owner at Mount Oliphant, in 1777, they moved to the farm of Lochlie, near Tarbolton. It was here that Burns and some friends founded the "Bachelors' Club", a debating society, and where, in 1781, Burns became a Freemason. Between 1781-2, Burns became a flax-dresser in Irvine: these were years of some unhappiness, and ended with Burns's return to Lochlie, where there had been a disastrous fire, a court action with their landlord, and where his father, who had been often at odds with his eldest son in his last years, died in 1784. His father's death left Burns feeling some guilt, but was also perhaps a liberating influence: certainly, the years of 1785-6 were the years when he composed the works published in the Kilmarnock edition. By 1784, Burns had discovered the poetry of Robert Fergusson and found in the use of the Scots vernacular an ideal outlet for his ridicule of the rigid Calvinism of the "Auld Lichts" in the local community. *Holy Willie's Prayer*, *The Holy Tulzie* and *The Twa Herds* represent just such powerful satires on hypocrisy and bigotry. His *The Holy Fair* is written in good humour, and shows much of the effect of Fergusson on Burns's writing. By late 1785, Burns had fallen in love with Jean Armour, the daughter of a prosperous stonemason in Mauchline, but after her father issued a writ against Burns once she had become pregnant, he was forced into considering emigration. An Ayr friend agreed to find Burns a position as book-keeper at Port Antonio in Jamaica, and it was owing to the emigration plan that Burns decided to publish: "'twas a delicious idea that I would be called a clever fellow, even tho' it should never reach my ears a poor Negro-driver, or perhaps a victim of that inhospitable clime gone to the world of the Spirits". In July 1786, the Kilmarnock edition, to which his Ayrshire friends had subscribed, was published, containing some of his best known poems : *The Cotter's Saturday Night*, *To a Mouse*, *Address to the Deil*, and *The Auld Farmer's New Year Morning Salutation*

A Literary Guide

to His Auld Mare Maggie. Emigration seemed less attractive when the edition was hailed as a success: Henry Mackenzie set the tone which described Burns as a "heaven-taught ploughman". In addition, Jean Armour had borne Burns twins. It was also in 1786 that he met "Highland Mary", beloved of Victorian artists, who was the byre-maid at Tarbolton, and nursemaid to Gavin Hamilton's children. In May, they famously met for the last time at a confluence of the River Ayr, exchanged Bibles and vows. Mary Campbell's death not long afterwards distressed Burns, and biographers have also anguished over the question as to whether she died bearing Burns's child. Robert Cromek told the story of the exchange of Bibles and **Currie** obfuscated the question, by writing of "Youthful passions.. the history of which it would be improper to reveal, were it even in one's power". As the success of the Kilmarnock edition became known, even the Armours softened their opposition to Burns. **Robert Heron** may have been typical in his excitement, when, on being given a copy of the poems as he prepared for bed, he was unable to stop reading until the book was finished. Through Dugald Stewart, who was a member of the Tarbolton Lodge, Burns began to make the acquaintance of influential people. Dr Lawrie, a clergyman at Newmilns, sent a copy of the poems to **Dr Blacklock**, and passed on Blacklock's favourable verdict to Burns. Already hesitant about emigration, Burns went to Edinburgh, where he was lionised and regarded by the gentry as something of a phenomenon. It was Blacklock who suggested an Edinburgh edition of the poems, and a second edition duly appeared in April 1787, published by William Creech. There is no doubt that women of high rank found his passionate nature attractive; one of the more lasting relationships he formed at this time was with Mrs. Frances Anna Dunlop, a descendant of William Wallace, who was 29 years older than Burns. It was a motherly relationship, and seems to have survived Burns's sexual adventures and Mrs. Dunlop's criticisms of Burns's poems, but foundered on his attitude to events in revolutionary France: Mrs Dunlop's daughters were married to aristocratic emigrés. Despite, or perhaps because of, his success in Edinburgh, Burns began to feel that he was merely a sideshow-attraction, and was frustrated at his failure to find permanent patronage. In the summer of 1787, he visited the Borders and the Highlands, and began to consider the offer by Patrick Miller of Dalswinton of a lease on his farm in Dumfriesshire. It was at this point that Burns began his important involvement with Scots song: James Johnston was experimenting with the printing of music and the *Scots Musical Museum* (1787-1803) eventually included about 160 of Burns's composition, the chief component of his creative activity once he moved to Dumfriesshire. He also became involved in a romantic affair with Mrs Maclehose, whom he addressed as "Clarinda", signing himself "Sylvander": the affair's best memorial is his *Ae Fond Kiss*. Since Jean Armour was pregnant again, and he was under financial pressure, in 1788 he finally took the lease of the farm at Ellisland. His marriage to Jean was regularised at Mauchline, and he began the hard work of preparing the farm for her coming. To this period belong *Of a' the Airts* and *I Hae a Wife o' My Ain*. In Dumfries and at the neighbouring estate of Friar's Carse belonging to the **Riddell** family, Burns was accepted as an honoured guest: in 1790, he wrote *Tam O' Shanter* as a result of the contact he had made with Francis Grose at Friar's Carse, who requested a poem to accompany an illustration of Alloway Kirk in his *Antiquities of Scotland*. The failing farm was eventually given up and Patrick Miller bought back the lease from Burns, whose health and nerves were increasingly fragile. Burns had had to take on an excise appointment to support his growing family and, from 1791, he worked from Dumfries, holding the post – despite the authorities' disapproval of his unwisely expressed sympathy for the French revolutionaries – until his death in 1796. In the later years of his life, Burns worked hard on song-writing, and collaborated with George Thomson, who produced the *Select Collection of Original Scottish Airs* (1793-1818): the greatest of these was perhaps *Scots Wha Ha'e* and the best-known his re-working of *Auld Lang Syne*. In Dumfries, where Jean was pregnant again, and had also had to take on a love-child of Burns by the barmaid Ann Park, the family moved from an apartment into the house at Mill Hole Brae. In 1793, the second Edinburgh edition appeared, this time including *Tam O'Shanter*. By New Year 1794, Burns's relations with the **Riddells** were shattered almost irretrievably by the "Rape of the Sabines" disaster, when Burns disgraced himself at Friars' Carse by an over-enthusiastic imitation of the classical incident. In 1796, Burns was becoming ill with rheumatic fever, and a course of sea-bathing, to be undertaken at the village of Brow, was recommended by Dr William Maxwell. On 21st July 1796, he died at Dumfries and, as he was being buried, Jean gave birth to their last child. Friends of Burns, like John Syme and Alexander Cunningham, rallied round to ensure that Jean Armour would not be in need, and the much-criticised edition of Burns's works, together with a biography by **Dr Currie,** eventually raised £2000 for the family. His death was, however, only the beginning of his cult, which was expressed not only in the building of monuments at the various Burns shrines, but also in an immense literary industry in many countries, and in the institution of "Burns Nights" on 25th January, which are now a world-wide phenomenon.

* * *

There is probably no aspect of Burns's life, no reference in his poetry, and no obscure link which has not been discussed in the huge literature surrounding his life and work; fortunately, the emotional and linguistic immediacy of his poetry and songs is such that one has to know little about this much-trampled ground in order to respond to his work. Burns's concerns – with nature, politics and with liberty in particular, with the plight of the poor, with love and lust – have perhaps enabled him to reach a wider audience than any other poet. The different moods of Burns's early poetry – ranging between masterpieces of invective and nostalgic and reverent pictures of the peasantry – may be seen in his *Holy Willie's Prayer* and in *The Cotter's Saturday Night.* The *Prayer* was written in defence of Burns's friend, Gavin Hamilton, who had been involved in a "Sessional process" with "Holy Willie": it satirises the Calvinist doctrine of predestination and allows Holy Willie to condemn himself through his own words, with their combination of unctuous religiosity and temporal self-interest. This is the ironic conclusion: "But L-d, remember me and mine / Wi' mercies temporal and divine!/ That I for grace and gear may shine, / Excell'd by nane!/ And a' the glory shall be thine! / AMEN! AMEN!" By contrast, the tempo and temper of *The Cotter's Saturday Night,* where one can hear the classical influence of Gray's *Elegy,* is a world apart: "The toil-worn Cotter frae his labour goes, / This night his weekly moil is at an end,/ Collects his spades, his mattocks and his hoes, / Hoping the morn in ease and rest to spend, / And weary, o'er the muir, his course does hameward bend". It is characteristic of Burns that the density of his use of Scots varies widely, according to the subject; he also makes skilful use of a particular illustration to pass to general, philosophical conclusions. In *To a Mouse* he condenses complex Romantic political theory and egalitarian sentiment into a reflection on the mouse's reaction to his destruction of her nest: "I'm truly sorry Man's dominion /Has broken Nature's social union, /

An' justifies that ill-opinion, / Which makes thee startle, / At me, thy poor earth-born companion, / An' fellow-mortal!". His gift for reviving and re-working the folk-heritage of stories about the supernatural had a far-reaching impact on succeeding developments in Scots poetry and writing: poems such as *Tam O'Shanter* and *Address to the Deil* did much to articulate the curious and uniquely Scots familiarity with the devil, who is part Christian image and (much more largely) supernatural being, and who is treated with a blend of comedy and horror. Nationalism also received its imprint from Burns in his fiery song of liberty, *Scots Wha Ha'e*, and *To a Haggis*, with its mockery of foreign customs, now ritually recited at Burns Suppers. Many of the songs from the Dumfries years have entered the language, as with: "O my Luve's like a red, red rose / That's newly sprung in June; / O my Luve's like the melodie/ That's sweetly play'd in tune". There is little doubt that his concentrated efforts to collect, and modify, Scots songs in his last years did much to rescue folksong from oblivion; his revival of Scots language, which both expressed local tradition and was capable of appealing to a world-audience, had an incalculable effect on the future of Scottish literature.

BIBLIOGRAPHY:
Poems, Chiefly in the Scottish Dialect (1786, Kilmarnock; 2nd ed. 1787, Edinburgh); James Johnson, *The Scots Musical Museum* (1787-1803); George Thomson, *A Select Collection of Original Scottish Airs* (1793-1818)

PLACES TO VISIT: Ellisland Farm, and Burns's House in Dumfries are both open to the public; many places associated with the Bard, like the Brow Well, are also signposted.

A Literary Guide

JM Barrie
1860-1937
Dumfries

Although the inspiration of JM Barrie's early successes undoubtedly lay in his childhood – and his mother's childhood – home of Kirriemuir in Angus, and the later stimulus to the composition of "Peter Pan" came from his acquaintance with the Llewelyn Davies boys, his boyhood sojourn at Dumfries deserves mention: at the Academy, he received encouragement for his dramatic talents and interests, and he was later to claim that his days at Dumfries were the happiest of his life.

James Matthew Barrie was born in 1860 at Kirriemuir, the seventh child of an independent and self-educated Forfarshire weaver. When his talented elder brother died in an accident, Barrie became his living substitute in the eyes of his mother, Margaret Ogilvy, and the two exchanged tales and reminiscences in a fantasy existence, closed to the rest of the world. Barrie's education was promoted by his eldest brother, Alexander, a teacher, whom he followed first to Glasgow Academy, and then to Dumfries, where Alexander Barrie became School Inspector for the district. Barrie joined his brother at Dumfries in 1873, and on his first day at the Academy, he befriended Stuart Gordon, the son of the Sheriff Clerk. The Gordons lived at Moat Brae, on the banks of the Nith, and the brothers and their new friend formed a pirate band, whose adventures took place along the river bank. Barrie also walked the countryside around the town with his brother, and came to love the names of Caerlaverock, Lincluden and Criffel; later, on the outskirts of the town, an awe-struck Barrie was to take his cap off to Mr **Carlyle**, seen out walking. Later in his career at the Academy, he met Wellwood Anderson, son of a Dumfries bookdealer, who founded a school manuscript journal *The Clown*; when Barrie contributed "Reckolections of a Skoolmaster", revealing the strain of whimsy which was to make him famous, Anderson invited further contributions from its author, and discovered that they shared a fascination for the theatre. Dumfries had a surprisingly good theatre for a small town, and was on the circuit of reputable theatre companies; Barrie attended every performance he could and took an interest in the stagecraft and management of the plays. Anderson proposed a dramatic club for the Academy, which he called "Dumfries Amateur Dramatic Club", and the second play of their first season, in 1876, was written by JM Barrie, under the inspiration of Fenimore Cooper. The Club gained sudden notoriety, when a local clergyman publicly attacked its performances as immoral and the affair was taken up in the press. The Rector obtained the support of influential patrons, including famous actors, for the group, and as a result of the press attention, the Club played to packed houses. Barrie was later to keep in touch with Anderson, and to write to him, with excitement, that he had been chosen as dramatic critic for the *Edinburgh Courant*, when starting out as a struggling journalist. By this time, Barrie's ambition was to become a writer, despite the family disapproval he dreaded. Partly to satisfy his family, he did take the English Literature MA course at Edinburgh University : Barrie was a freshman just as **SR Crockett**, with whose name Barrie's was later to be coupled as a leading exponent of the "Kailyard school" of Scottish literature, was leaving the university. At the University, he joined the Dumfriesshire and Galloway Literary Society, and met the young Dumfriesshire explorer, **Joseph Thomson**, who was to become a firm friend and appears in Barrie's affectionate sketch in his *An Edinburgh Eleven*.

* * *

Barrie's *Peter Pan* is quite simply the most famous children's play ever written, emerging from the stories he spun for the five Llewelyn Davies brothers, whom he was ultimately to adopt and support. Success had come much earlier, however, with sketches from his mother's recollections about bygone Kirriemuir, or "Thrums". It was his Thrums stories (*Auld Licht Idylls, When a Man's Single, A Window in Thrums*) and his novels *The Little Minister*, and *Sentimental Tommy*, with its sequel, *Tommy and Grizel* which earned Barrie his unsolicited title as master of the "Kailyarders", a term used to describe a brand of pastoral writing about Scotland, which seemed to critics to be a nostalgic refusal of the emerging values of her industrialising society. Barrie was bracketed with, although always acknowledged as a superior writer to, **Crockett** and Ian MacLaren, and certainly all had in common their having been discovered and promoted by Robertson Nicoll. Nonetheless, the label, although helpful in identifying a popular trend in Scottish writing, may conceal more than it reveals, since it describes a literary effort which ranges from the psychological complexities of *Peter Pan* to adventure stories such as Crockett's *The Raiders*, which has a greater affinity with Stevenson and Scott than with Barrie.

BIBLIOGRAPHY:
Auld Licht Idylls (1888); *When a Man's Single* (1888); *A Window in Thrums* (1889); *An Edinburgh Eleven* (1889); *The Little Minister* (1891); *Sentimental Tommy* (1896); *Tommy and Grizel* (1900); *Peter Pan* (1904)

PLACES TO VISIT: Dumfries Academy, as it was when Barrie attended it, has been replaced by modern buildings. Moat Brae, home of the Anderson family, is still standing.

Dumfries and Galloway

Maria Riddell
1772-1808
Dumfries

Maria Riddell, wife to Walter Riddell of Woodley Park, near Dumfries, was the most accomplished of all **Burns**'s *female acquaintances. She was an authoress in her own right and exchanged verses with the poet. She was notoriously involved in the breach with Burns over what has become known as the "Rape of the Sabines" incident, but showed her humanity in a reconciliation with him before his death, and in her balanced and perceptive appreciation of his personality published a fortnight after his death.*

Maria Woodley was the daughter of the Governor of St Kitts and the Leeward Islands. She was high-spirited and intelligent, exchanging rhyming badinage with the London wits at the age of fifteen and writing an account of her voyage to the Leeward Islands, including the incident where the ship was chased by a pirate, at the age of sixteen. She returned to England, but went back to Antigua in 1790, where she met her future husband, Walter Riddell, who had come into a property in Antigua by his deceased wife, Ann Doig. Walter's brother, Robert Riddell, was the well-known and good-humoured proprietor of Friar's Carse, which was adjacent to **Robert Burns's** farm at Ellisland, near Dumfries. Riddell admitted Burns to the grounds, which he had adorned – according to current antiquarian taste – with a Druid's Circle and Hermitage, and he became an honoured guest. It was owing to Riddell's antiquarian enthusiasms that the Glenriddell manuscripts were composed, consisting of poems and prose by Burns, to form part of Riddell's own collection. At Friar's Carse too, Burns met Francis Grose, the antiquarian, who was in Dumfriesshire collecting material for his *Antiquities of Scotland*. Grose consented to the insertion of a drawing of

Alloway Kirk in the volume, if Burns would give him a witch tale, and so originated *Tam O' Shanter*. Another of Burns's poems, *The Whistle* celebrates the drinking competition between the lairds of Maxwelton, Craigdarroch and Friar's Carse. It was here, in this somewhat Falstaffian company, that he met Robert Riddell's sister-in-law, Maria, who had moved to a property known as the "Holm of Dalscairth", but renamed "Woodley Park" in her honour. Maria, barely twenty, was fascinated by Burns, enjoying a trip with him to Wanlockhead and soliciting his influence with William Smellie, the printer and naturalist, for the publication of her *Voyages to the Madeira and Leeward Carribean Isles* in 1792. Burns wrote - in praise which sounds slightly faint-hearted - to Smellie, who subsequently befriended Maria, that "she was much beyond the common run of Lady-Poetesses of the day". But there was no doubting that there developed a literary intimacy between them, involving the exchange of letters, confidences, poetry and – once – a contraband pair of French gloves, which Burns obtained for her through his excise duties. Maria was the heroine of *Bonnie Wee Thing* and Burns named a daughter (who died in infancy) "Elizabeth Riddell Burns" after her sister-in-law. This degree of intimacy only added intensity to the sense of injury on both sides which was to occur as a result of the famous "Rape of the Sabines" incident. In the winter of 1793, a drunken episode occurred, probably at Friar's Carse, when the gentlemen decided to re-enact the classical incident of the Rape of the Sabine Women ; Burns was allocated Maria Riddell as his "Sabine" and when he carried out his part, breaking into the drawing room and probably kissing or manhandling her, the punishment of the society which had encouraged it was swift and decisive. Maria and her brother-in-law's household immediately broke off all contact with Burns, who then wrote in apology the abject "Letter from Hell". It begins "I daresay this is the first epistle you ever received from this nether world". The interpretation of the incident has been dogged by scholarly controversy, and no part of it - the questions as to where it took place, whether it was a deliberate "setting up "of Burns by the gentry, and to whom the letter was addressed – has been exempt from doubt. It now seems that Burns wrote to Mrs Robert Riddell, wife of the host, and that Maria felt obliged to break off contact to show solidarity with her family. When Burns's various overtures were ignored, he turned to vituperation in verse: his *Monody on a Lady Famed for her Caprice*,

From Esopus to Maria (though its authorship is doubted) and his unkind *Lines Pinned on Mrs. Walter Riddell's carriage* were circulated amongst friends, but, fortunately, not published. He also wrote some lines in mockery of her husband. There were attempts at reconciliation, including his heartfelt sonnet on the death of Robert Riddell and the exchange of verses "Canst thou leave me thus, my Katy?' to which she replied "Stay my Willie – yet believe me.." Eventually, they began to correspond again, after Maria had been forced to move from Woodley Park, and returned to Tinwald House and then to Halleaths, near Lochmaben in 1794. The friendship strengthened once more and eventually appears to have been fully re-established by the time she was called to the Brow Well, where Burns was already dying. He famously greeted her, in an ironic echo of the "letter from Hell" with the words: "Well, madam, have you any commands for the other world?' According to her own testimony, he expressed regret for "letters and verses written with unguarded and improper freedom". That the reconciliation was complete and heart-felt on Maria's side was demonstrated in her going by night to plant laurels on his grave, five days after he was buried. She was requested by John Syme to contribute a memorial on Burns to the *Dumfries Weekly Journal*, which is a generous and considered tribute to his genius. In financial embarrassment, the Riddells moved to England for good in 1797, and Walter Riddell eventually died in Antigua, where he was on business, in 1802. Maria continued her interest in the Burns family affairs, corresponding frequently with Burns's biographer **Dr James Currie**, to whose research she contributed (and perhaps filtered) information and verses relating to the time of her acquaintance with Burns. She received a letter from Mrs. Burns in 1804 and had been active in collecting subscribers for the new edition of his works. She had doubts, however, about the erection of an elaborate stone for his tomb and did not fail to express her impatience with the "parcel of Dumfries mechanics [who] wanted to dictate to me, so I deserted them; and it too". In 1807, she met Walter Scott and sent him some of Burns's election songs. She married again, to a Colonel Fletcher in Flintshire, but died shortly afterwards, on December 15th, 1808.

* * *

A Literary Guide

Apart from the interesting account of her travels to the West Indies, Maria Riddell published *The Metrical Miscellany* including 16 lyrics by her own hand, and one by Mrs McLehose, or Burns's "Clarinda". *Corin's Adieu* in this collection is certainly in memory of Burns. Her accomplished *The Kiss* beginning "Humid seal of soft affections, /Tenderest pledge of future bliss;/ Dearest tye of young connexions, / Love's first snow-drop – Virgin-kiss" was at least once published as the work of Burns himself. Other contributors to the volume included Dr Darwin and Henry Erskine. Perhaps her most moving work is the one she sent Burns in reconciliation in 1795, a song on the Nith: "For there he roved that broke my heart, / Yet to that heart, ah, still how dear.." Her assessment of Burns' character, written in 1796, is an invaluable first-hand account of the poet, of the wit and repartee of his conversation, and she shows a mature appreciation of the way in which his quick sensibility to slights was a symptom or a consequence of the very disposition which was also the source of his talent - of, as she puts it, "his splenetic warmth of spirit".

BIBLIOGRAPHY:
Voyages to the Madeira and the Leeward Carribean Isles (1792); *The Metrical Miscellany* (1802)

PLACES TO VISIT: Ellisland Farm is open to the public and there is a marked footpath to The Hermitage, Friar's Carse, home of Robert Riddells. Goldielea, once Woodley Park, is now a nursing home

Benjamin Bell
1749-1806
Dumfries

Benjamin Bell, born of a landed family in Dumfriesshire, was author of one of the best-selling works on surgery of his day; it became the textbook for the Edinburgh school of medicine. His essays on agriculture and political economy were recommended by Adam Smith.

Benjamin Bell was the eldest son of George Bell, descended from Dumfriesshire landed proprietors and owner of Woodhouselee; Benjamin was the eldest of fifteen children. His father, George Bell, worked on the agricultural improvement of his estate. Benjamin was educated at the Grammar School at Dumfries, and apprenticed to Mr. James Hill, surgeon of Dumfries and author of a work on surgery. At the age of 17, Bell was sent to Edinburgh medical school, which was growing famous under the tutelage of a group of famous professors. Bell became house-surgeon at the Royal Infirmary for two years. He then went to Paris: as he explained in his copious and affectionate letters home, he could learn techniques of surgery in Paris, which were not known in Edinburgh. He studied there under Baron Portal, who had recently published a textbook on surgery. On his return, in 1772, Bell was appointed surgeon to the Royal Infirmary, a position which he held for twenty-one years. He married Grizel Hamilton, and, after an accident caused by a fall from a horse, took a farm outside Edinburgh at Liberton. There he could occupy the leisure time required by his recuperation in working on his *System of Surgery*, eventually published in seven volumes. In 1778, he became surgeon at Watson's Hospital and published his *Treatise on the Theory and Management of Ulcers*, which attracted some attention and was translated into French and German. Between 1782 and 1787, his *System of Surgery* appeared, became the textbook of the Edinburgh school, and was also translated. It is clear that Bell's reputation was that of a skilful and careful surgeon, and his practice prospered. Both his letters home and his works on political economy show him as a canny manager of finance, and, as his affairs prospered, he was able to move into a larger house and purchase a considerable estate. Eventually, he possessed the greater part of Newington, a suburb of Edinburgh. When pressure of work began to tell on his health, he was compelled to travel south to recuperate, and the story is told that, when he was passing Harwich in 1798, a group of sailors, hearing that the carriage was conveying Benjamin Bell, who had cured Admiral Duncan, victor of Camperdown, unyoked the horses, and dragged the post-chaise in triumph. His health finally dictated that he give up practice, and he died at Newington House in 1806.

* * *

The *System of Surgery* went through seven editions in 13 years. In it, he refers to his own technique of saving as much skin as possible in amputations and other operations, a measure whose neglect he had noted, and which retarded healing. The plates in the *System* include interesting engravings of medical equipment of the day, including the prostheses used after amputations, and fearsome operating knives and saws. His other treatises include several on urology and venereal disease. It is not difficult to see why Adam Smith praised Bell's *Essays on Agriculture* (1802), since they were ahead of their time in attacking the corn laws, discussing the effect of the Window Tax on health (since windows were boarded up in order to avoid tax), and in recognising the need for good communications and "new modes of conveyance" to open up markets. Bell's letters home to his father include detailed discussions of estate management , and the topics of his *Essays* range over "The Taxation of Income", "The National Debt", "The Sale of Land Tax", and "Scarcity of Provisions of Dearth". He also reprinted a memorial he had written to the government recommending an agricultural census for the entire country, a suggestion which was not taken up until some years later. The *Life, Character and Writings of Benjamin Bell* (1868) was written by his grandson, who was a member of the medical dynasty founded by Bell.

BIBLIOGRAPHY:
A Treatise on the Theory and Management of Ulcers (1778); *A System of Surgery* (1782-1787); *Essays on Agriculture* (1802); *The Life, Character, and Writings of Benjamin Bell* (1868)

A Literary Guide

Sir John Richardson
1787-1865
Dumfries

Sir John Richardson, born in Dumfries, was one of the principal Arctic explorers in the era when the North West passage between the Pacific and Atlantic Oceans and the extremity of the American continent were topics of intense scientific and geographical interest. He made no less than three expeditions northwards, sometimes under conditions of extreme hardship, but nevertheless managed to collect scientific specimens and to write up learned accounts of the observed phenomena.

John Richardson was born on 5th November 1787 at Nith Place, Dumfries, in a well-to-do and close-knit family. His father, Gabriel, was Provost of Dumfries, JP for the county and a friend of **Robert Burns,** who regularly spent Sunday evenings at Nith Place between 1790 and 1796. Burns lent the young John Richardson a copy of Spenser's *"Faerie Queen"* and his eldest son, Robert Burns, entered Dumfries Grammar School on the same day as Richardson. Richardson's mother was a daughter of Peter Mundell, of Rosebank, near Dumfries. In 1800, Richardson was apprenticed to his uncle, a surgeon in Dumfries, and in 1801, entered university in Edinburgh. In 1804, he became a house surgeon at Dumfries Infirmary, but returned to Edinburgh, as he was to do throughout his life, for further study. By 1807, he was qualified as a member of the Royal College of Surgeons. At the height of the Napoleonic wars, he became assistant – surgeon on board the frigate "Nymphe", which was present at the bombardment of Copenhagen. He successively obtained appointments aboard different ships, including those involved on convoy duty to Spain and Quebec. In 1810, he obtained leave to study anatomy in London; in 1814, was appointed surgeon to the first battalion of marines, then in North America. After seeing active service there, he returned to Edinburgh to study botany and mineralogy and completed a thesis on yellow fever in 1816. At this point, he began a medical practice, without much success, in Leith, and married in 1818. At this point he obtained an appointment as surgeon and naturalist to John Franklin's polar expedition and was to collect specimens of plants, animals and minerals. While Parry and **Captain John Ross** were appointed to pass through the Davis Straits, Franklin's mission was to go overland and determine the extreme limits of the American continent. The expedition crossed the Atlantic along with passengers destined for **Lord Selkirk's** Red River colony ; Richardson gives graphic descriptions in his letters home of the icebergs encountered en route. The explorers started from the chief northern post of the North West Company, accompanied by Indian guides, and completed a voyage of 1350 miles in 1820. In 1821, they travelled down the Coppermine River in birch-bark canoes, reaching the coast and penetrating as far east as Cape Turnagain. Their journey was hampered by inadequate supplies and uneasy relations with the Indians : at the Barren Grounds, where the expedition was experiencing great hardship through lack of food, Richardson shot and killed an Iroquois, who had murdered a member of the group. He was nearly drowned while attempting heroically to swim a river, in order to get his party across on a raft, and the party was finally rescued by an Indian who took them to Fort Providence. They reached Fort York in the following June and arrived in England in 1822. In 1823, the *Narrative* of the expedition was published by Franklin, including Richardson's notices of fish, geology and remarks on the aurora. He moved to Edinburgh and devoted himself to making a zoological commentary on the appendix to Parry's *Journal* of his second voyage. Although appointed to a division of marines at Chatham, he obtained leave to accompany Franklin on a second voyage to the mouth of the Mackenzie river, where the aim was for Richardson to explore the 900 miles of coast between there and the Coppermine river. As he explained in his *Polar Regions*, a book which was expanded from an article he wrote for the *Encyclopaedia Britannica*, these surveys, together with Captain Beechy's, defined an

A Literary Guide

outline of the American continent from Behring's Strait eastwards and ultimately contributed to ending a three centuries' search for the North-West Passage. With his indefatigable energy, Richardson travelled 2000 miles in ten weeks. When travelling homewards, they were feted in New York and arrived in England with important collections of scientific specimens. Richardson prepared a narrative of his segment of the expedition, with comments on solar radiation and meteorological tables. In 1828, he returned to Chatham to resume his medical duties and devoted his energies to the *Fauna Boreali-Americana*, to which he contributed all observations on quadrupeds and fishes, while other naturalists wrote the sections on birds and insects. In 1832, he was instrumental in beginning a campaign to interest the public in the plight of **Captain John Ross**, whose expedition had sailed in 1829; he was ultimately defeated in his wish for a search expedition by opposition at the Admiralty. In 1838, he was appointed physician to the Royal Hospital at Haslar, near Plymouth, where he concentrated his efforts on persuading the admiralty to treat lunatics with more humane methods; later, he was to meet another eminent medical reformer, Florence Nightingale, with whom he discussed conditions in naval hospitals. Here, he was visited by Sir Joseph Hooker, who was preparing to accompany **Sir James Ross** on his voyage to the Antarctic. In 1840, he was appointed Inspector of Hospitals. When fears-which turned out to be well justified – were expressed for the safety of Sir John Franklin's expedition, Richardson once more set out for the shores of the Arctic Sea. Despite ice-floes at Cape Kendall, he reached Fort Confidence, but ultimately left his second-in-command, Dr Rae, in charge of discovering the whereabouts of the distressed expedition. Later, he claimed that Franklin had discovered the North-West Passage, though none of the members of his expedition had lived to tell the tale. The *Journal* of his voyage, published in 1851, included notes on magnetic phenomena and on temperatures. He finally retired to his mother-in-law's estate near Grasmere in the Lake District, and worked on articles on ichthyology and on Sir John Franklin for the *Encyclopaedia Britannica*. He was also known for his willingness to give medical aid to the poor, for his enthusiasm for gardening, and for his work as a magistrate, and he concluded his energetic career by a tour of the art galleries of Europe and trips to see antiquities at Ruthwell, Dumfriesshire, and Dowalton Loch in Wigtownshire. He had been knighted in 1846 and was made companion of the Bath in 1850; he was married three times, once to a niece of Franklin. He died in 1865 and was buried at Grasmere.

* * *

Perhaps Richardson's most human testimony of his voyages is contained in the frequent and devoted letters back to his family in Dumfries, which are quoted at length in the biography by Rev. John McIlraith (1868). The details were graphic enough, including his experience of having to singe the hair off a buffalo blanket in order to boil and eat the hide, during the time of dangerous hardship at Barren Grounds. Other fascinating glimpses from the correspondence include his account of a New Year's ball at a northern outpost, including a description of the clothing of the Indian guests. His interest in exploration was perhaps dictated by his wish to pursue the inquiries initiated by Humboldt into the geographical distribution of vegetable and animal forms ; his *Fauna* was for long a standard work on North America and he was able to make significant contributions to ichthyology, especially of China and Japan. His *Polar Regions* (1861) shows him as a writer of elegant and scholarly prose, with a profound sense of the history of exploration, charting the progress of discovery, from ancient times to the expeditions of his contemporaries - **Ross**, Franklin, Parry, Beechy, Rae and Back. His *Arctic Searching Expedition: a Journal of a Boat Voyage through Rupert's Land and the Arctic Sea* is aimed at an exhaustive cataloguing of phenomena of all kinds, including minute observations on the Inuit and the Kutchin people, their customs and language. He was contributing to the *Dictionary* of the Philological Society when he died.

BIBLIOGRAPHY:
Fauna Boreali-Americana (1829-1837); *Arctic Searching Expedition: a Journal of a Boat Voyage through Rupert's Land and the Arctic Sea* (1851); *The Polar Regions* (1861); John Franklin, *Narrative of a Journey to the Shores of the Polar Sea* (1823); John McIlraith, *Life of Sir John Richardson* (1868)

A Literary Guide

RW MacKenna
1874-1930
Dumfries

RW MacKenna, born at Martyr's Manse, Irving Street, Dumfries, became a doctor and specialist in dermatology. Possessed both of medical expertise and of a deep religious faith, he published during the First World War on aspects of death and suffering, which he came to justify by reference to the workings of providence and purpose. His later historical novels, set in the times of the Covenanters, incorporate much Galloway scenery and characters, in a form reminiscent of **Crockett**.

Dr R. W. MacKenna.

RW MacKenna was the son of the Rev R MacKenna, minister at the Martyrs' Free Church in Dumfries. His father, from Girvan, had studied at the Reformed Presbyterian College in Edinburgh; his mother was Margaret Wright, of Ballantrae. The family, which came to consist of six children, moved to Nunholm, on the outskirts of Dumfries, and regularly spent summers at Ballantrae. MacKenna entered Dumfries Academy in 1883 and was taught by John Neilson, also the teacher of **JM Barrie**. At the age of 15, he entered the Royal High School, where he was tutored in Latin and Greek, and then took an arts bursary at Edinburgh University in 1892. He was the first to complete arts and medical course simultaneously, completing the degrees in six years. He won university prizes, edited the Dumfries and Galloway Literary Magazine, *The Student*, and published some verses in 1897, including *Carmina Cadaveris*, which attracted some attention for their medical themes. At this time, he aimed to specialise in gynaecology, and left Britain to study in Vienna. There, he met his future wife, Harriet Bird, also a student. He began practice in Liverpool, hoping to specialise. Since his practice was struggling to establish itself, he contributed to the two Dumfries papers, including a poem *Spring*, and wrote for Liverpool papers, to earn cash. He obtained a post at the Liverpool Skin Hospital, then a private hospital, and retained his general practice. In 1907, he devoted himself entirely to a specialist practice in dermatology and obtained his degree of Doctor of Medicine from Edinburgh in 1908. In 1914, he was called to join a territorial division of the Royal Army Medical Corps at Fazackerly, as a Captain. In 1917, he was ordered to the General Hospital under canvas at Boulogne, and thereafter travelled with it to Marseilles. His war service had the effect of stimulating his literary talents, and he published *The Adventure of Death* in 1916, *The Adventure of Life* in 1919, and *Through a Tent Door*, written at the General Hospital in France. After demobilisation in 1919, he tried to re-establish his private practice, but was appointed Honorary Dermatologist to the Liverpool Infirmary and became Lecturer at the University. His major work *Diseases of the Skin* was published in 1923, but the 'twenties saw his significant foray into the territory of the historical novel, with *Bracken and Thistledown* (first published in the *People's Friend*), *Flower o' the Heather* (first serialised in the *Scotsman*), *Through Flood and Fire* and lastly *O Rowan Tree*, 1928. He died in 1930 and *As Shadows Lengthen* was a collection of essays, collected posthumously by his son.

* * *

MacKenna's first works drew on his knowledge as a doctor and his religious feelings as the son of a minister, in dealing with the problem of the theological justification of pain. His *Adventure of Death*, 1916, had its origins in a lecture to a Church literary society and was amplified for publication, with a particularly topical section on the feelings of soldiers facing death in battle. His *Adventure of Life* gives a teleological justification of life, which emerges as the purpose of nature, with the development of intelligence as its summit and knowledge of God as the crowning glory of intelligence. *Through a Tent Door* made use of his medical experience of the psychological states of men under the stress of battle and the encounter with death. His historical novels return to the Southern Scottish landscapes of his youth. *Flower o' the Heather* returns to Covenanting times, and has flavours of both Scott (in his semi-comic character of Hector the Packman) and **Crockett** (in the interwoven love-story), his two illustrious predecessors in the novel of the Covenanting

A Literary Guide

period. It interweaves well-known historical incidents, such as the notorious drowning of the two Margarets at Wigtown, and well-known historical characters, such as the persecutor, Grierson of Lag, who belongs to the demonology of Southern Scotland, into the fictional story.

BIBLIOGRAPHY:
The Adventure of Death (1916); *The Adventure of Life* (1919); *Through a Tent Door* (1919); *Flower o' the Heather* (1922); *Bracken and Thistledown* (1923); *Diseases of the Skin* (1923); *Through Flood and Fire* (1925); *O Rowan Tree* (1928); *As Shadows Lengthen* (1932)

William McDowall
1815-1888
Maxwelltown, Dumfries

William McDowall, born in Maxwelltown, spent most of his life as the editor of the influential and moderately Liberal "Dumfries and Galloway Standard". His work on the history of Dumfries, which went into four editions, remains the sole full-length history of the town.

William McDowall's father was a traveller employed by the firm of Gregan and Creighton, cabinet-makers and upholsterers. William McDowall was educated at Oliver's School and at Dumfries Academy. He was then apprenticed to Mr John Sinclair, bookbinder, and then became a journeyman with Messrs. M'Kinnel and M'Kie, working in Glasgow and London. He was already publishing articles in the Dumfries newspapers, such as *The Dumfries Times*, and showing a marked interest in political and theological questions, in which he tended towards Liberal views. After the Disruption of the Church of Scotland in 1843, he was on the side of Non-Intrusion and joined the Free Church of Scotland, and also became secretary to the local Chartist movement. In 1844, he published his book of poetry, *The Man of the Woods*, which was reviewed favourably by the editors of the *Dumfries Herald* and *Courier*. His enthusiasm for Chartism meanwhile declined, as those in favour of violent protest gained ascendancy. Robert Somers, a native of Wigtownshire, asked him to Edinburgh to manage the *Scottish Herald*, a non-Intrusionist publication. Subsequently, he went to Belfast, to manage the *Banner of Ulster*, which promulgated similar views; there, McDowall became an early and moderate advocate of Irish Home-Rule. In Dumfries, the *Dumfries and*

Galloway Standard had been established by, among others, **Rev Dr Henry Duncan**, who wrote a prospectus detailing the aim of the newspaper, to promote the view of the Evangelical majority in the church. By 1846, McDowall had been offered the editorship, and saving a brief interlude when he edited a journal in Sunderland, he remained at the *Standard* for the rest of his career. During his editorship, he constantly advocated the cause of social and political reform, reported the proceedings of the Town Council in detail for the first time, and gave encouragement to young writers of the area. He was himself at one time elected to the Council, was active in the Antiquarian Society, and played a conspicuous part in the Scott and **Burns** Centenaries, particularly in the erection of Burns' Statue at the head of the High Street. He died after weakening bouts of rheumatic fever, having just completed an article promoting the advent of the railways to the Glenkens district of the Stewartry. He was buried in the churchyard at Troqueer.

* * *

His poem *The Man of the Woods* (of which the later edition included a connecting narrative) was based on the mystic and Emersonian belief that "there is an occult relation between man and the vegetable" and endeavours to establish the essential humanity of famous trees in the Dumfries district. The ash at Troqueer churchyard, where McDowall was himself buried, is apostrophised: "'Ere long to death thy head must bow, / And thou shalt be as these below; / Thy youth – thy prime- thy autumn past,-/ Be levelled with the earth at last". A similar mysticism marks his *The Mind in the Face*, where he drew the consequences of Lavater's science of physiognomy, where moral character could be predicted from physical attributes, particularly of the face. *Memorials of St Michael's, the Old Parish Churchyard of Dumfries* draws on painstaking research about those buried there: most famously, of course, St Michael's is the site of the original tomb of **Burns** and the later Mausoleum, as well as being the site of burial for many of his friends and acquaintances, like Colonel de Peyster, his commanding officer in the Dumfries Volunteers. But McDowall's tour of the graveyard gives a fascinating guide to the memorials of lesser Dumfries characters such as John Gas, barber to Bonnie Prince Charlie when he visited Dumfries in 1745, and who features in **John Mayne's** *Siller Gun*. Literary memorials, to which McDowall appends biographical information, include those of **Thomas Aird, John McDiarmid, Benjamin Bell's** family, the **Kirkpatrick Sharpes, Clark Kennedys,** and **Thomas Blacklock's** father (for whom Blacklock himself wrote the epitaph: "A mind content itself and God to know"). McDowall's greatest and most lasting work, however, is his weighty *History of the Burgh of Dumfries*, which ran to three editions, the second one of which included two additional chapters on **Burns** and Dumfries, research which was also embodied in a separate monograph *Burns in Dumfriesshire*. Reading about the vicissitudes of the burgh, as it was criss-crossed by the ambitions and the armed retinues of Scottish barons and English kings (who on more than one occasion set fire to the town in passing), it is hard to imagine how civil order survived at all. Certainly, the history of the burgh provides McDowall with plenty of dramatic material, and his description of the meeting of the Bruce and the Red Comyn on the streets of Dumfries, prior to the Bruce's slaying of Comyn in Greyfriars Church should not be missed. *Burns in Dumfriesshire* includes a number of anecdotes which were preserved in the Dumfries folk-memory of Burns, including some demonstrating his indulgence to local people found violating the excise law. One interesting Dumfries Burns relic McDowall describes was a French book Burns had apparently presented to Dumfries Library, and in which he had written an incautiously pro-Revolutionary sentiment in the fly-leaf; later, thinking better of it, he returned and pasted it together. The account of Dumfries social round and of Burns' routine as a gauger do much to correct the picture of unmitigated debauchery given by earlier writers. McDowall gives useful details of many of the Dumfries worthies, now canonised because they were apostrophised or vilified by Burns, including John Syme and Gabriel Richardson, father of **Sir John Richardson**. He concludes with an account of the moving of Burns's body to the mausoleum, when the body was allegedly found incorrupt until the air reached it. The appendix listing Burns relics in Dumfries in the year 1870 is a useful reference and an interesting reflection on the growing cult leading up to the centenary.

BIBLIOGRAPHY:
The Man of the Woods, and Other Poems (1844); *History of the Burgh*

A Literary Guide

of Dumfries (1867); *Memorials of St. Michael's, the Old Parish Churchyard of Dumfries* (1876); *Burns in Dumfriesshire* (1881); *The Mind in the Face* (1882)

PLACES TO VISIT: Burns' Statue, erected partly through the industry of William McDowall, stands at the head of Dumfries High Street. There is a memorial plaque to McDowall in the Ewart Library, Dumfries.

Thomas Aird
1802-1876
Dumfries

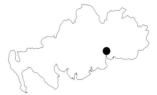

Thomas Aird became editor of the "Dumfries and Galloway Herald" from 1835-1863; he published several editions of his poetry, which shows a particular descriptive power when dealing with the natural world, and some plays.

Thomas Aird was the second of nine children born to James Aird and Isabella Paisley, at Bowden, Roxburghshire. His parents were respectable "Portioners" who cultivated their own land, and were strong "Anti-Burghers" in religion. Aird attended the parish school, and then the school at Melrose. In 1816, he went to Edinburgh University, where he became firm friends with **Thomas Carlyle**, who in later years visited him regularly at Dumfries. During his studies, he was a tutor in Selkirkshire, where he made the acquaintance of James Hogg, and later attended the dinner held in Hogg's honour at Peebles. He gradually abandoned all idea of entering the church, and, in 1826, embarked on his literary career with *Murtzoufle*, a tragedy in three Acts, and some poems, which included the popular and sentimental *My Mother's Grave*. His *Religious Characteristics*, on the psychology of sin, caught the attention of the influential Professor Wilson, who reviewed it in *Blackwood's Magazine*. He was by now supporting himself by teaching and contributing articles to reviews; in 1832, he edited the *Edinburgh Weekly Journal* for a year. In 1835, he left Edinburgh, and joined the *Herald*, a paper of Conservative principles, in Dumfries, partly thanks to a recommendation from Professor Wilson. His own verses appeared in the paper, and he gave encouragement to others in their literary efforts:

they included **Robert Burns's** eldest son, Robert, and **Dr Duncan's** son, George. His most popular work appeared in 1845: *The Old Bachelor in the Old Scottish Village*, which consisted of descriptive sketches of character and of the changing seasons of the year. The full edition of his poems appeared in 1848, including *The Devil's Dream on Mount Aksbeck*, which at the time was compared, for its portrayal of Satan, to Milton's *Paradise Lost*. After the age of 50, he wrote little and suffered from a nervous disposition, which was easily affected by noise; even the crowing of a cock disturbed him, as he described : "Your keen and nervous spirit cannot sleep,/ Hearing him nightly from some neighbouring court!" In 1847, he attended the public banquet to honour **John McDiarmid**, owner and editor of the rival *Dumfries Courier*; he himself was similarly honoured on his retirement in 1863, after 28 years at the *Herald*. He was required to attend many literary functions, including Burns suppers, and also presided over the dinner in honour of Scott at Dumfries in 1871. Thomas Aird is buried in St. Michael's Churchyard.

* * *

Aird had a remarkably fresh and sensitive eye for nature; his description of autumn in *The Old Bachelor* is indicative of the immediacy he can achieve in prose: "To saunter through the rustling woodlands; to stalk across the stubble-field, yellow with the last glare of day; to skirt the loin of the hill, and, overleaping the dyke, tumble away among the ferns, and reach your door just as the great, red, round moon comes up in the east, - how invigorating!" **Carlyle** wrote to him of the book : "The descriptions of <u>weather</u> and rural physiognomy of nature in earth and sky seem to me excellent. More of the like when you please!" His lyrical poetry is far more successful than his long narrative poems or attempts at drama, and is in fact notably experimental in its use of image and in its sensitivity to the sound of language . In *Songs of the Seasons*, he writes of an icy night: "Blue breathing Night, down from her styptick noon, / Makes her young ice; the pools all plated gleam. / Bold speed defies her : down the dashing stream / Flashes the shattered moon". In his *The River*, the breathless onrush of the verse imitates the tumbling of the stream as it grows into a river: "Infant of the weeping hills, Nursling of the springs and rills, Growing River, flowing ever, / Wimpling, dimpling, staying never,- / Lisping, gurgling, ever going, / Lipping , slipping, ever flowing, / Toying round the polished stone". His *Devil's Dream on Mount Aksbeck* includes some good Miltonic description of Satan's tortured soul, when confronted with "(t)he silent magnanimity of Nature and her God", and is full of descriptive touches to evoke the mood of defiance and dread: "Above them lightnings to and fro ran crossing evermore, / Till like a red bewildered map, the skies were scribbled o'er".

BIBLIOGRAPHY:
Murtzoufle (1826); *Religious Characteristics* (1827); *The Captive of Fez* (1830); *Othuriel, and Other Poems* (1840); *The Old Bachelor in the Old Scottish Village* (1845); *The Poetical Works of Thomas Aird* (1848)

A Literary Guide

John McDiarmid
1790-1852
Dumfries

John McDiarmid, one of the founders of the "Scotsman" newspaper, was editor of the "Dumfries Courier" for 36 years and had a marked impact on public opinion and standards of reporting in Dumfriesshire. He also published the "Dumfries Monthly Magazine" to provide a platform to local literary talent, and wrote his "Sketches from Nature", from articles which had previously appeared in the "Courier".

JOHN M'DIARMID.

John McDiarmid was born in 1790, and was the son of the Rev Hugh McDiarmid, minister of the Highland Church in Glasgow. He lost his father early in life, received some education in Edinburgh, and eventually became a clerk in a counting house associated with a bleachfield at Roslin. Later, he obtained a position at the head office of the Commercial Bank. While working, he began a course of extensive reading, and acted as amanuensis when Professor Playfair was tutor to Lord John Russell. His employers, recognising his gifts, gave him access to the library and to classes. He became active in College debating clubs, and became a leading light in the Edinburgh Forum. Some of his essays appeared in *Blackwood's Magazine* and his name became known when he wrote some lines for the inauguration of the Waterloo monument at New Abbey, the first to be erected in the country. He was known to figures important in the Edinburgh literary scene, such as "Christopher North", Francis Jeffrey, and James Hogg. Jeffrey offered him some work on the new and influential *Edinburgh Review*, but since the opportunity for his first article – on the struggle for democracy in South America – was offered on condition that he declare the unripeness of the continent for freedom, he declined the work. At the end of 1816, he, along with Charles Maclaren and William Ritchie, proposed to found a new weekly journal, a proposal which eventually resulted in the first printing of *The Scotsman* on 25th January 1817. McDiarmid retained his share in the copyright, but by 1817, he had left for Dumfries to work on the *Dumfries and Galloway Courier*. The *Courier* had been edited by its founder, **Henry Duncan**, until 1816. When McDiarmid took over, he left his own stamp on the newspaper, concentrating on the themes of agricultural improvement, natural history, and antiquities. He supported the Whig cause, and spoke out for the abolition of the Test and Corporation Acts; when he also spoke for Roman Catholic Emancipation, the windows of the *Courier* office were broken, and he was burnt in effigy outside it. In 1832, he stayed at his post throughout the outbreak of Asiatic cholera, which raged in Dumfries, and helped in the administration of relief funds; he also promoted a Soup Kitchen for the poor. He also knew and befriended **Burns's** widow and his sons. In 1819, he married Anne McKnight from Dumfries, and his position at the *Courier* was further established when, in 1820, he was offered a stake in its proprietorship, as surety against his departure for the *Caledonian Mercury*, from which he had received an offer. He was later (1837) to become sole proprietor, and his son, William Ritchie McDiarmid, succeeded him. In 1817, he published an edition of Cowper's poetry, and in 1820, he issued the first edition of his *Scrap Book*, a highly successful set of selections from prose and poetry. In 1823, he edited Goldsmith's *Vicar of Wakefield*, with a memoir of the author. He began publishing the *Dumfries Monthly Magazine* in 1825 to encourage native literary talent, and in an early issue, he printed **William Nicholson's** *Brownie of Blednoch*; he was later to write a *Memoir* of Nicholson, to accompany a new edition of his poems. The *Sketches from Nature* (1830) were selected from pieces in the *Courier*. His *Picture of Dumfries* (1832) contains engravings by Andrew S Masson, and gives a fascinating contemporary account of its natural history, antiquities, trade and schooling. In 1847, he had become such a well-respected figure in Dumfries that he was entertained to a public banquet, attended by, among other local dignitaries, **Thomas Aird**, editor of the rival newspaper, the *Standard*. He suffered an attack of erysipelas, and died in Dumfries in 1852. He was buried at St. Michael's Churchyard.

* * *

A Literary Guide

McDiarmid's *Sketches from Nature* demonstrate the quality of writing in the *Courier* and show his particular interests in natural history and agricultural improvement. The farmer, he wrote, "presses art into the service of nature , and has to do with the weighty concerns of soil, season and climate – his workshop is the fruitful earth – his machinery the sun, moon, and clouds; and, aided by these, he produces the elements of every comfort, irrigating the parched plain, draining the morass, inclosing the common, and reclaiming the barren waste." The first part of the book includes sketches of Galloway, where he had been on a walking tour in 1828, and includes an account of the surviving eagles at Loch Dungeon, and of the magnificence of the Mull of Galloway. The second part consists largely of biographical sketches, including some of Gilbert Burns, **James Hyslop**, and **Hugh Clapperton.**

BIBLIOGRAPHY:
The Scrap Book (1820); *Memoir* in William Nicholson, *Poems* (1828); *Sketches from Nature* (1830); *Picture of Dumfries* (1832); WR McDiarmid, *Memoir of John McDiarmid* (1852)

John Mayne
1759-1836
Dumfries

John Mayne was born in Dumfries on 26th March 1759, just two months after his greater contemporary, **Robert Burns.** *Their careers as poets indeed touched at two points, when two of Mayne's poems, which were early examples of the revival of Scots dialect in poetic diction, inspired compositions on similar themes by Burns. Mayne is best remembered, however, for his poem "The Siller Gun", describing a shooting competition, or "waponshaw" at Dumfries.*

John Mayne was educated at Chapman's Grammar School at Dumfries and later entered the offices of the *Dumfries Weekly Journal*, the town's first newspaper. It was in 1777 that he published the first version of *The Siller Gun*, having witnessed the competition by the Incorporated Trades of the town for a small silver gun, said to have been presented by James VI to encourage the burgesses of Dumfries in the practice of arms. He left Dumfries shortly after joining the newspaper, when his parents moved to Glasgow. There he was employed for five years as a compositor's apprentice under the Foulis family. He remained a printer and journalist for the rest of his life, but moved to London , where he became printer, editor and proprietor of *The Star and Evening Advertiser*. Mayne continued, however, to write as a poet, contributing verses, usually in Scots, to his own newspaper and to the *Gentleman's Magazine*. Between 1777 and 1836, he continued to expand and re-work *The Siller Gun*, the final version of which, with notes, appeared in the year he died. He was buried in his family's vault at Paddington.

* * *

The Siller Gun is, like most of Mayne's work, written in lively Scots verse and is a worthwhile and enjoyable example in the Scottish tradition of mock-heroic poems, originating with *Christ's Kirk on the Green* (which Mayne quotes) and of which **Burns**'s *Holy Fair* was perhaps the most notable representative. The characteristic theme was the celebration of local festivals with gentle observer's irony. In the case of Mayne's poem, the grandiose military tone adds spice to the humour, enabling Mayne to underline the particularly unwarlike characteristics of his Dumfries contemporaries: "Swords that, unsheath'd, since Prestonpans, / Neglected lay, / Were furbish'd up , to grace the hands / O' Chiefs, this day!" Mayne was an early pioneer in the revival of the vernacular and the poem received favourable mention in the Fifth Canto to Sir Walter Scott's *Lady of the Lake* and the final edition included, among its subscribers, Mayne's friend and admirer **Allan Cunningham**, the critic and poet, Thomas Campbell, and JG Lockhart, the son-in-law of Sir Walter Scott. His *Logan Braes*, which achieved some popularity, possesses considerable charm: "By Logan's stream that rin sae deep, / Fu' aft wi' glee, I've herded sheep, / I've herded sheep, or gathered slaes, / Wi' my dear lad on Logan braes". It appeared in a version with three stanzas in the *Star* in 1789, and its popularity and the naïve vigour of its refrain, where the speaker laments the absence of her lover who "maun face his faes, / Far, far frae me and Logan Braes", was such that **Burns**, who knew the tune and these two lines, believed it to be a traditional ballad and quoted it in his own *Logan Water*. Mayne's *Hallowe'en*, published in *Ruddiman's Magazine* 1780, may also have inspired Burns's better known poem, and certainly has some success in conjuring up a picture of the uniquely Scottish celebration of Hallowe'en, and of the "bleezing ingleside, / Where nowther cauld nor hunger bide", where the farmer's wife makes preparations for the communal meal and tells of old superstitions, while the young simmer with anticipation of seeing their future betrothed revealed. That Mayne was aware of his greater contemporary is clear from his *Glasgow*, a poem which also appeared in several versions, in which he laments: "O! for the Muse o' Burns, sae rare, / To paint the groups that gather there !" The poem conjures up a picture of the city of Glasgow as a bustling trading city ("Whatever makes ae penny twa, / By wind or tide, / Is wafted to the Broomielaw,/ On bonny Clyde!") before the full onset of industrialisation. The poem's praise of Glasgow's learned tradition is piquantly couched in pithy Scots : "If ye've a knacky son or twa, / To Glasgow-College send them a'/.." There follows an invocation of Glasgow's famous sons, a formula which Mayne was to re-use in the later versions of *The Siller Gun*. Like **Stewart Lewis** and many others, Mayne also tried his hand at a version of the traditional ballad *Fair*

Helen of Kirkconnel Lee (see also under **Frank Miller**), but as with other revised versions, his fuller poem fails to live up to the haunting strangeness of the original fragment. Other works included patriotic addresses to *English, Scots and Irishmen* (1803) and a eulogy hailing the visit to Scotland in 1822 of George IV.

BIBLIOGRAPHY:
The Siller Gun: a Poem (1777, also editions of 1779, 1780, 1808, & 1836); *Glasgow: a Poem* (1783, & 1803); *English, Scots and Irishmen* (1803)

PLACES TO VISIT: The original "Siller Gun" is on display at The Observatory, Dumfries Museum.

John Maxwell Wood
1868-1925
Dumfries

Maxwell Wood was the editor of the influential literary periodical "The Gallovidian" from 1900-1911 and again at a later period, until just before his death in 1925. He also published on Dumfriesshire and Galloway folklore, smuggling, and on Burns' friendship with the Riddell family.

John Maxwell Wood was born in a house at Assembly Street, Dumfries, son of John Wood, dentist and also magistrate and Councillor in Dumfries. He was educated at Dumfries Academy, and then trained at Edinburgh University for medicine. He took honours in several classes and graduated in 1891. Early on in life, he had to take on family responsibilities, after the death of his father during his college course, and as a result, he returned to Dumfries. In Dumfries, he became involved extensively in civic life, obtaining a commission in the KOSB territorials under Colonel Dudgeon; he promoted the Mechanics' Institute and was much involved in the cataloguing of its library. He was himself a bibliophile and had a collection of Dumfries and Galloway books and antiquities. He was active in organising the centenary commemoration of Burns' death, was President of the Burns Club in 1907, and was also a prominent Freemason. In 1906, he helped organise the banquet which was held to honour **SR Crockett**. He took over the editorship of the *Gallovidian* in the year after its inception, and it became one of the most highly regarded provincial magazines. He frequently contributed reviews to it, wrote biographies in the *Sons of the South* series, and his articles included a diversity of subjects, such as the Troqueer ghost, the drowning of Commander Thurot, and the history of lifeboats. His two works *Witchcraft and Superstitious Record in the South-Western District of Scotland* and *Smuggling in the Solway and Around the Galloway Seaboard* were both first serialised in the *Gallovidian*. In the sphere of medicine, he was a pioneer in the use of Chloride of Ethyl as a general anaesthetic, and designed an inhaler, which appeared in *The Lancet* for 1904. In 1910, he left Dumfries to join the White Star Line as a ship's surgeon, and a public dinner was held in his honour, attended by – amongst others - **Malcolm Harper** (whom he had assisted with revisions to *Rambles in Galloway*), Provost **McCormick** of Newton Stewart, and Lord Ardwall. He returned to Dumfries, after travels abroad, and continued his editorship until the year of his death, in 1925. He is buried at Troqueer.

* * *

Maxwell Wood made several contributions to **Burns** studies, including articles on *The influence of Dr. Blacklock on Robert Burns, Burns as a Patron of the Drama*, and *A Burns Landmark of Dumfries about to Pass*. His longest work on Burns was his *Robert Burns and the Riddell Family*, 1922, which despite some inaccuracies about the family properties and the avoidance of some issues surrounding the "Rape of the Sabines" incident (in which Burns caused grave offence to the Riddell family by a drunken re-enactment of the Classical "rape of the Sabine women"; see **Maria Riddell**) , includes some interesting information on the Riddell descent and good contemporary illustrations. Maxwell Wood's *Smuggling in the Solway* (1908) was probably the first attempt to gather together information about this significant phenomenon in Dumfries and Galloway history. It systematically deals with locations, literary references (of which the most famous are, of course, those of Sir Walter Scott in *Guy Mannering*), the revenue service and the social effect of the smuggling trade. Like its successor *Witchcraft and Superstitious Record*, it is illustrated by the artist, J Copland. The *Witchcraft* volume quotes plentifully from past authorities on the subject of superstitions, tales of Brownies, and death-customs: from **William Todd**'s *Galloway Traditions* articles on Rhins superstitions for the Stranraer publication *The Galloway Register*, from **Allan Cunningham**'s poem *The Witch-Cake*, and from **Robert de B Trotter** on the cure of changeling babies by "riddlin' the

A Literary Guide

reek". Maxwell Wood's record of famous hauntings goes back as early as the late seventeenth century, when the persecution of one Gilbert Campbell, weaver, and his wife at Glenluce, attracted the attention of the professor of Hydrostaticks at Glasgow, George Sinclair, who published an account of the phenomenon in 1672.

BIBLIOGRAPHY:
Smuggling in the Solway and Around the Galloway Seaboard (1908); *Witchcraft and Superstitious Record in the South-Western District of Scotland* (1911); *Robert Burns and the Riddell Family* (1922)

Allan Cunningham
1784-1842
Blackwood, Dalswinton, Dumfries

Allan Cunningham, born near Dumfries, who was a prolific author of poetry, collector and creator of folklore, and who was known, because of his biographies of artists, as the "Scottish Vasari", is a significant figure in the early Romantic literature of Scotland. He was acquainted with and admired by Hogg, Southey and Scott and is now remembered for the lyrical beauty of such pieces such as "A Wet Sheet and a Flowing Sea" and "The Lovely Lass of Preston Mill".

Allan Cunningham was born in the parish of Keir in Dumfriesshire, where his father was overseer on the Blackwood estate. He was the fourth son in a talented family of nine, of whom the eldest, James, published poetry in local newspapers and corresponded with **James Hogg**, and another brother, Thomas Mounsey Cunningham, published poems in the *Scots Magazine*, including *The Hills of Gallowa'*, which was attributed variously to both Burns and Hogg. The youngest, Peter, became a surgeon in the navy and, when in America, became a friend of **Hugh Clapperton**, the explorer; he published accounts of his own voyages to New South Wales and to the Falklands and scientific writings. The family moved early to Dalswinton, where Cunningham's father became factor to **Burns's** friend and neighbour, Patrick Miller. Burns was farming nearby Ellisland and was on friendly terms with John Cunningham; Allan later recalled hearing the poet reciting *Tam O' Shanter* in the kitchen at their home at Sandbed. He was sent to a dame school at Quarrelwood and, by the age of eleven, was placed under the tutelage of his brother James to become a stone-mason. He read avidly in private and attended local festivities, at which he picked up snatches of local tradition and ballads. At twelve years of age, he walked in **Burns's** funeral cortege. His worship of the giants of literature at the time was such that he walked to Edinburgh to catch a glimpse of Scott, after the publication of *Marmion* and had committed the entirety of the *Lay of the Last Minstrel*, which he could barely afford on his wages, to memory. He met James Hogg, when Hogg was engaged as shepherd to a Mr Harkness of Mitchelslacks, in the parish of Closeburn. Their meeting, which both afterwards recorded, took place on the side of Queensberry Hill, where Hogg had a makeshift hut. Cunningham seemed to Hogg "the very model of Burns" and recited to him his songs and ballads. A friendship sprang up, so strongly that Hogg and his wife later fostered one of Allan's nieces, whom they introduced to Sir Walter Scott. Perhaps it was not surprising that when, nourished on this rarefied literary atmosphere, Cunningham asked for advice on his future from the local minister, Rev John Wightman, he was advised against "loving poetry too much". Far from being discouraged, however, he began publishing under the pseudonym "Hidallan" in *Literary Recreations* and in 1809 received his first real literary opportunity, when RH Cromek, an engraver, visited Dumfriesshire in search of poetic material. Cromek had published a supplement to **Currie's** edition of Burns and was preparing a *Collection of Scottish Songs*, with notes and memoranda of Burns. Cromek was astonished by Cunningham's breadth of knowledge of local poetry and folklore, but was not encouraging about Cunningham's own original work. "No one," he advised "should try to write songs after Robert Burns, unless he could either write like him or some of the old minstrels". Cunningham quickly conceived that if he could pass off his own work as genuine fragments of ancient poesy, he would find a route to publication through this enthusiast for the antiquarianism of Scott and Bishop Percy. He therefore agreed to search out the relics of Dumfriesshire poetry, and so originated, almost entirely from the fertile imagination and prolific pen of Allan Cunningham, a largely bogus *Remains of Nithsdale and Galloway Song*, edited by Cromek. To his brother he wrote "I could cheat a whole General Assembly of Antiquarians with my original manner of writing and forging ballads". If Cromek suspected the fraud, he never revealed his hand, but more experienced observers, such as Scott, Hogg and Bishop Percy recognised

Cunningham's trademark. "Christopher North", or Professor Wilson, later wrote an appreciative piece in the *Edinburgh Review*, crediting the poems to their rightful and talented author. Cunningham went to London, before publication, to earn his living by literary means, but found that Cromek's enterprise did not pay. He took on some parliamentary reporting, but found that he would have to rely on his talents as a mason for a living. Through Cromek, he was eventually introduced to Francis Chantrey, for whom he became superintendent of works and amanuensis for 28 years. By 1811, he had sent to Scotland for his wife-to-be, Jean Walker, to join him in London, and , throughout their long and happy marriage, "bonnie Jean" was the subject of many of his poems. Some of these appeared in *Songs: Chiefly in the Rural Language of Scotland*, 1813. His tales of Scottish character and life, chiefly relating to Dumfriesshire, which were published in *Blackwood's Magazine*, later became *Recollections of Mark Macrabin, the Cameronian*, and included satirical material on the Buchanite sect, a record of the tradition of the harvest kirn and of the Witch of Ae. He met his boyhood idol, Scott, when Scott came to London in 1820 to receive his baronetcy, and sat to have his bust sculpted by Chantrey. He became a personal friend, but even he could not praise Cunningham's drama *Marmaduke Maxwell*, which lacked dramatic unity, though not poetic luxuriance. With characteristic generosity, he did, however, refer to it in a kindly way in the introduction to the *Fortunes of Nigel*, praised Cunningham's poem *It's Hame and it's Hame* as equal to Burns, and gave him the nickname by which he was often referred to : "Honest Allan – a leal and true Scotchman of the old cast". Scott also later obtained Indian commissions for two of Cunningham's sons. Cunningham's other romances, such as *The Maid of Elvar, Sir Michael Scott* and *Lord Roldan* were similarly unsuccessful, but his *Traditional Tales of the English and Scottish Peasantry* were a success and included interesting local colour, such as *The Placing of a Scottish Minister*, set in the days of patronage, and folklore, such as *Elphin Irving, the Fairies' Cupbearer*. He also published an article in the *London Magazine*, on his acquaintance with **Burns** and an account of his death and of Byron's; the accuracy of some details relating to Burns has been questioned. In 1825, he published *The Songs of Scotland*, partly based on scraps collected from friends at Kirkmahoe, and prefaced with a long essay, giving Cunningham's own personal view of the history of Scottish song. Six of these are wholly his own composition, including his best known nautical ballad *A Wet Sheet and a Flowing Sea*. In 1829, he edited an anthology or *The Anniversary*, for which he recruited many well-known Scottish writers, including Wilson, Lockhart, Hogg and **Edward Irving**. He was inspired by Johnson's *Lives of the Poets* to compose a six-volume *Lives of the Most Eminent British Painters, Sculptors, and Architects*, for which undertaking his own acquaintance with the techniques of sculpting and with many artists uniquely fitted him; the volumes won praise from Robert Southey for its style. Still indefatigable, he edited a new *Works of **Robert Burns***, with a biography, a new arrangement of his works, addition of new material and excision of inauthentic material. Just before his death, he had finished the proofs of a *Life of Sir David Wilkie* to whom the earlier *Lives* had been dedicated. In 1831, he returned to Dumfriesshire, and was feted at a public dinner at Dumfries, under the presidency of **John McDiarmid**, the influential editor of the Dumfries Courier. Cunningham was presented with the freedom of the Incorporated Trades of the town, and heard **Thomas Carlyle** make his first public speech, having come to Dumfries from the wilds of Craigenputtock, especially to honour him. Later they met in London and Carlyle always referred in kindly terms to the "solid Dumfries stonemason". By 1840, Cunningham's health was impaired, and in 1842, he was stricken with a final paralysis. He died at the age of 57 and was buried at Kensal Green cemetery.

* * *

With his interest in folklore, the language of the peasantry, the supernatural, and even with his flirtations with literary imposture, Cunningham is recognisable as part of the Europe-wide Romantic movement in literature and was certainly in personal contact with its major figures in Scotland – Scott and Hogg. The *Remains of Nithsdale and Galloway Song* includes an introduction explaining how the Scots peasantry had been able to preserve a pure strain of ancient song and gives an entire ideal (and largely mythical) history of Scots song. There is a touching description of "taking the beuk" and the appendix includes a lively account of fairies and the detail of their clothing. Of the four classes of ballads (sentimental, humorous, Jacobite and old fragments) very few had not undergone extensive revision at Cunningham's hands, even if he had received original fragments from informants like Mrs Copland of Dalbeattie, and almost all the sentimental ballads are of his own making. These, however, include much of merit, such as the appealing *Lovely Lass of Preston Mill*, in part based on his own courtship of Jean Walker: "Sweet lass, will ye gang wi' me, / Where blackcocks craw, and plovers cry?/ Six hills are woolly wi' my sheep / Six vales are lowing wi' my kye". Other pieces which can stand on their merits include "*A weary bodie's blythe when the sun gangs down*, and the long narrative poem *The Mermaid of Galloway*. In the *Songs: Chiefly in the Rural Language of Scotland*, where he establishes a canon of what he believes to be the true tradition of Scots song, he often echoes Burns, but is at his best when introducing closely observed touches from nature: "Erewhile the hare denn'd close from view, / Licks from her fleece the clover dew" (*Awake my love*) . When writing of **Burns** and his life, he has been accused of romanticising his own personal recollections of the poet and of the effect of his death on Dumfries, and also of unfounded innuendo when describing Burns's relations with various women. For all that, Cunningham was held in respect and affection by the writers of his generation, the prolific corpus of his writings contains much deserving resurrection and he remains a pivotal figure in the Scots literature of the early nineteenth century.

BIBLIOGRAPHY:
Songs: Chiefly in the Rural Language of Scotland (1813); *Traditional Tales of the English and Scottish Peasantry* (1822); *The Songs of Scotland* (1825); *Sir Michael Scott* (1828); *The Anniversary* (1829); *The Lives of the Most Eminent British Painters, Sculptors, and Architects* (1830); *The Maid of Elvar* (1832); *The Works of Robert Burns* (1834); *Lord Roldan* (1836); *The Life of Sir David Wilkie* (1843); RH Cromek, *Remains of Nithsdale and Galloway Song* (1810)

A Literary Guide

Robert Service
1854-1911
Dumfries

Robert Service, who lived from childhood and worked in Maxwellton, Dumfries, became the most noted naturalist of the area, taking on the mantle of Sir William Jardine, and specialising particularly in the subject of bird migration. Although he did not produce a magnum opus, his 200 articles on zoology and his regular contributions to local newspapers under the pseudonym "Mabie Moss", constitute a formidable corpus of observation on the changing scene of the natural world on the Solway.

Robert Service was born at Netherplace, near Mauchline, where his father, James Service, was a gardener. After a brief interlude at Carlisle, his father set up business as a nurseryman in the suburbs of Dumfries, and then at Maxwellton, where his two sons were eventually to inherit the business. Robert Service attended the old Free Kirk School in Maxwellton, and then entered his father's business. In his leisure hours, he kept up a keen interest in the sciences, especially astronomy, and began publishing papers in the *Transactions of the Dumfriesshire and Galloway Natural History and Antiquarian Society* (of which he was secretary and had been one of those who helped set the society on a new footing in 1876), in the *Scottish Naturalist*, and the *Entomologist*, among others. In 1879, he married Jemima Margaret Glendinning of Maxwellton, and they had a family of five children. Probably because of his family commitments and his duty to run his father's business, in which he became a noted seedsman and plantsman, he refused the opportunity to accompany **Joseph Thomson** in 1882, on his journey to East Africa. Locally, however, he threw himself into public service, on local councils, in the Dumfries Volunteers, and as secretary and curator of Dumfries Observatory and Museum, to which he gave many of his specimens. He established his reputation as the leading authority on the birds of the Solway by his meticulous recording of sightings and his tireless fieldwork. In 1884, for example, in the company of Mr TB Bruce of Slogarie, he spent days on Ailsa Craig, observing bird-life. His manuscript notebooks, in the possession of Broughton House, Kirkcudbright, are a treasure-house for naturalists interested in the changing patterns of population and depopulation of different species. He often acted as expert witness for departmental committees of the Board of Agriculture: for example, he was questioned by **Sir Herbert Maxwell** on the plague of field voles in Scotland, on the predators, habitat and life-cycle of these mammals, and also gave evidence to the Solway Fisheries Commission.

* * *

Robert Service was a prolific writer, but his articles are widely scattered, and an astonishing variety of species. His pseudonymous articles in the *Kirkcudbrightshire Advertiser* are full of anecdote and invite reports of sightings from local contributors. A manuscript notebook at Broughton House shows that, in pursuit of a complete picture of the changing life of the Solway, he had conscientiously extracted reports relating to natural history from every issue of the *Dumfries and Galloway Courier* for the years from 1810 and 1874, so that the scrapbook now forms a uniquely comprehensive record for naturalists. Some of his articles show too that he had a wider cultural interest in natural history: for example, he wrote an article on the former existence of wild white cattle in Galloway, last herded at Cally until 1846. He also wrote on the Dumfries fur market, which was so significant that it used to dictate the prices for the rest of Britain: the furs included those of otter, foumart, hares and rabbits. He surveys the evidence for the existence of the ptarmigan in Galloway, probably last sighted in 1820, and for the decline in the population of choughs. While his projected work on the *Fauna of the Solway Area* was never written, he influenced the future writing of natural history in the region by selflessly putting his manuscript notes and notebooks at the disposal of **Hugh Gladstone**, who wrote the classic *Birds of Dumfriesshire*.

A Literary Guide

BIBLIOGRAPHY:
Articles in *Transactions of the Dumfriesshire and Galloway Natural History and Antiquarian Society*; Notebooks and other manuscripts in Hornel Library, Broughton House, Kirkcudbright

William Paterson
1658-1719
Dumfries

William Paterson, born at Skipmyre, near Dumfries, was the founder of the Bank of England, and the chief mover behind the ill-fated Darien expedition to found a Scots colony in Central America. His writings on trade, including the founding of a Council of Trade, his opposition to paper currency, and his reflections on the Union with England and its commercial advantages, were extremely influential at the time, though his name became largely forgotten.

Details of William Paterson's early life are hard to ascertain, but it seems that he was born to the family of John Paterson, of Skipmyre, in the old parish of Trailflatt (now Tinwald), and to his wife Elizabeth (Bethia). His father was a well-to-do tenant, having lands of his own nearby. They may have moved at some point to Kinharvie, a small estate near New Abbey. It is possible that the family suffered during the persecutions of the Covenanters and that William Paterson was brought up with his mother's family near Bristol for this reason. The early part of his commercial career is also obscure, but it seems that until the Revolution of 1688, when William of Orange gained the British throne, he was abroad gaining financial experience, and that this included trips to the West Indies and to New England, where he married his first wife. Like the **Earl of Stair,** who later was one of the chief supporters of his scheme for the colonisation of the Darien peninsula, he was one of those Scots who took an active part in Holland in the planning of the Revolution. By 1691, he was a man of influence in the

A Literary Guide

City of London and had accumulated a fortune. In that year, he and other City merchants proposed the founding of the Bank of England, and argued for the restoration of the standard of the currency. Only in 1694 did the proposal bear fruit, and, although Paterson became one of the first directors, he was disappointed in its early performance, and after a difference with the directors, he took the opportunity to resign. He had some engineering ability and had apparently surveyed the Hampstead and Highgate hills for the supply of water to North London; he retained a considerable interest in the Hampstead Water Company throughout his life. His early experience in the West Indies had led him for some time to contemplate the idea of a colony in Central America and his proposal for colonising the Darien peninsula clearly took account of its pivotal position between the Indian and Atlantic oceans. At first, his proposal was eagerly taken up in both Scotland and England, and received the support of King William. Paterson was himself in charge of drafting the act establishing the Scottish Africa and India Company in 1695. The English government and the King, however, were soon under pressure from other interested parties, including the East India Company and powers within Europe, to abandon the scheme, and the King dismissed his Scottish ministers, including the Earl of Stair. The lack of support from England was to prove fatal to the success of the expedition, since governors of American and West Indian colonies were instructed to refuse supplies to the colonists; but at this point, there was still great enthusiasm for the scheme in Scotland. As with Paterson's previous plan for the Bank of England, subscriptions poured in and the sum of £400,000 was raised in Scotland within a matter of weeks. Most Scottish burghs became shareholders, including Paterson's native Dumfries, which contributed £11,600 to the scheme. The colony was founded on the principle of religious, social and political freedom and many thought that it would be the means of bringing the Christian Church to Central America. Paterson himself had a substantial investment in the company and abandoned his City interests to devote himself to the scheme. He was commissioned to purchase stores for the expedition, but was betrayed by a dishonest agent and was therefore not appointed Director of the company he had proposed. He embarked with 1200 other colonists, including his own servant and his wife and child (both of whom were to die in Darien), disenchanted or unemployed soldiers from the continental wars and many young men of noble Scottish families. Although the expedition arrived without mishap and began to build a capital called New Edinburgh, within a country they called "Caledonia", the disarray of the directors without Paterson's guidance, and the fatal lack of supplies from friendly neighbours, meant that a promising beginning deteriorated into chaos, as illness and hunger devastated the colony. Although more supplies were eventually dispatched from Scotland, and Paterson himself was appointed to the Council, the damage inflicted on the enterprise was too great to be repaired. The colony, seen to be exposed and friendless by the neighbouring Spanish, came under attack, and by the time the second wave of supplies and recruits arrived, it had been largely abandoned. Paterson, himself weak from disease, returned to Edinburgh in 1699 and prepared a report on the scheme, remaining optimistic that it could be revived with English support. He did much to calm Scottish anger at what was seen to be a betrayal of the colonists by the English, one which had led to the huge financial losses sustained throughout the country. By 1701, he had been taken into the counsels of King William and was advising him on investigations into the probity of those conducting the revenue, on a scheme to rescue the national debt, on the Union with Scotland, and on a further West Indian expedition, which he planned as a counterbalance to Franco-Spanish influence in Central America. At this point, his influence with ministers, who frequently consulted him on matters particularly relating to supplies, was at its height, and he recommended the establishment of a "Sinking Fund", ultimately a policy pursued by Walpole. In 1703, he offered to put his own library on commerce and trade at public disposal, in order to promote the understanding of commercial matters. In 1705, he entered a controversy with John Law, vigorously attacking his promotion of an inconvertible paper currency, which Paterson effectively prevented from being introduced in Scotland, where Law was proposing it as a panacea for the country's great economic distress. During the negotiations relating to the Treaty of Union with England, he helped frame the articles on trade and finance and attended the Scottish Parliament, in order to ensure the smooth passage of the treaty: for these services, the Scots Parliament recommended him to Queen Anne. It was a measure of his personal standing, that despite the fact that the articles of the Act of Union were burnt publicly in Dumfries, he himself obtained a seat at the first

Parliament of the Union. It was, however, a "double return" with William Johnstoun, and he failed to keep his seat. From the early 1700's, he was living in Queen Square, Westminster, probably with the step-children from his first and second marriages. His own fortune had been severely diminished by his involvement in the Darien scheme, and he is said to have taught mathematics and navigation while awaiting for compensation under the terms agreed in the Act of Union. Although his claim was eventually acknowledged, by the time of his death, his substantial fortune had been largely absorbed by his losses.

* * *

Paterson seems to have exemplified the rise to power of the cautious, moderate Scottish financier, both willing to and capable of wielding extraordinary influence at the helm of government, at a time when political economy was beginning to emerge as a fledgling professional discipline. The edition of his work *Central America* well describes him on the title page as "Merchant Statesman". His own disposition, despite his personal losses, never seems to have become embittered and he writes in his work on *Proposals and Reasons for Constituting a Council of Trade* that "revengeful resentments and redress always were and will ever be inconsistent". This work was written amid general unrest in Scotland, after the failure of the Darien scheme, and it recommends a blueprint for what we would now recognise as a development company for Scotland, to supervise weights and measures, control fraud, hold a supply of corn, end protection in fisheries, and diminish the amount of poor relief by the provision of suitable labour. Throughout his life, he was aware of the need for those in charge of trade to be professionally equipped with the special knowledge required for its successful promotion and stated that Council members would have to be mathematically competent, and "with an inclination and genius for the knowledge and study of matters relating to trade and improvements..". In writing both of Scotland's relations with England (*An Enquiry into the State of the Union of Great Britain, and the Past and Present State of the Trade and Public Revenues thereof*) and of Britain's relations with foreign powers, he never ceased to recommend trade as the most powerful and least wasteful means to achieving political ascendancy. A characteristic passage on the advantages of the Darien scheme as a weapon of foreign policy, recommends " this door of the seas and key of the universe, with anything of reasonable management, will of course, enable its proprietors to give laws to both oceans, without being liable to the fatigues, expenses and dangers, or contracting the guilt and blood, of Alexander and Caesar".

BIBLIOGRAPHY
A Discourse of Trade, Coyn and Paper Credit: and of Ways and Means to Gain, and Retain Riches (1697); *Proposals and Reasons for Constituting a Council of Trade* (1701); *Central America* (1701); *An Enquiry into the State of the Union of Great Britain, and the Past and Present State of the Trade and Public Revenues thereof* (1717); John Prebble, *The Darien Disaster* (1968)

A Literary Guide

William Beattie, MD
1793-1875
Dalton

William Beattie, born at Dalton in Annandale, trained in medicine, but was extensively engaged in the composition of lavishly illustrated travel books on Scotland and Switzerland, still well-known for their engravings by Bartlett and Allom. He was also on close terms with the literary men and women of his day, and gave medical treatment free of charge to many in the world of letters, including the poet Thomas Campbell, whose life and works he edited.

William Beattie's father was educated as an architect and surveyor, but apparently worked as a builder. He was killed in an accident in 1809. William Beattie attended Clarencefield Academy, where he was well-grounded in Latin, Greek and French. By 1812, he was a medical student at Edinburgh, and had gained his degree with credit by 1818. He supported himself by teaching during his studies, and even after gaining his diploma, he continued to lecture and translate, while conducting a small practice. Early pieces include *The Lay of a Graduate*, *Rosalie* and *The Swiss Relic*. He started a practice in Cumbria, but in 1822 was in London, apparently preparing to emigrate. His plans, however, were forestalled, when he became engaged to Elizabeth Limner, who was the heiress to a fortune. He spent some time in Paris, studying methods in hospitals there, returned to marry Miss Limner, and was on the point of beginning a practice in Dover, when he was asked to accompany the Duke of Clarence (later William IV) and his family on a visit to the courts of Germany. On his return, he resumed his studies in Paris and for the following two years studied in Italy, Switzerland, and on the Rhine. It was the picturesque scenes on the continent of Europe which were to form the subject of his travel guides and poetry, and which were to appeal particularly to an audience whose appetite for the literature of travel was being whetted by the founders of the new tourist industry, including Thomas Cook. In 1824, Beattie began medical practice, but was again summoned to accompany the Duke to Germany, where he investigated the medical effects of spa treatments. On his return, he published the poem *The Heliotrope* and *The Courts of Germany*. In 1826, he was on his third trip with the Duke, an attendance which included the duty of private secretary and for which he appears never to have been recompensed, except with some favours and keepsakes from members of the royal household. In 1827, he became a Licentiate of the Royal College of Physicians, and established himself at Hampstead with a large practice. In 1835-6, he again travelled in Switzerland, and published a poem *John Huss* and *Ports and Harbours of the Danube*, one volume in a series of illustrated historical works, which were to prove hugely successful. He seems to have had a generous temperament, helping the poet Thomas Campbell with his *Scenic Annual*, for which Beattie composed most of the pieces, and attempting to rescue the Countess of Blessington (to whose *Book of Beauty* he contributed) from financial crisis. He was also on confidential terms with Lady Byron. Thomas Campbell, best known for his popular Victorian recitation pieces *Hohenlinden* and *Lord Ullin's daughter*, and for his first poem *The Pleasures of Hope* which begins with the well-known line " 'Tis distance lends enchantment to the view", used to retreat to Beattie's house at Hampstead for rest and recuperation. Campbell's career was also promoted by assistance from **James Currie** and **Thomas Telford**. It was Beattie, however, who edited his *Life and Letters* in 1849 and hastened to Campbell's death-bed at Boulogne. Campbell's *Pilgrim of Glencoe* was dedicated to Beattie, and it was Beattie, one of Campbell's executors, raised the subscriptions to place a bust of the poet in Poet's Corner in Westminster Abbey, supplementing the subscriptions by a substantial personal contribution. In 1845, Beattie's wife died and he ceased from general medical practice, though he continued to give free medical help to men of letters. He composed a memoir for the benefit of his friend

A Literary Guide

and engraver, WH Bartlett, and obtained a pension for his widow. He contributed to the Archaeological Society publications and to many reviews; he was Foreign Secretary to the British Archaeological Society, and fellow of the Ethnological Society, member of the Historical Institute, and of the Institut d'Afrique, Paris. Later on in life, he lost money on the failure of the Albert Assurance office. He died at Portman Square, London, and is buried at Brighton, alongside his wife. It is said that he had composed an unpublished autobiography.

* * *

Beattie's literary works have been a victim of their own success: his development of a highly successful partnership with the engravers, Bartlett and Allom, with whom he travelled to Switzerland and throughout Scotland, has had the effect that his works are now plundered chiefly for the accomplished plates, rather than for their own merit as travel guides. His lavishly illustrated *Scotland* was particularly popular. It ministered to the growing **Burns** cult , by describing a pilgrimage to Burns country, accompanied by what are today familiar plates of sites of Burns interest – including Ayr town centre with thatched roofs and Dumfries town with ramshackle luckenbooths – and gives lucid and elegant accounts of the historical and folkloric background to the places visited. Beattie's works on Switzerland and Italy appealed to the Romantic yearning for travel in classical lands and places with literary and artistic associations. In his *The Heliotrope*, expanded into the *Pilgrim in Italy*, where artistic pilgrimage is seen as a cure for a distempered soul, he writes of Boccaccio: "The Poet's Song and sanctifying dust, / Here left, and living, stamp upon the soil / The seal of immortality!..". Of Thomas Campbell's death, which he personally attended, both as physician, literary man and friend, he writes : "While I – who saw the vital flame expire, / And heard the last tones of that broken lyre - / Closed the dim eye, and propped the drooping head - / And caught the spirit's farewell as it fled - ." Beattie's *Life and Letters of Thomas Campbell* makes extensive use of original letters of a poet who was more highly regarded in his day than now, and whose correspondence gives a useful insight into the life and network of acquaintances of a well-connected man of letters of the era: he was acquainted with Scott, **Telford, Currie, Alexander Murray,** and **Thomas Brown**. The biography concludes with extracts from Beattie's diary of the poet's last moments at Boulogne and includes an appendix listing subscribers to the Campbell monument at Westminster Abbey and of the pall-bearers at his funeral, who included Sir Robert Peel, Lord Brougham and Lord Aberdeen.

BIBLIOGRAPHY:

The Heliotrope (1832); *Switzerland* (1836); *Scotland, illustrated in a Series of Views ...* (1838); *The Danube: its History, Scenery and Topography* (1844); *Life and Letters of Thomas Campbell* (1849); *The Pilgrim in Italy* (1850)

A Literary Guide

John Morrison
1782-1853
Terregles

John Morrison, born near Terregles, in Dumfriesshire, was a minor poet and an artist of some talent, whose friendship with Sir Walter Scott and James Hogg, with Sir Henry Raeburn and Sir Thomas Lawrence, and with Thomas Telford, meant that he had access to the elite literary, artistic and engineering circles of his day.

John Morrison was born in 1782, the son of a small farmer, whose land was on the banks of the Glen water. The young Morrison's education was fostered by a clergyman, William Wright, who had once been amanuensis to **Dr Blacklock**, but who had lost his reason, either through a disappointed love-affair, or, according to other versions, as a result of the shock of John Paul Jones's raid on the Kirkcudbright coast. Wright taught Morrison to read and to fish; Morrison celebrated the memory of his benefactor, who was found dead on the banks of Lochenkit, in one of his poems. In 1778, the Morrison family moved nearer Kirkcudbright, and there Morrison attracted the notice of the **5th Earl of Selkirk**, who lent him books, taught him Euclid, and promoted his education, sending him first to Dumfries and then to Edinburgh. The Earl's aim was to train Morrison as a land surveyor, who would serve in the colonies in Canada which the Earl was planning. In Edinburgh, Morrison studied painting under the distinguished artist, Alexander Nasmyth. Morrison's tastes, however, tended towards literature, and when it came to the point that the Earl's colonists were leaving for Red River, Morrison took advantage of a delay, went on a tour of the Highlands and missed the sailing. He returned to Tongland, where he obtained some farm and surveying work, and also painted portraits. **Thomas Telford** at the time was engaged in building the Tongland Bridge, outside Kirkcudbright, and, always willing to promote talent, employed Morrison in the survey of a railway from Glasgow to Berwick, and on roads and bridges in England, Wales and Scotland. Morrison made the acquaintance of Walter Scott, after having written to him in 1803 to correct an error in *Minstrelsy of the Scottish*

Border and later wrote *Reminiscences of Scott, the Ettrick Shepherd and Sir Henry Raeburn*, recalling these illustrious friendships. Scott was interested in all that Morrison had to relate about Galloway tradition (**Joseph Train,** Scott's other faithful informant on all things Gallovidian, later recalled meeting Morrison, whom he found aloof and difficult, at Scott's home), particularly about the Douglases and about stories of the supernatural. Morrison also told Scott of his meeting with James Hogg, then employed in Dumfriesshire at the farm of Mitchelslacks. Hogg later referred to Morrison in his *Queen's Wake*, in a passage which confirms Train's assessment of Morrison's character: "The fifth was from a western shore, / Where rolls the dark and sullen Orr; / Of peasant make and doubtful mien, / Affecting airs of great disdain". Morrison continued to make surveys for Telford, and his work included plans for the harbour of Portpatrick. He later acted as surveyor for John Rennie, and worked on important constructions at the Waterloo and Southwark Bridge, London, and the Albert Dock, Liverpool. He retired from surveying, to help his father with the farm at Fellend, but was unsuccessful as a farmer; after his father's death in 1818, he returned to surveying, drawing plans of estates and painting for a livelihood. His surveys included one of Abbotsford and he painted Walter Scott's uncle and his servant. His intimacy with Scott, despite Morrison's often difficult manner, continued to strengthen, and he was introduced by him to Sir Henry Raeburn, Maria Edgeworth and Lady Byron. He sketched a series of castles for Scott, and these were printed in a limited edition, and some of his sketches appeared in the Abbotsford edition of the Waverley novels. Sir Walter did his best to recommend Morrison for employment in Liverpool, but he failed to find regular employment. After paying a visit to London, where he met the great portraitist, Sir Thomas Lawrence, Morrison returned to Scotland from his tour in the south. In 1832, he published his *Poems*, dedicated to his old landlord at Fellend; his *Reminiscences*, with their documentation of friendships with important literary and artistic figures of his time, were published in Tait's *Edinburgh Magazine* in 1843. He continued to earn a living from painting and surveying, and took an early interest in daguerreotypes, the early photographic prints; characteristically, he refused to accept an annuity raised through charity. He died in June 1853. The "epitaph", composed by James Hogg, was in fact written many years before his death, and sums up Hogg's impressions

A Literary Guide

of Morrison's contradictions and talents: "How solid as gold, and how light as a feather, / What sense and what nonsense were jumbled together.."

* * *

Morrison's *Poems* tend towards the grotesque : their subjects are death, murder, decline, madness and disease. His *The Welsh Harper* relates to the tragic story of the real-life counterpart of Scott's Wandering Willie, whose entire family were smothered in a gravel pit, just after Morrison had met them in Stranraer and after they had failed to obtain any lodging for the night. **Joseph Train** was also acquainted with the story and supplied it to Scott. His *On Ascending Cairnsmoor at Night*, however, contains passages of real lyrical beauty : "The curling mist arising from the lake / A thousand fancy figures seems to take,/ Arising from the pool, in columns white, / Illumined by the wan moon's parting light.." His *On the Death of a Bullfinch* is addressed to a bird which was his companion while painting, and which apparently stood on Morrison's coffin after he died. A notebook of manuscript poems, dated 1853, exists at Broughton House, Kirkcudbright, and includes several bewailing Morrison's survival of his near contemporaries and others accepting death with resignation.

BIBLIOGRAPHY:
Poems (1832); *Reminiscences of Scott, the Ettrick Shepherd and Sir Henry Raeburn* in *Tait's Edinburgh Magazine* (1843)

John Gerrond
1765-1832
Kirkpatrick Durham

John Gerrond, born at Kirkpatrick Durham, was author of a slim volume of poems and prose work, the latter largely a description of his travels in America. Though MacTaggart dealt scathingly with his works and personality, and Harper also dismisses his verses, few of which, he says, contain "much, if any, poetic talent", Gerrond's reputation has been under reconstruction of late, and his poem, "The Peat Moss", and others on regional events ("Dumfries Rood Fair"), the pleasures of the chase and of drink, are lively descriptions of rural life.

Gerrond, with perhaps characteristic self-preoccupation, gives us an extended autobiography in his introduction to his *Poetical and Prose Works* of 1811. He was born at Gateside of Bar in Kirkpatrick Durham where, as he later wrote, "clashing gossips heard me scream, / What hurry I was to begin / This world of wae". His father was a blacksmith, rented a small farm and kept an inn; he also wrote verse. When Gerrond was ten, the family moved to Causewayend, now Castle Douglas, where Gerrond learnt easily at school, but also helped his father with his trade. After his mother, Jean Halliday, died, he experienced difficulties at home with his stepmother and perhaps at this time there were already signs of the fatal Gerrond flaw: the tendency, which he observed but did not correct, to be a "rambling fellow" rather than "a steady industrious man". He was trying his hand at satirical verses, went on a trip to England, and returned to set up in business as a smith at Crossmichael. In 1791, he married Elizabeth McMinn, daughter of a farmer in Balmaghie, and

A Literary Guide

their courtship is poetically transmuted in *The Peat Moss*. The poem also unfortunately hints at the later course of their marriage: "After marriage what a pity, / Cloys so soon our youthful fires". After a period of ill health, Gerrond became depressed, attempted to run away from home, and sold up his business. He commenced smithing again near Dumfries; his unusual professional sign "Hit on mislucks a' – The case is altered" betrays his characteristic sense of being cursed with ill-luck, which recurs in his poems. His business might have thrived, but he neglected it for field sports, which he celebrates in his poems. Eventually, he decided to abandon his wife and left to seek his fortune in America, where he landed at New York. His business failed at Philadelphia, where he mentions having seen General Washington several times, after yellow fever devastated the city. He moved to Brandywine and worked as a farmer. His description of early American farm practices and harvest traditions are fascinating. He was particularly well qualified to give a view of the fledgling American nation, since he embarked on a round trip, visiting Boston, Connecticut (where he records the poor dental health of the ladies "from eating so much fruit") and went north into Canada, where he taught Highland Scots on the St Lawrence River. In 1799, he sailed from Halifax and returned to Dumfries seven years after leaving. His wife, who had set up as a milliner and "mantua-maker" to support their daughter, seems to have shown unusual forbearance, greeting him, as he tells us, "with the greatest cordiality". He began business as a licensed grocer in Castle Douglas under the banner "John Gerrond from Boston", but after "an arch-enemy" destroyed his enterprise, he "fell into dissipation". Before his death from cholera in 1832, he began smithing again, doing jobbing work and making "Gerrond hammers" which were apparently in much demand.

* * *

Editions of Gerrond's poems appeared in 1802, 1808, 1811 and finally in 1818; latterly, the publication was well-subscribed. The later versions included the interesting prose account of his travels in America. His *The Peat Moss* was successively extended and a moral turn given to its originally pastoral and descriptive intention. His poems tend to be Burnsian in their egalitarianism ("Could gentry stap great Sol to shine/ On poor folks' yard and poor folk's wean, / Could they on Atlas' shoulders climb/ And toll-bars fix/ The peasant's moon would soon be in/ Total eclipse") and their themes of love and drink; indeed, he addressed a poem to **Burns** from Pennsylvania in 1797. But there is a plaintiveness when describing his misfortunes and strand of misogyny in his thought, which is less attractive. **MacTaggart**, who had a particular dislike for Gerrond owing to his poetic praise for Miss Heron, "Star of Dungyle", criticism of whom had occasioned the suppression of MacTaggart's own book, perhaps perceived correctly that the reason for Gerrond's discontent was literary and cultural rather than personal: he belonged to a post-Burnsian generation whose creative energies were sapped by the sheer power of Burns's inheritance. Gerrond, however, perhaps had merits which MacTaggart was not prepared to allow: he is at his best in the serio-comic description of human nature as displayed at the Dumfries Rood Fair, where his description of the seasonal occupations in what was still a largely agricultural economy adds both charm and authenticity to the prevailing sense of anticipation on the eve of the fair: "The barnman's up now by daylight, / And berries on till ten at night , / Offers his help the corn to dight, / Or big a slap, / An' sae as a' things may gang right, / He theeks a stack". He is also on his own ground in his celebration of the pleasures of the field: "Of all the diversions Mortals here enjoy / Give me the sweet amusements of the field. / Above the rest they seem the least to cloy / And to a troubled Breast most comfort yield".

BIBLIOGRAPHY:
Poems on Several Occasions, Chiefly in the Scottish Dialect (1802); *The Poetical and Prose Works of John Gerrond* (1811); *The New Poetical Works of John Gerrond, the Galloway Poet* (1818)

James Currie
1756-1805
Kirkpatrick Durham

James Currie, first biographer of **Robert Burns**, *has been alternately revered and reviled for his role in being the first to fix popular perceptions of the national bard. By the time of the centenary in 1896, he came under heavy criticism for his treatment of the poet's "weaknesses" in the first critical edition of Burns's works, which he edited. Largely thanks to the efforts of RD Thornton, Currie's biographer, a more sympathetic image of Currie has emerged, as a writer under pressure to reconcile editorial standards of accuracy with the need to conciliate Burns's enemies, and to raise subscriptions by a popular sale of the works. Currie was also in his own right a noted medical writer, political thinker and philanthropist.*

James Currie was the son of the minister of Kirkpatrick Durham, and member of a close-knit family, consisting of ministers, farmers and small landowners in and around Dumfries. **Henry Duncan**, whose career he was later to aid, with characteristic selflessness, was a step-cousin. In 1762, Currie's father became the minister of Middlebie and he attended the parish school. His father taught him classics and politics in the evenings. In 1769, he was sent to Chapman's school at Dumfries, a school with an excellent reputation; this was at a time when his mother was dying in the last stages of consumption, the family disease. With a practical concern for the boy's future, his father took an opening for James with a tobacco company in Glasgow, where tobacco imports were centred. Perhaps somewhat envious of his cousins, who had gone to study medicine, he embarked on board the ship "Cochrane", destined to become an apprentice in the tobacco trade of Cunninghame and Company, on the James River in Virginia. His interest in the songs and traditions of the Border, and his habit of extensive reading did not desert him, however, nor did his wish to correspond regularly with his home. Unfortunately, his father died in 1773, when Currie was still struggling to establish himself and was as yet unable to take care of his sisters in Scotland. Worse was to come with the American Revolution, as the tobacco trade in general and Scots merchants in particular, came under attack. His experience of slavery as an integral part of the tobacco trade, and his experience of the discrimination against the Scots, formed in him liberal and patriotic opinions, which he was to maintain later in life. During this turbulent time, he fled to the home of a physician cousin in Virginia and was inspired to resolve on a medical career. His return home was turbulent, as might be expected for a Briton seeking a passage home from America at this time. Eventually, in 1777, he reached home, and announced his decision to leave for medical study in Edinburgh, where the medical faculty was renowned. There, he met old Dumfries associates, like John Syme, later friend, landlord and executor to **Robert Burns**. Upon qualifying, Currie still intended to leave the country for America, but was delayed by the American War; while trying to obtain a post in the Caribbean, he was in London during the Gordon Riots, which appalled him as an example of intolerance and demagogy, and which unleashed an unreasoning Scotophobia in London. He was forced into print, defending his countrymen once again, in three pseudonymous letters to the press. Reconsidering his decision to leave the country, he eventually fixed upon Liverpool as a place to set up his new practice, and arrived there in 1780. Within twenty years, he was to be considered the foremost physician on Merseyside. Currie had both medical skill and a humanitarian concern, which led him to campaign for the inoculation of the poor against smallpox, to improve medical standards for French prisoners of war and on board slave ships. His marriage to Lucy Wallace, daughter of one of the great merchant princes of Liverpool, increased both his fortune and his clientele. He began to be able to maintain his family in Scotland, although his sisters were early stricken, as he later was to be himself, with consumption. He also maintained friendships in Dumfriesshire – for example, with Robert and Elizabeth Riddell, brother-

and sister-in-law of **Maria Riddell,** who was later to help Currie assemble his biographical materials for the edition of Burns's works. Between the years of 1785 and 1805, Currie was associated with every medical advance in Liverpool – such as the Lunatic Asylum and the Fever Hospital – in the field of public health. He was also an active member of the Liverpool literary set, taking part in the Liverpool Philosophical and Literary Society, the foundation of the Liverpool Athenaum (1799), reading papers, particularly on the subject of his special interest, hypochondriasis, and encouraging the literary work of others, such as Thomas Campbell and Thomas de Quincey. From 1797 onwards, he began to publish his *Medical Reports* on the effects of water affusion on fevers and is remembered in medical history for being the first to insist on the safe and controlled use of water treatments and the precise thermometrical observation of fevers under treatment. By 1793, he was at the centre of agitation in Liverpool, the chief city benefiting from the profits of the slave trade, and was in touch with Wilberforce. In 1788, he had already composed *The African,* which no doubt drew on his own Virginian experiences. Inclining towards dissenting views in religion, he fought for the civil rights of dissenters, and entered into opposition to the Prime Minister, William Pitt, whose war policy he thought destructive and tyrannical. His *A Letter, Commercial and Political, Addressed to the Rt. Hon. William Pitt, by Jasper Wilson* drew him into such dangerous political controversy that he was considering emigration once again. In 1797, however, he threw himself into the defence of Liverpool against invasion, but was so influential in improving conditions for the French prisoners of war that he was honoured posthumously by the French government in 1924. Scotsmen passing through Liverpool were never slow to apply to James Currie for either hospitality or help and were rarely disappointed: **Henry Duncan,** a relative and son of a minister at Lochrutton, who was helped to a banking career in Liverpool, which enabled him to save for his training and career in the ministry; **Thomas Brown,** who was given a copy of Stewart's *Elements of the Philosophy of the Human Mind,* and **Thomas Telford,** all made their pilgrimage to Currie's door. He also attempted to treat the ailing Lord Daer, brother to the future **5th Earl of Selkirk,** whose entire family came to visit Currie in the hope of a cure for the talented heir. Currie had maintained a dream of retiring to Annandale and eventually purchased the estates of Stakeford, north west of Dumfries, and of Dumcrieff, near Moffat, in 1792. John Syme, the future executor of Burns' literary estate, was the manager of his Scottish properties. It was when Currie was visiting his Scottish estates in 1792 that he had his sole meeing with **Burns,** paying his respects and leaving with an impression of genius and a doctor's analysis of Burns's failing health. He was to return in 1804, to visit the poet's grave and his widow. Already in 1786, he had received a copy of the Kilmarnock edition of Burns from a friend of Mrs Dunlop, and had been excited by his discovery of the poet. He had also known the Riddells, Burns's friends, from childhood, and was related to the Duncans, of whom the Rev George Duncan, father to Henry and Thomas, helped Burns and advised his own sons: "Look well, boys, at Mr Burns, for you'll never again see so great a genius". Currie was therefore well-acquainted with the circle surrounding Burns, and it was no surprise that John Syme, concerned with launching a subscription for Burns' widow, should appeal to Currie, to raise subscriptions from Liverpool. The idea of a posthumous edition arose naturally in the context of raising financial support for Burns' family, and the executors began sifting manuscripts, though Syme lacked the time and feared he had not the competence to act as editor or biographer. Currie was meanwhile in correspondence with Syme, asking for information about Burns in order to counter rumours which circulated about the poet's "weaknesses" for wine and women, and suggesting that a competent biographer be found. Currie was not himself immediately enthusiastic to become that biographer, and there was indeed some suggestion that Dugald Stewart might undertake the duty; but when that prospect proved vain and Syme himself refused Currie's promptings, Currie undertook to write the biography anonymously. After some hesitation, occasioned at least partly by his being in charge of a new edition of his own *Medical Reports,* Currie began the huge task of sifting through the unsorted manuscripts : his edition of Burns appeared in 1800, published in Liverpool. By 1804, Currie's own recurrent bouts of consumptive coughing gave cause for concern, and he was forced to leave his busy life in Liverpool for Clifton. He considered that the establishment of a less strenuous medical practice at Bath might help his declining health, but his health continued to deteriorate as the family toured the South West of England. He died in 1805, in Sidmouth, Devon, and John Syme was the executor of the will, which included a justification

A Literary Guide

of Currie's past political acts, including his pseudonymous publication as "Jasper Wilson". He is interred in the parish Church at Sidmouth. It reflects interestingly on the view taken of Currie's achievements by his contemporaries that the rhyming couplet inscribed on his gravestone and written by Professor Smyth of Cambridge, refers not to his connection with Burns, but to his medical discoveries: "Art taught by thee shall o'er the burning frame / The healing freshness pour and bless thy name". His son, William Wallace, wrote a memoir of his father, recording in a phrase what sums up Currie's career – his "ardent humanity".

* * *

As the cult of Burns grew during the nineteenth century, attacks on Currie's edition and biography reached a crescendo: he was accused of proceeding on hearsay, on the accounts of only one or two witnesses, of being timid, teetotal and insensible to literary merit. These latter characteristics have been proved to be fictitious by a closer examination of Currie's own career, but it is clear that in his understanding of "where we must tread rapidly and lightly", he belonged to his own time. He writes of his own immediate impressions of the manuscript mass forwarded to him by the executors that "I read them with sympathy, with sorrow, with pity, and with admiration: and, at times, with strong though transient disgust". The range of emotions seems not unreasonable, given some of the material he must have encountered for the first time in Burns's letters. It should be remembered that the sting of incidents, such as the "Rape of the Sabines", of Burns's epigrams, of his remarks on revolution, monarchy, class, and the impact of his bawdry, were still fresh and involved many people still living. As it was, Currie had both to tolerate and withstand pressures from all those who wished evidence of their involvement with Burns destroyed, like "Clarinda" (Mrs Maclehose) and **Maria Riddell**, who visited Currie at Liverpool, apparently to help his efforts, but who also insisted on controlling the information relating to her own involvement with Burns. No doubt, with such informants, Currie had to achieve a balance between suppressing the information which they insisted be withdrawn and grasping the opportunity such acquaintances of Burns offered of supplying him with first-hand accounts of the poet. Gilbert Burns stayed with Currie and provided him with information, but insisted later that the account was flawed. Currie himself, like all biographers, had his own theory of biography, which included an interest, as it were, in the pathology of the man of genius, and of the flaws which were inherent in a poetic character. He was also influenced by his knowledge of contemporary philosophical theories, relating to the role of imagination in strengthening the passions, and wished to give an account of the Scottish peasantry, as the seed-bed of Burns' genius. This, **Carlyle** was later to complain, gives him a "certain patronising apologetic air", as if marvelling that such a rustic could have been a man of genius. There is no denying, however, that the constraints on Currie were considerable, given his own political unpopularity after the "Jasper Wilson" affair and given the explosive nature of his subject: there was the overriding pragmatic need to raise money for the family; his wish to counter the circulation of memoirs like **Heron's**, who was viewed as venting a grudge; the need to counter English criticism that the Scots nobility and literati had simply abandoned Burns to destitution; and the requirement to deal with the wish of those involved with Burns to minimise or alter their real roles. It is little wonder that, on occasion, he seems euphemistic.

BIBLIOGRAPHY:
A Letter, Commercial and Political, Addressed to the Rt. Hon. William Pitt, by "Jasper Wilson" (1793); *Medical Reports on the Effects of Water as a Remedy in Fever and Other Cases* (1797); *The Works of Robert Burns: with an Account of his Life* ...(1800); William Wallace Currie, *Memoir of the Life and Writings of James Currie* (1831); RD Thornton, *James Currie: the Entire Stranger and Robert Burns* (1963)

PLACES TO VISIT: Burns Centre, Dumfries, Burns's House and mausoleum, Dumfries, Ellisland Farm, Dumfries.

A Literary Guide

Joseph Thomson
1858-1895
Penpont, Thornhill

Joseph Thomson, born at a house built by his father at Penpont, and brought up and educated at Thornhill, became one of the great African explorers of the nineteenth century, ranking with Livingstone and Mungo Park. His expeditions, particularly that through the dangerous territory of the Masai, resulted in the opening up of vast stretches of East Africa to British influence, and in successful trade treaties with the Sudanese kingdoms. His proudest boast, however, was that he never shot an African during an expedition, and never lost one of his own men on his expeditions, except by sickness or accident.

Joseph Thomson was born in 1858, the fifth son of William Thomson by Agnes Brown, in a house at Penpont built by his father, a journeyman mason. In 1868, the family moved to Gatelawbridge, where his father became tenant of a farm and of the freestone quarry, made famous by its having been previously leased by the real prototype of Scott's "Old Mortality". He was educated at a small school at Gatelawbridge, intended for the children of the quarry-workers, and then at the parish school at Thornhill, under the master, Alexander Hewison, father of the **Rev JK Hewison**, who wrote that Thomson was "the indubitable favourite of the school". Thornhill proved to be a stimulating environment, and Thomson attended meetings of the Literary Society, and was encouraged by his father and by Thornhill's redoubtable Dr Grierson in an interest in geology. He contributed substantive geological papers to Dr Grierson's "Society of Inquiry" and met Professor Archibald Geikie at Crichope Linn, when Geikie was engaged on the geological survey of Annandale in 1871. Geikie confirmed at the time that Thomson had discovered some new types of fossil ferns. Thomson read widely, including Shakespeare, Scott, Verne and RM Ballantyne; he also showed a marked interest in explorers, such as Park, Bruce and Livingstone, about whose fate there was then public concern. After he left school in 1873, he spent a time at his father's quarry, but then left for the University of Edinburgh, where he studied and excelled at natural history and geology. At age 20, he saw a newspaper advertisement for a naturalist on a mission to explore East Central Africa, under the leadership of Alexander Keith Johnston. When he had received an appointment to the expedition, and undaunted by his inexperience, he took lodgings at Kew and plunged into the study of the flora and fauna, and of any facts known about the region. Thomson's letters of this period are full of ebullient high spirits about his future prospects. In 1879, the expedition reached Zanzibar, but Johnston soon showed signs of sickness, and died soon after they left the coast. Thomson decided not to turn back, but took command, and pressed towards Lake Tanganyika, where he confirmed Stanley's theory that the apparently muddy and sluggish outlet of the lake was at times enlarged to become a full flowing river. Thomson was keen to go west to the headwaters of the Congo, but his men were fearful and mutinied. He went north from the Lake and was the first European to see Lake Hikwa (Leopold). His account of his experiences and the extraordinary distances covered is contained in *To the Central African Lakes and Back*, 1881. On his return to Dumfriesshire, he found a welcoming party, including Dr Grierson, and the poet, **Alexander Anderson**, with whom he was to cement a lasting friendship, and was treated as a guest of honour at Thornhill. His next expedition was for the purely commercial purpose of investigating for the Sultan a possible source of coal, noted by Livingstone, in the Rovuma valley, but this proved to be shale. A more challenging prospect offered, however, when the Royal Geographical Society chose him to open up a route, in 1883-4, in the wholly unknown territory between the seaboard of Africa and Lake Victoria Nyanza. This entailed Thomson's entering the dangerous Masai territory, where he managed to reach Mount Kilimanjaro and ascend it to a height of 9,000 feet. He made a detour to see Mount Kenya and named a range of mountains after Lord Aberdare, the president of the Royal Geographical Society. At Lake Baringo, he took a much-needed rest, and then slowly

A Literary Guide

returned to Lake Victoria-Nyanza. On his return journey, he made a detour to Mount Elgon, where he noted evidence for very early civilisation, and suffered from the menace of the Masai, from bouts of dysentery, and from a buffalo, which gored him and resulted in his being carried for miles in a litter. Fortunately, the expedition was able to fall in with a friendly caravan, and continued for Mombasa, via Teita. It was during this voyage that he discovered Thomson's Falls, and sighted the gazelle named after him, now the best known gazelle in East Africa. On his return to London, he was greeted as a hero, who had succeeded in Masailand where others had failed, and he received the Royal Geographical Society's Founder's medal in 1885. In the early 1880's, he had met **JM Barrie**, who later recalled his boyish enthusiasm on Thomson's entering the room, "how we gathered round him like an African tribe". Barrie was to declare that there was no man whom he had admired more than Joseph Thomson and throughout the 1880's and until his death, Thomson's letters are littered with references to his friendship with Barrie, which included a walking tour of the continent. In the mid-1880's, Thomson was engaged in an expedition to counter German attempts to cement relations in the Sudan with the kings of Sokoto and Maliki; Thomson's treaties with these potentates was an immense commercial advantage to Britain. From 1885-7, he spent time on his literary work and in recuperating his health. Without activity, however, his spirits tended to decline into depression and his failure to be engaged in going to the relief of Emin Pasha – for which he advocated a route through Masailand – contributed to his sense of frustration. In 1888, he went to North Africa, to explore the Atlas mountains on his own account: despite being hampered by the Moroccan authorities, he was making geological observations, and noting, as he had done in Africa, the more favourable effect of Islam, rather than Christianity, on the level of civilisation of the native population. In 1888-9, he became involved in policy statements at home on the British foreign policy of withdrawing from East Africa, and vigorously denounced government pusillanimity and treachery. Thomson's own view was that a system of Chartered Companies could be adopted to develop Britain's African interests, where the government could not or would not take on the responsibility, and therefore, in 1890, Thomson willingly took on a mission from the British South Africa Company. He took personal instructions from Cecil Rhodes at Kimberley, but the march was dogged by a deadly outbreak of smallpox, the need to out-manoeuvre the Portuguese, and Thomson's own failing health, which had been affected by earlier injuries. He had to rely upon his two lieutenants, Grant and Wilson, and barely managed to return to London in 1891. Compelled to inactivity by illness, he occupied his time with literary work, and composed his paper *To Lake Bangweolo and the Unexplored Region of British Central Africa* for the Royal Geographical Society. He was in fact only to return to Africa for his health's sake, when he returned to the Cape and stayed with Cecil Rhodes. Despite making plans for an expedition to Mashonaland, he returned home to Scotland, but was compelled , in an ever more desperate search for health, to travel to a milder climate in France. He died in 1895, commenting "I have been face to face with death for years, and I need not be alarmed at it now". He was buried at Morton cemetery, Thornhill, his funeral being attended by **Barrie** . A commemorative poem was composed by **Alexander Anderson** for the biography written by Thomson's brother, and it describes his burial in his native Thornhill : "O better thus than that he should lie / To mingle with no kindred earth,/ In the lone desert where the sky/ Burns all things into fiery dearth,/ And where not even one kindly eye/ Could note the grave wherein he slept". A bust was sculpted by Charles McBride and was erected in 1897, near his old school at Thornhill.

*   *   *

Thomson's prose ranks high in the literature of travel and, judging by the numbers of reprints and translations of his works into German and French, the public appreciated the heroism of his journeys and the exoticism of their setting, in the high era of empire-building. Thomson was capable not only of precise geological observation (he also had several plant species named after him and his collections were sent to the museums at South Kensington, London), but of an appealing immediacy of description, bringing his audience close to the unfamiliar reality of Africa: " If you want to get some idea of what an African road is like, I would advise you to go out to some moorland place after rain, and march up and down in one of the drains for two or three hours. If there is a loch near at hand, vary your walk with a ramble in to it, and now and then perambulate over some piece of dry ground. The effect will be highly

A Literary Guide

realistic". The drama of *"Through Masai Land"* was highly appreciated by Victorian audiences: "Here I was, on my knee, behind a small skeleton bush, positively looking up at an enormous wild elephant, the head of which was almost over me.." He wrote prolifically for the Royal Geographical Society, and early works appear in the *Transactions of the Dumfriesshire and Galloway Natural History and Antiquarian Society.* He lectured extensively, always including lectures at Thornhill when in Scotland. Despite his undoubted contribution to British interests in Africa, he continued to meditate his first-hand experience of the effect of colonising and Christianity on African culture, and was not afraid to confront the public with unpleasant truths about the supposed beneficence of British influence. In his lecture *On European Intercourse with Africa,* delivered in Edinburgh and other places, he pulls few punches, asking: "(w)here.. was the compensation to Africa for the frightful legacy of crime and degradation they had left behind? Where was the reparation and atonement for the millions torn from their homes and the millions massacred for a land laid waste, for the further warping of the rudimentary moral ideas of myriads of people, and the driving of them into ten-fold lower depths of savagery than they had known before the European era?" In his life of Mungo Park, in which he describes the later expeditions of **Clapperton** and Landers, he makes clear – as also in his oration at the unveiling of Livingstone's bust at Stirling – the qualities in Park which he admires in any explorer of the African scene: his sense of a higher, peaceful and civilising mission in Africa, over and above mere conquest. His *Ulu* (1888) was his only attempt at fiction, written with Miss E Harris-Smith as a psychological study of the African mind, set in the unknown territory of Masailand at the foot of Mount Kilimanjaro, and aiming to counter what Thomson viewed as the nonsense of Rider Haggard's *She.* Perhaps what does not emerge in Thomson's prose is the immense fortitude, good humour and ebullience of which he was capable in his letters and which emerges in **JM Barrie's** humorous account of him in *An Edinburgh Eleven,* which concludes: "Perhaps his most remarkable feat consisted in taking a bottle of brandy into the heart of Africa and bringing it back intact".

BIBLIOGRAPHY: *To the Central African Lakes and Back* (1881);

Through Masai Land (1885); *Mungo Park and the Niger* (1890); with Miss E. Harris Smith, *Ulu: an African Romance* (1888); J.M. Barrie, *An Edinburgh Eleven* (1889); J.B. Thomson, *Joseph Thomson, African Explorer* (1896)

PLACES TO VISIT: Thomson's birthplace at Penpont is marked by a plaque; his bust outside his school at Thornhill still stands.

Hugh Steuart Gladstone
1877-1949
Capenoch, by Thornhill

Hugh Gladstone, who lived at Capenoch, Thornhill, and was prominent in civic life in Dumfriesshire, was the most eminent writer on ornithology in the region: his "Birds of Dumfriesshire" is authoritative, and is now a rare book. He was also an authority on aspects of **Burns's** *life.*

Hugh Steuart Gladstone, Esq. of Capenoch.

Hugh Gladstone, whose father was a cousin to the great politician WE Gladstone, was born in 1877 and educated at Eton and Trinity Hall, Cambridge. The family estate of Capenoch is in the parish of Keir, near Thornhill. Gladstone served in the South African War in the KOSB, and was again gazetted Captain during the 1914-18 war, when he was attached to the general staff of the War Office. He took up an active role in county government, beginning as a County Councillor in 1904; by 1930, he was Convener of the Council, a Director of the Crichton Royal Institution, and of the Dumfries and Galloway Royal Infirmary, and in 1946, he was Lord Lieutenant of Dumfriesshire. His ornithological knowledge was put to use when he was chosen as a member of government committees on the protection of wild birds, on game and on heather-burning. He was also President of the Dumfries and Galloway Natural History and Antiquarian Society, and wrote its history on the occasion of its jubilee in 1913. His *Birds of Dumfriesshire*, 1910, was the fruit of much study, collection of records, and the accumulation of an immense ornithological library and of specimens at Capenoch. It was followed by *A Catalogue of Vertebrate Fauna of Dumfriesshire*, 1912, and *Birds and the War*, 1919. Gladstone was a renowned shot, and had been big-game hunting in India and East Africa: he published *Shooting with Surtees*, in 1927, and had earlier published *Record Bags and Shooting Records* in 1922. His own game books were marked by the same meticulous care which he devoted to his ornithological observations.

* * *

Birds of Dumfriesshire, printed in a small run of only 300 copies, was the best county avifauna of its day. It opens with an invaluable set of biographies of naturalists of the region, including **Sir William Jardine, Thomas Aird**, and **Captain AWM Clark-Kennedy**. Gladstone also acknowledges the contribution of **Robert Service**, who had put at his disposal many records and manuscript notebooks. 218 species of bird are listed, with chronological details of sightings and discussion of migration patterns, but the scientific content of the prose is also enlivened by quotations from poetry and by historical observations. A supplementary volume *Notes on the Birds of Dumfriesshire: a Continuation of the Birds of Dumfriesshire*, was published in 1923. *Birds and the War* was a survey of the role of birds in the war and its effect on them, including accounts of the life-saving feats of carrier pigeons returning home with critical messages. Gladstone belonged to the generation when a talent for hunting was entirely compatible with a talent for natural history, and indeed when the one often promoted the other. His *Shooting with Surtees*, 1927 is a confessedly nostalgic set of extracts from the hunting incidents in the works of Robert Smith Surtees; his *Record Bags and Shooting Records*, 1922, recording the largest bags of game-birds and wild-fowl taken in the British Isles (and often in Dumfries and Galloway) and compiled from private records to which Gladstone had access, can now serve us as a testimony to the huge numbers of birds, such as black grouse, once existing in the countryside and now virtually vanished. His life-long interest in the works of **Burns** found expression in a scholarly and balanced article on *Maria Riddell, the Friend of Burns*, 1915, which is still a useful reference work.

BIBLIOGRAPHY:
The Birds of Dumfriesshire (1910); *A Catalogue of Vertebrate Fauna of*

Dumfriesshire (1912); *Maria Riddell, the Friend of Burns* (1915); *Birds and the War* (1919); *Record Bags and Shooting Records* (1922); *Notes on the Birds of Dumfriesshire: a Continuation of the 'Birds of Dumfriesshire'* (1923); *Shooting with Surtees* (1927)

Rev Dr James King Hewison
1853-1938
Thornhill

James King Hewison was born at Morton Schoolhouse, the son of Alexander Hewison, a respected parish schoolmaster. By profession a minister, Hewison was an historical scholar of some note, writing particularly on ecclesiastical history, including his classic work on the Covenanters, and work on the Ruthwell and Bewcastle crosses.

REV. JAMES KING HEWISON, D.D.

James King Hewison was son of the parish schoolmaster at Thornhill, Alexander Hewison, who was affectionately remembered by his pupils, **Joseph Thomson** and **Joseph Laing Waugh**. At 16, Hewison entered Edinburgh University and graduated MA in 1875. He wrote a small geography of Dumfriesshire, now rare, and in 1874, began a series of articles for the *Dumfries Standard*. He became a private tutor to the family of Mr WP Adam of Blairadam, who was Governor General of Madras, and Liberal Whip. In 1878, Hewison continued his studies at Leipzig, where he cultivated his knowledge of European languages, and in 1879 was licensed by the Presbytery of Edinburgh to preach in the Church of Scotland. He briefly assisted Dr MacLeod at the Park Church, Glasgow, and was then elected parish minister for the Ayrshire parish of Stair. In 1884, he was called to the charge of Rothesay, where he found much material to inspire his historical interest and study. In 1887, he edited for the Scottish Text Society the works of Abbot Ninian Winzet, and his several papers on the archaeology of Bute culminated in his classic *The Isle of Bute in the Olden Time*, 1893. By 1902, he had received an honorary doctorate from Edinburgh for his historical work . His weighty and classic *The Covenanters*, on a

A Literary Guide

subject which had long interested him, appeared in 1908. In 1912, he returned to his early interest and issued a County Geography of Dumfries. His work *Notes on the Runic Roods of Ruthwell and Bewcastle* occasioned controversy, as did his newspaper articles on the subject of "Old Mortality", on the portraits of Robert Burns and the story of Annie Laurie, the subject of the ballad. During the First World War, he acted as chaplain to the Bute Battery Territorials. In 1923, he published the *Romance of the Bewcastle Cross*. He retired to "Kingsmede" in Thornhill and reissued his *Chiselprints of Old Mortality*. His interest in the Covenanting period resulted in the erection of a cross in memory of the 57 Nithsdale martyrs at Dalgarnock churchyard, just south of Thornhill, in 1928.

* * *

Several of Hewison's important works are concerned with the dating and interpretation of the Bewcastle and Ruthwell crosses. His *The Runic Roods of Ruthwell and Bewcastle* contains a general history of the cross and crucifix as symbol, and then a detailed discussion of the mistaken interpretation of the runes on the Ruthwell cross, which had been preserved and re-erected by the **Rev Henry Duncan**. The *Dream of the Rood*, the moving Anglo-Saxon poem which tells the story of the cross itself and part of which was discovered to be inscribed on the cross at Ruthwell, was translated into English verse by Hewison : "Methought I saw a wondrous tree on high, Begirt with light and moving through the sky; / It was the Cross Itself, effulgent bright,/ And ever glowing as a beacon-light". Hewison's *Isle of Bute in the Olden Time*, 1893, was written at a time when the archaeology and history of Bute were being vigorously re-examined under the auspices of the **Third Marquess of Bute**, whose antiquarian and architectural tastes led him to the restoration of record numbers of ecclesiastical buildings during his lifetime. Occasional pieces by Hewison concern items of local interest as diverse as Burns' acquaintance with the members of the Buchanite sect (including the apparently beautiful Jean Gardiner, one of Burns' "Jeans") , an article on Hewison's friend and Glasgow School artist, EA Hornel, and his *The Tryst of Dalgarnoc* (1927) which celebrated the role of the Nithsdale Covenanters, and particularly that of the Harkness family, which rescued prisoners from the hands of Claverhouse's dragoons at the Enterkin Pass, on 29th July, 1684. The eventual fate of members of the family makes grim reading: the mother of James Harkness was sentenced to transportation to the colonies and other family members were scourged through the streets of Dumfries. Hewison's magisterial work on *The Covenanters* runs to two quarto volumes and covers the period from the Reformation, in which he traces the movement's formative influences, to the "Killing Times". His research was meticulous, and included previously unknown manuscripts; the text is illustrated with facsimiles of the Covenants, portraits, photographs of gravestones, battlefields and prisons. Hewison includes a dramatic account of the Pentland Rising, which began in an alehouse in the clachan of St John's Town of Dalry, in the Glenkens. Perceptive character sketches are given of Claverhouse, whose contradictory qualities have given rise to an equally contradictory attitude to him by critics and historians, of the martyr Renwick, and of **Rutherford,** whom Hewison describes as a "legalist, and yet a lover of all; a philosopher, and yet a prose-poet; a narrow-minded patriot, and yet a citizen warring for heaven; a man of 'passions wild and strong', wrestling with himself in a mystic's dream". Hewison's gift for summarising character in a pungent phrase may be demonstrated by his description of Charles II, who "finally put on Popery as a comfortable shroud to die in".

BIBLIOGRAPHY:
The Isle of Bute in the Olden Time (1893); *The Covenanters* (1908); *The Dream of the Rood* (1911); *The Runic Roods of Ruthwell and Bewcastle* (1914); *The Romance of the Bewcastle Cross* (1923); *The Tryst of Dalgarnoc* (1927)

PLACES TO VISIT: The monument at Dalgarnock Churchyard may be seen just south of Thornhill. The Ruthwell Cross, housed in the church at Ruthwell, is open to the public, and is interpreted through the display at the Ruthwell Savings Bank museum, which relates the contribution of the **Rev Henry Duncan** to its rescue.

A Literary Guide

Joseph Laing Waugh
1868-1928
Thornhill

Joseph Laing Waugh, born in Thornhill and intensely attached to his native village, is remembered for his serio-comic fictional works, written in the vernacular and set in Thornhill, and for his collection of traditions, portrayal of "worthies", and record of dialect in the village.

Joseph Laing Waugh was born in 1868 to John Waugh, master painter and to his wife, Helen Cook in North Drumlanrig Street, Thornhill. In his later *A Hallowed Memory*, he refers to his early experience of his parents' reverence for the Bible and for Burns: he was himself later to propose the "Immortal Memory" on 34 separate occasions. He was educated at the parish school under Mr. Hewison, known in Waugh works as "The Maister", who was father of the historian, **Dr J King Hewison**. He also attended Wallace Hall Academy, while Mr. Stevens was rector. His chief education, however, was perhaps on the streets of Thornhill, where he formed an abiding nostalgia for the village in former times: "I counted among my early friends many old worthies, who daily graced with their venerable presence the steps of the old grey cross, and who in their conversation lived in the past – in the quiet days of the hand-loom and stage-coach" (*Thornhill and its Worthies*). He was first apprenticed to his father, but then went on to Edinburgh to study art; he also wrote some articles on art and lectures on **Burns** at this early stage of his career. Feeling the need, however, to earn a living, he became apprenticed to a wallpaper and paint firm, and eventually became senior partner in the firm McCrie, Waugh and Co., wholesale wallpaper merchants, George Street, Edinburgh. His first works *And A Little Child Shall lead Them* and *Mumper* were published in the 1890's. *Thornhill*

and its Worthies was first serialised in the *Dumfries and Galloway Standard* before its publication in book form, but it was the fictionalised accounts of the master-mason of Thornhill (whose prototype was apparently a neighbour of the Waughs), "Robbie Doo", who established Waugh's popularity. *Robbie Doo, Cracks with Robbie Doo, Betty Grier* and *Cute McCheyne* followed each other in quick succession, the latter being dramatised for the stage. In *Betty Grier*, whose first edition rapidly sold out, Thornhill characters, such as Dr Grierson, and places such as the Cross and Gillfoot appear without fictional disguise. Waugh was apparently an eloquent performer of his own works and gave popular public lectures. Upon his death, subscriptions were collected by the Scottish Vernacular Association of Edinburgh for a memorial in Dean Cemetery, but such was the response, that a further bust could be erected in Thornhill. Those speaking at the unveiling of the memorial in Thornhill, a bust by HS Gamley, included the artist, EA Hornel, **Dr J King Hewison** and **Andrew McCormick.**

* * *

If the "Kailyard" school of Scottish literature is defined by its setting in small agricultural communities, preferably harking back to a generation which could remember a pre-industrial era, and where village elders indulge in moral reflections of unquestioned authority, then Waugh is a worthy member of the Kailyard group. His characters tend to be from the older generation – such as Robbie Doo – and there is little reference to the world outside the secure village community of skilled craftsmen, local dominies and ministers. Waugh's recording of the vernacular, however, and his half-amused observation of human frailties and the often unconscious humour of local wisdom give his prose a quality which lifts it above the worst sentimentality of the group: in *Thornhill and its Worthies*, an old woman comments that "Thornhill gets the name of being a bad place to get mairret in – everything is raked up, ye ken, but nae place bates it to dee in. Ay, I houp I'll dee at hame.." Older dialect words are frequent and local idiom, such as the peculiar mild expletives ("Lovenanty!") are faithfully recorded, to the extent that parts of *Robbie Doo* were used as specimen texts in the *Manual of Modern Scots*. The vernacular is often used for poetic effect, as when Doo describes how "My wark has taen me oot in the early morn, when the eyelid o' nicht

A Literary Guide

had been lifted from the eyeball o'earth, and left it brichtened wi' pulsin' life and skinklin' wi' tear draps o' dew". In his more truly documentary work, *Thornhill and its Worthies*, Waugh records snippets of literary history and folklore : **Burns**' Thornhill bootmaker, for example, who preserved for history the fact that Burns was "uncommon thick" in the leg, was late with the bard's new boots and declared that he was "terrible feart he wad mak' poetry about it". Dr Grierson, who accumulated an extraordinary museum of relics, both ancient and modern at Thornhill, was the son of a provost of Dumfries who had a major part in erecting Burns' mausoleum in St. Michael's Churchyard, and was himself baptised out of Burns's punchbowl. Waugh also gives us pictures of Sir Walter Scott's carriage being mobbed by admirers at Thornhill, of **Carlyle** visiting Templand farm and Morton Old Kirk, and of the explorer, **Joseph Thomson,** a pupil, along with Waugh, of Mr Hewison, the parish schoolmaster.

BIBLIOGRAPHY:
And a Little Child Shall Lead Them (1890); *"Mumper" and Other Stories* (1892); *Thornhill and its Worthies* (c.1906); *Robbie Doo* (1912); *Cracks wi' Robbie Doo* (1914); *Betty Grier* (1915); *Cute McCheyne* (1917); *Heroes in Homespun* (1920)

PLACES TO VISIT: A Memorial tablet to Waugh may be seen at Thornhill.

Dumfries and Galloway

William Wilson and Tom Wilson
1830-1908 ; 1864-1930
Sanquhar

William and Tom Wilson, father and son, whose family came to the Sanquhar area in the 1690's to develop lead mines at Wanlockhead, were indefatigable collectors of tradition, history and anecdote related to the burgh of Sanquhar, and have therefore ensured that the town has one of the most documented histories in the region.

William Wilson

Tom Wilson

William Wilson was born in Sanquhar in 1830; his wife, Agnes McCririck, came from Cairn in Kirkconnel parish. William Wilson was brought up by his mother and grandmother, who regaled him with traditional tales, of which he made use in later life. He was educated by James Kennedy and at the Crichton School, Sanquhar. He became a bookseller and stationer at High Street, Sanquhar, where he remained in business from 1850-1887. He regularly contributed, for almost half a century, to various national newspapers, both local and national, and during the Crimean War published his own weekly *Sanquhar Times* and a *The Sanquhar Monthly Magazine*. He was a friend of the Dumfries editor, Thomas Aird. He composed the *Visitor's Guide to Sanquhar and Neighbourhood*, the comic *Sanquhar Town Council Drama*, first published in his own newspaper, and his most important work, *Folk Lore and Genealogies of Uppermost Nithsdale*, 1904. He was a staunch opponent of Home Rule, and was agent of the Unionist Association from 1886; he was superintendant of the Sunday School at Sanquhar, and took a leading part in the Burns centenary in 1859. Tom Wilson, his son, was born in 1864, at their home on the High Street of Sanquhar. Tom was educated at the Crichton School and at the public school. He became a pupil teacher there, and then accepted a situation in Christ Church School at Bolton, run by the Church of England, of which he remained a loyal member. After a year, he left to take up journalism, with a post on the *Ardrossan and Saltcoats Herald*. Later, he joined the *Weekly News*, published by Messrs DC Thomson of Dundee. For some years, he was the representative of that firm at Aberdeen and was on the executive committee of the Institute of Journalists. In 1893, he joined the *Sheffield Telegraph*, where he remained for nine years. From 1902 until 1927, he became a member of the commercial staff of Messrs. James Clarke and Co., publishers of the *Christian World*. During his entire career, he regularly returned to Sanquhar, married Flora Austin of Blawearie, Sanquhar, and was chosen as the first Cornet for the newly revived Riding of the Marches in 1910. In 1914, he was the recipient of a public testimonial from the people of Sanquhar. He retired to "Blawcarie" and remained there until his death in 1930.

* * *

William Wilson's *Folk Lore and Genealogies of Uppermost Nithsdale* is an idiosyncratic selection of fact and folktale relating to Sanquhar. The sketches had originally appeared as articles in the press, and include many tales relating to the supernatural, including the story of the ghost of Abraham Crichton, whose uneasy posthumous haunting was ascribed to his guilty part in pulling down old Kirkbride church; the book also includes many accounts of town "worthies". The genealogies, which were intended as the basis for a history of the barony of Sanquhar, particularly relate to the Crichton family, of whom the most famous member was the "Admirable Crichton" of Eliock, master of twelve languages and victor in learned disputes in the universities of Paris, Padua and Venice. At an early age, he was stabbed to death by his pupil, the jealous heir to the duke of Mantua. The history of Sanquhar Castle, plundered by those building the Sanquhar Town House, is brought up to contemporary date, with a description of its purchase by the **Third**

Marquess of Bute. Tom Wilson's *Burns and Black Joan* documents the poet's connection with Sanquhar, his excise duty and his stops at the Whigham's Inn. Sanquhar, as one of the Dumfries burghs, jointly returned a Member of Parliament and features in **Burns'** *Five Carlins*: "Black Joan, frae Crichton Peel / O gipsy kith and kin". Wilson's *Memorials of Sanquhar Kirkyard* is a fund of information on Sanquhar history and includes details of many of the Sanquhar characters mentioned by his father, who first encouraged him to write the book. The book is organised as a perambulation round the monuments in the churchyard and those documented include the poet, **James Hyslop,** and the historian of Sanquhar's vigorous Covenanting past, the **Rev James Simpson, DD.** Tom Wilson's *Annals of Sanquhar*, published posthumously by the Rev W McMillan, is a serious attempt to give a continuous history of the burgh, but includes lively descriptions of the last clan battle in Scotland, fought on Dryfe Sands, between the Johnstones and the Crichtons, the origin of the ballad *The Lads of Wamphray*, and of the circumstances of the Sanquhar Declaration (1680) and the subsequent martyrdom of the Cameronians at Airdsmoss.

BIBLIOGRAPHY:
William Wilson
The Sanquhar Town Council Drama (n.d.); *The Visitor's Guide to Sanquhar and Neighbourhood* (1886); *Folk Lore and Genealogies of Uppermost Nithsdale* (1904)

Tom Wilson
Burns and Black Joan (1904); *Memorials of Sanquhar Kirkyard* (1912); *Annals of Sanquhar* (1931)

PLACES TO VISIT: Sanquhar Castle and Cameron's monument are in the town of Sanquhar. There is a good display of local history at the Sanquhar Town House.

A Literary Guide

Rev Robert Simpson
1795-1867
Sanquhar

The Rev Robert Simpson DD was pastor of the United Presbyterian Church, Sanquhar, for 47 years. He collected the numerous stories preserved in the oral tradition of the area relating to Covenanting times and embodied them in his tremendously popular "Traditions of the Covenanters", which went through many editions and was at one time as common in the south of Scotland as the Bible itself.

Robert Simpson was the son of Robert Simpson, a farmer, and Helen Ketchen, and was born in Edinburgh. He was taken as a child to Peeblesshire, where he was brought up by his grandfather, an overseer to Sir James Montgomery. He entered Edinburgh University, with the intention of entering the Established Church, but decided to join the Original Secessionists, and studied at the Theological Hall, Selkirk. He was the first pastor of the United Presbyterian North Church in Sanquhar, from 1820 and he remained there for the entire term of his ministry. His wife was Jean Faulds, daughter of a banker in Leith, and they had several children. The original church to which he was called was threatened with collapse, because of the coal workings beneath it, and a new church was erected in 1849. In 1853, he received the degree of Doctor of Divinity from Princeton University, for his historical work. Simpson travelled throughout his parish in search of Covenanting traditions, often related by the descendants of those who had hidden in the Upper Nithsdale hills from Claverhouse's and Lag's dragoons: the notes appended to the

Traditions of the Covenanters document the sources from which he collected his narratives. It was Simpson who met the poet, **James Hyslop**, soon after Simpson's arrival in the parish, and it was he who encouraged Hyslop to write *The Cameronian's Vision*.

* * *

Simpson describes in the introduction to his *Traditions of the Covenanters* how his comprehensive survey originated in one or two articles for a newspaper and then developed as he realised that "(t)here is scarcely a place around Sanquhar that does not tell its tale of persecuting outrage". Certainly, the plethora of stories of dramatic escapes (most famously, at the Enterkin Pass), cold-blooded shootings, and of the hide-outs in the caves and linns on the north-western moors and hills of Sanquhar parish, bring home how the supporters of the Covenant engaged in a vast exercise in civil disobedience, aided and abetted by the support of the farming communities of Dumfries and Galloway. The book is a strange cross between a Protestant martyrology and a stirring story of resistance and adventure; certainly, the young **SR Crockett** was brought up on the stories of Simpson and returned to Covenanting territory for several of his novels. The names of the leaders of the Covenanting resistance – Peden and Renwick among others – and those of their martyred followers – Harknesses, M'Haffies, Browns , Bells, Campbells – as well as the infamous names of their persecutors, and the respective victories and defeats of the Pentland Rising, Bothwell Brig, Airds Moss, Drumclog, became part of the mythology and demonology of southern Scotland for two hundred years. The illustrations to Simpson's *Traditions..* demonstrate how Scottish artists responded to the ideal of the Covenanters, which Simpson did much to popularise. Other works by Simpson are fictionalised accounts of the Covenanting resistance, such as *Martyrland, or the Perils of the Persecution* which concerns the worst of the persecutions during the "Killing Times", or *The Cottars of the Glen*, an over-idealised attempt to convey the context behind the support for the Covenant, amongst a deeply religious "peasantry". Simpson's *History of Sanquhar*, 1853, which ran to a second edition, shows his more general interest in antiquities of the area, and records some interesting archaeological facts : for example, Simpson recounts that during the demolition of the old church at Sanquhar, human bones,

A Literary Guide

possibly of an ecclesiastic, were found under the altar, but that subsequently the evidence was destroyed or vanished. His poem on the taking of Sanquhar Castle shows that he was capable of writing a stirring heroic ballad : "O heard ye o' that dire affray / Befell at Crichton Peel, man, / How the reiving bands o' Annandale / Of a' the border thieves the wale, / In heaps fell on the field, man".

BIBLIOGRAPHY:
Traditions of the Covenanters (1842); *History of Sanquhar* (1853); *Martyrland, or the Perils of the Persecution* (1861); *The Cottars of the Glen* (1866)

PLACES TO VISIT: An obelisk to the memory of Robert Simpson was erected outside the North Church, Sanquhar. The monument to commemorate the Sanquhar Declaration, 1680, was set up in 1864 and stands on the main street of Sanquhar.

James Hyslop
1798-1827
Sanquhar, Kirkconnel

James Hyslop, born at the Vennel in the parish of Kirkconnel, and later a cow-herd and shepherd in Muirkirk parish, Ayrshire, was the author of "The Cameronian Dream", a poem relating to a vision of the famous Covenanting martyrs at Airds Moss. The poem was often reprinted, learnt by heart in the south of Scotland and even achieved much celebrity as far afield as the United States.

James Hyslop's father early abandoned his mother, Margaret Lammie, and he was brought up by his maternal grandfather, a customer weaver, George Lammie. His grandfather apparently taught him his letters from the alphabet printed inside the Catechism, but was unable to afford much education for him. Early on, he was employed as a cow-herd, but was keen and intelligent enough to do much for himself in the way of education: his first poem, *The Beacon* is said to have been composed when he was aged 12. Later, when he was sent to live with his paternal grandfather, he was nearer to Sanquhar, where he was able to attend the parish school - at least when not required for farm-work. His mother re-married John Lammie, who became shepherd on Glenmuir Water. Hyslop grew up with a familiarity with these remote landscapes, imbued with the tales of the Covenanters. In 1812, he became the shepherd at Nether Wellwood in Muirkirk parish, Ayrshire, just over the county border from Kirkconnel, where he befriended another ambitious farm-worker, John McCartney. He then became shepherd at Corsebank on the Crawick Water, a landscape which features in many of his poems. At this time, he read during his spare time, studied at evening classes, and was helped on by an enlightened farmer, his master, and the schoolmaster of Kirkconnel. It was here that he acquired a technique in shorthand which was his own invention. By the age of 20, he was a good classical scholar, had learnt some modern languages and some mathematics. In 1819, he left for Greenock, where he tried to start an adventure school, but the enterprise was apparently ruined by an unwise involvement in a security held for a dishonest partner. Hyslop narrowly escaped being jailed by his landlord, and it was at this time that poems such as *Despair* were written. He had by this time met the "Lydia" or "Annie" of his poems, a lady supposed to be beyond his reach in social station or fortune. As a result of this financial ruin, he was forced to return to the Crawick Water before two years were up. His time in Greenock, however, was not wholly wasted, since his two best known poems *The Cameronian's Dream* and *The Scottish National Melody*, along with some prose pieces on the folklore of Dumfriesshire, were published in the *Edinburgh Magazine*, edited by Dr Morehead, who introduced him to Lord Jeffrey. It was Lord Jeffrey who eventually procured for him a post as schoolmaster aboard the HMS "Doris". Before he left for a three year trip, he met and paid a visit to James Hogg at Yarrow. On board the "Doris", he saw Rio and Peru, and his experiences were chronicled in eleven letters published by the *Edinburgh Magazine* on his return. He also composed many of his love-songs while abroad. After returning home to Sanquhar, he left again for London in 1825, where he tried his hand at journalism; finding that this life did not suit him, he found a post as a master in a charity school. At this point, like many expatriate Scotsmen in London, he attended one of **Edward Irving's** sermons and apparently impressed him with the speed and accuracy of his shorthand method. Irving is said to have given him a Hebrew Bible. He also met and found congenial company in **Allan Cunningham**. Thanks to the patronage of Lord Spencer, he obtained another teaching post aboard a man-of-war, and sailed aboard the "Tweed" in 1827 for the Cape of Good Hope. At the Cape Verde Islands, the crew spent a night ashore, and most were infected with a tropical fever. Seven of them died in two days; Hyslop survived for another ten days, but died eventually on the 4th November, 1827, and was buried at sea. In 1887, his poems were collected by the Rev Peter Mearns of Coldstream, and in 1898, the centenary of his birth, a granite obelisk was erected in the parish of Kirkconnel, overlooking the Crawick Water.

Dumfries and Galloway

* * *

The poem *The Cameronian's Dream* acquired almost canonical status in the Covenanting country of Sanquhar, Kirkconnel and south Ayrshire. James Hyslop, as a shepherd on the farm of Nether Wellwood, must have passed daily the grave of the famous martyr, Richard Cameron, responsible for the Sanquhar Declaration, and slaughtered at the battle with the dragoons at Aird's Moss. Hyslop's poem was inspired by an experience of his fellow worker, John McCartney, who was known as something of a free thinker and sceptic. Hyslop wrote that he spent his time "in driving carts, making songs, forming theories, and forming ditches". McCartney's sweetheart at the time lived at Tarrioch, and, after visiting her one night, he rode home for Nether Wellwood, past the "Through-stane" which marked the grave of Cameron and his fellow-martyrs. On the monument are engraved an open Bible, and a minister and his sword. McCartney claimed that he had an awe-inspiring vision at the monument, in which a fiery chariot descended from heaven and circled the pillar, without burning the grass. Stupefied, he lost his way, though he had taken it hundreds of times and only returned to the farmhouse, where he awoke Hyslop to tell him of his experience, towards morning. McCartney's "road to Damascus" was eventually transformed by Hyslop into the poem , which describes how "When the righteous had fallen and the combat had ended,/ A chariot of fire through the dark clouds descended. / The drivers were angels, on horses of whiteness; / And its burning wheels turned upon axles of brightness". His later and longer *The Cameronian's Vision* was suggested by **Rev Dr Simpson**, minister of Sanquhar, and related to the martyrdom of John Brown of Priesthill, Muirkirk, who, in 1685, was shot to death at his door , in the presence of his wife and children, by Claverhouse, whose "..dark picture, painted in blood, shall remain, / While the heather waves green o'er the graves of the slain".

BIBLIOGRAPHY:
The Cameronian's Vision (1874); *Poems, with a Sketch of his Life* (1887)

A Literary Guide

PLACES TO VISIT: Richard Cameron's grave at Aird's Moss is marked by a memorial. Hyslop's monument on the Crawick Water can be glimpsed from the front of the parish church in Sanquhar.

Alexander Anderson ("Surfaceman") 1845-1909
Kirkconnel

Alexander Anderson, born at Kirkconnel in Upper Nithsdale, lived much of his life as a worker on the railway there. He attained celebrity when he began publishing poetry under the pseudonym "Surfaceman", particularly with his "A Song of Labour". It was his vernacular poems, however, which made him a household name in southern Scotland: "Cuddle Doon" became a favourite nursery poem.

Alexander Anderson was born at John McLatchie's entry in Kirkconnel on 30th April 1845, the youngest of six sons and one daughter born to James Anderson and Isabella Cowan. His father, who was sometime ploughman, miner, roadmaker and quarry foreman, was intelligent and well-educated, reading his son Scott, Burns and Hogg. The family moved, when their youngest son was three years old, to Crocketford, where he was educated at the parish school. There he became interested in painting, joining a group of boys who fiercely criticised each others' work, and then began to read and write poetry. When he was sixteen, he returned to Kirkconnel, where his father built a house for the family, and first was employed in a quarry, then with the Glasgow and South Western Railway Company as a surfaceman. In his spare time, he studied Wordsworth, Tennyson, Keats and Shelley. During pauses at work, he taught himself French, in order to read Racine and Moliere, and then acquired German and Italian. He also had a slight knowledge of Latin and Greek. He was a member of the Evangelical Union Church and of the teetotal order of Good Templars. His first mature poem was written after the death of a brother, aged 26: *To One in Eternity*.

His local reputation was established when he wrote *In Memoriam* for a fellow surfaceman killed on the railway, and his published career began when he sent *John Keats* to the *People's Friend*, a periodical for which he continued to write throughout his life. He also contributed to *Chambers's Journal*, *Cassell's Magazine* and other miscellanies. In 1873, he published his first collected edition of verse *A Song of Labour*, which attracted favourable attention of the critics and public, who, in a post-Burnsian context, were appreciative of the appearance of another working-man poet. Two years later, *The Two Angels and Other Poems* appeared, with a biographical introduction by the Rev George Gilfillan, including the sonnets *In Rome*, written before he had ever visited Italy. Later, in the company of Archibald Cameron Corbett MP (who became Lord Rowallan), he was to travel through France, Germany and Italy. The volume also includes the vernacular poems *Cuddle Doon, Jenny with the Airn Teeth* and *May Middleton's Tam*, which established him – perhaps unexpectedly for a bachelor – as a favourite nursery poet. His later *Songs of the Rail* (1878) and *Ballads and Sonnets* (1879) largely consisted of the re-issue of earlier pieces. By 1880, he had obtained an appointment at Edinburgh University Library, where he learnt the trade of librarian. In 1885, he left the library for a brief appointment as secretary to the Edinburgh Philosophical Institution, where he had the opportunity of meeting lecturers and writers of the day such as Andrew Lang, Dean Farrar and JA Froude. Thanks to Dr Grierson of Thornhill, he was introduced to **Thomas Carlyle**, about whom he wrote a poem. He returned to the Edinburgh University Library in 1886 and was eventually made Chief Librarian. At a complimentary banquet in Edinburgh, he was presented with his portrait in oils by the Stewartry artist, WS MacGeorge. Despite his increasing celebrity, Anderson continued to return to Kirkconnel, which remained his inspiration; certainly, he published less after leaving Nithsdale and the unpublished *Lazarus of Bethany*, much influenced by Tennyson, shows little of his earlier passion. He helped establish a library in Kirkconnel and was well known for his acts of private charity. His health began to fail in later years, which did not improve his always uncertain temper, and he died on 11th July 1909. As a testimony to his popularity, a monument was erected to him, by subscription, in Kirkconnel, with a bronze relief by the sculptor, HS Gamley.

* * *

Many of Anderson's railway poems are accounts of the dangers and real tragedies on the line which were personally known to him: *Nottman*, for example, was based on the incident of a driver's stopping his engine just in time to save the life of his own child, which had fallen asleep on the line. As such, the poems were well calculated to appeal to late Victorian sentiment. There is, however, in the longer poems (*Song of Labour, To my Readers, What the Engine Says*) a greater sophistication of vision: the personification of the "iron horse" as a sort of Leviathan, created and controlled by man and yet able to crush him, together with the onward rush of the rhythm mimicking the train's speed, lend passion to Anderson's reflection on double-edged nature of technological conquest. The opening of *To my Readers* is marked by typical Anderson touches, including its celebration of the role of the worker as a link in the chain towards civilisation and liberation , which will come thanks to man's inventive powers: "A worker on the rail, where, day by day, / The engine storms along, / And sends forth, as he thunders on his way, / Wild strains of eagle song". Likewise, in the case of his vernacular poems, like the *Cuddle Doon* series, while some compositions may be well within the sentimental tradition of nineteenth century Scots verse, *Cuddle Doon* itself shows a delicacy of touch and a precise observation of children, which gave it a deserved place amongst nursery favourites: "The bairnies cuddle doon at night, / Wi' muckle faucht an' din- / 'O try and sleep, ye waukrife rogues, / Your faither's comin' in'". The poem also possesses a complexity, which makes it more than an atmospheric description of childhood antics; it gradually acquires depth as Anderson develops a metaphorical meaning for "bairnies", since we all retain a childish standing in relation to God. The repetition of the phrase "Cuddle doon", acquires force from its use in different contexts throughout the poem, finally coming to symbolise divine comfort and ending with an appeal that He may "who rules aboon / Aye whisper, though their pows be bald, / 'O bairnies, cuddle doon'". Later poems in the series recount the tribulations inflicted by age and experience on the "bairnies" of the original poem, and the refrain "Cuddle doon", is developed ironically, and ultimately comfortingly, to mean death. Other poems, such as *Holy Jamie's Prayer* show Anderson's gift for sarcasm and ability to poke fun at village elders, while yet others, like the *Covenanter's Tryst* show him in different mood, inspired by the Covenanting history and landscapes in his native parish.

A Literary Guide

BIBLIOGRAPHY:
A Song of Labour and Other Poems (1873); *The Two Angels and Other Poems* (1875); *Songs of the Rail* (1878); *Ballads and Sonnets* (1879)

PLACES TO VISIT: Kirkconnel Station has a plaque in Anderson's honour, while the red sandstone monument, with bust of Anderson in relief, stands in the corner of Kirkconnel cemetery.

Peter Rae
1671-1748
Kirkconnel, Kirkbride and Dumfries

Peter Rae, from a family of Dumfriesshire tradesmen and small farmers, became minister of Kirkbride in Penpont parish, and later of Kirkconnel; he was a mechanic, mathematician and divine, but most importantly, he began a small printing press while minister at Kirkbride, so that his books were the first to be printed in the south of Scotland, at a time when there were barely half a dozen presses in the country. The "Drumfries Mercury", likely to have been printed by him, and first appearing probably in 1722, is one of the first newspapers to appear outside Edinburgh.

Peter Rae was born, probably at Mouswald in Dumfriesshire; a likely relative was the deacon of the freshers' trade in Dumfries. He was late in entering the university, since he appears as a freshman at Glasgow in 1692, but this may have been because of a conflict between his own Presbyterian background and the accommodationist views of the university authorities; attempts were made only after the "Glorious Revolution" of 1688 to redress the balance and send students to university who had previously been unacceptable on grounds of their religious views. Certainly, his name appears on a bursary from Dumfries session. Prior to his leaving for university, he had acted as clerk to the Presbytery of Dumfries. He was a student of divinity in 1697 and was licensed to preach by the Presbytery of Penpont in 1699. In 1697, he married Agnes Corsane, daughter of a prominent Dumfries

A Literary Guide

family, which included several Provosts and parliamentarians. Rae accepted the call from Kirkbride church and was ordained in 1703. He reassumed his old role as clerk to the Presbytery, at Penpont, until 1718. His term of ministry, however, appears to have been fraught with controversy and there was mounting feeling against him within the parish. The main ground of complaint appears to have been that he was "so taken up with mechanics and worldly business that it takes him off his ministerial office". It may be, however, that the hostility to him was due to his taking the Oath of Abjuration, against which there had been much agitation locally. Certainly, the controversy was of concern to him, since seven out of seventeen imprints issuing from the Rae Press were concerned with the dispute. It is probably true, however, that he was engaged on many outside interests, since in 1702, he was appointed Freeman of the Incorporation of Hammermen of Dumfries, an honour given him for his technical expertise, and he had been engaged in compiling, from 1706, his unpublished *Natural and Genealogical History of the Shire of Dumfries*. He had also taken an interest and possibly some responsibility in the Duke of Queensberry's lead-mines and probably carried out some experiments in type-founding, at a time when all Scottish type was imported from England or Holland. But the most important cause of complaint concerned his printing an obscene ballad, *Maggie Lauder*, and, though he was exonerated of this charge, his printing activities continued to be a matter of controversy right up until 1715, when a ballad appeared by Robert Ker, who, in a resounding attack on worldly earnings by ministers, wrote : "If he a right Watch-man were bred, / Durst he take up the Printing Trade; ..They have sufficient stipends here / That may suffice them for their Hire". It was probably the controversial nature of his printing activities which led him to print all his books under his son's name, Robert Rae, even though at the time the boy could not have been old enough to be involved in the business, as later he certainly was. His defamers in Kirkbride held meetings and presented their grievances to the authorities, and the issue went to a lengthy trial, interrupted only by the Rebellion of 1715. Eventually, Rae was largely vindicated, owing to the complainants' inability to present trustworthy testimony in favour of their complaints. The printing press was probably moved to Dumfries after this, because of the dispute, and it was run from Kirkgate, Dumfries, by Rae's son, Robert. After compiling his *History of the Late Rebellion*,

Rae seemed to turn more to parish duties and, after his wife inherited her brother's estates, his press fell silent. By 1727, Kirkbride parish was suppressed, and he was translated to Kirkconnel. While there, he constructed an astronomical clock for Charles, 3rd Duke of Queensberry, and also contributed notes to the first Agricultural Society in Scotland in 1740. In 1748, the year of his death, he was elected Moderator of the Presbytery there. In later years, a tablet was erected to Peter Rae by one of his successors on the wall of the Kirkconnel Church, which was newly built in his day. He left some money to the poor of Kirkconnel, and at least ten children, who pursued his interests in printing, clock-making, lead-mining and farming.

* * *

Rae's own *History of the Late Rebellion: Rais'd Against His Majesty King George, by the Friends of the Popish Pretender*, published in 1718 is of interest in that it shows Rae's meticulous attention to "authentic doubles of letters, manifestos, Declarations, Proclamations, speeches, Addresses, and associations". His unpublished manuscript history *Natural and Genealogical History of the Shire of Dumfries, Presbytery of Penpont* was transcribed by **Dr James King Hewison** and is held at Broughton House, Kirkcudbright: it includes interesting notes on the old Dumfriesshire families, including his wife's family, the Corsanes of Meiklenox. Rae takes a lively interest in the derivation of local place-names and in antiquities, such as the Roman roadway from Nithsdale towards Biggar. His own writings also include *Gospel Ministers, Christ's Ambassadors* (1733) and *A Treatise on Lawful Oaths and Perjury* (1749). The Rae Press of Kirkbride opened in its inaugural year with a popular textbook *A New Method of Teaching the Latine Tongue, by John Hunter, Minister at Air*, 1711. The first Dumfries book was Matthew Henry's *Sober-Mindedness press'd upon Young People*, 1715. His imprints are good examples of contemporary typography and his achievement is remarkable, when one considers the obscurity of the parish and the distance from technical or literary centres of excellence, such as those in Edinburgh or London.

A Literary Guide

BIBLIOGRAPHY:
The History of the Late Rebellion: Rais'd Against His Majesty King George, by the Friends of the Popish Pretender (1718); *Gospel Ministers, Christ's Ambassadors* (1733); *A Treatise on Lawful Oaths and Perjury* (1749); *Natural and Genealogical History of the Shire of Dumfries, Presbytery of Penpont* (1706 - unpublished ms. in Hornel Library, Broughton House, Kirkcudbright); John Hunter, *A New Method of Teaching the Latine Tongue* (1711); Matthew Henry, *Sober-Mindedness Press'd upon Young People ...* (1715)

PLACES TO VISIT: Rae memorial, Kirkconnel churchyard

Dumfries and Galloway

Robert de Bruce Trotter
1833-1912
St John's Town of Dalry /
Auchencairn / Dalbeattie

Dr Robert de Bruce Trotter was descended from a dynasty of Glenkens doctors, who were also keen collectors of Galloway traditions. Dr Trotter's father, **Robert Trotter,** *wrote novels and poetry, and collected Galloway antiquities and curiosities, as did his brothers,* **James** *and* **Alexander***. Robert de Bruce Trotter's two volumes of "Galloway Gossip", one for Wigtownshire and one for the Stewartry of Kirkcudbright, are perhaps the best exemplification of the family knack for recording the unique flavour of life and language in Galloway.*

DR ROBERT D. B. TROTTER,
PERTH.
(Author of "Galloway Gossip.")

Robert de Bruce Trotter was the eldest son of **Robert Trotter,** doctor at Dalry, who knew Burns and corresponded with Scott, and was himself author of several novels. His mother was Maria Nithsdale Maxwell, who originated from the Machars of Wigtownshire. Robert de Bruce's parents moved from Creetown, to Dalbeattie (where Robert was born) and then Auchencairn, where his father successively established practices. It was at Auchencairn where he and his brother **Alexander** composed a youthful, unpublished work, *Adventures in and around Auchencairn*; he also began composing poetry. His parents moved on to Kintyre and Skye, but Robert attended the medical course at Glasgow University, and then travelled all over the world, particularly in the East and West Indies. He had a successful medical practice at Bedlington,

A Literary Guide

Northumberland for ten years, ultimately in partnership with his brother, James. Thereafter he moved to Wigtownshire, where he spent four years, contributing frequently to local newspapers and magazines on the subject of antiquities and archaeology. The articles on Galloway antiquities and curiosities ultimately formed the basis of the *Galloway Gossip* volumes; a further volume was projected for Nithsdale, but was never completed. It was presumably also at this time of his residence in Wigtownshire that he engaged in an amateur excavation of the cave of St Medan on the Rhins peninsula(May 1870), of which he gives an account in Volume VI of the *Ayrshire and Galloway Archaeological Collections*. The Rhins traditions of bathing in the wells at the cave on "Co' Sunday" and their thinly disguised pagan origin attracted his antiquarian eye just as much as the details of excavation. He then moved to Perth, where he acted as medical officer to the General Post Office, Perth and was president of the British Medical Association, Perthshire branch. Like his brother, James, he became a long-serving town councillor. Some of his poetry was published in **Harper's** *Bards of Galloway*. Several of his sons succeeded him in the medical profession.

* * *

In his introduction to the second, Stewartry, volume of *Galloway Gossip* **SR Crockett**, surely justly, places it and its predecessor volume in the idiosyncratic tradition of Galloway literature begun by **John MacTaggart**, with his *Scottish Gallovidian Encyclopaedia*. The book betrays a literary debt to one member of the family who did not publish, since it is written in the persona of – and is presumably at least in part a record of the stories and traditional lore handed to her children by – his mother, Maria Trotter, born at Barraer in Penninghame Parish in 1803 and whose father also farmed at Barlaughlan. Throughout the two volumes, we catch snatches of Maria Trotter's biography – how she and her husband, Dr Robert Trotter, settled at Creetown to begin a medical practice, then moved to Dalbeattie and finally to Auchencairn, where her sons were born. Trotter may have had other family debts for his repertoire of stories: the insight into the human condition which the Trotters must have acquired during several generations' practice of medicine would have given them a store of anecdotes and a tolerant and amused view of the world, and of Galloway in particular. Possibly, Trotter had other literary mentors than his parents: perhaps his vigorous portrayal of the superstitions and prejudices of the Rhins owed something to a personal acquaintance with **William Todd**, whom Trotter explicitly mentions in his wry opening section warning of the dangers to an author of a frank portrait of the local population. In the later volume, it is clear that Trotter was actively appealing to the public for anecdotes, preparatory to a third volume, on condition that the stories were true and referred to real people, while he guaranteed for his part that he would avoid personal offence in their recounting. Beyond the slight unifying thread of Maria Trotter's narrative, the books' concerns and subjects are manifold and their prejudices, even if tongue-in-cheek, are pronounced: the content ranges from records of superstitions, such as cures at holy wells, marriage and Hogmanay customs and visits by the fairies, to snatches of traditional ballads, renderings of local dialect and language (such as the unusual use of intensifiers in the Rhins – "maist odious splendid") and records of antiquities and well-known characters, whether local worthies or celebrated men like **Thomas Carlyle** and **Captain Denniston**. Trotter was writing, in 1878 and still more in 1901 when his second volume was published, at a time when it was perceived the traditional Gallovidian society was changing for good under the influence of Irish immigration and the taking up of farm tenancies by Ayrshire farmers. The attitudes expressed in the stories towards both these groups is revealing. Ministers, the clergy as a whole and antiquarians (such as **Joseph Train**) all come in for brutal exposure, but above all, Trotter's narrator's scorn is reserved for those "doubly refined people who consider a Scotch origin to be the lowest possible depth of degradation", and who seek to alter original Galloway pronunciations, place – or personal names. For Trotter, Galloway language and names are at the heart of its traditional identity. Anglicising Scots authors, such as Sir Walter Scott and, more locally, **Samuel Robinson,** come in for particularly severe criticism, though in the following passage, where there is perhaps a little gentle self-mockery , the literary profession as a whole does not fare well: "A suppose ye ken yt Gallowa's hotchin' wi' poets; a wasp-bike's naething till't! gude-for-little doylocks, maist o' them, fond o' onything but wark. Some o' them haes nae objection tae drink, though". In fact, by time the second volume was written, the use of dialect throughout the book was far more dense and the plea for the preservation of the Scots language, including

A Literary Guide

instructions for its correct pronunciation, was more intense. Perhaps Trotter's lasting contribution was less in the recording of superstitions and anecdotes, but in the way his stories, told in dialect, act as a good-humoured and far from sentimental reminder of the uniqueness of Galloway dialect, and as an argument for retaining its racy vigour.

BIBLIOGRAPHY:
Galloway Gossip Sixty Years Ago (1877) - Wigtownshire; *Galloway Gossip, or the Southern Albanich* (1901) - Stewartry of Kirkcudbright; *Notice of the Excavation of St. Medan's Cave and Chapel, Kirkmaiden, Wigtownshire* in *Proceedings of the Society of Antiquaries* (1886), and in Vol. VI of *Archaeological Collections of Ayrshire and Galloway* (1889).

Dr James Trotter
1842-1899
Auchencairn

James Trotter, one of the three literary sons of a literary father, Dr Robert Trotter of Dalry, was a member of the fourth generation of Trotters to write poetry and practise medicine. Trotter is chiefly remembered for his "The Clachan Fair", and the "Song of Freedom", which attained particular popularity in America.

DR. JAMES TROTTER.

James Trotter was born at Auchencairn in 1842, the fourth son of **Dr Robert Trotter**, who at the time was practising in that village, and Maria Nithsdale Maxwell; his brothers were **Robert de Bruce Trotter** and **Alexander Trotter**, and his aunt was **Isabella Trotter**. His father moved to Campbeltown in Kintyre, when he was ten years old, and James was educated at the parish school there. He followed his father in his taste for antiquities and heraldry, and frequently sketched the ecclesiastical remains of the area. In Skye, where the family next moved, he collected traditions, which were contributed to the *Traditions of the West Highlands*, by Campbell of Islay. When he was eighteen, he began the study of medicine at Glasgow, and simultaneously published some verse. In the vacations, he assisted his brothers, Robert and Alexander, who were settled in medical practice at Bedlington and Blyth respectively. He joined in a partnership with his eldest brother at Bedlington and became a prominent and popular Radical politican in the district. He joined the Northumberland County Council and the Bedlington District Council and the Morpeth Board of Guardians.

He fought for the miners' right to a vote, on the basis that they were also householders, and his victory led to the election success at Morpeth of Thomas Burt, the first working man in Parliament. He was a prolific writer of election literature and local poetry, such as *The Devil's Visit to Bedlington in search of an honest man, and failure to find one*, so that he is as much known in the North of England as in Southern Scotland. He was the joint founder of the *Fraser's Blyth and Tyneside Comic and Pictorial Annual*. In his longest poem, however, he returned to Scots language and it was printed as *The Clachan Fair* in pamphlet form. Poems and humorous prose sketches appeared in the *Kirkcudbrightshire Advertiser*. His *The Song of Freedom* and *The Wee Bruckit Lassie* were much reprinted. He was a member of the Northumberland Antiquarian Society, and was in correspondence with literary and scientific men of his day. His last poem was written a fortnight before his death, for the *Gallovidian*, and described the Glenkens, where he was buried at Kells Churchyard. His funeral was attended by politicians of all complexions and after his death, a drinking fountain crowned by his bust was erected by public subscription in the High Street of Bedlington.

* * *

Trotter's best work is in the vernacular and his *The Wee Bruckit Lassie* is an appealing example of a sentimental genre: "The sun has set, the gloamin's come, the day has glided by, / The lassies liltin' through the broom, are ca'in' hame their kye;/ I'll daunder doun the clachan brae to meet the ane I lo'e - / My wee, wee bruckit lassie, that milks her mammie's coo". His *The Clachan Fair: a Descriptive Poem, by Bartholomew Powhead*, 1872, was a satirical poem, sent in person to many of those satirised, including his own father, and the original work is now very rare. It includes some good description of the excitement of the preparations for the Fair, in the best tradition of Scots poems about popular festivals: "Our shepherd blades, wi' streamin' plaids, / Wear in their pantin' sheep, man; / Their collies wide, on ilka side, / Ca' roon them wi' a sweep, man. / Alang the moors, in teamin' scores, The droves theigether draw, man; / Amang the rocks, the fleecy flocks / Come doon like driftin' snaw, man". It also describes the inevitable consequences of the Fair's jollities: "We maun confess, we shouldna guess / What hasna seen the light, man; / But mony a lass will sell the pass / Nine nonths that very night, man!" . His *Song of Freedom*, appearing in **Harper's** *Bards of Galloway* and written in classical English, gives vigorous expression to his progressive political views: "Not with sounding drum or tabor, / Seek we for a world's applause.. / Heart and brain our weapons ever, / Logic clear and reason strong, / Striving in one grand endeavour, / Aiding right, repelling wrong".

BIBLIOGRAPHY:
The Clachan Fair: a Descriptive Poem, by Bartholomew Powhead (1872); Malcolm McL Harper, *The Bards of Galloway* (1889)

PLACES TO VISIT: Trotter's tomb is in Kells churchyard, New Galloway.

A Literary Guide

Joseph Heughan
1837-1902
Auchencairn

Joseph Heughan was born in Auchencairn, in a house built by his father, and remained there throughout his life, as village blacksmith. He is noted for the density of classical and Biblical allusion in his poetry, together with the use of archaic Galloway words. He wrote a version of the satirical poem "The Gallowa' Herds".

Joseph Heughan was born on the 1st January 1837, but was orphaned shortly after birth: he was looked after by his maternal grandfather, James Milligan at West Knockwhillan croft. He learnt Latin at Auchencairn school, could translate it freely, and throughout his life collected books, showing his large collection freely to interested visitors. He was apprenticed as a blacksmith, a trade which he followed throughout his life, and samples of his metalwork exist in the Stewartry Museum in Kirkcudbright. He was a strong Liberal in politics. Though well known locally and through publications in newspapers, no collection of his verse exists. He was a close friend of **Alexander Trotter,** whose death affected him deeply. His Liberalism led him to a lively sympathy with the Boers in their struggle for independence, and he followed the news of their battles and of the subsequent peace, to within a few days of his death on 18th June 1902.

* * *

Two of Heughan's love poems, *Amor redivivus* and *The Wooer's Plicht* are published in **Harper's** *Bards of Galloway* and like several of his on this theme, deal – perhaps somewhat tongue-in-cheek – the vicissitudes of love. The *Wooer's Plicht* begins : "Puir ell-wan' Johnnie canna sleep, / Since Jeanie gaed awa' / The saut tears thro' his winkers dreep, / His e'en's like meltin' snaw / He's blearie and weary, / The chiel's gane nearly doylt.." He also wrote a two hundred verse appreciation of **Burns**, including these lines referring to his *Hallowe'en* and to the seasonal custom for girls to try to obtain a clue as to the identity of their future husbands: "When runkled spinster, bloomin' queen/ Did laughin' try / To rive keek-hole in future's screen, / Guid-man to spy". An unpublished didactic poem deals with Heughan's thoughts on human affairs and on the nature of the Deity. His version of the satirical *Gallowa' Herds* is interesting; no doubt the robust language of the original appealed to Heughan; there exist several copies of his version with his own amendments, which are different in each copy, and written in his characteristically elaborate script. The theme of the poem, originally written in 1821 by Andrew Sturgeon, schoolmaster at Clauchanpluck (now Laurieston), was the cruelty suffered by Queen Caroline, after her separation from the King and, more particularly, after the edict preventing "loyal black-coat" clergy from praying for the Queen's soul. The Reverend **William Gillespie** of Kells had been arrested for refusing to obey the royal command and is one of the few to receive favourable mention in the poem. Heughan's version is a fair sample of his use of Scots language: his verse on Gillespie runs "Up to scorn hing the cuifs, a wheen cauve lick ma-loofs / Wha Levite gang bye destreest bodie/ Yet sky-heich-roose the king, bent on swallin' Hell's bing / His harn-pan aye soomin wi' toddy". Among others receiving summary treatment in the poem is **Thomas Murray,** author of the *Literary History of Galloway*, whose fruitless pursuit of literary immortality is mocked. **Robert de Bruce Trotter** also wrote a version of the *Gallowa' Herds* and Thomas Fraser, publisher in Dalbeattie, brought out a version of the old text in 1901. **Alexander Trotter** refers to Heughan's *Reminiscences of Auchencairn*, which are unpublished.

BIBLIOGRAPHY:
Revised edition of *The Gallowa' Herds* (MSS.); Malcolm McL Harper, *The Bards of Galloway* (1889)

PLACES TO VISIT
Some fine examples of Heughan's metalwork are to be seen at the Stewartry Museum

A Literary Guide

Dr James Muirhead, DD
1742-1808
Haugh of Urr, Buittle

James Muirhead originated from an old Galloway family, with an estate in the parish of Buittle. He became minister of Urr, and engaged **Alexander Murray** *as his assistant, shortly before he died. He is best remembered for his poem "Bess the Gawkie", which was admired by Burns, but he also engaged in a sharp exchange with the poet, after* **Burns** *lampooned him in an election ballad. Muirhead's reply was said to have wounded the poet keenly.*

James Muirhead was the eldest son of a family which had, for centuries, had estates in Galloway; at the time of his birth, the family was proprietor of Logan estate in the parish of Buittle. He was educated at Dumfries Grammar School, where he showed early signs of promise, and was sent to Edinburgh to study law, at the early age of twelve. He abandoned law for divinity, and attracted the attention and friendship of scholars there, including David Hume, Dr John Brown and the circle engaged in writing and editing the *Edinburgh Magazine* and *Review*. Some articles of Muirhead's appeared in the *Review*. He was also noted for his interest in natural science and mathematics. In 1765, he was licensed to preach by the Presbytery of Kirkcudbright and in 1769 he was presented to the living of Urr, near his ancestral estate, by the Crown. In 1777, he married Jean Loudon and had two sons by her. His sense of humour, sometimes sardonic, especially when it was exercised at the expense of his brother ministers, was remembered in many parish anecdotes. For example, he gave an

185

extemporaneous blessing at a fellow minister's table: "Bless, O Lord! These three small dishes, / As thou didst the loaves and fishes;/ For if they do our bellies fill, / 'Twill be a wondrous miracle". On another occasion, he preached a sermon to "kirk" a newly married minister of Terregles, who had married an exceptionally tall lady, called Miss Grace, and led the service from the text: "Unto me who am less than the least of all saints is this great grace given". As a Tory, and one with political influence, he came into collision with **Burns,** who lampooned him in his election ballads, calling him sarcastically "Muirhead, wha's as guid as he's true". Muirhead replied in a clever parody of Martial's epigram "Ad Vacerram", in which Vacerras appears as a gauger of loose principles, whom his patrons kept as poor as a church rat. It is said that no other reply to Burns ever left him as sore from the encounter. Burns further ridiculed Muirhead's genealogical and heraldic interests, in the last of the Heron ballads: "Here's armorial bearings/ Frae the Manse of Urr, / The crest, an auld crab apple,/ Rotten at the core". Muirhead obtained the degree of Doctor of Divinity from Edinburgh in 1796, and became known as Dr Muirhead of Logan. He seems to have been an efficient administrator of his parish funds and a devoted pastor. He was first assisted and then succeeded by **Dr Alexander Murray,** the oriental scholar and linguist. In 1808, he died at Spottes Hall, an estate acquired by his son, and Murray preached his funeral sermon.

* * *

Muirhead is remembered mainly for his Scots vernacular poem *Bess the Gawkie,* which was much re-printed and was admired by **Burns** as "a beautiful song and in the genuine Scots taste" (*Reliques of Burns*, RH Cromek) . It is supposed to relate to a love affair in Muirhead's own life; if so, it is written with humour. Bess, apparently duped by the faithless Jamie, who deceives her with Maggie, has the best of him in the end: "As they gaed ower the muir, they sang, / The hills and dales wi' echoes rang, / 'Gang o'er the muir to Maggie'". Muirhead also wrote one of the best entries in the *Statistical Account of Scotland*, for his own parish of Urr. His humour also emerges in his article, where he comments on the military road "which passes through Urr in a line so preposterous that mere folly could hardly have stumbled upon it, is the only benefit we stand indebted to public benevolence for". His antiquarian tastes are also reflected in the article, where he reports Roman finds near the Motte of Urr and Covenanting monuments, which, as he says, were more effective in keeping the countryside loyal during the Jacobite rebellions than a substantial militia of troops. His account of the new town at Dalbeattie and his liberal views on the necessity of high educational standards are of interest.

BIBLIOGRAPHY:
Bess the Gawkie in Malcolm McL Harper, *The Bards of Galloway* (1889); *Parish of Urr* in *The Statistical Account of Scotland* (1794)

Robert Kerr
1811-1848
Haugh of Urr

Robert Kerr (sometimes Ker) was born at Midtown of Spottes and in later life lived at Redcastle Farm, near Haugh of Urr, where he was a ploughman. He attained some celebrity for his sentimental poems, written largely in Scots, " The First Fee" and "The Widow's Ae Coo". "Maggie o' the Moss" is a long narrative poem, drawing on the tradition of "Tam o' Shanter" for its mixture of humour and the supernatural with moral reflection.

Robert Kerr was born at Midtown of Spottes to parents who, themselves labourers, belonged to families which produced writers on both sides. He was the eldest of four sons and two daughters. His mother was Janet Shennan, who came from Kirkpatrick Durham. At Hardgate school, he was something of a boy phenomenon, composing verses which he presented to an enlightened teacher, William Allan. He worked on the land until he saw an advertisement in the *Dumfries Courier* for a packman, in Colchester. At the time, the packman's trade offered a road to success and prosperity: by serving five or six years' apprenticeship, during which time board and clothing were free, the packman would then have acquired a business, which would then be sold on by instalments to another aspirant to fortune. Kerr's temperament agreed little with the trade, at least by his own account in *The Pedlar and his Pack*, though he spent the years between 1826 and 1835 at the trade. He then returned to Urr and became a ploughman at Redcastle, which his father had leased; his earnings at

A Literary Guide

peddling may, indeed, have helped his father to take on the farm. Urr was the parish of **Rev Dr Muirhead** and **Alexander Murray**, and it is clear that Kerr relished following the tradition of Burns, as a ploughman-poet. He kept *a Bosom Book* which he subtitled: "A few of the daft ideas of Robert Kerr, loosely thrashed into rhyme and written here for the gratification of his own whims, and for the perusal of a friend or two of his own kind of material and calibre, in the year o' good, 1838". It is clear, however, that he devoted study to Ramsay, Hogg and Burns, and his reflective conclusion to the *Lines on Digging Up an Old Moss Oak*, are a meditation on his own probable poetic fate: "And such is our lot, soon unseen – forgot / When my bones may be cast on the green, / It is but like a day till the living will say - / ' Ah ! look here where some dead man's been'". Ironically, his poems did in fact achieve their best success posthumously, when **Malcolm McL Harper** resurrected two of his poems for his *Bards of Galloway*, and this led to a demand for a larger edition of his poems, ultimately published, with a memoir of the author, by Harper in 1891. Kerr in fact prospered enough by 1848 to leave Redcastle and rent a farm on his own account at Boghouse, near Garlieston. There has been speculation that he took the farm prior to making a proposal of marriage to Agnes Marchbanks of Buittle Mains. Sadly, his new prosperity was short-lived and his plans came to nothing: he caught a chill while sea-bathing, which developed into consumption. He returned to Redcastle and died aged 37, in 1848. He is buried in Urr churchyard.

* * *

Kerr is at his best in Scots verse and his two poems *The First Fee* and *The Widow's Ae Coo* appealed to the early Victorian taste for sentimental verse. Malcolm Harper was the first to attribute the poems to Kerr, since they had been incorrectly ascribed to Hyslop, author of *The Cameronian's Dream*. They are appealingly and simply written, and *The First Fee*, of which a correct version appears in Harper's "*Bards*" opens: "My mither was wae, for my faither was deid, / And they threatened to tak' the auld hoose owre oor heid". The poem was highly praised by reviewers, with WS Stewart writing: " It is a brief and simple entry in the annals of the poor". *The Widow's Ae Coo* contains some reflections on the contrast of the older ways with the more organised society of his day: "An' where are we better though police gae by / To pummel our beggars or pound our stray kye?". Epigrams published in his works, and the long poem *Maggie o' the Moss*, however, prove that he was capable of pithy humour. The story of Maggie was apparently based on a real person, living near Redcastle, who was thought to be a witch. A reverend doctor, apparently as a joke, promised her a pair of shoes, if she would lift one McLelland, a man whom he disliked, up into the air and give him a ride. The local story goes that Maggie did so, but landed too soon, and was therefore rewarded only with clogs. This story was repeated in the locality and was apparently firmly believed by the population, who held Maggie in dread. Kerr, whose version was published in three parts in **Nicholson's** *Traditional Tales of Galloway*, (Harper published the first unified text of the poem) uses the story for boisterous descriptions of the witches' meeting at the North Pole: "Here sturdy witches of the arctic / Kiss'd warlocks frae the far Antarctic: / And mony a Caledonian grannie / Flown aff wi' some auld nei'bour Sawnie/ Some rode on ragworts, some on docks, / Some lang kail runts and cabbage stocks; / Some on a cat, some on a hen, / And some upon their ain guidmen." His description of Satan is penetrating in its grasp of the psychology of evil: "An ! Satan is it thus with thee? / Above, below, thou'rt never free.../ Locality's a small affair, / When hell is with thee everywhere". The moral of the tale, in the tradition of *Tam o' Shanter*, is deliberately understated: "Maggie doesna rank alone, / Nor yet is Nick the only one, / Who oft has guiltless caught the blame, / By having first a wicked name".

BIBLIOGRAPHY:

Malcolm McL Harper, ed., *Maggie o' the Moss: and Other Poems* (1891)

A Literary Guide

James Clerk Maxwell
1831-1879
Glenlair, parish of Parton

The name of James Clerk Maxwell, whose family estate was at Glenlair, near the village of Parton in the Stewartry of Kirkcudbright, is perhaps the only one in physics which might be mentioned in the same breath as that of Newton and Einstein. Like Newton, he gave a mathematical account of processes in nature – in Clerk Maxwell's case, a coherent notion of the electro-magnetic field – and revealed the electro-magnetic nature of light itself. His notion of the field, as a mathematically configured system, sensitive in each part to change in any other of its parts, was revolutionary, overcoming the problem of the Newtonian "action at a distance"; and it was the contradictions implicit in the notion of a field which stimulated Einstein's thought, and Maxwell's notion of light as a form of electro-magnetic radiation which enabled Einstein to determine the connection between Energy, Mass, and the speed of light, which is the foundation of the Theory of Relativity and the basis for the development of atomic energy. Clerk Maxwell's contribution to the kinetic theory of gases, which was elaborated by Boltzmann into the foundations of statistical mechanics, became one of the pillars of quantum theory. He was therefore a pivotal figure, in a sense perfecting Newtonian science, and yet providing all the material for the great changes in physics which were to rock its foundations in the twentieth century.

James Clerk Maxwell's father, John Clerk, brother to Sir George Clerk of Penicuik, added the name "Maxwell" to his own when he succeeded to the Kirkcudbrightshire estate of Middlebie, acquired through a female relative of that name. The residual Middlebie estate had no mansion, and so John Clerk Maxwell set about building a house on the Lair burn, which he called "Glenlair". It was

Dumfries and Galloway

to Glenlair that he brought his already precocious two-year-old son, James, whom he brought up to study the Bible and to whose curiosity and perpetual question "What's the go o' that? What's the *particular* go o' that?" he gave devoted encouragement. Maxwell's religious belief, his devotion to the parish church at Corsock, his Parton accent and his affection for Glenlair were never to leave him. The boy's mother was Frances Cay, of Charlton, Northumberland, but she died in 1839, and this induced the first major change in the household, when James Clerk Maxwell was sent to Edinburgh to attend the Academy, staying at an aunt's house. At the Academy, he cut an awkward and rustic figure, partly due to the fact that his father cut and made his son's clothes and shoes himself. At age 15, he had already contributed a paper to the Edinburgh Royal Society on the *Description of Oval Curves*. In 1847, he entered Edinburgh University to study mathematics, natural and mental philosophy, and chemistry. The philosophical influences which he came under at Edinburgh – that of William Hamilton among others– gave him a sense of the unity of nature, which probably predisposed him later to appreciate the work of Michael Faraday, who was struggling to articulate the notion of a field. In 1850, he left Edinburgh for Cambridge, where he was taught by tutors famous in the history of physics: William Hopkins, GG Stokes, the Lucasian Professor, and William Whewell, master of Trinity, Clerk Maxwell's college. It was at Cambridge that he acquired his mathematical sophistication, particularly from the work of Lagrange and Laplace. In 1854, he became second Wrangler in the Tripos and in 1855, was elected Fellow of Trinity. The illness of his father, to whom he remained extremely close, was by now of concern and this induced him to seek a Scottish appointment, at Marischal College, Aberdeen, which he held until its amalgamation into the University in 1860. In the 1850's, he was working on the theory of colours in relation to colour blindness, and a famous photograph shows him conducting his experiments with rapidly rotating colour discs. For his research, which confirmed the conclusion that colour blindness was due to the absence of one of three primary sensations, he was awarded the Rumford medal of the Royal Society in 1860. It was, as a result of these researches, Clerk Maxwell who developed the principle of the three colour process in colour photography. Another prize essay of this period was *On the Stability of Motion of Saturn's Rings*, where he supported the conclusion that the

A Literary Guide

rings were likely to consist of discrete particles. In 1858, he had married Katherine Mary Dewar, daughter of the principal of Marischal College, to whom he retained an unflinching and almost mystical devotion throughout her life. Also at this period, he had written his first paper on the kinetic theory of gases. In 1860, he became professor at King's College, London and it was at this period that he began his work on electro-magnetism, which was to result in the final joining of two apparently distinct aspects of physical reality – light and electricity. This aspect of his work was influenced by the brilliant Scottish physicist, William Thomson, later Lord Kelvin, who was seven years older than Maxwell, and who was applying results from the theories of heat and fluids to the problems of electro-magnetism; it was probably Thomson who encouraged Clerk Maxwell to think highly of the unorthodox and mathematically innumerate Faraday. Clerk Maxwell's experiments were conducted both at his home and at his laboratory at King's. In 1862, he became member of the new electrical standards committee of the British Association, at a time when the laying of the cross-Atlantic cable was adding commercial impetus to the theoretical problem of establishing exact units of measurement for electrical resistance. The results of the committee's deliberations added a new unit to the world of measurement: the British Association ohm. In 1865, he retired to private life at Glenlair, where he wrote his massive *Treatise of Electricity and Magnetism*. In 1871, however, he seemed the obvious candidate for the new chair of Experimental Physics at Cambridge, and he returned there to embark on the huge practical project of establishing the Cavendish Laboratory, which set physical experimentation on an entirely new footing and was opened in 1874. For the five years he was at Cambridge, he returned to Glenlair for the long summer vacations, never omitting to return to Corsock church, where he acted as elder in administering the Communion. He also actively supported the parish school, and was proposing to support it in the face of threatened closure, when his final and fatal illness overtook him in 1879. He returned to Cambridge to be closer to expert medical help, but died in November 1879. His bust by Boehm was placed in the Cavendish Laboratory, and a portrait was hung at Trinity. His was the only portrait which Einstein allowed to be hung in his study, and he wrote that "One scientific epoch ended and another began with James Clerk Maxwell". In his will, Clerk Maxwell left funds to establish a studentship in experimental physics.

Dumfries and Galloway

* * *

Clerk Maxwell's own words in his epoch-making *On a Dynamical Theory of the Electro-Magnetic Field* probably best summarise the electromagnetic theory which he created: "Light itself (including radiant and other radiations, if any) is an electro-magnetic disturbance in the form of waves propagated through the electromagnetic field according to electromagnetic laws". In fact, this statement, couched in characteristically lucid prose, was the culmination of several papers, in which the process of scientific creativity can be classically observed. First had come *On Faraday's Lines of Force*, 1855, where he speculated about the flow of an ideal fluid, in order to envisage the geometry of Faraday's lines of force, observed by Faraday in the "magnetic curves" traced out by lines of iron filings. Faraday wholly rejected the notion of "action at a distance" and sought to demonstrate his theory of electrical induction which involved contiguous molecules transmitting the force. In the second paper *On Physical Lines of Force*, 1861, Maxwell envisages how effects are transmitted through an electro-magnetic medium with the same velocity as light, thereby suggesting that light might be a phenomenon of electromagnetic processes. It was only in his *On a Dynamical Theory of the Electro-Magnetic Field* of 1864 that he applies Lagrangian mathematics to introduce the field as an energy-bearing continuum. The two aspects of physical reality, light and heat, can only be unified if the ratio of electrostatic to electromagnetic units of measure take on a specific value, namely, the speed of propagation of electromagnetic waves. If this in turn equals the velocity of light, the theory explains the nature of light itself as an electromagnetic process. The revolutionary nature of this thought enabled successors like Hertz, after Clerk Maxwell's death, to discover radio waves, generated electro-magnetically in a laboratory. An area of Mars was named "Maxwell" because his electromagnetic theories led to the invention of the radio telescope. Clerk Maxwell's work on the kinetic theory of gases shows a similar process of maturing thought, stimulated by his correspondence and professional contact with the German physicist, Clausius. Ultimately, it was Clerk Maxwell, in his *On the Dynamical Theory of Gases* which applied statistical ideas of Laplace and Gauss to describe the molecular motions of a gas, and thence derived a description of the measurable properties of gases. Its offspring was the statistical mechanics of Boltzmann and Gibbs. Despite the mathematical

A Literary Guide

sophistication of Maxwell's work, he retained an essential interest in the clear exposition of his works, and, having been influenced at a young age by Frederick Dennison Maurice, a Christian Socialist, wrote his *Matter and Motion* to explain the concepts of physics to working men. Clerk Maxwell's high level of literary ability shows clearly in the selection of poems, which appeared in an appendix of his biography, and reveal much of the philosophical and religious thinking which underpinned his scientific work. His *Student's Evening Hymn* repays study for its insight into his classically metaphysical vision of nature, whose disparate phenomena are unified – at least for the visionary – beyond appearances: "Through the creatures Thou hast made, /Show the brightness of Thy glory..". In his *Recollections of Dreamland*, the vision of unity is only obscured through our own wilful intrusion: " And I heard how all Nature rejoices, / And moves with a musical flow / .. we are drowning in wilful confusion, / The notes of that wonderful song". Other poems speak directly of scientific work, but are able to reveal the well-known and irrepressible Clerk Maxwell sense of humour, such as *In memory of Edward Wilson*, which reads "Gin a body meet a body / Flyin' through the air, /Gin a body hit a body, / Will it fly ? and where ?" When he playfully envisages a Valentine sent down a wire between two telegraph clerks, he refers to the discovery of the new units of measurement which enabled long-distance electrical connections to perform to satisfactory technical standards, and in which he had personally been extensively involved: "Through many an Ohm the Weber flew, / And clicked this answer back to me ,-/ 'I am they Farad, staunch and true/ Charged to a Volt with love for thee'".

BIBLIOGRAPHY:
On a Dynamical Theory of the Electro-magnetic Field (1864); *On the Dynamical Theory of Gases* (1866); *A Treatise on Electricity and Magnetism* (1873); *Matter and Motion* (1888); Lewis Campbell & William Garnett, *The Life of James Clerk Maxwell* (1882) - this also includes Maxwell's *Poems*

PLACES TO VISIT: Parton churchyard contains a memorial to Clerk Maxwell and his tomb; in Corsock church there is a stained glass window in his memory.

John Wilson and Samuel Wilson
1737-1806 ; 1784-1863
Crossmichael

John and Samuel Wilson were uncle and nephew from an old family from Burnbrae, a small estate near Clarebrand village. Both had a gift for polemic in verse and Samuel had undoubted poetic talent for a wide variety of forms, but, in the absence of a collected volume of his work, became quickly and undeservedly forgotten.

John Wilson, the son of James Wilson, was born at Crossmichael, educated at Crossmichael and at Dumfries Academy. In 1759-60, he became a tutor to the family of McGhie of Airds, which included Mary McGhie who was to become the celebrated subject of **John Lowe's** poem *Mary's Dream*. He became master of the parish school of Holywood, and then of Sanquhar; while at Sanquhar, he probably made the acquaintance of Lowe. He apparently attended some sessions at the Divinity Hall of the University of Edinburgh, but in 1777, appears to have relinquished his plans to enter the ministry and became master of the Grammar School of South Leith for a period of ten years. He was then elected one of the four Masters of the Grammar School of Glasgow, an appointment he kept until his retirement in 1806. While absent from Galloway, John Wilson founded the Glasgow-Galloway Brotherly Society and the Glasgow-Dumfriesshire Society. In his later years, he had accumulated enough capital to buy back the property of Burnbrae, which had been lost by an ancestor, and then acquired the mansion place of Upper Clarebrand. He had always had a close bond with his brother, James, who lived with him on the estate, and then inherited it after John Wilson's death. James Wilson, who was first a weaver, and then a field labourer, was father to Samuel Wilson, born in 1784. He was educated at Ringanwhey Public School, then at Crossmichael parish school , and appears to have attended Glasgow University for a session. When his uncle died, he returned to Clarebrand, and went into business: first, he was in partnership in the timber business, but during this time he unfortunately lost a leg as the result of an accident in 1820. Earlier in his

A Literary Guide

career, he had begun to be known as an antiquary, and had travelled throughout Scotland, acquiring a thorough knowledge of Gaelic and of the bagpipe. When his father died in 1810, and left him the property at Clarebrand, Wilson started a grocer's business in a small house in the village, and the shop became a centre for parish politics. Apparently, the place where Wilson stood behind the counter became worn by the point of his artificial limb, and could be seen years later, as one of the curiosities of the village. His poetical pieces were published in the *Castle Douglas Miscellany* and *Dumfries Courier*, but, though much reprinted in contemporary anthologies, were never collected in book-form. The inscription on his tomb-stone at Crossmichael reads: "This marks the resting place of an individual who in his time was recognised as one of the greatest of the numerous poets in Galloway during the latter part of the 18th century".

* * *

Both Wilsons composed satirical poems on events of their day ; the most elaborate is the *Daviad* by John Wilson, published in the *Dumfries Weekly Magazine* in 1774. The circumstances which gave rise to the poem were that an impromptu dance had been got up in Sanquhar, which John Wilson had attended, and that those excluded had written a scurrilous piece of the *Dumfries Weekly Magazine*, misrepresenting the ball and those who attended it. Wilson's reply was called the *Daviad* after one of those who had condemned the dance in print, Davy Crotchet. As Wilson comments: "Tis grown the fahsion of the times, / To tell our tales in doggrel rhymes /..Each written by some curious blade, / Who sees with fond parental eyes/ The labours of his head arise". Wilson clearly had the better of his antagonists, both in wit, versification, and grammar, as he does not hesitate to remind them; but he does not scruple to stoop to some coarse humour at their expense. Samuel Wilson, like his uncle, was capable of polemical verse: for example, in the *Christmas Carol*, which is preserved in the *Burnbrae Papers* at Broughton House, Kirkcudbright, he complains of the state of contemporary literature, making obvious allusions to current writers: "What de'ils o' a' our bards become? / Our prose-men, too, are they grown dumb?" But the selection of Wilson's works published in **John Nicholson's** *Historical and Traditional Tales.. Connected with the South of Scotland* shows that he was capable of writing in a wide variety of styles and moods. The prose selections are from a spirited sketch of smuggling on the Solway coast, while the poetry includes two vivid pieces, no doubt inspired by Scott, *The Galloway Raid* and *Aylmer Gray*. The *Galloway Raid* features his own ancestor, Wudsword of Clairbrand, who, he believed, had inhabited Clarebrand and acquired the nickname through carrying a naked broadsword under his arm like a staff, and who enters the fray against a marauding party of Johnstones and Jardines from the Borders; the coup de grace in the fight is actually delivered by Wudsword's daughter. Doubtful as the history may be, there is no questioning the ballad's sense of drama: "All silent the moss-trooper's now, / Save their steed's hollow tramp on the wild mountain's brow; / They scared not the wild fowl that swam on the lake, / Nor in hamlet nor hall did the sleepers awake". Similar in spirit is his *Battle of Spearford*, set in the Glenkens, but betraying an antiquarian's nostalgia for the Highland host: "Proudly paraded the hardy Glenkensmen, / Their broad tartans wav'd in the winds of the hill;/ Gordon's loud pibroch cheers on his bold clansmen, / The turrets of Kenmure resound to the peal." His *Gaberlunzie Man* was printed without permission by **Barbour** (who later apologised in his own inimitable style) in his *Lights and Shadows of Scottish Character and Scenery* (1824), and tells the story of a beggar, who was staying in Balmaclellan and was drowned in the Garpel water. Its evocation of the Kelpie, its hair hung with "faem bells" is in the best tradition of the Scottish supernatural. Both the *Gaberlunzie* and *May of Craignair* were extensively anthologised and were popular in Wilson's life time. *May*, an evocative poem of tragic love, shows Wilson in yet another mood: "Saw ye my true-love on yon misty mountain, / Or down the dark glen was he chasing the deer, / Or heard ye his staghounds on Raeberry hunting? / He promis'd ere now to hae' met wi' me here." Given the range and quality of his productions, it is a pity they are now to be found only in the pages of scarce periodicals or in out-of-print anthologies.

BIBLIOGRAPHY:
Burnbrae Papers (mss. in Hornel Library, Broughton House, Kirkcudbright); John Gordon Barbour, *Lights and Shadows of Scottish Character and Scenery* (1824); John Nicholson, *Historical and Traditional Tales in Prose and Verse, Connected with the South of Scotland* (1843); Malcolm McL Harper, *The Bards of Galloway* (1889)

A Literary Guide

Malcolm McLachlan Harper
1839-1914
Castle Douglas

Malcolm Harper was one of the most significant collectors and promoters of Galloway literature during the nineteenth century; he was responsible for reviving the works of **William Nicholson, Robert Kerr,** *of republishing minor Galloway poets, and for writing a life of* **Crockett.** *He also wrote an excellent guide to the historical, etymological, and folkloric material of the province in his "Rambles in Galloway". The illustrations to this book demonstrate the intimate links between the literary and artistic circles in Galloway at this time, particularly in the Stewartry, where Harper was closely acquainted with the Kirkcudbright school of painters, such as EA Hornel, WS MacGeorge, Blacklock, Henry and Mouncey.*

Malcolm Harper was born in 1839 in comfortable circumstances: his father was a merchant in Castle Douglas and his mother's brother was a minister in the town. He attended the school of a Mr Morgan and early became a clerk in the British Linen Bank in Castle Douglas, where he served as a clerk, accountant and agent for 57 years. Only two years before his death did he leave the Bank House, and purchased "Strathmore", where he died in 1914. He held a respected position in the community, where he was burgh treasurer, collector of the Parish council rates, secretary of the Agricultural Society, of the Galloway Rifle Association, and of the Soldiers' and Sailors' Family Association, JP for the Stewartry, factor for several estates and a member of Kelton Parish Church. From 1864, he and TR Bruce of Slogarie were the main supporters of the Galloway Volunteers, where he rose to the rank of Major. It is clear, however, that his main interests were literary and artistic, and he describes himself ironically as a "notched and cropt scrivener; one that sucks his sustenance as a sick person through a quill". His extensive antiquarian collection of books and his acquaintance with writers such as **Crockett,** whom he knew for more than 30 years, made him the ideal editor of Galloway texts. There is little doubt that the revival of interest in Nicholson and Kerr would not have occurred without his intervention and his alliance with Thomas Fraser, the publisher, of Dalbeattie. His own verses appeared in local newspapers such as the *Dumfries Courier, Kirkcudbrightshire Advertiser* and *Galloway Gazette.* He also exhibited paintings of his own, some of which appeared as illustrations to his *Rambles..,* at the Royal Scottish Academy and the Royal Glasgow Institute. His obituary describes how , each season, he would set up an artists' camp at "The Lake", outside Kirkcudbright, with William Mouncey and Tom Blacklock. He also certainly acquired a collection of paintings by his artist friends, including some by EA Hornel. His own paintings tend to be of pastoral and nostalgic subjects; Professor Reid, writing in the *Gallovidian* wrote that in the pictures "[t]here is, too, the vague presence of toil-worn men and women, leading lonely grave lives and becoming gradually part and parcel of the wild landscapes around them".

* * *

Harper's *Rambles in Galloway* ranks with **CH Dick's** later work, as a classic of Galloway guide books. But like Dick's book, it is something more; it is the expression of Harper's immense reservoir of knowledge of Galloway, his sense of the presence of its history, and of his devotion to its landscapes and people. Written first in chapter form in the *Kirkcudbrightshire Advertiser,* it eventually appeared in book form in 1876, and includes information on archaeology, literary associations, folklore and topology. The second edition of 1896 was expanded to take account of recent excavations at Whithorn, of new material from the burgh archives at Kirkcudbright, and includes illustrations of famous sons of Galloway, such as **Alexander Murray, Hannay, William Nicholson, Kerr** and **Stair.** Like **Alexander Trotter,** Harper did much to record information about and illustrations of writers of Galloway, which might otherwise have been lost. For a de-luxe edition , published in the same year, Harper enlisted the help of his friend, Hornel, to illustrate

A Literary Guide

Nicholson's famous poem *The Brownie of Blednoch*; other Galloway artists who provided illustrations include the Faeds from Gatehouse of Fleet, Muirhead, Robert Burns, Tom Scott, Maxwell and Mouncey. Harper's own portrait in the frontispiece is by WS MacGeorge. The heraldic lion embossed on the front cover was designed by John Duncan. Harper's early recognition of the merit of **William Nicholson**, whose works with a "memoir" he published in 1878, did much to rescue the poet's reputation from oblivion. His *The Bards of Galloway*, published in 1889, contains a fascinating set of biographical notes for each author, compiled from the rich store of Harper's knowledge of even the most obscure corners of Galloway literature, and its illustrations once again serve as an index to the working Galloway artists of his time. His *Crockett and Grey Galloway* was issued on the occasion of a banquet given to honour the novelist in 1906, and a minute account is given, both of Crockett's childhood as it was personally known to Harper, and of the distinguished guests proposing the health of the novelist at the celebration. The guest list for the banquet, presided over by **Sir Herbert Maxwell** of Monreith, reads like a directory of the Galloway cultural establishment of the time, and it is a measure of Harper's position within this elite that he was asked to compile the testimonial to Crockett. A small selection of Harper's own poems appears in *The Bards of Galloway*: though some are too sentimental for modern taste, and others from the newspapers – such as those on the death of Queen Victoria or the King's accession – are merely occasional, his poem on a favourite terrier, "Snap", shows some vigour and humour.

BIBLIOGRAPHY:
Rambles in Galloway (1876, also editions of 1896 & 1908); *The Poetical Works of William Nicholson* (1878); *The Bards of Galloway* (1889); *Crockett and Grey Galloway* (1907)

Samuel Rutherford Crockett
1859-1914
Little Duchrae, near Laurieston

*Although SR Crockett only lived in Galloway for the first fifteen years of his life, it was to Galloway that Crockett's imagination returned throughout his life and his extraordinarily prolific and varied output, for the inspiration for his best novels and stories. Galloway, particularly in the vicinity of Crockett's birthplace at Little Duchrae, and in the hill country of the Southern Uplands, therefore has the distinction of being one of the three defining landscapes of the "Kailyard" school of Scottish writing, along with **JM Barrie**'s "Thrums" and Ian Maclaren's "Drumtochty". "Kailyard" is not, or does not have to be, a term of opprobrium, but defines an extraordinarily popular literary phenomenon, one which was perhaps a necessary outcome of the success of Burns and Scott in defining the Scottish identity and language, and which has certain characteristic features. Crockett's novels, or at least his most successful ones, have in common a generally pre-industrial landscape, a background in which religion plays a strong role, a sentimental love-story and a certain brand of arch humour, of which the two last have aged least well. His best-known novel, "The Raiders", which sold out within a day of publication, is more than this, however: it is a breathless adventure story in the best tradition of Stevenson and Scott.*

Samuel Rutherford Crockett (the middle name and the extra "t" were added later, when his literary reputation was on the rise) was born an illegitimate son to Annie Crocket, dairymaid, and daughter to William and Mary Crocket of Little Duchrae. The Crockets came of stern Covenanting stock, and Crockett remembered later how he was brought up among aunts and uncles, but chiefly by his grandparents, who remained the prototypes of all his family portraits. Crockett was brought up on a diet of

A Literary Guide

Covenanting traditions, on **Simpson's** account of these, and on the Bible. He attended the Free Church School at Laurieston. In 1867, William Crocket, patriarch of the family, retired from farming to 24 Cotton Street, Castle Douglas (the "Cairn Edward" of Crockett's stories). There, Crockett also attended the Free Church school, and befriended, if somewhat boisterously and commandingly, AS Penman and WS MacGeorge, later a well-known Galloway painter. This group of boys spent a memorable summer holiday on Rough Island in the Solway Firth, which was to become the inspiration for the scene on "Hestan Island" in *The Raiders*. By his uncle Robert, Crockett was encouraged to read Shakespeare, Tennyson, Milton, Carlyle and Scott. Crockett stayed on as a pupil-teacher at the school, and was coached for a bursary to Edinburgh, which was offered by the Edinburgh Galloway Association. This incident, and his successful winning of the bursary, are imaginatively reused in the semi-autobiographical *Kit Kennedy*. At Edinburgh, he first shared rooms with cousins, and later with MacGeorge. Having to support himself, he wrote articles and acquired the habit, never shaken off, of composing at speed. He also acquired an abiding passion for book-collecting. He graduated MA in 1879, but went through some years of indecision, during which he acted as a tutor to a rich young American touring Germany and Switzerland, composed some verses, and engaged in some scientific work and some journalism. He also fell in love with Ruth Milner, daughter of a Manchester mill-owner and some of that romance is reflected in his published collection of poetry, *Dulce Cor*, drawing deeply on the Tennysonian tradition. Perhaps his courtship was the stimulus to the choice of a settled career, but, whatever the reason, in 1879, he enrolled as a Divinity student. With an energy which was to remain characteristic, he threw himself into missionary work in the Edinburgh slums and befriended the street urchins, one of whom was to appear transformed into the eponymous hero of the extremely successful novel, *Cleg Kelly*. By 1886, he had completed his course at New College, and became assistant to the minister at the Free Abbey Kirk. Subsequently, he accepted a call from Penicuik and, once established at the Free Church Manse, he married Ruth Milner. In his parish, he began a vigorous and popular series of educational lectures for parishioners, wrote passionately about the nearby Mauricewood pit disaster in 1889, and conducted evangelical missions outside Penicuik. At this time, a correspondence grew up with Robert Louis Stevenson, who gave him the good advice, upon receiving a copy of *Dulce Cor*: "Write .. my Timothy, no longer verse, but use good Galloway Scots for your stomach's sake - and mine". In response to this challenge, Crockett began writing the series of articles on parishes, parishioners, and ministers, which eventually appeared in one volume, in 1893, as *The Stickit Minister*. The anthology achieved virtual overnight fame for its author and stimulated an appetite for the unfamiliar Galloway scenery in an audience whose taste had already been shaped by JM Barrie's "Scotch" fiction. The book eventually went into luxury editions, with artists providing illustrations free of charge, and with Robert Louis Stevenson's evocative dedication reproduced in facsimile in the frontispiece : "that grey Galloway land/ where about the graves of the martyrs/ the whaups are crying - / his heart remembers how". Crockett's work was in demand, and commanded high prices; he also had gained literary contacts, including those with **Ruskin, Sir Herbert Maxwell, JM Barrie,** and Andrew Lang. He was able to move his growing family to the larger Bank House, at Penicuik, and built a wooden annexe for his immense and choice library. In 1894, he had been the guest of the Pen and Pencil Club in Edinburgh, the dinner being completed with a menu illustrated with Galloway scenes and a recitation of a poem by **Alexander Anderson** on *The Raiders*, published in 1894 and sold out on the day of issue. Eventually and inevitably in the face of such overwhelming popularity, the calls on his literary time forced him to reconsider his commitment to the ministry, and he announced, in 1895, that he would leave his charge. In 1896, he was investigating the Ayrshire coast, in preparation for *The Grey Man*, perhaps his most artistically mastered work, which was serialised before appearing as a book. Crockett's happy family life also found reflection in his publications for children, with his *The Surprising Adventures of Sir Toady Lion*, based on his own son's fictitious adventures , reaching the top of his publisher's sales lists. As Crockett's novels emerged thick and fast, however, his energy and health began to show signs of decline; in inverse relation, his plots grew more sensational, and his care and his control of his material less assured. Nonetheless, although he returned again and again to the landscape which had proved successful for him in his classic novels, as in *Kit Kennedy*, he was still capable of conquering new ground, as in *Cleg Kelly*, where he displays his knowledge of the Edinburgh slums and betrays

A Literary Guide

the influence of Christian Socialist ideals; later novels included some explicitly concerned with social comment, such as *Vida or the Iron Lord of Kirktown*. There was little doubt, however, that Crockett's classic period was over by the late 1890's and yet he was still compelled to write extensively to support his family and the lifestyle to which they had grown accustomed. There was little sign of public disillusionment with his work, and in his lifetime postcards of Galloway scenes, including his birthplace, were issued, tours of "Raiderland" were a commercial proposition, and he acquired an audience in the Far East, the US and Australia. He was apparently painted by James McNeill Whistler, and reached the acme of fame by being caricatured in *Vanity Fair*; Lord Kitchener wrote that he had read *The Grey Man* on the eve of the battle of Omdurman. The critics, however, grew increasingly scathing. The term "Kailyard" had first appeared in an article by JH Millar, who took the term from a motto of Ian McLaren's; **John Buchan**, early on, had allied Crockett with this movement, when he wrote that Crockett "was all for the wind and the sunshine, hills and heather, lilac and adventure, kisses and well-churned butter". Crockett himself was seeking refuge abroad for increasing bouts of ill-health and returned to Scotland only in summers, to the cottage left him by his uncles at Auchencairn, on the Solway coast. In 1901, he ceased to be an elder at Penicuik, because of his numerous absences, and in 1906, the family had to leave Bank House, when its lease terminated, and, taking with them the entire wooden annexe and Crockett's immense library of nearly 40,000 books, set up at Torwood House, Peebles. It was at this point that the Dalbeattie General Improvement Society issued an invitation to a public celebratory dinner, of which **Malcolm Harper**, who had helped Crockett with information on traditional tales of the area, gives a circumstantial account in his *Crockett and Grey Galloway*. By 1911 and 1912, the income from sales of his books had declined sufficiently that he had to sell off some of his library. In 1914, while he was abroad, he died suddenly. His funeral cortege travelled through Castle Douglas and was escorted in procession through the streets. He was buried in the family plot at Balmaghie Kirk. Several of his books were published posthumously, including *Rogues' Island*, based on his own experiences at Rough Island in the Solway, and *Silver Sand*, a return to the successful territory of *The Raiders* and the early life of its ambiguous hero, Silver Sand, during Covenanting times.

Dumfries and Galloway

* * *

It is impossible to comment in detail on an output so large and so varying in quality as that of Crockett, but some features of his best-known works may be noted. *The Stickit Minister*, which established Crockett's reputation, while containing some sentimental and unbelievable stories such as his *Accepted of the Beasts*, contains also some caustic observations on the Kirk and some perceptive recording of the thinking of the "unco' guid", whose unconscious hypocrisy both amuses and appals us: in the *Tragedy of Duncan Duncanson*, a minister addicted to the bottle, he writes "(t)here were those in the presbytery, who had often fallen down at their back doors, but then this made a great difference, and they all prayed fervently for the great sinner and backslider who had slidden at his front door in the sight of men". *The Raiders*, like *The Grey Man* is written through one of Crockett's favourite narrative voices, that of an adolescent and inexperienced boy, whose rather prim self-satisfaction in recounting events and whose self-deception in relation to his feelings for the heroine allows the reader and other characters a superior and amused insight into the story and its likely development. As an astonished Patrick is told, in relation to May Mischief's liking for him, in *The Raiders*: "Ye surely wore your e'en in the tail o' your coat. Ye micht hae kenned by the way she flyted on ye". There is not simply humour in the novel, however, but an excitement in the best tradition of the adventure story, and one which opens with the subtle suspense of the first sentence of the book: "It was upon Rathan Head that I first heard their bridle-reins jingling clear..." This paves the way for some atmospheric descriptions of the Galloway uplands, where Crockett had carried out his research during strenuous walks in the company of an expert guide - the tenant farmer at Glenhead of Trool, John McMillan. Crockett's manuscript letters to John and Marion McMillan, written in dialect and preserved at Broughton House, Kirkcudbright, provide delightful reading. *The Raiders* is one of the examples of Crockett's imaginative transformation of genuine Galloway tradition and legend, such as that of the Murder Hole, recorded in **John Nicholson's** *Traditional Tales of Galloway*, and transported by Crockett from its traditional location near the Rowantree toll, to the corner of Loch Neldricken. *The Grey Man* makes use of Ayrshire history from the time of the Kennedy ascendancy in Carrick, and of the ballad tradition of the Ayrshire cannibal, Sawney Bean. More classic Crockett territory appears in *The Men of the Moss Hags*, a dramatisation of the events surrounding the persecution of the Covenanters by Lag, and their defeat at Bothwell Brig. Crockett achieves a masterly touch of the supernatural when, after the battle, a horse returns to the door of its accustomed home alone, without its much awaited rider, "and in the holster on that side, where the great pistol ought to have been, a thing yet more fearsome – a man's bloody forefinger, taken off above the second joint with a clean drawing cut".

BIBLIOGRAPHY:
Dulce Cor (1886); *The Stickit Minister* (1893); *The Raiders* (1894); *The Men of the Moss-Hags* (1895); *Cleg Kelly: Arab of the City* (1896); *The Grey Man* (1896); *The Surprising Adventures of Sir Toady Lion* (1897); *Kit Kennedy* (1899); *Vida or the Iron Lord of Kirktown* (1907); *Silver Sand* (1914); *Rogues' Island* (1926); Malcolm McL Harper, *Crockett and Grey Galloway* (1907); Islay M Donaldson, *The Life and Work of Samuel Rutherford Crockett* (1989)

PLACES TO VISIT: A memorial to Crockett stands in the village of Laurieston, and his grave is at Balmaghie Church. Classic Crockett country may be visited by walking into the Galloway Hills from Glen Trool.

Professor HMB Reid
1856-1927
Balmaghie parish

Professor Reid was minister of Balmaghie, the "Kirk above Dee Water", which was SR Crockett's parish church and is his place of burial. Reid published extensively on theology, being latterly professor of Divinity at Glasgow University, but his contribution to Galloway literature rests on his sketches of local character, and, particularly, on his documenting his predecessors at Balmaghie, including John MacMillan, one of the founders of the Reformed Presbyterian Church.

H. M. B. REID.

HMB Reid was born in 1856, son of Alexander Reid, who was chaplain to HM Prison, and of Elizabeth Beckwith. He was educated at the High School, Dundee, and at St Andrew's, where he had a distinguished academic record as a student. He was assistant to the Professor of Humanity at St Andrews from 1878-9, and then was licensed to preach by the Presbytery of St. Andrews in 1879. Before being ordained to Balmaghie in 1882, he assisted at Anderston and St Mungo, in Glasgow. He was minister at Balmaghie for the long period of 22 years, before being appointed Professor of Divinity in Glasgow in 1904, as successor to Professor William Hastie. He gave the Lee Lectures at Edinburgh in 1899 on *The Historical Significance of the Episcopacy in Scotland*. In 1900, he had already been appointed additional examiner in Theology and Church History at St. Andrews, was Synod Clerk of Galloway, and received the degree of Doctor of Divinity. From 1900-1911, he edited *The Layman's Book*.

* * *

A Literary Guide

Reid's earliest Galloway work was his anonymous *About Galloway Folk, by a Galloway Herd*, written in 1889. The term "herd", short for "shepherd", was taken from the satirical poem *The Galloway Herds* (see under **Joseph Heughan**), which described the self-serving conduct of the clergy, when commanded to refrain from saying prayers for Queen Caroline. The book draws amusingly on Reid's experience of the Galloway character from the day when he came as a candidate to Balmaghie kirk and left with "a drenched satin hat and a cold". Reid ascribes many local characteristics – its hardiness, caution, self-reliance and "pawkiness" – to the constant battle of man with the landscape and the weather. A certain cunning is relished in Galloway: he notes a "fresh respect for the man who can pass off a lame or blind horse as sound, and so make two or three hundred per cent profit". Clearly, even at the end of the nineteenth century, isolation from the mainstream of industrial and cultural development meant that superstitions lingered in the Glenkens: Reid describes the burial of unbaptised infants after sundown, and the decoration of doorsteps and hearths with chalk hieroglyphics. New ways coming from the city were not always appreciated and severe judgements were meted out on any young minister "whose town-bred stomach rises at potato-scones and whisky; and whose opinion on a 'beast' is not worth a straw". Given Reid's gift for delineating character and his obvious affection for his stiff-necked parishioners, it is not surprising to find **SR Crockett** accepting an invitation to write the introduction to Reid's main Galloway work: *The Kirk Above Dee Water*. Crockett's introduction includes his own reminiscences of Laurieston characters, such as the shopkeeper, Jean, who would warn youngsters like Crockett against the lasses, those "feckless, fleein' heverals". The work began as a lecture given in aid of church funds, on *Some Old Ministers of Balmaghie, with Illustrative Pictures and Other Objects*, but was expanded to include a description of the Church and churchyard, and particularly to give a biography of John MacMillan, Balmaghie's seventeenth century minister. Reid was later to expand the biography further into his full-length *A Cameronian Apostle*. MacMillan originated from stern Covenanting stock at Barncauchlaw, Minnigaff, where he was born in 1669. After training at Edinburgh, where he was influenced by the "Societies" which stood outside the mainstream of the Church of Scotland, he was for a short time chaplain to the Murrays of Broughton, near Gatehouse of Fleet, and then became minister of Balmaghie in 1701. He soon became increasingly alienated from his own Presbytery, as he came to accept the view that the Solemn League and Covenant were being ignored and that, in various ways, the Church's freedom was becoming invaded by the State. The Presbytery at first took various moderate measures to discipline the unruly minister, and he probably hoped, even after being deposed in 1703, to be peaceably reinstated, given the evident and staunch support of his congregation. Matters became violent after he ignored Church court rulings and his congregation prevented any new minister from entering the church building, despite the threat of arrest and the advent of the Sheriff and 100 yeomanry, who came to force acceptance in 1708. Because of the persistence of MacMillan and his followers, the new minister, Mr McKie, was forced to live alongside his deposed predecessor until 1729, making use of a meeting house, while MacMillan continued to occupy the manse and Church. This peculiar situation gave rise to stories such as that of the *Twice Christened Bairn*, told in **John Nicholson's** *Historical and Traditional Tales..* of 1843. MacMillan eventually became the first minister to the United Societies, and the Reformed Presbyterian Church, founded in 1743, was often known as the Macmillanite church. Reid pursued his interest in Covenanting history with his edition of *One of King William's Men*, an annotated diary of Colonel William Maxwell of Cardoness, who was the son of the minister of Minnigaff, sailed with William of Orange from Leyden in 1688, and defended Glasgow during the 1715 rebellion.

BIBLIOGRAPHY:
About Galloway Folk (1889); *The Kirk Above Dee Water* (1895); *A Cameronian Apostle* (1896); *One of King William's Men* (1898)

PLACES TO VISIT: The Balmaghie church may be visited, and a tablet to John MacMillan may be found in the churchyard.

Robert Heron
1764-1807
New Galloway

*Author of a huge and voluminous range of historical and other material, Robert Heron, born in New Galloway in the Glenkens, had an unstable character which prevented his early promise from coming to fruition. He is remembered for composing the first full-length biography of **Burns**, whose contemporary he was and whom he had met, but is blamed for starting a trend in Burns biography which exaggerated the poet's tendency to debauchery. His best work is his first-hand "Observations made in a Journey through the Western Counties of Scotland", 1793, which gives fascinating insight into conditions in Scotland at the turn of the nineteenth century.*

Robert Heron was born in New Galloway, son to a weaver and his wife who seem to have been highly literate and to have encouraged their precocious son. Certainly, there were literary influences in the family, since Heron's grandmother, Margaret Murray, was aunt to the linguist, **Alexander Murray** and John Heron, his father, employed **John Lowe**, author of *Mary's Dream*. After being taught at home by his mother until the age of nine, he attended the parish school; but by the age of eleven, he was capable of teaching the children of neighbouring farmers. By the age of 14, he was master of the parochial school of Kelton. By saving money earned through teaching and translating from the French, he saved enough money to enter Edinburgh University to study divinity. Here too, he was forced to support himself by writing. In Edinburgh, he made the acquaintance of **Dr Thomas Blacklock**, whom he later described as "an angel upon earth" and frequently met him, taking him for walks on the green. It was in fact Blacklock who formed the point of contact between Heron and **Burns**, when they met at Ellisland in 1789: the poet asked Heron to take Dr Blacklock a letter, but, typically, Heron failed to deliver it. It was this failure which gave rise to Burns's lampoon on Heron: "But aiblins, honest Master Heron / Had at the time some dainty fair one, / To waste his theologic care on". In fact, unreliability was one of Heron's

211

few constant traits, as he disarmingly reveals in his unpublished *Journal of My Conduct* which is composed of a strange mixture of self-mortification and vanity, and documents both punishing industry and extreme indolence. Though he intended his stay in Edinburgh to be of financial help to his family in New Galloway, he did not take up holy orders (though he was for some time assistant to Dr Blair) but concentrated on an uncertain literary career, beginning with a critical edition of Thomson's *Seasons* in 1789. He declares in the Preface to his later *History of Scotland* that literary exertion was for him the means to self-betterment: "It is literature alone, would I whisper to myself, that equals the fate of the poorest to that of the externally greatest of mankind". It was perhaps the fact that his writing was so directly the means to an end that his prolific output was often poor in quality, and that he neglected writing as soon as he had sufficient income to indulge his taste for being a gentleman of leisure. In 1790-1, he researched a historical course of lectures on the law, but these failed to attract an audience. He had brought his brother John and sister Mary to live with him in Edinburgh, but his poor habits of economy and bouts of extravagance when his affairs occasionally prospered, eventually led him to seek asylum from the debtor's prison in the sanctuary of the Abbey of Holyrood. He and Thomas de Quincey were the last literary men to appeal to this ancient legal protection. Debtors had the freedom to enter the city on a Sunday until midnight, and it is said that he so narrowly escaped from his pursuers that he left his decayed and threadbare coat-tails in their hands, as he managed to reach the sanctuary just before the end of the day. His friends and creditors, however, agreed on a scheme whereby he would compose a *History of Scotland* to pay off his debts, and the first volume of six was written entirely in jail. Though he blamed its inaccuracies and hurry on these unusual circumstances, the lack of profound scholarship was to be a Heron hallmark. On his liberation from jail, he took a pony and began on the journey through Scotland which was to form the basis of his most successful work, on the condition of the Western counties of Scotland; in 1797, he issued a more condensed guidebook to Scotland, entitled *Scotland Described*. Also at this time, he completed the memoir of **Burns**, only a year after the poet's death, in 1797. Invincibly optimistic, he now tried his hand at drama and launched a comedy, *St Kilda*, on the stage at the Theatre Royal, Edinburgh. Whether for its ribaldry or its poor quality,

A Literary Guide

it was hissed off before the second act, but Heron revived from his disappointment to the conviction that his enemies had tried to ruin his production out of jealousy. The comedy was therefore published with an ill-tempered preface, but this, not surprisingly, failed to improve its literary reception. Perhaps rather incongruously, he was elected ruling elder for New Galloway and spoke frequently and memorably at the General Assembly of the Church of Scotland, particularly on the subject of "Foreign Missions". He was also in charge of editing material for the *Statistical Account of Scotland* under the supervision of Sir John Sinclair, and according to **Thomas Murray,** who includes an extensive note on Heron in his *Literary History of Galloway,* revised those entries which were incomplete or inelegantly phrased. He had attempted to help out his family's finances by bringing his elder brother to the university, and his sister Mary to live with him; she is commemorated in the preface to his *History of Scotland.* Her death in 1798 came near to unhinging his mind, but he eventually recovered from his sense of overwhelming guilt and decided to try his fortune in London, where the booksellers did not know of his unreliability. From 1799, he was engaged in Parliamentary reporting and in journalism in London, including the editing of a French Royalist publication , funded by the British government. His occasional successes contributed to revive his extravagance, and he began to keep a pair of horses and a groom in livery. When poverty loomed once again, he would work feverishly, with a green cloth over his head to shield his inflamed eyes. In 1806, he wrote a letter to Wilberforce on the *Justice and Expediency of the Slave Trade,* published in the *Encyclopaedia Britannica,* translated works on chemistry and geography, and contributed ephemeral articles to huge numbers of journals and newspapers – more than any other living author, he was to claim, perhaps with justification. Despite his evident capacity to earn a living, he was once again arrested for debt and this time was confined to Newgate jail. It was from here that he wrote a letter "in the very extremity of bodily and pecuniary distress", conserved by Isaac d'Israeli in *Calamities of Authors,* appealing for help from the Literary Fund and detailing his contributions to literature. Although probably already afflicted with the "putrid fever" which was to end his life at St Pancras hospital, it is characteristic that he had time to write, while in Newgate, the *Comforts of Human Life* which ran to two editions in a week. He died in 1807.

Dumfries and Galloway

* * *

Despite the ire of Burns scholars, the account of Burns ("a great man, solely of God Almighty's making such") does not wholly bear out the theory that Heron deliberately set out to depict Burns as the uncrowned king of drunken debauchery and heretical scoffing. Though he has a tendency to moralise, especially about Burns's life after his arrival in Dumfriesshire, his methodology is interesting in that he claims to consider the influences on Burns which may have contributed to his genius, and his assessment of the parish school system and the influence of the "taking the Beuk" on Burns's literary education is not without interest. Whatever later sections of the *Memoir* insinuate to Burns' detriment, Heron's description of his own discovery of Burns has the authentic flavour of literary wonder, and shows him as other than a jealous and carping rival: "I closed it [the Kilmarnock edition] not, till a late hour on the rising Sunday morn, after I had read over every syllable it contained". Heron's *Observations made in a Journey Through the Western Counties of Scotland* contains further material on Burns in the description of Ayrshire, where he states that his poems "are in every person's hands". It is hard to avoid the conclusion that Heron's description of Burns's alleged dissipation includes a certain amount of self-confession: "We resist, and resist, and resist; but, at last, suddenly turn and passionately embrace the enchantress". Heron's own unpublished *Journal* shows that he was neither stranger to temptation nor to a morbid analysing of his own failings and a compulsive pattern of failure, followed by self-reproof. The *Journal* is a revealing and touching example of eighteenth century confessional literature. The *History of Scotland* is a literary work, rather than one of profound historical scholarship. Heron's *Observations made in a Journey through the Western Counties of Scotland*, 1793, adopts a similar method to that of his biography, since it is devoted to an analysis of the causes, both natural and accidental, which lead to the "industry, the virtue, the wealth, the happiness of the inhabitants of the different parts of Scotland". His range of interests on his travels echoes that of the *Statistical Account of Scotland*, on which he was then actively engaged as editor of the Galloway material: geography, antiquities, manufactures, domestic customs and folktales. One of the most revealing and lengthy passages deals with his own native New Galloway, where he assesses the

A Literary Guide

advantages and disadvantages of the development of industry and concludes conservatively that man may be happier and certainly more virtuous in primitive circumstances, rather than in a thriving town, with all its attendant risks. He also gives a full account of the new cotton mills at Gatehouse of Fleet and a description of the Galloway gypsies, including the famous Billy Marshall.

BIBLIOGRAPHY:
Observations made in a Journey through the Western Counties of Scotland (1793); *A New General History of Scotland* (1794-1799); *Scotland Described: or a Topographical Description of all the Counties of Scotland* (1797); *A Memoir of the Life of the Late Robert Burns* (1797); *St. Kilda in Edinburgh* (1798); *Letter to William Wilberforce ...on the Justice and Expediency of the Slave Trade* (1806); *The Comforts of Human Life* (1807)

Rev William Gillespie
1776-1825
New Galloway

Rev. William Gillespie, minister of Kells Church, was one of a cluster of poets and writers from the Glenkens of Galloway at the turn of the nineteenth century; he studied at Edinburgh University during the most stimulating period of its Enlightenment, and was in touch with many of the literary men of his day. He was a prolific, though never popular, poet. His principled and unassuming disposition appears to have inspired much respect in his contemporaries.

REV. WILLIAM GILLESPIE.

William Gillespie was the son of the Rev John Gillespie, minister of Kells for 42 years, and Dorothea McEwan, from Kirkcudbright. Gillespie attended the Grammar School of New Galloway (where he was a school-fellow of **Alexander Murray**) and went on to University at Edinburgh in 1792. There, he joined in the talented circle, which included **Thomas Brown** and many of the leading lights of the Edinburgh Enlightenment, and which founded the "Academy of Physics" and eventually the *Edinburgh Review*. He was tutor in the family of Sir Alexander Don of Newton, and was then licensed to preach by the Presbytery of Kirkcudbright. In 1801, he became helper, and was eventually successor, to his father in the parish of Kells. In 1805, he published *The Progress of Refinement*, an allegory. In the Stewartry, he made contact with most of the literary men of his day: **John Barbour** (who published a Memoir of Gillespie's life in his *Tributes to Scottish Genius*) **Robert Heron, Dr Thomas Brown, John McDiarmid,** and wrote an obituary of **Dr Muirhead**. He was also a devotee of Burns and attended the Burns dinners at Dumfries; it was

William Gillespie's father who met **Burns** on his Galloway Tour of 1793, and whom Burns – ignoring jokes about his being "priest-ridden" – carried ashore from a boat trip down Loch Ken. William Gillespie's poetry was inspired by various walking tours – to the West Highlands, and to the Lake District. In 1815, he published *Consolation, with Other Poems*, but the most celebrated and popular of his writings was the sermon he preached on the occasion when he defied a Royal edict forbidding prayers for Queen Caroline, estranged wife of George IV. He was arrested for his refusal to omit the Queen's name from prayers, and the feeling in Scotland against the edict was such that Gillespie's sermon, published in justification of his conduct, went through three editions. A popular poem of the time, *The Galloway Herds* (see entry under **Joseph Heughan**) which lampoons the "loyal Black-coats" who did confirm to the edict, refers to Gillespie's defiance: "Poet Wull! Poet Wull!/ Ye've cracked your skull / Against our mean sinecure vermin;/ But when you're perplex'd, / Just stick to your text, / And ye'll get a good sale for your sermon". Gillespie married Miss Charlotte Hoggan of Waterside in Dumfriesshire in July of 1825 after a long engagement, but died only three months later, in October 1825, when he returned to Kells Manse from his honeymoon tour.

* * *

Gillespie's *Progress of Refinement* is written in Spenserian stanzas and consists of a mythical history of Britain, and its emergence from savagery. Some shorter pieces, which contain some pleasing touches are appended to it, such as *Ode to Frost*: "..'neath the starry arch serene, / Hang'st in the atmosphere unseen; / Or in thy chrystal chariot driv'n , / Sparkling in the moon-beams pale". His *Consolation* is a didactic poem, spelling out the consolations offered by religion: "Religion, hail! best solace of th' unblest/ As angel fair, and pure as is the light / That robes all-beauteous the eternal throne". His *Ruin* is a moral poem on the transitory nature of all human achievement, and concludes with a topical piece on the devastation inflicted by Napoleon in Russia, followed by his flight from Moscow. In 1810, he wrote a sympathetic *Memoir* of **John Lowe**, author of *Mary's Dream*, since Lowe had been personally known to Gillespie's father; the account of Lowe is printed in Cromek's *Remains of Nithsdale and Galloway Song*.

BIBLIOGRAPHY:
The Progress of Refinement (1805); *Consolation, with Other Poems* (1815); John Barbour, *Tributes to Scottish Genius* (1827); *The Galloway Herds* (1909 reprint by Thomas Fraser, Dalbeattie); RH Cromek, *Remains of Nithsdale and Galloway Song* (1810)

A Literary Guide

John Lowe
1750-1798
New Galloway

*John Lowe was born at New Galloway, though he later emigrated to Virginia, in the United States. He was known particularly for the affecting ballad "Mary's Dream" and his poetry, though not extensive, was sufficiently known to **Burns** for him to visit the peninsula between the Ken and the Dee, known as "Lowe's arbour", where the ballad was thought to be composed.*

John Lowe was the eldest of a numerous family; his father was gardener to Mr. Gordon of Kenmure, whose own father had supported the rebel cause in 1715. He attended the parish school of Kells, but despite his early promise and ambition, was forced to become apprenticed to a weaver in New Galloway, who was himself father to **Robert Heron**, the historian and translator. He struggled to escape his circumstances, learning under the schoolmaster of neighbouring Carsphairn, and teaching church music and violin in the evenings. He gained the friendship of those who were able to assist him with his career and he was particularly indebted in this respect to Rev John Gillespie, minister of Kells, whose son, **William Gillespie**, later wrote a memoir of Lowe (published in RH Cromek's and **Allan Cunningham's** *Remains of Nithsdale and Galloway Song*). He became a student of divinity at the University of Edinburgh in 1771, thanks to the help of such friends. He returned to his native parish and became tutor to the McGhies of Airds, between the Ken and the Dee; he also became an admirer of Miss Jessie McGhie. Here, he began composing verse, often from a viewpoint where he erected a seat overlooking the Ken, which became known as "Lowe's Seat". In his *Morning*, he wrote "High on a rock his favourite arbor stood, / Near Ken's fair bank, amid a verdant wood; / Beneath its grateful shade, at ease he lay.." It was this arbour which **Burns** visited, lingering, according to Syme "as if expecting the passing spirit to appear as in 'Mary's Dream'". The occasion of this well-known poem of Lowe's was the news which shocked the household of Airds, that Alexander Miller, a surgeon, who had been engaged to Mary, one of the daughters of the house, had perished at sea. Lowe returned to Edinburgh in 1772 and was possibly licensed to preach in 1773. Finding it difficult to obtain a living, and wishing to support his mother and family at home, he decided to emigrate to America and, receiving an invitation to be a tutor to the family of Washington's brother, embarked for Virginia. Shortly afterwards, he opened an academy of his own at Fredericksburg, Virginia, and this succeeded until there was a hard winter in 1784, when he could no longer procure supplies for his pupil boarders. He then took orders in the Episcopal church and became a fashionable preacher. This might have been a point at which he could have sent for Jessie McGhie to become his wife, but the lengthy ode he sent her indicates a faltering commitment: "Where are the wishes that our souls employed? / Ah! Where the moments that we once enjoyed?". Shortly thereafter, he declared his love for a lady from Virginia, who rejected his addresses, but whose sister became attached to him. Perhaps in a fit of pique, he eventually married her, but the marriage proved disastrous. He drowned his sorrows in the bottle and eventually escaped his home, to die at the house of a fellow Scot. He is buried in an unmarked grave at Fredericksburg, Virginia. His wife apparently eventually sent for the horse on which he had ridden away to his death, only to find that it had been sold to defray funeral expenses.

* * *

Lowe is remembered almost entirely for the ballad *Mary's Dream*, and the poem deserves its reputation for its haunting beauty. Mary's fiancé appears to her in sleep: "When soft and low a voice was heard / Saying 'Mary, weep no more for me'". Before her, stands her Sandy, "With visage pale and hollow e'e / 'O Mary dear, cold is my clay - / It lies beneath a stormy sea." **Allan Cunningham**, in Cromek's *Remains*, composed a Scots "original", upon which Lowe's version was supposed to have been based, and provides a critical analysis to prove that the Scots version was the earlier. Lowe's poem and authorship was, however, too well known to allow Cunningham's literary subterfuge to be successful.

BIBLIOGRAPHY:
RH Cromek, *Remains of Nithsdale and Galloway Song* (1810)

A Literary Guide

John Gordon Barbour
1775-1843
St John's Town of Dalry

*John Gordon Barbour came from an old Glenkens family and lived at Bogue House near St John's Town of Dalry, the setting for many of his tales and poems. Like **Denniston** and **Cunningham**, he was a collector of local traditions, and for him, Galloway landscapes were densely populated with legend and figures of history and literature. His "Lights and Shadows of Scottish Character and Scenery" are treasuries of many local legends. His "Queries Connected with Christianity" show a man of intense radical conviction, often painfully at odds with the society of his day.*

The Barbour family laid claim to a long tradition of landownership in the Glenkens, including a descent from the famous Barbour, author of *The Bruce*. John Barbour was brother to the laird of Barlay and their father was a farmer at Gordonstone. As an adult, he took on a lease of the farm of Bogue House, on the Garple burn, not far from his father's farm and in the vicinity of St John's Town of Dalry. Both Barbour and his wife, Margaret Wilson, whose famous namesake and relative was drowned at the stake in Wigtown, were descended from Covenanting stock. The interest in Covenanting history is evident from the number of Barbour tales and traditions from the period of the "Killing Times". His first work was *Lights and Shadows of Scottish Character and Scenery*, which he published under the pseudonym of "Cincinnatus Caledonius" and contained mainly traditions from Galloway. The radicalism of his subsequent volume *Queries Connected with Christianity* was such that publishers shied away from backing a second series of his *Lights and Shadows*. His *Tributes to Scottish Genius* (1827) contained a long tribute to his late friend, Rev **William Gillespie** of Kells, and continued his celebration of the famous, particularly from Galloway, such as **Thomas Brown** (whom he knew), but also contained articles on Scots institutions such as Burns nights, the bagpipe and on Galloway literature. Two volumes of poetry, *Evenings in Greece* which included *Baronial*

Promenades (in which Kenmure Castle features) and *Helvetic Hours*, with the theme of the liberty of the Swiss peasants, followed in 1829 and 1831. In 1833, he published *Unique Traditions, Chiefly Connected with the West and the South of Scotland*, which included an account of the origin of the Carlin's Cairn on the Rhins of Kells, and of the standing stones near Anwoth known as "Rutherford's Witnesses". Barbour's traditional tales were collected on his summer rambles, "as he journeyed among the cottages and the cemeteries of his native Caledonia" (*Tributes..*"). The pithiness of his prose and his forthright opinions were not universally appreciated and he received round criticism in the *Castle Douglas Miscellany*, to which he replied equally robustly, under the name of "Lowran Glen". The newspaper followed up by publishing a weekly series of colloquies with "Lowran Glen", ridiculing Barbour, somewhat in the manner of the *Noctes Ambrosianae* of Christopher North. He was, in fact, visited at Bogue by both Christopher North and James Hogg. Even **MacTaggart** gives his tales some grudging praise ("The tales of his are tolerable"), but may have been responsible for some fun at Barbour's expense in the *Miscellany* : "The kintra's fu' o' rhyming cuifs, / There's scarce a mailen free o'them; / Tie their blethers to their tails / An' ower the Brig o' Dee wi' them". He died in 1843 and was buried at Dalry churchyard.

* * *

Barbour was probably at his best in prose. His tales in the first series of *Lights and Shadows* include a valuable selection relating to Galloway, particularly in connection with places with literary and historical echoes. Galloway landscapes clearly inspired him with an almost living vision of their historic past, and treating of Bruce's battle at Moss Raploch, he exclaims: "How many 'lights and shadows' of the south of Scotland pass before us, on this sacred spot!". He includes accounts of the martyrdom of Richard Cameron near Sanquhar, of **John Lowe**, and of "brownies" who appeared on his own farm at Bogue during Covenanting times. His rather peculiar *Dialogues of the Dead*, published in 1836, envisages conversations between famous Scots who may not have met in life, but whose dialogue could be employed to bring up important issues of the day. For example, **Alexander Murray** and **Robert Burns** discuss the uselessness of their recently erected monuments; **William Gillespie**

A Literary Guide

and **Thomas Brown** bemoan the lack of spiritual leadership in their county, while Jessie McGhie meets **John Lowe**, her fiancé, and reproaches him with his faithlessness. Barbour is at his most acid and characteristic in the *Queries Connected with Christianity*, whose radical sentiments caused a furore. He states his personal credo: "Neither do I believe that Washington or Jefferson were objects of divine reprobation, because they possessed not eight or ten palaces, pagodas and pavilions". Some of the heads of his questions indicate the style of the production and bear comparison with the most vigorous in the tradition of radical satire: "Can decorations and Orders put a Soul into any Man?"; "Are there no swine or swatter-mires, even upon thrones?" and "Is the Gout any criterion of Christianity?" His own ability to resist the pressures of public opinion and his Classical sense of the sufficiency unto itself of moral self-worth is well summarised in his own poem, *The Snowdrop* which, even in the wintry blast, "darest abroad thy petal fling,/ In spotless dignity alone".

BIBLIOGRAPHY:
Lights and Shadows of Scottish Character and Scenery (1824, 2nd Series 1825); *Queries Connected with Christianity* (1824); *Tributes to Scottish Genius* (1827); *Evenings in Greece* (1829); *Helvetic Hours* (1831); *Unique Traditions, Chiefly Connected with the West and the South of Scotland* (1833); *Dialogues of the Dead* (1836)

PLACES TO VISIT: Bruce's Stone at Moss Raploch (NTS) may be visited in the Galloway Forest Park. "Rutherford's Witnesses" stand on a moor above Anwoth village.

Rev David Landsborough
1779-1854
St John's Town of Dalry

David Landsborough, descended from the McClambrochs of Stranfasket, and sometime tutor to the family of Lord Glenlee, became a distinguished clergyman and naturalist, particularly known for his study of seaweeds and zoophytes, and his knowledge of the Clyde estuary and of the island of Arran.

DAVID LANDSBOROUGH, D.D.

David Landsborough, whose name was modernised from the older "McClambroch", was born the son of a weaver in Dalry, and educated at the Free Grammar School there. He attended Dumfries Academy, and then Edinburgh University. During this time, he was invited to act as tutor to the family of Lord Glenlee at his estate near Dalry, and thereafter Lord Glenlee exerted his influence on Landsborough's behalf once he was licensed to preach. In gratitude, Landsborough later dedicated his poem *Arran* to Lord Glenlee. While at Glenlee, Landsborough became acquainted with **Thomas Brown**, who invited him to attend his lectures at Edinburgh. Landsborough became an assistant at Ayr Auld Kirk to the Rev Dr Auld (**Burns**'s "Daddy Auld"), and was ordained in 1811 as the minister of Stevenston, one of the most lucrative livings in Ayrshire. His poem on *Arran* was inspired by the views of the island from his Stevenston manse. At Stevenston, he became a popular preacher, and a new church was built to accommodate 1200 sittings. His religious convictions tended towards the evangelical, and during the Kilsyth revival, he held prayer meetings assisted by Andrew and Horatius Bonar; he also organised a Temperance Society. He became

A Literary Guide

known for his scientific research, particularly on marine and land shells, and on fossil botany, which could be studied in the coal beds near Stevenston. He contributed some of his discoveries on seaweeds to Dr Hervey for his *Phycologia Britannica* and Hervey named one of the algae *Ectocarpus Landsburgii*. He also had a zoophyte, a New Zealand alga, and a shell named in his honour and kept up a learned correspondence with many of the natural historians of his day. In 1837, he wrote some sermons and papers for the *Scottish Christian Herald*, of which three were published as *Ayrshire Sketches* on religious personalities of the day, and also in this year, wrote the *Statistical Account of Stevenston*, a work for which he was well-prepared by the meticulous daily diaries he kept of natural phenomena and meteorology. In 1845, some of his papers on natural science appeared in *The Christian Treasury* and attracted the praise of Hugh Miller; they were published separately as *Excursions to Arran*. He was often accompanied on his trips by another native of Dalry, the Rev Nathaniel Paterson, DD, who was also to leave the Established Church of Scotland at the Disruption. In 1849, he published *A Popular History of British Sea-Weeds* and, in the same series, in 1852, *A Popular History of British Zoophytes, or Corallines*. For his work, he was elected a Fellow of the Linnaean Society, and was awarded the honorary degree of DD by an American university. At the time of the Disruption of the Church of Scotland in 1843, despite his having a lucrative living and despite having reached the age of 62, he left the church and, with his congregation, set about building a new church at Saltcoats, ultimately having charge of additional congregations at Kilwinning and Stevenston. He also assisted at the establishment of a Free Kirk at Bogue Tollbar, near Dalry in the Stewartry. He was able to return to scientific pursuits in 1844, and began a series of expeditions dredging in the Firth of Clyde from a friend's yacht: some species of the shells retrieved were new to science. In 1852, he chose to leave Scotland as the Free Church's delegate to a Presbyterian church at Gibraltar, where he became chaplain to the Cameronian regiment. From here, he visited Spain and North Africa. In 1854, when he had returned to Ayrshire, where Asiatic cholera was raging, he was seized with the disease himself, having contracted it during his many pastoral visits to the sick, and died in September. He is buried in Stevenston churchyard, with his wife, Margaret McLeish.

* * *

Landsborough's poem in blank verse, *Arran*, refers to his boyhood's inspiration, where "daily I saw the rich and fertile vale / Through which irriguous flowed the silver Ken;". Its descriptions of Arran and its botany, since they were written by the authority on the island's flora and fauna, make it a didactic poem in the true sense: "I've oft explored thy glens and tangled brakes,/Where every bank blooms with the primrose pale, / And drooping hyacinth; or where amidst / Her ensiformal leaves, on stately stem, / Sweet Epipactis, rarest of they plants, / Builds up her pyramid of snowy gems." The 1828 edition abounds with notes on history, geography, botany and personalities. The description of his excursions to Arran, *Arran: its Topography, Natural History, and Antiquities*, 1875, includes a memoir by his son, David, who also followed his father into the church and in his interests in conchology and algology. Landsborough's intense interest in natural science was without difficulty combined with his religious beliefs, and in his *Popular History of British Zoophytes, or Corallines*, which is aimed at a young audience, he writes that "(God) has also given us the book of Nature, making it accessible to all; and in many a delightful page of it does He plainly say, 'Come, see the works of my hand, so full of wonders, and so well-fitted to show forth my praise'".

BIBLIOGRAPHY:
Arran: a Poem (1828); *A Popular History of British Sea-Weeds* (1849); *Excursions to Arran, Ailsa Craig, and the Two Cumbraes* (1851); *A Popular History of British Zoophytes, or Corallines* (1852); *Arran: its Topography, Natural History, and Antiquities* (1875)

A Literary Guide

Robert Trotter, MD
1798-1875
St. John's Town of Dalry

Robert Trotter was the first in the Trotter dynasty of doctors and writers; he was born at New Galloway and returned to the Glenkens for the latter part of his life, having practised medicine throughout the Stewartry, and elsewhere. His novels, inspired by the Romantic taste for chivalry and the supernatural, are of minor interest, but his collecting of Galloway tales inspired a generation of sons to write on local subjects: **Robert de Bruce Trotter, Alexander and James Trotter.**

DR ROBERT TROTTER,
DALRY.

Robert Trotter's father was the "famous Muir-doctor", who introduced advances in medical care to the Glenkens. No doubt because of his father's connections as a well-respected practitioner, he was brought up in close proximity with the sons of the Gordons of Kenmure, and with whom he engaged in a variety of scrapes described by Alexander Trotter in his *East Galloway Sketches*. When he was fifteen, his father died and he began to earn a living, first as teacher at the parish school of New Galloway and later as a tutor to various families. At this stage of his career, he was helped out financially by **Professor Thomas Brown**, a native of Kirkmabreck and an old friend of his father's. His first publication, *Lowran Castle, or, the Wild Boar of Curridoo* dedicated to the Hon. John Gordon of Kenmure, was aimed at raising the means to put himself through a medical training at university, and received a good number of subscribers. He drew on his knowledge of the topography and folklore of Glenkens for contributions to the *Dumfries Magazine*, as his sons would do for their own writing. At this time, he was also projecting a study of heraldry of local families, and during the planning of this volume (which was never published, but appeared as appendices to future works), he met Sir Walter Scott. In 1825, he published *Derwentwater: or the Adherents of King James*, a novel set in the times of the 1715 rebellion, in which his ancestors had taken the part of the Stuart cause. His final and most ambitious historical novel, *Herbert Herries: or the Days of Queen Mary, a Tale of Dundrennan Abbey* was his least successful work and thereafter, he confined himself to contributing to periodicals on his favourite subjects of genealogy and folklore. The story of his attempts to set up medical practices in various parts of Wigtownshire, the Stewartry and Dumfriesshire, including Port William, Creetown, Moffat, Dalbeattie and Auchencairn, can be traced in the biographical snatches contained in his son Robert's *Galloway Gossip*. Between 1834 and 1853, he was largely resident at Auchencairn, where his sons began recording their impressions of village life. His literary interests continued unabated and he contributed to the *Scottish Antiquarian Magazine* and was consulted by the **Rev William Mackenzie** for material for his *History of Galloway*. In 1853, he was appointed medical officer in a parish in Kintyre and subsequently on the Isle of Skye, where he lived near Dunvegan Castle. From here, he was in a position to investigate the genealogy of the Highland chieftains and the antiquities of the islands, and contributed articles to periodicals on these subjects. In 1864, he retired to the Glenkens and became medical officer to the parish of Dalry. Tales and articles on Galloway families continued to appear in the *Kirkcudbrightshire Advertiser*, the *Dumfries Herald* and *Newcastle Weekly Chronicle*. He was an active member of the Dumfries and Galloway Natural History and Antiquarian Society and his museum of antiquities might have been the envy of Sir Walter Scott, containing relics of Bonnie Prince Charlie and the notorious persecutor of the Covenanters, Grierson of Lag, as well as Roman , Celtic and mediaeval finds. His funeral was attended by among others, the Auchencairn poet, **Joseph Heughan**, who wrote a tribute in verse to Trotter's interest in "coats o' airms and legends queer / And names o' folk and places here".

* * *

The title tale of *Lowran Castle* is written in tribute to the Gordon family, Trotter's friends and patrons, the origin of whose name is explained in the tale as deriving from "Gore-down", after the hero "gores down" a wild boar in the woods of the Glenkens, and, as a result, contrives to win the heroine, despite the attempted deceit of Archibald the Grim. The Romantic inspiration of the tales, and, in particular, the influence of Ossian, are evident in both the high-flown language and their concern with the days of chivalry, with the Stuart cause, with witches and the supernatural. Contemporary reviewers, like **MacTaggart,** who accords Trotter's work and rich fantasy a rare note of praise in his *Encyclopaedia* seem to have appreciated Trotter's touch in this genre. The tales are almost invariably set in the parish of Kells, in places such as Balmaclellan and Cairnsmore of Cairsphairn. *Derwentwater,* which was, according to the author, published on the advice of Sir Walter Scott, is a yet more highly coloured picture of life in the days of the Stuart rebellion and includes, as part of the appendix, details of the Trotter descent from a standard bearer of Robert the Bruce, a connection of which he was inordinately proud. Other genealogical details were received from the heads of local noble families and, as with the previous work, the historical notes are often now of more interest than the text. In *Herbert Herries,* Trotter includes a rather optimistic appeal to the Crown for the fulfilment of a promise of lands which had been made to one of his ancestors by Prince Charles in 1745.

BIBLIOGRAPHY:
Lowran Castle, or, the Wild Boar of Curridoo (1822); Derwentwater: or the Adherents of King James (1825); Herbert Herries: or the Days of Queen Mary, a Tale of Dundrennan Abbey (1827)

Isabella Trotter
1796-1847
New Galloway

*Isabella Trotter was the only woman of the Trotter dynasty to write: she was the sister of **Robert Trotter**, and aunt to **Robert de Bruce Trotter**, **Alexander** and **James Trotter**, all medical men, who celebrated their Galloway birth and inheritance in poetry and prose.*

Isabella Trotter was born in 1796 at Viewfield, the Trotter family home built by her father, Robert Trotter, the "Muir-doctor"; her mother was Grizel Stevenson, descended from Ayrshire Covenanting stock. She was educated at the Parish School of Kells, and at the Free Grammar School of Balmaclellan. Her father was an excellent tutor, knowing both Latin and Greek, but a less excellent man of business, since he left the family with debts contracted under an ungenerous landlord. Isabella Trotter in later life gave an account of the forced sale of the family possessions to pay the debt. A distant relative helped the family out in their extremity, and Isabella Trotter was sent to a school in Glasgow, and later to Dumfries Academy, where she was to qualify as a teacher or governess. She was governess in Peebles to children of the Selkirk family, by whom a pension was obtained for Miss Trotter, from the Royal Bounty Fund for the Relief of Decayed Gentlewomen. She also held a post at Bogue, home of **John Barbour**, who read to her his manuscripts. Perhaps while she held this situation, she acquired the ambition to write. She composed a biography of her father *Memoirs of the Late Robert Trotter, Esq., Surgeon, New Galloway*, who also receives a mention in **MacTaggart's** *Scottish Gallovidian Encyclopaedia*. In 1826, she wrote *The Four Glenkens' Ministers*, which first appeared in Bennet's *Dumfries Monthly Magazine*: Bennet also made her a proposal of marriage, which was declined. Her proposed volume of *Poems and Essays: Descriptive, Moral and Religious* was never published; her diary, from which her nephew, **Alexander Trotter**, gives some extracts appears to give fascinating insights into Glenkens social life, including details of her acquaintance with the **Rev William Gillespie** and his wife, and with Mr **McDiarmid** of the *Dumfries Courier*. She held various positions at schools in Castle Douglas,

A Literary Guide

Ballantrae, and at Leven Lodge School, Edinburgh . She joined the Free Kirk in 1843, and was obliged to leave her position, finally being appointed to a school near Lasswade. There, she died in 1847 of typhoid fever.

* * *

The Four Glenkens' Ministers is a fictionalised account of a real event, referred to by **Barbour** in his life of the **Rev William Gillespie**, namely the sudden coincidental deaths of all of the incumbents of the churches in the Glenkens within a short space of time. There is an interesting description in the sketch of the outdoor taking of the sacrament in the churchyard of Kells, to which the scattered communities came from miles around. Alexander Trotter gives a lengthy specimen of Isabella Trotter's blank verse - one with a twist in its tale - entitled *Home*: "The summer sun had sped his lengthened course, / And calmly tranquil now had sunk to rest/ As evening drew her curtains round, and night/ Advanced with slow and sober pace". The *Memoirs of the Late Robert Trotter*, are Isabella Trotter's recollections of her father who was a famed surgeon in the Glenkens and an important member of the medical dynasty of Trotters. The *Memoirs* are of interest in her description of the contemporary scene: she remembers his "buckled shoes, plain suit, black silk neckcloth and grey locks combed back with a black ribbon", the stud of racers he kept, which he ran at the race-course at Auchencairn, and his interest in cock-fighting. He superintended the building of "Viewfield", where she was born, on Lord Kenmure's estate, but apparently moved after a misunderstanding with his landlord. She describes how his practice extended to Ayrshire, Wigtownshire and Dumfriesshire. Dr Trotter also met **Burns** on his tour of the Glenkens in 1793 and accompanied him on some of his visits to places of interest in the area.

BIBLIOGRAPHY: *Memoirs of the Late Robert Trotter, Esq., Surgeon, New Galloway* (1822); *The Four Glenkens' Ministers* in - *The Dumfries Monthly Magazine* (Dec. 1826) and also in - John Nicholson, ed., *Historical and Traditional Tales in Prose and Verse, Connected with the South of Scotland* (1843); Alexander Trotter, *East Galloway Sketches* (1901)

Alexander Trotter
1835-1901
St John's Town of Dalry

Alexander Trotter was a third generation representative of a Galloway family which was unique in combining literary and medical skills: his father, **Dr Robert Trotter of Dalry**, *his aunt* **Isabella**, *and his brother* **James** *and* **Robert Trotter** *all wrote, and his grandfather, the "Famous Muir-Doctor" featured in* **McTaggart**'*s "Scottish Gallovidian Encyclopaedia", had taken* **Robert Burns** *on a tour of several places of interest in the Glenkens in 1793. Alexander Trotter's own chief literary contribution was through his newspaper articles on Galloway literature and tradition, chiefly published in the "Kirkcudbrightshire Advertiser", and which were ultimately embodied in his "East Galloway Sketches": these contributed to preserve many biographical details and photographs of Galloway writers.*

ALEXANDER TROTTER, M.D.

Alexander Trotter was born in 1835 at Auchencairn, the second of five sons of **Dr Robert Trotter**, who corresponded with Sir Walter Scott, had composed a number of novels set in Galloway and collected its antiquarian traditions. Dr Trotter communicated both the family literary and medical traditions to his sons: all four of them qualified as doctors, as had their father, grandfather and great-grandfather, one of the founders of the Royal College of Physicians. Alexander was educated at the parish school of Rerwick; aged fifteen, he entered an office at Birkenhead, and at nineteen, began medical classes at Glasgow University. He qualified as a surgeon and physician in 1858, and in 1863, became MD from the University of St Andrews; during his training, like many young doctors, he had acted as ship's surgeon on a whaling ship and his account of the

A Literary Guide

voyage in his *Journal of the Voyage of the Ship Enterprise, from Fraserburgh to Greenland* (1856) has been published. It offers an intriguing insight into the traditions and the brutishness of life aboard ship, the whaling industry, and an account of places, such as the Shetlands, at which the ship anchored. This was not , however, Alexander Trotter's first essay as a writer: at the age of 17, he had already written *Scenes and Adventures in and about Auchencairn*, extracts of which were later published. In 1858, he was medical officer aboard an emigrant ship and visited Niagara Falls. He followed his brothers into medical practice in the north of England , became a newspaper proprietor, a shipowner and county councillor. His articles for the *Newcastle Weekly Chronicle* were often on antiquarian and heraldic subjects. He was a prominent and popular town and county councillor, was surgeon to the local artillery volunteers, and published in the *Lancet*. He purchased the estate of Dalshangan, near Dalry, the home of his father and grandfather, for summer holidays and for his retirement. *East Galloway Sketches*, published in 1901 was the summation of his contributions written over a twenty year period for the *Kirkcudbrightshire Advertiser*.

* * *

Trotter wrote at a time when a certain local patriotism was fostering a vigorous interest in the tradition of Galloway literature, and when some significant collections were being formed. It is thanks to the industry of Trotter and others, like the publisher, Thomas Fraser of Dalbeattie, and **Malcolm McL Harper,** whose help he enlisted in compiling the *Sketches*, that a corpus of knowledge and a series of illustrations were preserved relating to Galloway's more and less obscure poets and writers, and men and women of note. Trotter's articles are still often the first, and sometimes the only, source for literary historians today for details on the lives of poets and writers such as **John Gerrond, John Morrison, Samuel Wilson** and **John Lowe,** a fact which bears out his own prediction in the Preface to the *Sketches*, that, such biographies, "if not written by the author, would probably never have been written at all". The literary biographies are interspersed with Trotter's observations on the history, folklore, villages and towns, and industrial and commercial development of Galloway, and on his own family's considerable contribution to the literature of the area, and the whole contributes to a picture of an astonishingly productive period between the eighteenth and nineteenth centuries, in the history of the area, particularly in the Trotters' beloved Glenkens.

BIBLIOGRAPHY: *Journal of the Voyage of the Ship Enterprise, from Fraserburgh to Greenland* (1856 - ms. in Hornel Library, Broughton House, Kirkcudbright); *East Galloway Sketches: or, Biographical, Historical, and Descriptive Notices of Kirkcudbrightshire, Chiefly in the Nineteenth Century* (1901); Innes Macleod, ed., *To the Greenland Whaling* (1979)

A Literary Guide

Captain Alexander William Maxwell Clark-Kennedy
1851-1894
Knockgray, by Carsphairn

Captain AWM Clark-Kennedy, born to a family of landed proprietors at Knockgray, near Carsphairn, wrote on ornithology and travel; he also composed poetry, including a poem "Robert the Bruce", inspired by Walter Scott and describing the places in the hills of Galloway associated with Bruce's military campaigns.

CAPT. A. W. M. CLARK-KENNEDY.

AWM Clark-Kennedy came from a line of distinguished military men; because of his father's military posting as colonel in an Irish regiment, he was born in Rochester in 1851 and brought up at Aldershot. At Eton, he started a school magazine, and, at the age of sixteen, wrote *The Birds of Berkshire and Buckinghamshire* dedicated to Prince Leopold, Duke of Albany, who was a school friend of Clark-Kennedy's. In 1870, he became an ensign in the Coldstream Guards and rose rapidly to the rank of captain; he sold his commission in 1874. He acquired an estate near Castle Douglas, at Meikle Ernambrie, but continued to live at his ancestral estate at Carsphairn. He was a noted sportsman, composed shooting songs for *Baily's Magazine*, and wrote articles on zoology, ornithology and antiquities for the *Field, Land and Water* and the *Zoologist*. He married a daughter of an Irish peer, Viscount Lifford, and expressed strong views on Irish politics, vigorously opposing Home Rule. Among other compositions on the subject of Irish affairs, he wrote a song *Rouse ye, Ulster!*, which was sung at a political meeting in Belfast in 1894 and he appeared on the platform brandishing a flag of the Grenadier Guards which had been carried at Waterloo. His *Robert the Bruce* was published in 1884, and an account of his *To the Arctic Regions and Back in Six Weeks* in 1878. Though he died in London, he had constructed a tomb on the slope of Knockgray Craig, overlooking the hills surrounding Loch Doon, and was buried there at his own request.

* * *

Clark-Kennedy's poetry is marked by his affection for Galloway, and particularly for the landscape round Carsphairn: "Where the Dungeon of Buchan its summit uprears/ And the Merrick, gigantic, in glory appears/ And their footsteps to-day have been wandering far / From the braes of Craigmulloch to grim Mullwharchar, / To grey Millyea with its rampart of rocks / The home of the badger, the wolf, and the fox". His poem, *Robert the Bruce*, which acknowledges its inspiration by Sir Walter Scott, is set during Bruce's Galloway campaign, and features many local landmarks, such as Garlies and Cruggleton Castles. Each Canto is dedicated to a different lady from local landowning families, whose estates covered part of the territory where the poem is set, and the last hundred pages of the poem consist of detailed historical notes. The atmosphere of the Bruce's campaign and hideouts in the hills and their caves is well conveyed in the sort of vigorous verse Clark-Kennedy had used in his hunting songs: "The cavern walls from roof to ground / With warlike spoils were hung around, / While here and there in vacant space / Were trophies of the merry chase. / There high above the royal head / Saint Andrew's banner gay is spread". Clark Kennedy's geographical writings, such as *To the Arctic Regions and Back in Six Weeks*, consist of readable travel journals, with observations on the ornithology (such as the Eider ducks) and the native people, the Lapps.

BIBLIOGRAPHY:
The Birds of Berkshire and Buckinghamshire (1868); *To the Arctic Regions and Back in Six Weeks* (1878); *Robert the Bruce: a Poem, Historical and Romantic* (1884); Malcolm McL Harper, *The Bards of Galloway* (1889)

A Literary Guide

John Loudon McAdam
1756-1836
Waterhead by Carsphairn; Moffat

John Loudon McAdam, born to an old landed family with an estate at Waterhead, was one of the first to devote systematic attention to the method of road-building since the Romans. His contribution came at a point when access by road had a critical part to play in opening up markets for the increasing production of the agricultural and industrial revolutions.

J. L. MACADAM.

The McAdams had been established at Waterhead since 1581. John McAdam, father of the road-builder, was one of the founders of the first bank in Ayr; John Loudon was the youngest of ten children. His father built a new house for the family estate at Lagwine, near Carsphairn, but this was burnt to the ground. Thereafter, the family leased Blairquhan from Sir John Whiteford, and John Loudon McAdam attended Mr Doick's school at Maybole. Even there, he showed an early interest in roads and apparently made a model of the Girvan road. His grandmother had gone to live at Dumcrieff, near Moffat (an estate which was to be sold at a later date to **James Currie**), and this became a part of the country of which he remained particularly fond. McAdam was sent to New York, where he had an uncle who had made a fortune, and joined a prosperous and loyalist section of New York society. Soon, he was established on New Dock as an agent for naval prizes, and with his uncle, established the New York Chamber of Commerce. He made a fortunate marriage to Miss Gloriana Nicoll of Long Island, whose family had been among the founders of New York. When war threatened in the colony, McAdam

Dumfries and Galloway

joined a volunteer loyalist regiment and was appointed Commissioner for Naval Prizes. After British defeat in the war, all those who had fought against the new Republic were attainted and their property was made forfeit. Nonetheless, when he was repatriated in 1783, he had retained enough money to buy Sauchrie House, near Maybole. After the Militia Act, he became Deputy Lieutenant, and in 1794, when invasion by France threatened, he raised a corps of volunteer artillery and was given the rank of Major. It may have been the urgent necessity of transporting troops at speed across the execrable Scottish roads which stimulated him to think further of the method of road building, but it is certain that at this time, he was travelling, examining roads in the south of Scotland, and experimenting with his own methods. He was also involved, at this time, with the Earl of Dundonald, a relative of his, who had patented the extraction of coke, tar and varnish from coal at a plant at Muirkirk. When he was offered the post of Government agent for victualling the Navy, on the West coast of England, he moved to Bristol and also lived for a time at Falmouth, until peace seemed imminent in 1801. He decided to make the best of the influential connections he had made in Bristol and sold Sauchrie House, settling in Bristol. It was in 1816 that McAdam was invited by the Bristol Municipality to become General Surveyor, with the charge of 146 miles of road. He inherited a situation where the roads were often impassable, sometimes positively dangerous, maladministered by a plethora of turnpike trusts, lacking a body of trained road engineers, and raising extortionate tolls. McAdam applied his method of applying a layer of uniform stone, crushed to a size of not more than six ounces, with a small rise in the centre, to the Bristol system of roads. Soon his improvements were attracting attention and he spent much time explaining his methods. It was at this point that he brought out the first edition of his *Remarks on the Present System of Road Making*, 1816. McAdam's methods impressed Parliament, because they made an economical re-use of existing material, which when properly applied, McAdam calculated would cost only 1d or 2d a yard to lay. By 1819, he was giving advice to the Select Committee, inveighing against the use of "statute labour" on the roads (the use of paupers as unpaid labourers), arguing the need for trained surveyors, and explaining the superiority of his own system against that of rivals, like **Thomas Telford**, who advocated laying an expensive foundation of slabs of stone. It is not clear that

A Literary Guide

McAdam shared in the animosity which existed between his own and Telford's supporters, but the opposition was certainly bitter and was later to spill over into accusations that McAdam was profiting unduly from the widespread use of his system. The poet Southey, one of Telford's friends and admirers, punned that the country would suffer from "quackadamizing", but demand for "macadamized" roads grew, even in the centre of London and, later, in Edinburgh. In large part, the coaching era, from 1820-1836, and the improvements in the art of coach-building, were largely dependent on the improvements brought about by McAdam, and Dickens wrote, expressing public enthusiasm, that "Our shops, our horses' legs, our boots, our hearts, have all benefited by the introduction of Mr McAdam". In 1824, the pun, often supposed to describe Telford, was printed in *Life in London*, referring to McAdam: "That, though McAdam can't straddle the sea / Yet he's surely a Colossus of Roads". His workload had grown to such an extent that his three sons were drawn from their various professions to help their father spread the gospel of his road-building method. Despite the accusations levelled at him, even in Parliament, McAdam did not seem to have benefited as much from the widespread application of his method as seemed possible or likely: in 1823, he was petitioning Parliament for recognition of his services, and only in 1825 was some remuneration awarded him. He was nearly dismissed by the Bristol Corporation, whose fortunes had been transformed by his first venture, and, in 1825 after his wife's death, he resigned from it. He married again in 1827 to Anne Delancey, whose sister married the novelist, Fenimore Cooper, who became a frequent visitor to McAdam's home. He acquired a house in Hertfordshire, but returned to Scotland, particularly to the Moffat area, each summer. In 1830, the French government adopted his system and the term "macadamizing" had entered the language, used as a symbol, for better or worse, for the application of scientific method and for industrial progress. It was on one of his visits to the Moffat area that he died in 1836; he is buried at Moffat churchyard. Perhaps fortunately, he failed to see the deterioration of his roads in the era after his death, for lack of application of his principles of repair and waterproofing, but he would certainly have welcomed the realisation of one aim for which he had long campaigned: the abolition of the inefficient and corrupt turnpike trusts, which also occurred after his death.

Dumfries and Galloway

* * *

McAdam's own works are those of an essentially practical man, bent upon proselytising the world on behalf of his method: they are not the works of an engineer or an architect. The first edition of his *The Present State of Road Making* (1816) is now extremely rare, only a few copies being known to exist in libraries; later editions of 1819 and 1820 were expanded with a full account of his evidence given to the Parliamentary Select Committees. He puts his argument succinctly: "The anxious provisions of the Legislature for preservation of the roads have unfortunately taken precedence of measures for making the roads fit to be travelled upon, or worth the care of being preserved". After an explanation of his principles, which particularly involved keeping the bed of the road free of "underwater" and then laying upon it a mass of non-water-retentive stone, which, when compacted, would keep the bed of the road wholly dry, he goes on to argue for attention to the nature of the officers in charge of roads and the care of finances. He understood that the huge debts run up by turnpike trusts could only be reduced by efficient repair, which in turn would reduce bills and enable tolls to be lowered from their current crippling level. He lays some stress on the nature of the tools to be carried by surveyors, including a pair of scales and a six ounce weight , and those to be used by those laying roads. In his *Letter to Sir Alexander Muir McKenzie, Bart., on the Subject of Scottish Roads*, he republished letters first issued in America, in the *Rail Road Journal*, New York, 1832. He stresses, contrary to Telford, that the thickness of road metal to be used should be dictated only by the need to exclude water, not by its power to carry weight. In another sense, McAdam's achievements entered literature: only an appreciation of the state of British roads, of the anger of the public about turnpike roads, and of the revolution which any improvement effected, can explain why a road-engineer's name should have become a household word. Thomas Hood, who wrote a poem on McAdam and his achievement, waxed eulogistic when he summarised McAdam's contribution to the opening up of industrial markets and prosperity: "Dispenser of coagulated good, / Distributor of granite and of food! / ..Best benefactor ! Though thou giv'st a stone / To those who ask for bread!"

A Literary Guide

BIBLIOGRAPHY:
Remarks on the Present State of Road Making (1816); *A Practical Essay on the Scientific Repair and Preservation of Public Roads* (1819); *Letter to Sir Alexander Muir McKenzie, Bart., on the Subject of Scottish Roads* (1833); Roy Devereux, *John Loudon McAdam: Chapters in the History of Highways* (1936)

PLACES TO VISIT: McAdam's gravestone exists at Moffat; an informative display on his life and work at Carsphairn heritage centre is within a few miles of his ancestral estate at Waterhead.

Dumfries and Galloway

Dorothy Leigh Sayers
1893-1957
Kirkcudbright, Gatehouse of Fleet

Dorothy L Sayers was one of the most accomplished writers of detective fiction this century: her polished style, closely reasoned plots and detailed backgrounds established the genre as one worthy of serious literary attention. Her novel, "Five Red Herrings" was set in Kirkcudbright and Gatehouse of Fleet, where houses, personalities and even train times were described with minute and verifiable accuracy.

Dorothy Leigh Sayers was the only child of the Reverend Henry Sayers and was brought up at Bluntisham Rectory in Cambridgeshire. She attended Godolphin School, Salisbury and won a scholarship to Somerville College, Oxford. In 1915, she took a First Class Honours degree in Modern Languages, and joined the staff of Blackwell's publishing house. After holding various teaching positions, she took a post with Benson's, preparing copy for advertising, where she worked between 1921-32. After a series of unsuccessful love affairs, in 1926 she married a journalist, Oswald Arthur Fleming, known – because of his Scottish ancestry – as "Mac". He claimed an aristocratic descent, since a Malcolm Fleming had been created Earl of Wigton by King David II, son of Robert the Bruce, and he himself would, he said, have been fourteenth in the line of descent. It was at any rate through Mac that Dorothy Sayers first visited the Stewartry of Kirkcudbright. Mac had visited Kirkcudbright first in the company of a painter, Hamish Paterson, third son of James Paterson (the painter, who had a house in Moniaive). Mac's interests included fishing and painting, and the artistic colony at

242

A Literary Guide

Kirkcudbright must have appealed to him; Dorothy Sayers was later to describe this community where "one either fishes or paints" in the opening lines of the *Five Red Herrings*. He had also been gassed during the First World War and his health apparently benefited from the mild climate, so that Dorothy Sayers insisted on staying in Kirkcudbright for holidays. They rented a house at 14a High Street, from the painter, EA Hornel, in June 1929, May 1930, September 1930 and September 1932. They also stayed at the Anwoth Hotel at Gatehouse, where Dorothy Sayers got to know the landlord, Joe Dignam, to whom she addresses the *Foreword*. The *Five Red Herrings* was published in 1931 and she wrote to Victor Gollancz, the book's publisher, eighteen months after publication, that she had become one of the "local amenities" when in Kirkcudbright, with local proprietors sending to her autograph-hunters who were already visiting the town after reading the book. She went on to publish several more of the "Lord Peter Wimsey" mysteries and to develop an entirely separate career as a religious writer and broadcaster. She appears, however, to have kept up a correspondence with the family of Joe Dignam long after she had finished work on the novel.

* * *

The *Five Red Herrings* stands mid-way in the development of Dorothy Sayer's detective writings, since at this point she had already written six novels and published a collection of short stories, but had yet to give her mysteries the full psychological development which they attained in the later *The Nine Tailors* and *Gaudy Night*. The Sayers technique of developing a wholly detailed and accurate backdrop for her stories (in which she was influenced by her study of Wilkie Collins) was, however, already well established. It was a technique designed to capture the reader's confidence in order to predispose him or her to accept the incredible. Sayers fans have delighted in establishing the real locations, either identified or thinly disguised in the text, of events in the novel: The Anwoth and the Murray Arms in Gatehouse of Fleet, the Ellangowan Hotel in Creetown, the Galloway Arms in Newton Stewart, the viaduct and station house at the remote Gatehouse station, the lead mines, artists' studios in Kirkcudbright, and the murder-scene itself on the waters of the Minnoch, can all still be seen. More difficult have been the identifications of the characters of the six artist-suspects with the real artists of Kirkcudbright's flourishing artistic colony. Perhaps the most likely is the identification of the character Gowan, one of those artists who is described as having a studio "panelled and high , in strong stone houses filled with gleaming brass and polished oak", with the Australian-born artist, EA Hornel. The story is told that the sole meeting between Dorothy Sayers and Hornel was not a success; Jessie M King, who lived at Green Gate (on which Wimsey's Kirkcudbright lodgings were modelled), suggested that Sayers soothe her feelings and take a refined revenge by portraying him in one of her books. Certainly, Gowan comes out in the book as a vain and peevish character. Anderson, on the other hand, is a genial character, and was probably based on William Robson, an artist and sportsman, who attracted much of Kirkcudbright's social orbit to his house at 52 High Street. Dorothy Sayers was on friendly terms with Robson's daughters. Other suspects were probably composites borrowing traits belonging to real artists, like Oppenheimer, and Sayers took care to conflate recognisable artistic styles, so as to avoid potentially libellous identifications. The novel was later filmed for television, with Ian Carmichael in the starring role.

BIBLIOGRAPHY:
Five Red Herrings (1931); Barbara Reynolds, *Dorothy L Sayers: Her Life and Soul* (1993)

PLACES TO VISIT: EA Hornel's home, Broughton House, Kirkcudbright (The National Trust for Scotland).
Stewartry Museum, where a Five Red Herrings Trail leaflet is available. Gatehouse station is still visible, and all hotels mentioned are still open to the public.

A Literary Guide

Mr William Mackenzie and Rev William Mackenzie 1753-1852 and 1789-1854
Kirkcudbright

Both natives of Kirkcudbright, William Mackenzie senior was uncle to the Rev William Mackenzie, master at Kirkcudbright Academy and author of the important "History of Galloway". The elder Mackenzie was the prolific author of popular moral tracts, aimed at the improvement of young people.

William Mackenzie, born in Kirkcudbright in 1753, was educated at Kirkcudbright Academy under Dr Currie. He was known for his beautiful penmanship, and the copy lines which have survived certainly testify to his skill. He answered an advertisement for a writing master at Ayr Academy, where he remained for some years and also found much work as a private teacher. He then started for Edinburgh University, intending to study for the church, teaching for part of the day. He obtained the post of writing master at Heriot's Hospital, after a competitive examination, and, although he did deliver one or two lectures at Divinity Hall, found that his success as a teacher interfered with his vocation as a minister, and devoted himself to teaching. He was often called upon to write the Royal addresses and burgess tickets for the city of Edinburgh, and George III commented that the finest documents which he received came from Edinburgh. On leaving Heriot's Hospital after ten years, he returned to Castle Douglas and then to Kirkcudbright. His publications on education , mainly aimed at encouraging virtue in youth, were written in these years. He died at Kirkcudbright in his elder brother's house, in 1852. William Mackenzie, his nephew, was born at Kirkcudbright, the son of John Mackenzie and Janet Kelly. He was educated at the Academy and then at Edinburgh University, was licensed to preach by the Presbytery of Kirkcudbright, and ordained in 1843. He was English master at Kirkcudbright Academy for many years and offered a prize for the best scholar in English there. Upon his retirement from the Academy, he became involved in the writing of *The History of Galloway*, whose

Dumfries and Galloway

publication involved him in bitter controversy with **John Nicholson,** the Kirkcudbright printer and publisher of the book. The controversy and the circumstances surrounding the composition of the work were documented by Mackenzie's brother, John Mackenzie, in his *Statement of Facts,* 1882, written to promote his brother's claim to be author of the book. According to John Mackenzie, the original invitation to write the work was given by John Nicholson to William Mackenzie senior, the writing master, at a regatta at Kirkcudbright in 1837. The elder Mackenzie declined, but the younger intervened, saying: "You do not ask me to do the work." Nicholson's original wish was simply for an introduction to a new edition of **Andrew Symson's** *Large Description of Galloway,* but Mackenzie persuaded him that a general history of the region would make Symson more intelligible to the reader and bring his work up to date. Although at first Nicholson pressed Mackenzie to insert his own name on the title page, it appears that this agreement was abandoned by Nicholson, and that Mackenzie had great difficulty in persuading him to accept his Foreword. Eventually, some accommodation was reached and an introduction was written by a mutual friend, but the controversy broke out afresh when a Dumfries newspaper mistakenly quoted Nicholson as the author, an impression which Nicholson did little to dispel. It appears that Mackenzie received only £20 for his literary efforts, despite the success of the book, and that payment was made only after the threat of legal action. His brother's *Statement of Facts* includes a variety of testimonies from correspondents of Mackenzie and from those who knew Nicholson, including his compositor, James Stewart, who wrote that he was "a man who is not competent to connect six words". That testimony was supported in the pamphlet by samples of Nicholson's prose, which included large numbers of spelling and grammatical mistakes. Nicholson's treatment of MacKenzie was said to have "embittered his existence" and he wrote to **Thomas Murray:** " I believe I am the only author of a history.. who was ever prohibited from writing his own preface. I wish, however, now to consign the misunderstanding to the 'tomb of all the Capulets'". Eventually, he was called to be minister at Skirling, under the patronage of Sir Thomas Carmichael. Like his uncle, he died unmarried, in 1854.

* * *

A Literary Guide

The elder Mackenzie composed a vast range of didactic works, including the *Outlines of Education, Notes on Philosophy, Morality and Education, Literary Varieties,* and *The Rustic Bower*, a series of inspiring and moral reflections derived from nature, all written at Castle Douglas. His *The Friend of Youth, The Young Man's Counsellor* and *The Sorrows of Seduction*, inspired by his long experience in the teaching profession, ran into several editions and attracted widespread notices in the Press. A sample of verse from the moral tale of *The Sorrows of Seduction* will suffice to show its quality: "Forbid, great God! That Vice, in Virtue's guise, / Should e'er unguarded Innocence surprise". It concludes with the sage reflection: "The joys of age from youth reflective flow, / Imprudent youth is an old age of woe". His nephew's work *The History of Galloway*, however, remains a serious and scholarly attempt to give an account of the role of Galloway in Scottish history, from prehistory to Mackenzie's own day, and is one of the few full-length histories of the area. The account begins classically with an account of the topography of Galloway and, although the early chapters dealing with the Celts and the Roman invasion of Scotland have now to be corrected and supplemented by the up-to-date information gleaned from archaeological findings not available in Mackenzie's day, the chapters describing the Galloway campaigns during the Wars of Independence, the role of the powerful Douglases, the impact of the defeat of Mary, Queen of Scots and of the 1715 and 1745 Rebellions, and the extensive account of the Covenanters, are still a useful introduction to the dramatic role played by Galloway in significant phases of Scottish history. The Appendix to volume II includes extracts from original documents, including witchcraft trials and accounts of smuggling in the Solway, as well as a list of artefacts belonging to the antiquary, **Joseph Train**, who, along with **James Murray Denniston**, had originally intended to write a Galloway history. Most significantly, the appendix includes the full text of the seventeenth century *Large Description of Galloway* by **Andrew Symson**, the reprinting of which had been the original object of John Nicholson's invitation to Mackenzie and which was dwarfed by his massive "introduction". Mackenzie also contributed to the *Statistical Account* for the parish of Kirkcudbright and wrote some poetry, including *Lines on Taking Leave of the Old Church of Kirkcudbright*, written on the occasion of his leaving for Skirling in 1838.

BIBLIOGRAPHY:
William Mackenzie senior: *The Sorrows of Seduction* (1806); *Notes on Philosophy, Morality and Education* (1822); *Outlines of Education* (1824); *Literary Varieties* (1837); *The Friend of Youth* (1843); *The Rustic Bower* (1844); *The Young Man's Counsellor* (1851)
William Mackenzie junior: *The History of Galloway, from the Earliest Period to the Present Time* (1841)

A Literary Guide

John Nicholson
1778-1866
Kirkcudbright

John Nicholson was among those printers and publishers who, in the history of Dumfries and Galloway, have done much to promote the publication of local literature. His "Historical and Traditional Tales in Prose and Verse, Connected with the South of Scotland" remains a classic selection. He was brother to the famous "Bard of Galloway", **William Nicholson.**

John Nicholson was born in Tongland in 1778, the son of James Nicholson and Barbara Houston. We know little of his education, but it may have been scanty, like his brother William's. He became apprenticed to Bailie Heron of New Galloway, father of **Robert Heron** , the historian, as a weaver. He left for Glasgow, where he was well regarded as a weaver, but when trade was depressed, he enlisted in the Guards. He left the army in the peace of 1814, and managed to avoid his regiment's involvement in the Battle of Waterloo. He recommenced weaving in Glasgow, but finding that machinery was affecting the trade of the hand-loom, and that he had injured his hand, he became a pedlar in Lanark, Ayr, Galloway and Dumfries, selling books and stationery. In 1820, he settled in Kirkcudbright as a printer and bookseller, probably in a close off the High Street. The most important book to issue from his press was *The History of Galloway*, the idea for which arose from Nicholson's wish to reissue **Andrew Symson's** *Large Description of Galloway* and for which he was seeking a new introduction. The publication had unhappy consequences, in that it was upon Nicholson's apparent unwillingness to acknowledge the real authorship of the **Rev William MacKenzie** that a great deal of controversy and bitterness ensued.

In the dispute which followed, supporters of MacKenzie's undoubtedly justified claim to be author claimed that Nicholson was barely literate and published samples of letters to prove their point. James Nicholson, on the other hand, who followed his father into the printing business, continued to allege that his father had collected all the material for the *History*. Nicholson's *Historical and Traditional Tales in Prose and Verse, Connected with the South of Scotland*, published in 1843, however, contain a number of short pieces by the "Editor", which would indicate that he had some skill and certainly a good deal of antiquarian interest in the history of the area. This is supported by the fact that he left a collection of relics, when he died, including a ring with a miniature of Bonnie Prince Charlie, allegedly presented to Flora MacDonald. From the advertisements in the front of the *Tales*, we learn that he had also published a *Coloured Atlas of Galloway, The Remains of the Rev. James Monteith, Minister of Borgue, 1693-1741* and an edition of *The Cherrie and the Slae*, supposed to be by **Alexander Montgomerie.** He also published from manuscripts *The Register of the Synod of Galloway* and *Minute Book kept by the War Committee of the Covenanters in the Stewartry of Kirkcudbright* belonging to Covenanting times, and issued, for a brief period of 9 years, a newspaper *The Stewartry Times*, for which his son James was chief reporter. The general pattern of his publications suggests a man with an interest in promoting the literature of Galloway, and with a certain pretension to a knowledge of it and of Galloway history.

* * *

The introduction, written by Nicholson, to *Historical and Traditional Tales* is a fascinating combination of lofty aims and commercial savoir-faire: he assures us that the tales have the ethnological intention of illustrating the Gallovidian social customs "in the privacy of their homes and their various social relations", thereby aiming to supplement *The History of Galloway*, for which, he says – in an uneasy reference to the saga of MacKenzie's authorship - "he had been at much labour and expense in collecting books, manuscripts &c". The range of material, he claims, offers even some "entertainment for the Sabbath", and is published at the lowest possible price to reach a wide audience. If that audience so desires, he says, a sequel could be published, since he has a "considerable

A Literary Guide

stock of matter still on hand". The book, which consists of selections from poetry, stories of the supernatural, Covenanting traditions, and folklore, gives a fascinating cross-section of popular writing current in Galloway in 1843. Nicholson's own contributions include two pieces on Cardoness Castle and Rusco Castle, on the martyrs of Kirkconnel, and on Rutherford's Three Witnesses, a choice of subjects with a moral and religious message which may justify **Alexander Trotter's** description of Nicholson as a man who acquired deep religious convictions during his apprenticeship with Bailie Heron. Among the authors he selected for his anthology, including **John Barbour, Robert Simpson, Edward Irving, Allan Cunningham, John MacTaggart, Joseph Train** and **William Nicholson,** his brother, are most of the prominent Galloway and Dumfriesshire authors of the time .

BIBLIOGRAPHY: *Historical and Traditional Tales in Prose and Verse, Connected with the South of Scotland* (1843) Published by John Nicholson - William Mackenzie, *The History of Galloway* (1841); Alexander Montgomerie, *The Cherrie and the Slae* (1842); *Minute Book Kept by the War Committee of the Covenanters in the Stewartry of Kirkcudbright, in the Years 1640 and 1641* (1855); *The Register of the Synod of Galloway, from 1664 to 1671* (1856)

PLACES TO VISIT: John Nicholson's tomb is in St. Cuthbert's churchyard, Kirkcudbright.

Thomas Douglas, 5th Earl of Selkirk 1771-1820
St. Mary's Isle, Kirkcudbright

Thomas Douglas, seventh son of the Earl of Selkirk and member of a prominent Parliamentary and landowning family, inherited his father's and eldest brother's political concerns and devoted himself to the pressing problem of Highland emigrations. His solution to the crisis was to settle three colonies of Highlanders in western Canada, and thereby he came to found part of Manitoba and Prince Edward's Island. His schemes had varying success, and his name is still both revered and reviled in the history of Canadian settlement.

Thomas Douglas was born at the family mansion of St Mary's Isle, outside Kirkcudbright, and was the son of the Earl of Selkirk, who had formed the object of John Paul Jones' notorious raid on the Kirkcudbright coast. His family were noted for their liberal sympathies with the cause of Parliamentary reform, his brother going so far as to be outlawed by the British government for his radical sympathies during the French Revolution. Douglas was educated at Edinburgh University between 1786 and 1790, where he too became a member of a liberal political club, "The Club", of which many members were to become leading lights in the literature and politics of their generation. Among others, Douglas met and befriended Walter Scott, Adam Fergusson and Francis Jeffrey. He studied ethics under the famous Dugald Stewart (who, with his class, was at a future date to seek refuge at St Mary's Isle from an epidemic raging in Edinburgh) and Scots Law under David Hume, with Scott as his class mate. He took a Grand Tour of the Continent and met and made friends with Talleyrand, and stayed with Sir William

A Literary Guide

Hamilton in Italy. At home on the estate, he took a lively interest in agricultural improvement, especially in tree-planting. He unexpectedly inherited the family title in 1799, after the successive deaths of his seven brothers. He had taken an interest in the plight of the Highlands, where the collapse of the feudal clan system, in the wake of the crushing of the 1745 Rebellion, had intensified the economic pressures towards the enclosure of land and eviction of tenants. In 1792, he took a tour of the Highlands, making meticulous notes on what he found , which he later worked up into his classic *Observations on the Present State of the Highlands of Scotland, with a View of the Causes and Probable Consequences of Emigration* (1805). He was deeply sympathetic to the plight of the Highlanders (himself learning Gaelic early in his life), but felt that various pressures made emigration unavoidable and that what was required was for the unorganised trend to become an organised planting of colonists in British territories. During the Napoleonic Wars, he was putting together plans for an expedition, but the times were not ripe for proposing emigration to a government keen to recruit Highland soldiers. During the Irish rebellion, he made a tour of the country and put proposals to the Foreign Office for an Irish colony, an idea which was frostily received in official quarters. His attention was no doubt turned towards Canada, since he had inherited some lands in upper Canada (now Ontario). His first choice was the Red River valley in the Hudson Bay Company's territory, which was fertile and not settled, but the Government, while giving him encouragement to act on his own initiative, did not take up his suggestion. He was eventually advised to adopt a maritime situation, and chose St John's Island, now Prince Edward's Island. In 1803, his agents had gathered together 800 Highland emigrants and they left Britain just as war with Napoleon was reviving, a fact which his enemies were later to use against him. He himself made an extensive tour of the northern United States and Canada, and on his return found that the colonists, despite a winter of misery, had begun to thrive and harvest crops. At about the same time, he had established a colony in Kent County in Upper Canada, which he called "Baldoon" after part of his Wigtownshire estate. This was to be established as a farming community, with the home farm a model of improved agricultural technique. Unfortunately, the experiment foundered, since the lands were low-lying and mosquito-ridden, and most colonists succumbed to malaria, while others were attacked during hostilities with the Americans during the 1812 War. The costs of the Baldoon experiment came near to ruining the Earl, but, although the colony failed, some settlers clung on and eventually established farms, in what is now one of the most fertile farming areas of Canada. In 1806 and 1807, he was chosen as one of the Scottish peers for the House of Lords, and this enabled him to develop other political interests: these included Parliamentary reform, national defence, the abolition of the slave trade, and Spanish colonies in South America. In 1809, he wrote a pamphlet on Parliamentary Reform, which adopts a position of moderate Conservatism, showing that his American tour had disillusioned him with the traditionally democratic leanings of his family. He was elected Lord Lieutenant of the Stewartry of Kirkcudbright in 1807, married into a wealthy Conservative family, the Wedderburn Colvilles, and was elected, in 1808, a Fellow of the Royal Society. He was still cherishing his original proposal to colonise the Red River valley and in 1810 he took advantage of a radical fall in the value of Hudson Bay Company stock to acquire a dominant interest in the company, which he then persuaded, in 1811, to grant a huge tract of land, measuring some 45 million acres, in the area now comprising Manitoba and Minnesota. Immediately, there were signs of opposition, which were to imperil the new venture's existence and ultimately to break the Earl's health and spirit. The North West Fur company contested the right of the Hudson Bay company to make the grant, but the expedition, consisting largely of unmarried pioneers, set out nonetheless from Stornoway in 1811, under the command of Miles MacDonell, a soldier who had impressed Selkirk when he met him on his tour of America. After a hard winter, the colonists began building Forts Douglas and Daer, named in honour of Selkirk's family, in 1812-13. The foundation was dogged by hostility of the North West Fur Company, and by apathy and even fraud on the part of Selkirk's agents. Although progress was being made in the establishment of agriculture in the colony, things came to a head when MacDonell declared himself governor and, by 1815, had escalated into a full military engagement. After the colonists' defeat, there was hope that they would be allowed to stay on, but they received an order to leave, and the colony seemed to have been destroyed. More recruits arrived from Scotland, and an attempt was made to re-establish it, under the supervision of Governor Semple, who had been appointed

A Literary Guide

by Selkirk. In retaliation for the destruction of the forts belonging to the North West Fur Company, however, Governor Semple and his attendants were killed by a detachment approaching Fort Douglas. At the time of this second threatened extinction of his colony, the Earl of Selkirk and his long-suffering wife themselves arrived in America, where the Earl spent some time collecting legal evidence against the Fur Company, which was later published as *A Sketch of the British Fur Trade in North America* (1816). The Earl headed north with a troop of disbanded soldiers from the American war. Upon hearing of the outrage practised upon Governor Semple, the Earl sailed for Fort William, headquarters of the North West Fur Company, and seized its inmates. In the following year, he re-established Fort Douglas, made peace with local native Indians, and named the colony "Kildonan". He was, however, forced to pay a hefty fine for damaging the interests of the fur company, and on his return to England, launched a campaign against the miscarriage of justice in the Canadian courts, where, it emerged, North West Fur Company partners were acting as jurors and some of their families were linked to judges. Selkirk's health was broken by his long struggle and he retired to southern France, suffering from consumption, where he died in 1820, at Pau. Almost immediately after his death, the two fur companies amalgamated and peace was established in the province; the immediate past was forgotten, as was Selkirk's name, which was represented only in townships named by or after him. Owing to his rage for colonising, his estate was in debt to the tune of £160,000.

* * *

Selkirk's chief work, which became known simply as *Selkirk on Emigration*, gave rise to a wide variety of opinion among his contemporaries. Sir Walter Scott, who referred to Selkirk as the most disinterested and generous man he had ever known, stated in *Waverley* that Selkirk's was an entirely accurate account of the changes in Highland society and land tenure. In the *Edinburgh Review*, it was noted that Selkirk (who was acquainted with the works of Malthus, and classical economists) had addressed a complex part of political economy, where "the theory of wealth and the theory of population are examined in connection". The book is a model of lucid and reasoned prose, typical of Selkirk's approach, and reveals a mixture of romantic nostalgia for the

Highland way of life, which was being irretrievably lost, and of arguments from political and economic self-interest: for example, arguing against the Highland Society's opposition to emigration, he wrote that the capital apparently lost to Scotland through emigration could be recouped as "the forests of the colonies are brought into a productive state, the markets of Great Britain supplied with various articles of value, and the consumption of her manufactures extended". The Highlanders, distinct in culture and language, Selkirk reasoned, could act as a bulwark against American encroachment. It is interesting that the Highland Society's wishes and government concerns about Highland depopulation were ultimately addressed in an entirely different way, by the road and harbour-building programmes managed by **Thomas Telford**, and the use of Highland labour to carry out these massive public works, something Selkirk deemed to be impossible. Nonetheless, Selkirk's description of the condition of the Highlands demonstrates a historical sensibility to the uniqueness of its culture and to the new stresses to which it was subject, owing to enclosure. Writing of the destruction of the feudal dependency on the clan chief, he said that the inhabitants "are not yet accustomed to the habits of a commercial society, to the coldness which must be expected by those whose intercourse with their superiors is confined to the daily exchange of labour for its stipulated reward". He concluded the book with a modest assessment of the success of his colony on Prince Edward's Island, noting that the settlers were organised in small family groups, in order to echo their pattern of life in the Highland crofting communities. The description of his welcome, when visiting their makeshift wigwams during the first winter, sounds like the description of the arrival of a Highland chieftain amongst his loyal clanspeople. Selkirk's controversy with the North West Fur Company, which he exposed in *A Sketch of the British Fur Trade in North America*, led to a flurry of vituperative literature by Company partisans, including *A Narrative of Occurrences in the Indian Countries of North America since the Connexion of the Rt. Hon. the Earl of Selkirk with the Hudson's Bay Company*, by SH Wilcocke. Selkirk's other writings concerned his reasons for abandoning the cause of Parliamentary Reform - the *Letter to John Cartwright Esq* – and a pamphlet recommending the improvement of national defence by the institution of a system of local militias.

A Literary Guide

BIBLIOGRAPHY: *Observations on the Present State of the Highlands of Scotland, with a View of the Causes and Probable Consequences of Emigration* (1805); *On the Necessity of a More Effectual System of National Defence* (1808); *A Letter to John Cartwright Esq. on Parliamentary Reform* (1809); *A Sketch of the British Fur Trade in North America* (1816); S.H. Wilcocke, *A Narrative of Occurrences in the Indian Countries of North America since the Connexion of the Rt. Hon. the Earl of Selkirk with the Hudson's Bay Company* (1817)

PLACES TO VISIT: The Selkirk memorial in the centre of Kirkcudbright is to the 5th Earl's elder brother. St Mary's Isle was burnt to the ground in 1940.

Alexander Montgomerie
1555?-1597
Cumstoun, near Kirkcudbright

Alexander Montgomerie was one of the most prominent of the "Castalian" group of poets, formed by the young King James VI of Scotland to experiment with new forms and revive vernacular poetry. Despite his prominence as a poet, little reliable detail has come down to us about his life, but a persistent tradition associates him with the Cumstoun (or Compston) estate, near the junction of the Dee and the Tarff outside Kirkcudbright.

Timothy Pont, the cartographer, records that Montgomerie was born at Hazelhead (Hessilheid) Castle, Ayrshire, of a cadet branch of the powerful Eglinton family. **Andrew Symson,** perhaps 80 years after Montgomerie's death, records the tradition which associates him with Cumstoun: "I have heard it reported, (how true I know not) that it was this place, and the situation thereof, which contributed towards the quickening of Captain Alexander Montgomerie, his fancie, when he composed the poem intituled *The Cherrie and the Slae*". Other traditions associate him with Argyll and the Highlands. He received early tokens of favour from James VI , perhaps owing to a kinship through his mother, Lady Margaret Fraser, and three of his poems receive favourable mention in the king's *Rewlis and Cautelis* of 1584, intended to set a poetic canon for a revival in Scottish literature. Montgomerie's Catholic faith, however, meant that his career was bound up with the complex religious politics of his day. He travelled abroad, perhaps with the object of giving covert support to Philip of Spain, and was imprisoned in England after being found on board a ship manned by Scottish soldiers. A pension received from James VI had by this time been alienated to someone else and the bitterness of his involvement in a lengthy law suit finds frequent poetic utterance in later works. In the probable year of his death, he was found guilty of treason for involvement in a Catholic invasion plot, but was posthumously pardoned by James, who wrote a touching epitaph for the poet and permitted him to be buried in consecrated ground.

A Literary Guide

* * *

The Cherrie and the Slae, a long allegorical poem, consists of a contest between personified faculties of the narrator's mind, in which Hope, Courage and Will urge him to strive for the "Cherry", whose sweet fruits are suspended over a dangerous precipice and can only be won by effort, while Dread, Danger and Despair tempt him to be content with the lowly sloe, which is near at hand, but whose fruits are bitter. The allegory has often been interpreted biographically, as referring to a mistress whose station and abilities exalted her beyond the poet's reach; however, the allegory, performed in front of a sophisticated Court audience, is many-layered and may contain arguments aimed at persuading James VI not to abandon Catholicism. Certainly, the sheer virtuosity of the performance, sustained over 114 stanzas, composed in a form which may have been Montgomerie's own invention, was aimed at stimulating and flattering the abilities of an audience appreciative of argument, metrical brilliance, and alliterative inventiveness. The early part of the poem, which may have been composed some time before the later and more moralising sections, includes charming descriptions of the birds and animals "..skipping and tripping, / They plaid them all in paires" and of the river supposed to be located at Cumstoun: "I saw an river rin / Out ouir ane cragge rok of stane / Syne lichtit in ane lin, / With tumbling and rumbling / Amang the rochis round, / Devalling and falling / Into that pit profound". It is now appreciated that such works, like Montgomerie's other stylised polemic or "Flyting" with a fellow poet, Polwart, are best seen as having been performed as drama or even sung to music.

BIBLIOGRAPHY:
The Cherrie and the Slae (1597); H Harvey Wood, ed., *The Cherrie and the Slae* (1937); (David Irving, ed., *The Poems of Alexander Montgomery* (1821); James Cranstoun, ed., *Poems of Alexander Montgomerie* (1887); RDS Jack and P Rozendaal, ed., *The Mercat Anthology of Early Scottish Literature 1375-1707* (1997) includes the full text of *The Cherrie and the Slae*

PLACES TO VISIT: The Dee at Cumstoun is best viewed from the Tongland Bridge (constructed by **Thomas Telford**); the ruins of Cumstoun Castle are private.

John MacTaggart
1791-1830
Borgue

Born at Lennox Plunton, near Borgue, John MacTaggart is probably the most Gallovidian of all Galloway authors; his extraordinary "Scottish Gallovidian Encyclopaedia" has been well referred to as a "literary haggis" with its variegated and vigorous sketches of eccentric characters, unusual Galloway words (many of which were thus rescued from oblivion), poems, tales, traditions, antiquities and natural phenomena. The "Encyclopaedia" has borne out its author's confidence that, although the book " will never create much noise, yet it will not be in a hurry forgotten".

The best source for MacTaggart's biography is his characteristic entry for himself in his *Encyclopaedia*. He was born, the third of eleven children, in the shadow of Plunton Castle, at a farmhouse now entirely replaced by a more modern structure. His father rented the farm from the Murrays of Broughton; his mother had been a pupil of **Robert Heron,** as he describes under Heron's entry in the *Encyclopaedia*. He was taught at home and "lashed occasionally" by a tutor hired, as was usual, by a group of farmers who shared the costs of tuition; then he attended Borgue Academy, where the lashings became so frequent that he claims he was saved from danger to his life only when his father moved to a farm at Torrs. He attended a local school there, where a milder regime predominated and where he began to display an aptitude for arithmetic, and then attended Kirkcudbright Academy. He developed an aversion to formal methods of teaching, failing to learn French at school, which he afterwards learnt to speak fluently – along with some German – by himself. Since he had no liking for farm-work, he applied to become a printer, while educating himself by borrowing the *Encyclopaedia Britannica*. At 19, he began attending Edinburgh University, for classes in mathematics and physical sciences, but claimed "I never received any good from attending the University". He left and returned home to help on the land, but continued to pursue his literary interests, composing a

A Literary Guide

poem to celebrate his majority entitled *Mac is Major*, where his characteristically robust and fearless disposition is celebrated: "Nae cringing, nae whinging / Shall ever come frae me/ Nor fawning, nor yawning / My stars have born me free". It was at this point that he composed the *Encyclopaedia*, which he says was concocted "while at my rural employment, and wrote down on scraps of paper". After its publication, which caused a scandal, he set off for London (he had already visited England and parts of northern Scotland) and attempted, with the support of **Allan Cunningham** and **John Mayne**, to start a weekly newspaper *The London Scotchman*, which survived only briefly. He continued to publish poetry : his *Address to the Scotch Folk in London* ("How chirt ye on throu' life ava', / In this tremendous clachan") appeared in the *European Magazine* of 1823 and his *Mary Lee's Lament* was later quoted by Charlotte Bronte in *Shirley*. He also appears to have been at work on a comedy *Look out for Squalls*. In London, he familiarised himself with the millwright's trade and with engineering; he superintended the gas-lighting of Plymouth and found a post in France with a gas company. Ultimately, the engineer John Rennie, whose acquaintance he had made in London or possibly Plymouth (though one wonders, since Rennie had been active in designing the Ken Bridge at New Galloway, the Cree bridge at Newton Stewart, to say nothing of Portpatrick and Stranraer harbours, whether they had not met in Galloway) recommended him for a post as clerk of works on the Rideau Canal project, which was to provide a military supply route from Ottawa river to Lake Ontario, across 160 miles of unreclaimed wilderness. MacTaggart was subordinate to Colonel By, after whom Bytown, later Ottawa, was named, and who was deeply impressed with MacTaggart's engineering skills. He also renewed the acquaintance of the Ayrshire writer, John Galt, who was one of the founders of the Canada Company and with whose pawky humour he no doubt felt a literary fellowship. MacTaggart published many letters in Canadian newspapers, including his humorous advice to potential emigrants "Sax months here are frost and snaw/Up to the oxters wading,/But what o' that! Success to sleighs / To fun and cavalcading". He made excursions to the interior and visited Niagara Falls. In 1828, he contracted a fever and returned to England; his intended fiancée, a Miss Gray, died on board ship. On his return, he published *Three Years in Canada: an Account of the Actual State of the Country in 1826-7-8.*

He sent a set of these volumes with a friendly greeting to **Allan Cunningham**. His health, however, had not recovered from the illness contracted in Canada, and he died at Torrs of a pulmonary condition, at the early age of 39. He had apparently intended further publications, which, one may regret, never saw the light of day: an Encyclopaedia for Canada, a collection of French Voyagers' songs, and a history of explorers. He left an unfinished poem, *The Engineer*, which was given by **Malcolm Harper** to the Stewartry Museum in 1880.

* * *

The *Scottish Gallovidian Encyclopaedia* owes its curious blend of the scientific with the folkloric to two different literary currents which MacTaggart inherited and combined: first, he has a place within the lexicographic tradition of Dr. Johnson's famous and idiosyncratic *Dictionary* and Dr. Jamieson's *Scots Dictionary*, and secondly, he was writing in a context of the revived interest in the Scots vernacular, promoted and exemplified most notably by **Burns.** He also acknowledged the influence of the regional literary tradition, including **Allan Cunningham, William Nicholson,** Peden's Prophecies, and **Rutherford's** Letters. His sharpness of observation for "every curious thing belonging to my native country", his relish for the vigour of Galloway dialect and his fearless judgements on contemporaries combine to give the *Encyclopaedia* its characteristic and robust flavour. For example, **John Lowe** and **John Gerrond** "the Gow" are given short shrift, both personally and artistically, but there are characteristically warm appreciations of **John Mayne, Allan Cunningham,** and **William Nicholson.** Unfortunately, his frankness went so far as to injure the good name of a Miss Heron, "The Star of Dungyle", whose father threatened legal action unless the book were suppressed. MacTaggart was obliged to consent, and letters of his in the possession of the Stewartry Museum in Kirkcudbright show that he regretted his indiscretion as a "slip of my better sense" and was aware that at home he had caused distress to his father; he confessed that some of the "fiery natures ..are determined on blowing out my brains". Characteristically, he declares that Mac "may <u>regret</u>, but never will <u>quake</u>". Apart from the biographical entries, there are memorable items on , to name but a few, the eating of "braxy hams", the "Cleppie Bells" of Wigtown, on the Fyke's Fair at Auchencairn, and on children's

A Literary Guide

games, superstitions or "freets", and on now obsolete agricultural terms. As a result of the book's withdrawal from circulation, it became a collector's item (it was one of **Joseph Train's** favourite books); a small run of 250 copies was issued in 1876, but only in 1979 was a larger run reprinted. In comparison, the *Three Years in Canada* is a more classic and restrained work, with accounts of natural phenomena, of his trip to Niagara Falls, of encounters with characters, and advice to potential emigrants. MacTaggart's unpublished and unfinished poem, *The Engineer*, perhaps surprisingly for the author of the *Encylopaedia*, is written wholly in classical literary English, and lacks the vigour of his Scots poetry, but is interesting for its attempt to provide a versified history of engineering from Biblical and classical times, through to the contributions of great explorers, cathedral builders, road builders and cosmologists. Both Rennie and **Telford** "plotting and profound / [Who] With his canals a kingdom great can cleave" are singled out for their contribution to engineering. It is clear that here "engineering" stands for the essentially human act of intervention, which, according to classic Enlightenment thinking, brings civilisation and order to wildernesses and lifts the life of man above the animal.

BIBLIOGRAPHY:
The Scottish Gallovidian Encyclopaedia, or, the Original, Antiquated, and Natural Curiosities of the South of Scotland (1824); *Three Years in Canada: an Account of the Actual State of the Country in 1826-7-8* (1829)

PLACES TO VISIT: The Stewartry Museum holds an important collection of material about MacTaggart.

William Nicholson
1783-1854
Borgue

William Nicholson, packman and poet, was known simply as the "Bard of Galloway": he deserves the title not only for his subject matter, or his undoubted devotion to its countryside, but for his use of its living language. His poetry, composed for recitation and singing, includes the "Brownie of Blednoch", a classic in Scots verse, which has won comparison with "Tam o' Shanter" for its universal treatment of local traditions of the supernatural.

William Nicholson was born at Tannymaas, near Borgue, in 1783. His father, James Nicholson, was a carrier, a small farmer, and lastly, a publican at what became the village of Ringford. His mother, Barbara Houston of Borgue, had a store of songs and stories, and knew poetry by Ramsay and **Burns**. William Nicholson was the youngest of eight children, one of whom, his elder brother, **John Nicholson**, became the Kirkcudbright printer and publisher. When the family moved to Barncrosh, Nicholson attended the parish school at Ringford, but was ill-fitted to school routine. Although at school he barely learnt to read and count, beyond the narrow confines of its discipline he apparently read songs, ballads and penny histories; he probably began composing and picking up songs early in his career. Because of his short-sightedness, he was not suited to farm-work, and it was decided that he would "carry the pack". He stocked it with combs, thimbles, and also added fabrics and "gown-pieces" and became a popular figure throughout Ayrshire and Galloway, particularly when, after the age of 20, he acquired a pair of pipes on which he could perform for

A Literary Guide

dances and songs. Although he prospered for a while, and was able to lay out a sum on a larger stock, in 1812 he suffered various misfortunes, including the loss of his horse, which broke its neck. In 1813, he closed his business and decided what "prenting a book wad do for him". It seems that he consulted **Alexander Murray,** then minister of Urr (on the occasion of whose death he later wrote a poem), and **Dr Henry Duncan** of Ruthwell. Murray suggested that he add to his collection of verse a longer tale, and this was the origin of the *Country Lass*. It is a credit to his popularity and persistence that he was able to collect the names of 1500 subscribers. Nicholson himself records that James Hogg helped him when he arrived in Edinburgh "almost friendless and unknown", and it is said that Hogg may have altered four lines of the *Country Lass*. Nicholson set off from Edinburgh with the books in his pack, "delivering the copies and hauling in the siller", and was so successful that he paid off his debt and was able to re-stock his pack. Unfortunately, however, the taste of success may have also given him the opportunity to drink, and although he kept up his peddling until 1825, he began increasingly to experience hallucinations and felt that he was chosen to preach the doctrine of Universal Redemption. Inspired by his visions, of which his biographer, **John McDiarmid,** gives rather a mischievous account, he went to London, to speak to the king about political and religious matters. In London, as McDiarmid describes, he was "terribly bombazed with the interminable streets and the mighty tide of population which caught his eye". After various misadventures, he met **Allan Cunningham,** who fed him and put him in contact with a colony of Dumfriesshire and Galloway exiles. Since he was at risk in London from those who might prey upon his bemused condition, his fellow Scots obtained a passage for him, aboard a smack bound for Leith. He used the delay before sailing to try to gain access to the king, and even managed to get so far as to send in a letter, along with a copy of his poems. Eventually, he reached Dumfriesshire and home in 1826. His later adventures, however, were no happier, since he was robbed of his bagpipes on a journey south in 1827, narrowly escaped drowning in a canal, and had to be sent back home, again by exiled Scots, to Kirkcudbright. Several of those who appreciated his worth as a poet suggested that he print a new edition of his poems, and this was edited by **John McDiarmid,** editor of the Courier, who composed the *Memoir.* We know little of his last years, but he may have fallen on hard times, despite the praise of reviewers and his undoubted personal popularity. When he died in 1854 - and there is some dispute about where he did – his brother **John Nicholson** erected a family tombstone at Kirkandrews, inscribing for his brother the line: "No future age shall see his name expire". Fifty years after his death, influential writers and painters, including **Malcolm Harper** (who edited a new edition of the poems in 1878), Thomas Fraser, the publisher, William MacGeorge, William Mouncey and EA Hornel (who was later to paint his "Brownie of Bladnoch") , sponsored a memorial to his memory, in Borgue.

* * *

Several editions of Nicholson's work exist : the first volume of his poems appeared in 1814 as *Tales in Verse and Miscellaneous Poems: Descriptive of Rural Life and Manners*. In 1825, the famous *Brownie of Blednoch* appeared in the *Dumfries Monthly Magazine* and won critical acclaim from John McDiarmid, Dr John Brown in his *Horae Subsecivae*, and even from **John MacTaggart** in his *Scottish Gallovidian Encyclopaedia* entry under "Wull Nicholson, the 'Poet'". The 1828 edition was edited with a Memoir by **John McDiarmid** of the *Dumfries Courier* ; **Malcolm Harper** brought out a new edition in 1878 and again in 1898. Recently, when Nicholson's reputation has seen some considerable reconstruction, a new edition of the poems has been issued, including some previously unpublished material. Nicholson's poetry ranges in density of language from classical poetic English, to a polite Scots and finally to a full Galloway dialect. Perhaps because he himself was part of the oral tradition, he is able to write in the vernacular without seeming to be overshadowed by Burns. *The Brownie of Blednoch* appeals to local traditions of "brownies", goblin-like beings, who would work tirelessly for human beings on farms in exchange for their keep. The sole rule of protocol with respect to a brownie was not to leave for him a gift of second-hand clothes. To a public whose folk-memory had been re-awakened and perhaps re-shaped by *Tam o Shanter*, the *Brownie* offered the frisson of the supernatural, combined with shrewd sketches of character, as in the case of the canny good-wife, who realises the value of Aiken-drum's labour. Throughout, neither the tension, nor the economy and richness of the language articulating it, falters: "His matted head on his breast did rest, / A lang blue beard wan'ered down like a vest; But the glare o' his e'e nae bard hath exprest, / Nor the skimes of Aiken-drum". His longer poem *The Country Lass* shows Nicholson in a different mood, able to weave between the comedy of Bess's unsuitable suitors, the near-tragedy of Sandy's disappointment and then suddenly to move to a different plane and conclude philosophically: "There's nane exempt frae life's cares, / And few frae some domestic jars; / A' whiles are in and whiles are out, / For grief and joy come time about." Despite the claim Nicholson is once alleged to have made, that the fault of his poetry was that it had no moral, in fact, it is one of his gifts to make a whole chain of deductions from an apparently trivial beginning: for example, his *To Tobacco* – "Foul fa' thee, vile unchancie docken, / That e'er thou set thy neb in Scotlan'; For now, 'tween sneezin', chowin', smokin', / There's few are free;" – goes on to speculate, serio-comically, on the causes of Scotland's degeneracy.

BIBLIOGRAPHY:
Tales, in Verse, and Miscellaneous Poems: Descriptive of Rural Life and Manners (1814); John McDiarmid, ed., *Tales in Verse, and Miscellaneous Poems ...with a Memoir of the Author* (1828); Malcolm McL Harper, ed., *The Poetical Works of William Nicholson* (1878); John Hudson, ed., *The Collected Poems of William Nicholson* (1999)

PLACES TO VISIT: The memorial sculpture in Nicholson's memory is located at Borgue school; his tombstone may be seen at Kirkandrews.

Thomas Murray
1792-1872
Gatehouse of Fleet

Thomas Murray, born near Gatehouse of Fleet, made the sole systematic attempt to give a literary identity to Galloway, by tracing its literary traditions across the centuries. Murray lived in an era when regional identity in Scotland was felt and mattered more than it does today, and his own sustained loyalty to Galloway throughout his life made the task of a literary biography of its natives a pressing and appropriate one.

Thomas Murray was born at Bush, a clachan now obliterated, but standing about 300 yards south of Girthon Manse, outside Gatehouse of Fleet. His father worked on the Cally estate, but was tragically killed by a cannon fired on the occasion of the Cally heir's coming-of-age. Thereafter, the laird felt obliged to contribute to the education of Thomas Murray and his brother. At first, he attended a school at Girthon kirk and then a seminary at Gatehouse. In 1807, he opened his own school in Gatehouse, in order to save funds for a place at college in Edinburgh. In 1809, he was teaching at a subscription school near Tongland, and also at Buittle. With some help from the factor on the Broughton and Cally estates, he set off for Edinburgh in 1810; at Moffat, he met another scholar proceeding on foot to Edinburgh - the 15 year old **Thomas Carlyle**, who had begun studies at Edinburgh in 1809. He was to become well acquainted with Carlyle during the Edinburgh years and must have forecast a great future for his fellow student, since Carlyle replies in 1814 "Ah Tam! What a foolish flattering creature thou art to talk of future eminence in connection with the literary history of the nineteenth century!". He also met **Alexander Murray**, the linguist, on his return from college in 1811, when Murray had been engaged as minister in the neighbouring parish of Urr, and discussed literature and the doctrine of predestination with him. At about this time, he contributed an article on the historian **Robert Heron** to the *Dumfries Courier*. He was eventually licensed to preach, but though he did preach occasionally, like Carlyle, he began a career in private teaching. Both men at this time met **Stewart Lewis**, the poet and author of *Fair Helen of Kirkconnel Lea*. He made the acquaintance of another Gallovidian, the political economist **John Ramsay McCulloch,** of Whithorn and Glasserton, which was to prove a useful connection once McCulloch became Comptroller of the Stationery Office. Murray shared McCulloch's interests in political economy, and had already contributed to David Brewster's *Cyclopaedia*. Though he did not manage to succeed to McCulloch's chair in Edinburgh, he did receive an invitation to lecture on political economy in the United States and , as a result, saved sufficient money to start a publishing and printing business, Murray and Gibb. It was while he was in this business that McCulloch's Stationery Office contracts proved material to his success. In 1822, he published his most important work *The Literary History of Galloway*, which attracted the pithy comment of his contemporary, **John MacTaggart** , who wrote in his *Encyclopaedia*: "I only think it a pity he paid so much attention to a subject not worth the paying attention to". In 1828, he wrote his *Life of Samuel Rutherford*, an expansion on his entry in *The Literary History* and had already, in 1827, edited Rutherford's account of John, first Viscount Kenmure. He also edited letters of Archbishop Leighton, and of David Hume. He left an account, with an autobiographical notice, of his trip to London in 1840, when he visited **McCulloch** and **Carlyle**, who, rather uncharitably, found him "worldly, egoistic, small, vain, a poor grub, in whom, perhaps, was still some remnant of better instincts, whom one could not look at without impressive reminiscences" Throughout his life he maintained his Galloway connections and did his best to foster the careers of young Gallovidians, such as **Dr Robert Trotter** of Dalry. He was secretary to the committee for the erection of a monument to **Alexander Murray** in 1833, contributed to the Statistical Account for Girthon and Anwoth, and was an early Committee member of the Edinburgh Galloway Association, founded in 1842; **JR McCulloch** was vice-President. In Edinburgh, he was Secretary of the Edinburgh School of Arts, later the Heriot Watt College and a portrait of him hangs in the Principal's room; he joined Edinburgh Town Council and wrote a history of Colinton. He died at Lasswade, near Edinburgh, aged 80, in 1872 and was interred at Leith; his wife, who was a native of Newton Stewart, survived him until 1888.

Undoubtedly, of Murray's several works, his greatest contribution was his *Literary History of Galloway*. His connexions and disposition gave him the opportunity to meet many of the literary men of his generation; in his account of his journey to London in 1840, he describes his habit of associating landscapes with the great writers who had lived amongst them. Perhaps surprisingly in view of this, his first edition contains a high concentration of entries about post – Reformation ministers, and comparatively few entries relating to his contemporaries, about whom his personal testimony would have been uniquely interesting. He therefore fell foul of MacTaggart's strictures concerning his undue interest in obscure "priests". The second edition, however, completed in 1832, was, he claimed, almost a new book and contained 19 new entries, including **MacTaggart** himself, **the Earl of Selkirk, Professor Thomas Brown** and **Alexander Murray.** The interest of his accounts tend to centre on the biographical information he preserves – and are still invaluable contemporary records for many authors' biographies – rather than on any critical analysis of the texts. Unfortunately for posterity, he did not record details of his friendship with Carlyle and reserved his account of the life of JR McCulloch for the pages of his *Journey to London in 1840*, published long after his death in 1911.

BIBLIOGRAPHY:
The Literary History of Galloway (1822, 2nd ed. 1832); *The Life of Samuel Rutherford* (1828); *Life of Robert Leighton, DD* (1828); *Letters of David Hume* (1841); *Autobiographical Notes, also Reminiscences of a Journey to London in 1840* (1911)

A Literary Guide

Captain James Murray Denniston
1770-1852
Gatehouse of Fleet, Creetown

James Murray Denniston belonged to a family which had at one time farmed Rusco and remained in the vicinity of Gatehouse of Fleet, having connections with the Murrays of Broughton and Cally. Denniston was a collector of traditions and tales with a local setting, but his best work is his poem "The Battle of Craignilder", which consists of a vigorous and atmospheric description of the battle between the Black Douglases and the Gordons at Machermore, near what is now Newton Stewart.

James Murray Denniston was descended from a family which had occupied Rusco for many centuries and who feature in one of **Nicholson's** *Historical and Traditional Tales...* in a story of the sixteenth century. Though intermarried with the Murrays of Broughton, the Dennistons had fallen on harder times and James's father had become apprenticed as a tailor in Gatehouse of Fleet. He married the daughter of a minister at Balmaghie, a Miss McKie, and their only son was James Murray Denniston. He was educated at the parish school of Girthon, and became a good classical scholar. He assisted his father in his trade, tried the profession of solicitor at Kirkcudbright, and then entered into partnership in a cotton milling enterprise at Creetown. Although this enterprise failed, while at Creetown he had impressed Mr Stewart of Cairnsmore with his performance of his duties as Town Clerk and JP, and as a result obtained a commission in the Galloway Militia through his influence. He studied at Glasgow University and joined the radical "University Literary Association", where he wrote and recited a radical political poem on the French Revolution. During the Irish rebellion of 1798, he collected rents due to the Murrays from their Irish estates and, in the French wars, he was promoted to adjutant, being known thereafter as "Captain" Denniston. While stationed in Edinburgh, he met Sir Walter Scott, through **Joseph Train**, in whom he had discovered a fellow enthusiast for Galloway traditions. Lockhart reports that Train and Denniston were engaged in composing a history of Galloway, for which Scott was to contribute some financial help, but this was never completed. Denniston certainly helped to identify many of the sites in Scott's *Guy Mannering* with their Galloway originals: "Kippletringan" is Gatehouse; "Port an Ferry" is Creetown; "Ellangowan" is Barholm and "Woodburn" is Cassencary. Denniston also frequently met James Hogg and also saw **Robert Burns** standing at the door of the principal hostelry in Gatehouse. He was also known to **Robert Trotter** (senior), himself a resident of Creetown at one time, and he recorded some of the many comic anecdotes which survive about the Captain. Denniston married a wife much younger than himself, but divorced her after some scandal. He was a welcome visitor in the homes of the aristocracy, many of whose traditions feature in his stories, and he was a keen amateur actor when performances were laid on for charitable purposes. He was Deputy Steward Clerk for the lower district of the Stewartry and a pious member of the Established Church. In 1857, he died and was interred in the family plot at Anwoth churchyard.

* * *

Denniston's best work is his narrative poem *The Battle of Craignilder* (1832), which he asserts was recited to him by a Mrs Heron of Creebridge, only claiming that "where a stanza was limping about in a mutilated state, we may have occasionally supplied it with a leg or two; perhaps a crutch might have been a more or less proper designation". In fact, the claim to be editor of ancient material rather than the author of an original work, was a characteristic move in the Romantic literature of the time, common to Scott and **Cunningham,** whose folkloric and antiquarian enthusiasms he shared. Denniston gives a description of his method in collecting and reworking legends in the introduction to his unpublished *The Seige* [sic] *of Cragg Tumble*: "I at once resolved upon making a personal inspection of its localities and obtaining such information as I could regarding it from old inhabitants, who resided in this vicinity, as well as gathering whatever traditions might still be lingering in the country, respecting its more prosperous days". The battle centred around the harrying of Machermore by Archibald Douglas of Threave and there is a fast-moving and atmospheric description of the summoning of the local lords and their retainers to arms to support the Gordons of Lochinvar: "They laup the stanks wi' nimble sten, / And roused the wild boar frae his den./ Then loudly cheered the lads o' Ken, / Wha's valour kept the

A Literary Guide

fiel', man, / Then raised the targe, / And to the charge / They rushed wi' glaives o' steel, man". There is a detailed account of the use of the Galloway flail, which, in the hands of Geordie Grier of Garroch, decided the combat. It ends with reflective lines on the consequences of the slaughter: " Let Ken's fair maids/ Weave flowery braids / To deck the deadly flail, man". War-like legends of old Galloway were a favourite Denniston theme, and his *Legends of Galloway*, published in 1825, includes *The Standard of Denmark*, set at Cruggleton Castle near Whithorn: this is a tale of love, war, treachery and the supernatural involving the Kerlies of Cruggleton (the historian, **PH McKerlie**, was a representative of this family) and the Graemes of Kirkclaugh. The *Battle of Cairnholy* describes a battle belonging to the days of the Bruce, where the Bishop of Whithorn leads his troops across the Bishop Burn at Wigtown, and finally falls and is buried at Cairnholy. It appears that Denniston's unpublished *Old Paulin, a Tale of Plunton Castle* was forwarded in manuscript to Sir Walter Scott. *The Ghost of Trool* is a humorous tale, with the characteristic supernatural element, describing the posthumous revenge of an old rebel of the 1715 rising on a miller who had doubted the veracity of his reminiscences. The unquiet spirit plays "nocturnal football" across Loch Trool with the miller, until the clergy intervene and the ghost is condemned to carry about a millstone as punishment.

BIBLIOGRAPHY:
Legends of Galloway (1825); *The Battle of Craignilder* (1832); *The Ghost of Trool* (1878); *Old Paulin, a Tale of Plunton Castle* (n.d. - unpublished ms. In Hornel Library, Broughton House, Kirkcudbright); *The Seige of Cragg Tumble* (n.d. - unpublished ms. in Hornel Library)

PLACES TO VISIT: Cruggleton Castle is among the sites of Denniston's tales which remains open to the public: it may be reached by a cliff-top footpath from Rigg Bay, Garlieston.

Samuel Rutherford (Rutherfurd) c1600-1661
Anwoth

Samuel Rutherford became minister of Anwoth in 1628 and remained there until 1637. Though he published scholarly and devotional works throughout his life and later, after leaving Anwoth, attained to much distinction within the Presbyterian church, he is most remembered for his "Letters", often to parishioners in the neighbourhood of Anwoth and Kirkcudbright: by 1900, there had been over 30 successive editions. His most significant, though least accessible work, is his "Lex, Rex" which set out the mutual rights and relations of king and people, and gained him a reputation as the most considerable constitutional theorist of the Covenanters. His career, ranging from his appointment to a Professorship of Divinity at St Andrew's and his selection as one of the Commissioners to the Westminster Assembly, to citation for treason as he lay dying, demonstrates the extremes of distinction and disfavour to which those at the heart of the turbulent religious politics of the seventeenth century were subject.

Rutherford was born in about 1600 at either Nisbet or Crailing in Roxburghshire. He entered the university of Edinburgh in 1617 and received his MA in 1621. Shortly afterwards, he became a Professor of Humanity, but was forced to resign his post after an irregularity in his marriage was discovered, which caused a scandal. In 1627, he obtained the living of Anwoth, through the intervention of Viscount Kenmure, who with his wife, Lady Jane Campbell, was a noted adherent of Presbyterianism. John Livingstone, who had been minister of Stranraer, was the first choice, but as he wrote "the Lord provided a great deal better for the people of Anwoth, for they got that worthy servant of Christ, Mr. Samuel Rutherford, whose praise is in all

A Literary Guide

the reformed churches". There are descriptions of his life at the manse at Bushy Bield (demolished in 1826, three weeks before a visit to the site by Dr. Chalmers, who was to lead the Disruption in 1843), which show that he managed to combine his scholarly activities with a dedication to pastoral duty: he rose at 3am, spent the following hours in prayer, meditation and study, and then devoted himself to practical duties . The parish, though obscure and scattered in population, proved congenial ground for Rutherford, since the local landowners were prevailingly favourable to Presbyterianism: the Kenmures were resident first at Rusco, then at Kenmure Castle. Rutherford kept up a correspondence with Lady Kenmure throughout his life and dedicated some learned works to the Viscount, and wrote an elegy in Latin for Viscount Kenmure after his death, as well as an account of his deathbed repentance. The reformers felt that Kenmure had compromised his principles by failing to oppose Charles I's innovations to church liturgy, after receiving a peerage from the king, but Rutherford returned to him in his final illness and saw evidence of contrition and a state of grace. This *The Last and Heavenly Speeches, and Glorious Departure of John, Viscount Kenmure*, first published in 1649, was edited in 1827 by **Thomas Murray,** who also wrote a *Life of Samuel Rutherford* in 1828. The increasing polarisation of religious politics in the 1630's took its toll on Rutherford too: there were persecutions in the diocese under the intolerant Bishop Sydserf, and ultimately Rutherford, who was condemned for an extreme Calvinistic standpoint in his *Exercitationes Apologeticae pro Divina Gratia*, was condemned by the High Commission, deprived at Wigtown of his benefice in 1636, and exiled to Aberdeen until 1638. Many of his letters to Anwoth parishioners date to the time of his exile and testify to the feeling of loss on both sides: "I often think that the sparrows are blessed, who may resort to the house of God in Anwoth, from which I am banished", he wrote to Robert Gordon of Knockbrex in 1637. Though he managed to return to Anwoth in 1638, the reunion was to be brief: when he attended the General Assembly as a representative of the Presbytery of Kirkcudbright , both Edinburgh and St Andrew's petitioned for his services in their divinity schools, and despite his pleas and those of his flock at Anwoth, he was translated to the Chair of Divinity at St Mary's College, St Andrew's in 1639. During this time, he lectured on ecclesiastical history, systematic divinity and Hebrew, and continued –

as he did to the end of his life – a prolific literary output, contributing to learned controversies in the defence of Presbyterian polity and producing devotional works. Most significantly, he was appointed by the Assembly to be one of the six Scots commissioners who attended the Assembly of Divines at Westminster which was to reform the English Church, between 1643 and 1647, and which subsequently produced the Westminster Confession, the Directory of Public Worship and the two Westminster Catechisms. Although only approved temporarily in England, the documents were accepted by the Church of Scotland and remain a standard today. It was during this period that Rutherford published his most significant work, *Lex, Rex: the Law and the Prince; a Dispute for the Just Prerogative of King and People, Containing the Reasons and Causes of the Most Necessary Defensive Wars of the Kingdom of Scotland, and of Their Expedition for the Ayd and Help of their Dear Brethren of England* in reply to a treatise by John Maxwell, late Bishop of Ross and friend of Archbishop Laud, who was known for his high monarchical principles. Rutherford's reply, which effectively argued for the right of a people in extreme situations – such as that of tyranny – to revoke the right granted by it to a king to govern over it, addressed the burning question of its day in the most radical terms; the book was said to be in the hands of every Assembly member. At the Restoration of the monarchy in 1660, a proclamation was issued against *Lex, Rex* for "inveighing against monarchie, and laying ground for rebellion" and it was publicly burnt by the hangman at Edinburgh, as well as at the gate of his college. He was deprived of his position and charge at St Mary's College, of which he was by now Principal, and confined to his house. Though he was cited to appear before Parliament on a charge of treason, he was never able to appear, since he was already on his deathbed. His last letters show that he regretted the enforced loss of the opportunity for a Presbyterian martyrdom. He was buried in the churchyard of the Chapel of St Regulus in March 1661. In 1842, a granite obelisk was erected to his memory near Anwoth, on an eminence which now overlooks the A75 road.

* * *

Rutherford is remembered neither for his involved and scholarly works of controversy, his constitutional works on civil or church government,

A Literary Guide

or his devotional works, but above all for his *Letters*. The first edition appeared within three years of his death; the definitive edition, published in 1891 by Andrew Bonar, contained more than 150 of them. Though the *Letters* give us only glimpses of his personal situation and make occasional reference to the critical negotiations in which he was engaged in defence of Presbyterian principles, they speak eloquently for his concern on behalf of the spiritual welfare of his parishioners, particularly those he had left at Anwoth. Many are exhortatory and consolatory in tone and aim, which accounts for the popularity of the *Letters* as a Christian handbook throughout three centuries: he writes to "a Christian gentlewoman", enjoining faith despite the loss of her daughter, "sure I am, seeing her term was come, and your lease run out, you can no more justly quarrel against your great Superior for taking his own, at his just term-day, than a poor farmer can complain, that his master taketh a portion of his own land to himself, when his lease is expired." The style is a fine example of the way in which the rich language and imagery of the King James version of the Bible had been absorbed into the everyday conversation of committed Christians. His *Lex, Rex*, written in the form of repeated questions and answers characteristic of scholarly disputations of the time, took a standpoint in opposition to the modified monarchism of **Lord Stair** : Rutherford argued that , though government in general might be natural and instilled in man by God through his social instincts, its particular form of organisation – whether monarchical, aristocratic or democratic – was artificial, positive, had no divine licence and was therefore voluntary and revocable. Though Rutherford's work does not have the theoretical breadth of other constitutional theorists, like Locke or Grotius, it is an example of the way in which apparently abstruse points about the distinction between natural and positive law, and the nature of an original compact founding civil society, could be and were being applied to the pressing circumstances of the day, in the context of a royal regime seen, by its tyrannical acts in imposing religious forms and organisation, to be threatening the very basis of civil society.

BIBLIOGRAPHY:

Excercitationes Apologeticae pro Divina Gratia ...(1636); *Lex, Rex: the Law and the Prince, a Dispute for the Just Prerogative of King and People*

Dumfries and Galloway

(1644); *The Last and Heavenly Speeches, and Glorious Departure of John Viscount Kenmure* (1649 - also 1827 ed. By Thomas Murray); Andrew A Bonar, ed., *Letters of Samuel Rutherford* (1891); Thomas Murray, *The Life of Samuel Rutherford* (1828); Robert Gilmour, *Samuel Rutherford* (1904)

PLACES TO VISIT: The ruins of Anwoth Old Kirk, built in Rutherford's day, and Rutherford's Monument, reached by a path from the village, may be visited.

A Literary Guide

Thomas Brown
1778-1820
Kirkmabreck

Thomas Brown, born at Kirkmabreck, was successor in the Edinburgh University chair of Moral Philosophy to the famous Dugald Stewart, and was the predecessor of John Wilson, alias "Christopher North". He has perhaps been overshadowed by his more flamboyant colleagues, but at the time – which was the summit of the Edinburgh Enlightenment – he was thought to have one of the most acute metaphysical minds in the country.

Thomas Brown was born in 1778, the youngest of thirteen children to Rev Samuel Brown, minister of Kirkmabreck, and Mary Smith, from Wigtown. His father died when he was young, and the family moved on to Edinburgh, where his mother was tutor to his apparently precocious talent. His maternal uncle, Captain Smith, took him under his protection when he had reached the age of seven, and he was educated in London. He attended several schools – in Chiswick, Bromley, and Kensington – where he was remembered for his cheerful disposition, his feats of memory, and his ability to compose verse. When his uncle died in 1792, he returned to Edinburgh, entering the university, where he began studying logic. In the summer of 1792, he went on a visit to Liverpool, where, like many promising young Scots, he met **Dr Currie**, who gave him a copy of Dugald Stewart's *Elements of the Philosophy of the Human Mind*, with an admonition to attend Stewart's classes. When, in the next session, he did so, he presented a reasoned objection to one of Stewart's contentions, and thereby attracted Stewart's notice. Brown joined a talented circle, which included the linguist, John Leyden and those who were to found the *Edinburgh Review*; indeed, Brown was a founder member (and secretary) of the "Academy of Physics", which led directly to the foundation of the *Review*. He contributed an explanation of the philosophy of Kant to the journal's second issue. In fact, he had already attracted attention in the Edinburgh literary world, by writing a reply, based on notes he had begun at the age of 18, to Dr Darwin's *Zoonomia*, proving that Darwin's principles were not justified by the phenomena: **Dr Currie** wrote him a letter of appreciation for his production. Between 1798 and 1803, he studied medicine, having abandoned the intention of studying law, and produced a first edition of his poems, which included some elegant compositions in Latin. He entered the academic fray on behalf of Professor Leslie, whose clear right by merit to the chair of mathematics was being brought into question by the church party, on the grounds that Leslie had quoted the heretical Hume's doctrine of causation with approbation. Brown attempted to remove misconceptions surrounding Hume's teachings. In 1806, he entered medical practice in partnership with Dr Gregory, but when Dugald Stewart's health began to fail, Brown supplied lectures in his absence during the session of 1808-9. The lectures were a popular success, and were attended by professors, as well as students, who sent him a testimonial of their gratitude when Stewart returned to his post. Ultimately, Stewart asked Brown to share the professorship with him, and he became Stewart's successor and a contemporary with **Alexander Murray**, who became professor of Oriental Languages in 1813. It is rather alarming to read his biographer's comment that Brown, once having composed his lectures, "continued to read the same lectures until the time of his death", but this was certainly an established practice. Certainly, once settled in the routine of professorship, Brown returned to poetry, and in 1814, published a poem, which he had actually composed some years before, entitled *The Paradise of Coquettes*. There quickly followed *The Wanderer in Norway* in 1815, which tells "of the many miseries, in the endless unforeseen perplexities of distress, that follow the first great misery of having yielded to a guilty passion". *The Bower of Spring*, published in 1817, treated of the changes to temperature and seasons, which were then – as now – being noticed. He revisited Kirkmabreck in 1817, on the occasion of his mother's death, and, while staying with his brother-in-law, minister of Balmaclellan, wrote *Agnes* in memoriam of his mother. He was at work on a textbook of moral philosophy, when his health showed signs of deterioration. It was while he was on a visit to

A Literary Guide

London in 1820, in the hope of restoring it, that he died, and his body was brought back to Kirkmabreck for burial in a leaden coffin, by the side of his parents' grave. An obelisk was erected to his memory, at the old ruined church of Kirkmabreck, in the hills above Creetown.

* * *

Thomas Brown joined the almost apostolic succession of famous names in Scottish philosophy who had held the chair of moral philosophy at Edinburgh and articulated the ideas of its Enlightenment: the torch passed from Adam Smith to Thomas Reid, and from Reid to Dugald Stewart. He held the position of Professor of Moral Philosophy when that appointment represented the acme of an academic career, in a nation which respected academe. It is perhaps also not surprising that his name has been overshadowed by his more illustrious forbears, and that, by his time, there was a decline in the vigour and originality of thinking within that world of ideas. **Hugh MacDiarmid**, in his essay on "Christopher North", Brown's successor, quotes – with disapproval – a description of Brown's methods and the delicate oratory for which he was famed: "He .. composed his lectures with the same rapidity that he would have done a poem, and chiefly from the resources of his own highly gifted but excited mind. Difficulties which had appalled the stoutest hearts yielded to his bold analysis, and, despising the formalities of a siege, he entered the temple of pneumatology by storm". **Thomas Carlyle**, who attended Brown's lectures, was equally dismissive. Brown's examination of Hume's doctrine of causation (*Observations on the Nature and Tendency of the Doctrine of Mr Hume concerning the Relation of Cause and Effect*, 1804) has nothing of Hume's radicalism, and differs from Hume's position in concluding only that our belief in causes originates, not in custom, but in intuition. The subjects of Brown's lectures fill four volumes, and are classed into four categories: Physiology of Mind, Ethics, Political Economy, and Natural Theology. Brown's literary style when lecturing, and the way in which he illustrated his talks from poetry, was noted by contemporaries, and it certainly seems that the comment in his poem *The Hazards of an Unknown Poet* might be autobiographical: "What Powers all space pervade, - what dim control / Rules the quick changes of the realm of soul, / Oft has thou studious search'd; - and yet, O hard / To credit ! – yet thou hop'st to be a bard!" Brown's poetic style often imitates Pope's – for example, in his *Paradise of Coquettes*. His *Man and Nature* is enlivened by autobiographical recollections of the landscapes of his youth: "Hill of my infant sports, - and thou, fair Cree! / From whose bright waters first my sudden gaze/ Started, in terror of that wond'rous world / Of skies as blue and clouds as white, that shone / An unknown depth beneath thy calm expanse!".

BIBLIOGRAPHY:
Observations on the Zoonomia of Erasmus Darwin (1798); *Observations on the Nature and Tendency of the Doctrine of Mr Hume concerning the Relation of Cause and Effect* (1804); *Poems* (1804); *The Paradise of Coquettes, a Poem* (1814); *The Wanderer in Norway, with Other Poems* (1815); *The Bower of Spring, with Other Poems* (1817); *Agnes, a Poem* (1818); *Lectures on the Philosophy of the Human Mind* (1820); David Welsh, *Account of the Life and Writings of Thomas Brown* (1825)

PLACES TO VISIT: Kirkmabreck's ruined church stands on the exposed hills above Creetown, with spectacular views of Wigtown Bay and the Solway Firth.

A Literary Guide

Patrick Hannay
?1594 ; died after 1646
Kirkdale / Sorbie

Patrick Hannay was descended from the house of the Hannays of Sorbie, a branch of which acquired lands at Kirkdale in the Stewartry. He became an accomplished court poet under James VI and I, and his work deals with the characteristic courtly themes of the tortures of the unrequited love for a merciless mistress. It bristles with the elaborate logical and metaphorical conceits expected by a sophisticated and literate audience.

The details of Patrick Hannay's biography have been obscured and complicated by the fact that many generations of the same family bore the same Christian names, and by a lack of written evidence. It seems, however, on the basis of heraldic evidence, that he was the third son of Alexander Hannay, first laird of Kirkdale, who had become a burgess of Wigtown, made money in business and purchased estates at Kirkdale in 1532. Reference is made to his descent from the Hannays of Sorbie and to the new lands at Kirkdale in the eulogy to his poems by John Marshall: "Hannay thy worth bewrayes well whence thou'rt sprung / And that that honour'd Name thou does not wrong; / As if from Sorby's stock no branch could sprout/ But should with Rip'ning time beare golden fruit: / Thy Ancestors were ever worthy found, / Else Galdus grave had grac'd no Hannay's ground". Little is known of the detail of his life, but it can be deduced that he was well educated, probably took the degree of Master of Arts, and possibly took up residence in London, after James VI acceded to the crown of England and his court moved there. From a dedicatory ode he wrote, it is clear that he served under Sir Andrew Grey, Colonel of Foot and General of

283

Dumfries and Galloway

Artillery to the King of Bohemia, and that he supported the cause of the daughter of James I, wife of the elector Palatine and titular king of Bohemia. From one extended but uncomplimentary reference to Croydon in Surrey, it is possible to deduce that he lived there for a time: "In midst of these [downes] stands Croydon cloath'd in blacke, / In a low bottome sinke of all these hills.." He ends the description with a damning of all "proud dames" to a life in Croydon, a punishment which he apparently thought severe enough. In the Parliaments of Scotland held at Edinburgh, between 1639 and 1646, Hannay was returned as Commissioner for the Burgh of Wigtown, and on two occasions his name occurs as Provost, in the list of members on Committees of War. His works were published in 1622 and later became so scarce that only six copies were known to exist; they were subsequently edited, with a critical introduction, by David Laing, who presented the edition to the Hunterian Club in Glasgow. Laing was assisted with research into Hannay's genealogy by **PH McKerlie**.

* * *

Hannay's *Philomela, or the nightingale* written on the subject of Ovid's classical legend, is a work of over a hundred verses, on a pattern similar to **Montgomerie**'s *The Cherrie and the Slae*. It opens: "The Maple with a seary skin / Did spread broad pallid leaves; / The quaking Aspen, light and thin, / To th'air light passage gives; / Resembling still / The trembling ill/ Of tongues of woman-kind,/Which never rest/ But still are prest/ To wave with every wind". The affectation of unhappy love was to some extent a courtly commonplace: "love's not love, wherein are no disasters". Many of Hannay's sonnets are written to a haughty mistress, Coelia, and describe the poet's sufferings: "Sometimes I burne with an Etnean fire: / Sometimes I freeze; I swim, straight sinke to ground" . The description of the trials of love, however, are often an excuse for a brilliant display of poetic and metaphysical virtuosity, characteristic of the period: "I am oft absent when I am most neare, / And neare when as I greatest distance keepe:/ These wonders love doth worke, but yet I finde/ That love wants power to make my Mistress kinde". His *Happy Husband*, a didactic poem of advice to women choosing a husband, is written in imitation of Sir Thomas Overbury's *A Wife, now a Widdowe* and gives a more optimistic view of the married state. His *Sherentine and Mariana* purports to be based on the history of the Royal house of Hungary and Bohemia, and he also wrote elegies on the death of Queen Anne, which are patriotic pieces in honour of a royal patron.

BIBLIOGRAPHY:
Songs and Sonnets (1841 reprint); David Laing, ed., The Poetical Works of Patrick Hannay (1875); Malcolm McL Harper, The Bards of Galloway (1889)

PLACES TO VISIT: Sorbie Tower, Sorbie, ancestral home of the Hannays, is open to the public.

Joseph Train
1779-1852
Newton Stewart and Castle Douglas

Joseph Train, excise officer both at Newton Stewart and Castle Douglas, became one of Sir Walter Scott's most reliable and copious antiquarian researchers, during a correspondence which lasted eighteen years. It was Train's suggestions which prompted Scott to write of Old Mortality, and enabled him to add authentic detail to his story of the Solway Coast, "Guy Mannering". In his own right, Train wrote an authoritative history of the Isle of Man and of the Buchanite religious sect, based at Crocketford.

Joseph Train's family was probably of Ayrshire origin; certainly his father was the land-steward on the estate of Gilminscroft in the parish of Sorn. While Joseph Train was still an infant, the family moved to the Townhead of Ayr, where his father became a day-labourer. Early on in his career, he was apprenticed to a weaver, but in 1799, when ballots were being drawn for unpopular military service in the militia raised against France, Joseph Train joined up as a substitute for a farmer at Carsphairn. Despite his lack of opportunities, it is clear that he early developed an appetite for study and the anecdote is told that, while his regiment was at Inverness, he was saving for a copy of **Currie**'s edition of Burns. When his commanding officer, Sir David Hunter Blair, discovered from a bookseller that the book was reserved for one of his men, he gave instructions for the edition to be finely bound and sent to Train free of charge. In 1802, he returned to weaving in Ayr and became engaged to Mary Wilson. The favourable impression he had made on Sir David, however, was to prove of use to him in the advancement of his career, and he obtained, on Sir David's recommendation, a post as gauger for the Ayr district. His first poetical work *Poetical Reveries* was dedicated to Hunter Blair, and appeared in

A Literary Guide

1806. After four years in Ayr, he moved to Breadalbane, where there was an illicit distilling industry on a large scale, and where he occasionally found that enforcement of the excise was a hazardous activity. In 1811, he was moved to Largs, whose historical associations proved congenial to his developing antiquarian tastes. Newton Stewart was his next posting, and since his area included the undeveloped and mountainous regions north of the town towards Carrick, he found ample material for collecting folktales, customs and historical anecdotes. The first-fruits of his collecting were gathered together in his *Strains of the Mountain Muse*, 1814, and it was this volume which was to lead him to the most decisive connection of his life: Sir Walter Scott (then Mr Scott) happened to see the proofs of the book and wrote to ask for two copies. The correspondence thus begun lasted until Scott's death. Train's reply to Scott's initial request for information on Galloway legends is preserved in a manuscript letter at Broughton House, Kirkcudbright; he writes: "Every vale in Galloway is a cradle in which superstition has been unceasingly nursed.. In my wanderings thro' this mountainous District I have taken down several curious stories from the recitation of old people which it would give me much pleasure to communicate to you, as I am sure you are fond of such legends". One can only imagine the sense of anticipation which Scott must have felt on receiving such a letter, from an area of Scotland whose traditions were largely unexplored. From this moment on, Train's own literary ambition, as he wrote himself, "was superseded by a desire to serve the great novelist". Train's first effort for Scott was to gather information about Turnberry for Scott's *Lord of the Isles* and the collection of artefacts which he was to gather for Scott began with his finding a drinking cup from the leper colony, founded by Robert the Bruce at King's Case in Ayr. In Galloway, Train's enthusiasm for old tales became well-known and he received many visitors, particularly beggars and tramps, who claimed to have traditions to relate; he was also in a position through his work to visit many of the hill farms. He came to know **Captain James Denniston**, who shared his passion for old Galloway, and together they resolved to write a history of Galloway. Questionnaires were sent out to parish schoolmasters asking for particulars of antiquities and tradition, but the history was never written, owing to pressures of other work. It may be through this means that Train made contact with the Kirkmaiden schoolmaster, **William Todd**, from whom a letter of 1818 is extant, describing the Rhins tradition of the brownie at Barncorkrie. He also regularly met the schoolmaster from the Clachan of Penninghame, Mr Broadfoot, at the Shoulder of Mutton Inn, Newton Stewart, and Broadfoot became the prototype of Scott's Jedediah Cleishbotham. Although he did not complete his own history of the region, Train did, however, eventually contribute material to **MacKenzie's** *History of Galloway*, and is acknowledged in the Galloway sections to the *Statistical Account of Scotland*. Train also worked hard at his professional duties and produced an influential survey of defects and abuses of the excise statutes, which was eventually taken up in government legislation. In 1816, he eventually met Sir Walter Scott in person, then still the "Great Unknown" and still, at least nominally, concealing his authorship even from Train, who, if he knew of it, as was only likely, faithfully kept the secret. It was during this visit to Scott in Edinburgh that Train noted that the portrait of the notorious persecutor of the Covenanters, Graham of Claverhouse, hung on Scott's study wall. In the ensuing discussion as to how the story of Covenanting times could be effectively told, Train pondered: "And what if the story were to be delivered as if from the mouth of Old Mortality?" The story of the mason from Closeburn, who devotedly carved and repaired the tombstones of the Covenanting martyrs, was unknown to Scott, but his name was to become the title of one of Scott's best known novels. Scott returned the favour to Train, by conscientiously trying to use his influence for Train's promotion in the excise service; he also introduced him to the great antiquarian, Chalmers, telling him that Train was the person most likely to give him topographical and antiquarian information on Ayrshire and Galloway. It was Train who informed Chalmers about Rispain Camp outside Whithorn (then mistakenly believed to be evidence of Roman penetration into the Machars) and introduced him to the notion of the "Deil's Dyke", a mighty prehistoric earthwork, which Train believed to stretch from Loch Ryan to Lochmaben. In 1818, Scott procured for Train a rare history of the Isle of Man and encouraged him to write a history of the island, a suggestion which was only to bear fruit after Sir Walter's death. In 1820, Scott's efforts on behalf of Train's career seem to have borne fruit, and he was promoted to the rank of supervisor, and to a post at Cupar, Fife. Train appears to have inspired friendship and, once his antiquarian passions were known, to have attracted the trust of his informants

A Literary Guide

wherever he went: in this case, the authorities viewed his friendly relations with the community in Cupar with suspicion, on the ground that it might be inimical to the revenue, and Train was moved on to Queensferry in 1822. In 1823, he was removed to Falkirk and Scott was trying to get him appointed to the rank of Collector, a less demanding post. It appears, however, from contemporary accounts, that at this point the excise service was flooded with English officers, who were hostile to the appointment of native-born Scots. At any event, as the result of some chicanery, Train was removed to the inferior post of Wigtown. He applied successfully for a post at Dumfries, where he lived near the Wind Mill and was able to enjoy the congenial society of **John McDiarmid**, editor of the *Courier* and of the poet, William Bennet. Inevitably, while there, Train accumulated Burns relics for Scott. Unfortunately, as the result of an apparent failure to detect some illicit distilling in his own area, Train was reduced in rank, but on appeal he was restored and appointed to Castle Douglas. In 1829, he was collecting information for notes for a new edition of the Waverley Novels. While in the Stewartry, he interested himself in local history, discovered the famous brass horse-visor from Torrs, near Kirkcudbright, collected information on the cannon, Mons Meg, and recorded stories about Burns' visit to Loch Ken in the company of John Syme and the **Rev William Gillespie**. Scott's death in 1832 meant that the principal stimulus for Train's researches was suddenly withdrawn. On his retirement from the excise, Train lived at Lochvale, near Carlinwark Loch, where he was the object of many an antiquarian pilgrimages. Here, he worked on his *Historical and Statistical Account of the Isle of Man*, the history of the Buchanite religious sect, and published a previously composed work, *The Wild Scot of Galloway* (1848). Train died in 1852, leaving five children, and is buried at Kelton Churchyard. A memorial to his memory was largely sponsored and promoted by **Andrew McCormick**, then Provost of Newton Stewart, and two plaques were eventually unveiled in 1909, at both Newton Stewart and Castle Douglas.

* * *

Train's contributions to Scott's pool of information on Galloway, which held special appeal for the Romantic imagination for its remote and undeveloped character, were momentous: apart from providing him with the details of Old Mortality, he supplied Scott with information about a blind Welsh harpist, who ended his life tragically smothered in a gravel pit near Creetown, with his entire family, and who became the prototype of "Wandering Willie" in *Redgauntlet*; the fate of the harpist was commemorated in a poem by **John Morrison**, who had met the Welsh family prior to their tragic end, and who also knew Train and Scott. Train also gave Scott a Northern English ballad concerning the predictions of a mysterious astrologer, who emerges in the opening of Scott's Galloway novel, *Guy Mannering*. The dramatic figure of Madge Wildfire in *Heart of Midlothian* is also based on a Train original, as is Edie Ochiltree in *The Antiquary*, derived from Train's account of a "natural", Andrew Gemmil. Train's own verse tends to lack a technical mastery equal to its theme, but there is little doubt that he was in sympathy with the Romantic passion for the supernatural . His *Witch of Inverness* in the early *Poetical Reveries* has some atmospheric moments: "A troop o' Fairies riding by, / On hearing her in child-bed cry, / Made fast their courses to the moon, / An', as the gossips fuddl'd roun', / Bore off the bairn in little space, / But left another in its place." Sir Walter Scott, whose acquaintance with Train was triggered by his interest in his *Strains of the Mountain Muse*, 1814, was particularly struck by his *Elcine de Aggart*, a poem about a witch, based on the notorious Ayrshire witch, Maggie Osborne, who repels invasion from the sea by winding up a ball of blue twine from a headland near Turnberry: " Old Elcine de Aggart has taken in hand / To wind up their lives ere they win to our strand". Both in this work, and in his later *Wild Scot of Galloway*, published by **John Nicholson** and trading on the traditions about the ferocity of the Gallovidians, there is great interest in his antiquarian notes, appended to the main text. The Isle of Man must have come to Train's attention as an excise officer, because it was its anomalous position with regard to the kingdom's excise laws which made of it a centre for smuggling into the nineteenth century. His antiquarian interests, however, were, as always, paramount, and it was clear that the island appealed to him above all because of the rich intermixture of cultures superimposed one upon another by invasion and settlement, and because the "secluded situation of the Isle of Man has also led to the continuance of ancient customs and of superstitious observances." His *History* of the island, which paid meticulous attention to documents and was for long regarded as an authority, includes, in

A Literary Guide

addition to a chronological history, a chapter on the archaeology of "Mounds and Fortifications". Train's valuable account of *The Buchanites from First to Last* charts the extraordinary history of a religious sect, inspired by Elspeth Buchan, "Friend Mother" and the Rev. Mr. White, who convinced their followers of the possibility of an imminent ascent to heaven, without suffering the pains of death. The involved and often ludicrous attempts of the sect to account for the continuing failure of the prophecies, and the later macabre story of the abstraction of Friend Mother's corpse from its grave to a house at Crocketford, must be one of the oddest in the history of sects. Train was in touch with and received a manuscript account from one of the sect's most devoted followers, Andrew Innes, who kept the bones of Mrs. Buchan in a special compartment constructed at the back of his bedroom fire, and was eventually interred beside them. Train also received tragic correspondence from witnesses, who, as children, had been starved for forty days, which was supposed to be the pre-condition for an ascent to heaven. Interestingly, however, Train gives the later history of the Buchanites, after the departure of the Rev Mr White for America, and points out that some settled as successful farmers at Larghill, and that the women, who wove a special green cloth for the clothes of the brethren, were responsible for the introduction of the two-handed spinning wheel to the area.

BIBLIOGRAPHY:
The Poetical Reveries of Joseph Train (1806); *Strains of the Mountain Muse* (1814); *An Historical and Statistical Account of the Isle of Man* (1845); *The Buchanites from First to Last* (1846); *The Wild Scot of Galloway: a Poem* (1848)

PLACES TO VISIT: Plaques to Train's memory exist at the MacMillan Hall, Newton Stewart, and at Castle Douglas. The scenery of *Guy Mannering* and many of its fictitiously named locations, may be found along the coast in the vicinity of Creetown and Barholm.

Andrew McCormick
1867-1956
Newton Stewart

Andrew McCormick, who lived in , practised law in and was Provost of Newton Stewart, wrote the classic and now increasingly rare Galloway book "The Tinkler-Gypsies of Galloway". He was a noted authority on the travelling people, on Romany language and on "tinkler's cant".

Andrew McCormick was born at Glenluce in 1867, but moved with his family to Newton Stewart when he was two years old. He entered university at Edinburgh to study law, and there engaged in his pastime of hill-walking in the Pentlands, an abiding interest he was to pursue in the Galloway Hills. In 1890, he returned to Newton Stewart, and set up a law business, McCormick and Nicholson, which rapidly became one of the most respected in the area. After nine years' service on Newton Stewart Town Council, he was appointed Provost of the burgh, and remained so for six years. During this time, he fostered many public projects, including the construction of the suspension bridge over the Cree, to commemorate the Coronation of King George V and Queen Mary. He later served as Town Clerk of Newton Stewart for many years. Perhaps his real enthusiasms lay away from the busy civic and professional life he led, since he was an enthusiast for stories of Galloway tradition, and for the Galloway hills, about which he was to publish *Galloway: the Spell of its Hills and Glens* in 1932. His first publication, however, indicated an equally unorthodox interest for a Provost: *The Tinkler-Gypsies of Galloway*, 1906, embodied his fund of knowledge about the Galloway gypsies, whom he had got to know personally and had photographed at their temporary local encampments. *Words from the Wild-Wood*, 1912, whose title commemorates the Wildwood Hut, situated beyond Minnigaff village, where he accomplished much of his writing, continues the main strands of his interest in the hill-country and in the local gypsy tradition. Many of his articles and anecdotes relate also to his love for angling. At the outbreak of the 1914-18 war, McCormick obtained a commission in the KOSB, but, since he was, by the end of his training, beyond the age limit for combatants, he took charge of a Labour Company of 500 men, attached to the Royal Irish Regiment. He was promoted to the rank of Captain and given command of his Company. The Company was engaged in the vicinity of Arras, France. In his older age, he sold Walnut House, Newton Stewart, and built "Tir-nan-Og", overlooking the Galloway hills. During his career, he supported several ventures to commemorate the life and work of other writers, including the **Crockett** Memorial at Laurieston, the restoration of the **Murray** monument , and the erection of the **Joseph Train** memorial tablets at Newton Stewart and Castle Douglas. He was also active in many other civic organisations, such as the Dumfriesshire and Galloway Natural History and Antiquarian Society, the Glasgow Galloway Association, and the Old Parish Church at Penninghame. He was married to the daughter of Colonel James Porteous of Turfhills, Kinross, and had two sons and one daughter.

* * *

The *Tinkler-Gypsies of Galloway*, which McCormick describes as "gleanings along a literary Gypsy by-path", follows in the tradition of George Borrow and FH Groome, who had introduced the gypsy to literature as a figure of romance. "Only those who have caught the cult of Gypsyism", McCormick writes, " can tell what an extraordinary charm and fascination there is in studying and reading and writing about the Gypsy race". McCormick's book, episodic in its character, having been published in part as separate articles, seems to share this wayward charm and fascination, since there are few books which Galloway collectors are happier to own than a copy of the *Tinkler- Gypsies*. The articles deal chiefly with the myth and fact relating to Billy Marshall, king of the gypsies, with the gypsy material used by Sir Walter Scott in *Guy Mannering* (including a discussion of the information given to Scott by

Joseph Train, in relation to "Wandering Willie"), with McCormick's own personal encounters with the Galloway tinklers (for whom he had an undoubted affinity), and with gypsy vocabulary. As the references suggest, however, the book was only the most public and popular face to McCormick's involvement with the study of gypsy tradition and language, and his correspondence reveals numerous contacts with the Gypsy Lore Society, contributions to Government reports on the condition of the gypsies, and lectures, illustrated by his invaluable slide collection. McCormick's *Words from the Wild-Wood* includes a description of his writing-hut, which makes clear to what extent the hut was a compensation for being deprived by circumstances of the wandering life to which McCormick felt an obvious attraction: "As I may not spend long holidays in the ideal way of travelling about the country in a gypsy van, by way of compromise I have lived from the beginning of May to the end of October for the past four years in my hut". Some of the essays recall Galloway traditions, others are fantasias on the Galloway past (a more extended attempt is *The Gold Torque*) and two important articles record, respectively, **SR Crockett's** debt to the McMillans of Glenhead for his knowledge of the Galloway Hills, and the visit by George Borrow, the original "Romany Rye", to Galloway. *Galloway: the Spell of its Hills and Glens* succeeds well, through its description of climbs, encounters with Galloway shepherds and of angling trips to distant lochs, in passing on McCormick's enchantment with the uplands: the hills, at McCormick's hands, develop personalities of their own, which seem to be expressed by their remote and rugged-sounding names – Rig of the Jarkness, Wolf's Slock, Coran of Portmark, Nick of the Dungeon.

BIBLIOGRAPHY:
The Tinkler-Gypsies of Galloway (1906); *Words from the Wild-Wood* (1912); *Galloway: the Spell of its Hills and Glens* (1932); *The Gold Torque* (1951)

PLACES TO VISIT: Walks taken and described by McCormick can be taken by travelling to Bruce's Stone and Glentrool and following a variety of routes, including a marked climb to the summit of the Merrick.

A Literary Guide

Alexander Murray
1775-1813
Dunkitterick, parish of Minnigaff

Eighteenth and nineteenth century biographies are full of stories of Scots students who overcome great odds, educational and financial, to become students and prominent men in their field: even in these annals, the story of Alexander Murray, son of a shepherd in the wilds of Minnigaff, has something like legendary status. Murray had a phenomenal talent for languages, speaking and reading more than a dozen, and eventually became Professor of Oriental Philology at Edinburgh: before his early death aged 38, he was in the forefront of those who began to perceive a kinship between European and Indian languages, and thus to found the discipline of comparative philology.

Alexander Murray was born at Dunkitterick, son of a shepherd, Robert Murray, who herded for Mr Laidlaw of Clatteringshaws. His mother, Robert Murray's second wife, was Mary Cochrane. At the time, no road passed Dunkitterick and there was little opportunity to attend a school. Much of our information about Murray's early life comes from an autobiographical fragment, sent to Rev Mr Maitland of Minnigaff by Murray, about a year before he died. It recounts how Robert Murray taught his son letters from a catechism, which he bought in 1781, and how Alexander learnt by inscribing the letters on the back of a wool-card, writing with a "birn" or stub of heather charcoal. He rapidly devoured all reading he could find – largely the Bible, from which he learnt to recite long passages. He was a frail child, unlikely to be able to help his father herding on the moors, as his half-brothers had done, and when an uncle heard of his prowess at reading, he undertook to place him at New Galloway school, where he could lodge with his grandfather. He attended school in 1784, where he made rapid progress, but after an outbreak of skin disease, was forced to leave and had no more education for four years. Between 1785 and 1787, he read all the penny ballads he could acquire, borrowed Salmon's *Geographical Grammar* which included translations of the Lord's Prayer into many languages, and in 1788 was appointed tutor to the children of two families in Kirkcowan parish, where he acquired some textbooks on arithmetic. When his father moved in 1789 to Drigmorn, closer to Minnigaff, Murray was able to attend the school there. While tutor to families in Minnigaff in that year, he acquired more miscellaneous learning by borrowing books on book-keeping, Latin classics and Burns's poetry. The numbers and range of books which Murray was able to borrow in his course of self-education is an interesting reflection on the level of learning in remote parts of Galloway: French, Greek and Latin grammars, Hebrew psalms and a Hebrew dictionary, acquired from John Heron, a cousin of Murray's and father of the historian, **Robert Heron.** From alphabets printed in dictionaries, or in Bibles, Murray also acquired knowledge of Anglo-Saxon, Abyssinian and Arabic. Until 1793, Murray continued to have some schooling, and to earn fees through tutoring. He also composed an epic poem, and some comic poems in Scots verse (of which six are extant, including *The Battle of the Flies* on Robespierre and Murat), and translated Drackenburg's *Lectures* on the lives and writings of Roman authors. On visiting Dumfries in 1794, to promote his translation, he met **Robert Burns** "who treated me with great kindness" and gave him the good advice not to publish his poems, on the grounds that his taste and style were not mature. His introduction to Edinburgh and university life came through a friend, Mr McHarg, who consulted a printer, James Kinnear, on the prospects for publishing Murray's poetry, at the same time mentioning Murray's prodigies of untaught language-learning. Kinnear promised that if Murray would come to Edinburgh, Dr Baird and others at the university would examine him. Murray duly arrived in Edinburgh in 1794 and his ability to read from several languages "ad aperturam libri" astonished the examining professors. He was entered as a free student at the University. Lord Cockburn remembered him as a "little shivering creature, gentle, studious, timid and reserved", but his letters written home in the 1790's, preserved in manuscript at Broughton House, Kirkcudbright, give a livelier picture of a young man interested in the French war and family news. Murray reached Edinburgh at a high-point of the Enlightenment, and was taught by such men as John Playfair and Dugald Stewart; he was able to form friendships with John Leyden, the only man with a claim to rival Murray's linguistic abilities, and **Thomas Brown.** Murray passed from arts classes to Divinity Hall and was licensed to preach in 1802. At this point, Leyden was preparing to leave Edinburgh for India, and invited Murray to take over the editorship of the influential *Scots Magazine*, to which he had already contributed in verse and prose. One of the articles Murray published in the *Magazine* was a contribution to the famous controversy as to the authenticity of the poems by "Ossian", in March and April 1802. His relations with the publisher, Mr Constable, turned out to have fortunate consequences for Murray, who corresponded with Constable for the rest of his life; it was Constable who eventually almost adopted Murray's orphaned son, before he was drowned at sea on his first voyage as a ship's surgeon. Constable had taken over the copyright of James Bruce's *Travels to Abyssinia* and asked Murray to bring out a new edition from the journals and manuscripts surviving at Bruce's home, Kinnaird House. Murray had already mastered the Amharic and Geeze, or Tigre, dialects of Abyssinian, and was the only person capable of editing Bruce's extracts from five different dialects. Unfortunately, Murray seems to have encountered some lack of co-operation, and even hostility, from Bruce's son, and it was probably with relief that he left Kinnaird in 1803. The new edition of *Travels to Discover the Source of the Nile, in the Years 1768-1773* appeared in 1805; earlier, Murray had contributed an article on Bruce to the *Scots Magazine*. Murray had by now been licensed to preach for three years, and in 1805, William Douglas of Orchardton, near Castle Douglas, who had taken language lessons from Murray, secured Murray's appointment as assistant and successor to **Dr Muirhead** of the parish of Urr. In 1806, Murray's appointment was confirmed and he continued to assist Dr Muirhead until the old gentleman's death in 1808, when Murray read the funeral oration. Murray married a neighbouring farmer's daughter, Henrietta Affleck, and appears to have been a conscientious pastor. During this time, he was working on material which was to become his *History of the European Languages*, was considering a history of Dumfries and Galloway, about which he was corresponding with Scott and Constable, and was inspired by the publication of Chalmers' *Caledonia* and Scott's

Marmion. It was in 1811, after Murray had suffered the first of some bouts of ill-health, that Constable wrote to say that Henry Salt, Consul-General to Egypt, required Murray's services in translating a letter from the King of Abyssinia – a letter which turned out to concern the state of religious opinion in Abyssinia. The letter " in very plain and good Abyssinian" had fruitful consequences for Murray, in that his widow ultimately received a pension of £80 per annum from the government and Henry Salt was instrumental in his obtaining the professorship at Edinburgh, which became vacant in 1812. The list of testimonials sent on Murray's behalf to enable him to win the contest for the chair reads like an index of Edinburgh's *literati* : Walter Scott, Dugald Stewart, Francis Jeffrey, John Playfair, Lord Woodhouselee, Professor **Thomas Brown**, and "Sanskrit" Hamilton. Despite some opposition from a rival party, who claimed that Murray's health was too delicate to enable him to carry on the work of the professorship, Murray was elected in 1812. He immediately published for his students the *Outlines of Oriental Philology* and delivered a course of lectures on Oriental culture. Unfortunately, the auguries concerning Murray's weak state of health turned out to be all too true, and after a single session as Professor, he became seriously ill, probably with the asthma and consumption from which he had been suffering for some years. **Thomas Brown** summoned Mrs Murray from Urr, seeing that Murray's illness was progressing rapidly, and she arrived before he died on 15th April 1813. He is buried at Greyfriars' Churchyard, Edinburgh. In 1834-5, a monument, promoted by **Thomas Murray**, a personal friend of Murray's and his biographer in the *Literary History of Galloway*, was erected to his memory, in the valley overlooking his birthplace at Dunkitterick. On the occasion of Murray's centenary in 1913, a special issue of the *Galloway Gazette* was printed, and the principal speaker was the instigator of the celebrations, Mrs McMillan of Glenhead of Trool, friend and correspondent of **SR Crockett**.

* * *

Alexander Murray's *magnum opus* was in fact posthumous; one of his unsuccessful rivals for the Edinburgh chair, David Scot, edited the book from his manuscripts. It was written at a time when great advances were being made in the publication of Eastern texts, particularly Sanskrit, by the Asiatic Society and when scholars like Sir William Jones and, in

A Literary Guide

Germany, Friedrich Schlegel, were turning their attention to the affinity of Indian languages with the Persian, and towards ancient Indian culture in general. John Reith, who wrote the *Life and Writings of Rev. Alex. Murray* in 1903, makes a vigorous case for Alexander Murray's being the first scholar in Europe to recognise the family of languages we now know as "Indo-European", and attempts to promote Murray's claim over and above that of the great German linguists, Franz Bopp and the Grimm brothers, to be father of comparative philology. Reith reasons that Bopp's publication might have issued from the press earlier, but Murray's was actually composed first, and was only delayed by his death, finally appearing in 1823, more than ten years after its composition. It is certain that Murray was working on territory closely allied to that of the German researchers, and that, by 1811, he was writing to Constable and other correspondents of his being able to see "light through the extent of Europe in every direction", which would enable him to unify the histories and literatures of Europe and Asia. Perhaps what hampered Murray's claim to having given the first scientific demonstration of the unity of Indo-European linguistic forms was less the delay of his publication than his lengthy narrative exposition and the metaphysical account he gave of the origin of linguistic forms from a primal syllable denoting vehement action. According to Murray, nine primitive syllables "are the foundations of language, on which an edifice has been erected of a more useful and wonderful kind, than any which have exercised human ingenuity"; language progressed, and ultimately split into the several families of Indo-European, when these nine radical monosyllables were varied by permutations, distinguishing case, number and gender. Whatever the truth of Murray's claim to have fathered comparative philology, he was certainly part of a movement in the study of language which was breaking away from the theological account of linguistic origins, and recognising the law-governed nature of language-change and a unity of languages behind a vast number of surface variations: "The progress of language", wrote Murray, " is not nearly so irregular as has been supposed.. and ..the mode of composition, derivation, inflection, alters its appearance, but retains its essential power through vast intervals of time and place".

BIBLIOGRAPHY: *Outlines of Oriental Philology* (1812); *History of the European Languages* (1823); James Bruce, *Travels to Discover the Source of the Nile, in the Years 1768-1773* (1805); Thomas Murray, *The Literary History of Galloway* (1822); John Reith, *The Life and Writings of Rev. Alex. Murray* (1903)

PLACES TO VISIT: Murray's birthplace at Dunkitterick has been preserved by Forest Enterprise, and the monument to his memory is a prominent feature of the Galloway Forest Park

A Literary Guide

John McNeillie (Ian Niall) 1916 -
North Clutag, near Wigtown

Ian Niall, who first published under his family name, John McNeillie, has celebrated the countryside in more than forty books; he claimed that his "Galloway Childhood" describing his life with his grandparents near Wigtown, was his best work. His work is marked by a profound understanding of the natural world, a crystalline prose style and by the quality of the illustrations accompanying his texts.

Since Ian Niall's work consists largely of autobiographical musings on his love for and involvement with nature, details of his biography can be gleaned from throughout the corpus of his writings. In particular, his autobiographical novel *A Galloway Childhood* is an informative and affectionate account of his upbringing in Wigtownshire, but *Feathered Friends, Country Matters, Around my House* and *The Idler's Companion* also include Galloway recollections. He was born at Old Kilpatrick on the Clyde, where his father, who had been apprenticed to an engineering firm on the Clyde at the age of 16, was employed in the aircraft industry from the beginning of the 1914-18 war. The McNeillie family, however, had originally come from Garlieston, on the eastern coast of the Machars, but had moved to Monreith, after Ian Niall's grandfather had applied for a smithy there. Niall's grandfather, who features as a larger-than-life figure in *A Galloway Childhood* and in other works, received the favourable notice of the local laird, **Sir Herbert Maxwell**, for his inventiveness and interest in constructing labour-saving farm machinery. He bequeathed both his engineering ability and his interest in prize poultry and birds to his son, Niall's father. When he was eighteen months old and his parents – who were already nursing a sick daughter – considered him a sickly child, Ian Niall was sent to Galloway, where his paternal grandfather had by then acquired a farm at North Clutag, near Wigtown, "on the proceeds of his inventions". He lived in Galloway until he was eight. Despite his happiness at his grandfather's home, his own vocation lay elsewhere: "I had picked up my pen to write and somehow cut myself off from my peasant heritage". He first moved south with his parents to Middlesex, where his father was in charge of the drawing office at Fairey Aviation at Hayes, and, as a young man, he took up journalism. It was then that he wrote his first book, the only one to be written under his own name of John McNeillie, about the Wigtown area : the *Wigtown Ploughman*. The book was serialised in the *Glasgow Sunday Mail* and then published by Putnam in 1939. The exactitude of the locations and the frankness with which some of the brutalities of the life of a Wigtownshire farm labourer were portrayed caused some offence in the local area. His father had retired to Wales, and Niall went to live in North Wales, near Llandudno, in the 1940's, as a full-time writer, and many of his books feature the Welsh countryside. Throughout his childhood, he had continued to return to Galloway during school holidays, and later returned on nostalgic trips recorded in his articles. After his grandfather's death, the farm near Wigtown was sold. He has written over forty books, eleven of which are novels, and one is a biography of his friend, Charles Tunnicliffe, bird artist, whose illustrations feature in several of Niall's works. He contributed *Countryman's Notes* to *Country Life* for many years. He married, and has two sons and one daughter. He now lives in England.

* * *

John McNeillie leaves one in no doubt, at the very opening *of Wigtown Ploughman* that the era of the "Kailyard" is long past : its earthy stress on poverty, grime, and sexuality – "untidy fireplaces, torn clothes, creaking bedsteads, faded willow-pattern crockery, smoked ceilings of wood, and the same pungent smell of baby napkins"– could not be further from the wholesomeness of **Crockett's** *Lilac Sunbonnet*. Place-names and locations are all described with accuracy, and there is an expert's rendering of the North Machars dialect: "dinna scraich at me. A'm no' argyin' wi'

A Literary Guide

ye"; "A micht get the len' o' a kert an' tak the twa three bits o' duds ower tae ma mither's". After the endless unwanted pregnancies, the drunkenness and violence, the book ends on a more optimistic note: "The old man put his hand on his arm. 'There's nae finer place, boy, than working in the fiels. There's jist you an' the Lord God and the green grass. Nocht metters...There's aye anither day tae work; there's the hills and the dykes lik' they wur whun yer granfether wus a boy. Bit ye gang tae the toon an' ye're eye wonnerin' whut time o' day it is. Every man is lik' the next. Every body eats an' sleeps at the same time. They ken nocht aboot the fiels an' the wee birds, the snigger o' a horse, whaur the fairy tatties grow or whaur the hare beds in the holla". The old man's speech sounds the beginning of a dialogue about the merits of a life close to nature and a reflection on technology and the spread of urbanisation, which was to pervade Niall's future work. The way in which the countryside may reveal what McNeillie calls in his *Wigtown Ploughman* preface "true beauty", and offers us a special access to what is real and fundamental, is still the subject of Niall's *A Galloway Childhood*, a much brighter and more optimistic work, written thirty years later. It is not merely that nostalgia magnifies the memories, as Niall admits it does, but that the life led by his grandparents and their contemporaries was uniquely designed to sharpen the perceptions, and allowed them a closeness to the cycles of nature which made them – paradoxically perhaps – better human beings. The deceptively simple accounts of victories at Wigtown show, milking, trips to the seaside, the crises of harvest, and of close family ties, contrive to build up a powerfully nostalgic picture of the countryside prior to mechanisation. In a few economical phrases, Niall can evoke an entire lost world of sensation: of milking-time, he writes: "The pump-handle squealed as someone drew fresh water, and far down in the mist-hung fields, the peewits took wing and called their spring call. Miles away the same sounds were filling the air in places lying in the shelter of round green hills and milkers were squatting on stools, their cheeks pressed to the great round, rumbling bellies of Ayrshire, Friesian or Galloway cows, while their deft hands sent milk spurting and ringing into their milking-pails". The theme that, as Niall says, "Man is not God", or that, when he tries to be, as master of technology, there are irretrievable losses to balance the gains in time and speed, informs later works. *To Speed the Plough*, for example, gives detailed descriptions of farming techniques prior to the advent of "horsepower", but it is also informed by a real sense of loss which is more than nostalgia, but a concern for the health of society and the place of man in the scheme of nature. The pervasive note of pessimism about the often disastrous intervention of man in nature is explicitly sounded in *Feathered Friends*, where he writes: "In a vague way, I began to realise, when I was three years old, that there is something lacking in man". Here, this defectiveness, which, for Niall, is the mark of man's fall from grace amid the Eden of nature, is personified in the advent of the bird-catcher, a sinister figure, who entraps with bird-lime and gins, and who "came like a flapping crow that couldn't quite take off". The pessimism, however, is always tempered by the sense of wonder which nature inspires, by a sense of its resilience and indestructibility, and the figures of evil are counterbalanced by the battery of sympathetic characters, once common in the countryside, such as tinkers, smiths, poachers and "idlers"; the diversity, the colourfulness and the sheer fieldcraft of characters such as "Bob in the Whins", Paddy who lived in a cave on the Garheugh shore, and "Snib", the farm tramp, are celebrated in Niall books such as *The Idler's Companion, The Poacher's Handbook, The New Poacher's Handbook* and *Country Matters*. It is a characteristic of Niall's style that his descriptions of rambles or night-time poaching expeditions do not remain at the descriptive level, but that he develops a conspiratorial companionship with the reader, who becomes his accomplice and initiate in the skills of field or river, and an escapee from more regimented modes of life. *Fresh Woods* ends with: "Brush the moss from your jacket and throw away your whittled stick. What company you have been in! What an idle timewaster you have been these past few days! Haste you away across the field, back home with your bag of hazel nuts, your elderberries, your excuses for being where you have been." No account of Niall's work would be complete without mention of his happy collaboration with a variety of distinguished illustrators, including Donald Watson, the Galloway bird artist, Barbara Greg, Louis MacKay, and CF Tunnicliffe, about whom he wrote the acclaimed *Portrait of a Country Artist*. He has also written novels, such as *The Harmless Albatross*, set in Wales, and *The Galloway Shepherd*, and a variety of natural history books for children.

A Literary Guide

BIBLIOGRAPHY:
Wigtown Ploughman (1939); *The Poacher's Handbook* (1950); *Fresh Woods* (1951); *The Harmless Albatross* (1961); *A Galloway Childhood* (1967); *The Galloway Shepherd* (1970); *The New Poacher's Handbook* (1970); *Around My House* (1973); *To Speed the Plough* (1977); *The Idler's Companion* (1978); *Portrait of a Country Artist: CF Tunnicliffe* (1980); *Country Matters* (1984); *Feathered Friends* (1984)

John Ruskin
1819-1900
Wigtown

*The Wigtownshire connections of one of the most significant art and social critics of the nineteenth century, John Ruskin, are a little known part of his history. Not only was Ruskin related, through his parents, to many of the chief Wigtownshire families (including the **Agnews** of Lochnaw, **the Rosses** of Balsarroch, and the McTaggarts of Ardwell among others) but the person who devoted herself to his care, after the death of his father and during the increasingly serious bouts of "brain fever", was Joan Agnew (Mrs Arthur Severn) who was born in Wigtown. Through her, he gained an affection for the towns of the Solway, which is revealed in his most accessible work, his autobiography "Praeterita".*

Only the parts of Ruskin's history which are directly related to Wigtownshire are of interest to us in the context of this book and it is in the final chapter, entitled "Joanie's Care", in his autobiography *Praeterita* that his connections are detailed and a family tree explains his intimate relationships with many of the chief Wigtownshire families. Ruskin's grandmother's family, the Tweddales, upheld a long and proud religious tradition in Wigtownshire, it being recounted that it was to Catherine Tweddale, aunt of a minister of Glenluce and Ruskin's great-grandfather, that the Solemn League and Covenant was delivered in 1685. A descendant, Mrs Agnew, lived in a house in Wigtown, on a site now occupied by the County Buildings, and her daughter Joan was brought up there. Ruskin was to write of Wigtown and of the small burghs in southern Scotland that "there was more refinement in them and more honorable pride at that time [the 1860's] than in any other district of Europe; a certain pathetic power of tradition consecrating nearly every scene with some

A Literary Guide

past light, either of heroism or religion". When Ruskin's father died, "Joanie" came to stay the night, and ended up staying with the Ruskins right up until Ruskin's death in 1900. When Joan Agnew met **Thomas Carlyle** at Ruskin's house, they came to realise that Carlyle had been hospitably entertained by Joan's grandfather at Wigtown; it was to her that Carlyle recounted the famous story as to how his enthusiasm for the coastal scenery of the Solway led to his pinioning Queen Victoria's dress with the leg of his chair. Joanie nursed Ruskin through the increasing instabilities which seemed to be aggravated by, and were evident in, his later works of social and political criticism. *Praeterita* was itself written in intervals between attacks of brain fever, and was embarked upon as a sedative, "passing in total silence things which I have no pleasure in reviewing". These naturally included his disastrous marriage to Euphemia Gray, which was dissolved on grounds of Ruskin's impotence, and his later, equally unfortunate, pursuit of the young girl, Rose de la Touche. The clarity of the early chapters of *Praeterita*, which make it a delight to read, were part of the device to return him to sanity, but this became clouded after a further serious attack in 1888, and the chapter on Joanie betrays a grasp on form which was already slipping.

* * *

It is impossible to review here the range and influence of Ruskin's writings, but it may be worth noticing some especially Scottish influences. He noted in later life how his preferred writers were Scott and Carlyle, of whom he had "read every word". **Crockett's** *The Raiders* was read to him as soon as it appeared, and Crockett is said to have been a close friend, visiting him in his retirement at Coniston in the Lake District. **Carlyle** directly influenced the ejaculatory style of *Fors Clavigera*, a series of letters which Ruskin issued between 1871-1884, attacking the utilitarian philosophy and capitalist economy which he loathed, with increasing violence. Interestingly, in Volume IV, in a letter dated October 10th 1883, Ruskin writes from Whithorn , Wigtownshire, describing two different classes of children seen on the main street. One group was neatly and cleanly dressed; then "up and down the earth broadway between the desolate looking houses which form the main street of Whithorn, I saw wistfully neglected children". In a passage typical of Ruskin's comparison of contemporary conditions with the nobler spiritual possibilities derived from history and art, he mourns the passing of St Ninian's missionary spirit and asks rhetorically: "Of what kingdom of Heaven are these children the nascent citizens? To what Christ are these to be allowed to come for benediction, unforbidden?" Informed by Joan Agnew, he once again returns to the salutary moral and intellectual influences of the Solway coast and its history in *Praeterita*. It is hard not to draw a parallel between Ruskin's increasing isolation from the mainstream of English thought, his vehement opposition to the age of the machine and his promotion of Christian, feudal and heroic ideals, with **Carlyle's** similar alienation; indeed, politically, they often found themselves on the same side. At least in Carlyle's case, his sense of unease with the direction of Victorian English culture was at least partly induced by the severe religious temper of his Annandale past, which, despite his long exile from Scotland, moved with him to contemporary London and accorded ill with the atmosphere of its sophisticated literary and political circles. Perhaps for Ruskin too, the remoteness and simplicity of his Scottish influences and connections seemed increasingly attractive by contrast with what he had come to reject.

BIBLIOGRAPHY:
Praeterita (1885-1889); *Fors Clavigera* (1871-1884)

PLACES TO VISIT: Wigtown County Buildings now stand on the site of Joan Agnew's home.

A Literary Guide

Peter Handyside McKerlie
1817-1900
Cruggleton, near Garlieston

McKerlie's "History of the Lands and their Owners in Galloway" has long been a classic of Galloway literature. Though many of his conclusions about early Galloway history have been overturned by more accurate etymological analysis and techniques of archaeological excavation unknown in his time, the value of his recording of family histories and early estate names renders his work still invaluable in the analysis of the shift and continuities of power and land in the hands of the main Galloway families.

Peter McKerlie was born in Duddingston, near Edinburgh, of a Wigtown family, with a strong allegiance to its Galloway roots. His father, whose autobiographical notes on his military career were published by a granddaughter, E Marianne H McKerlie, was stationed at Edinburgh and his son attended Edinburgh High School. He was also tutored by a talented Frenchman, Joseph Cauvin, whose eventual career as a reader at Longman's and Green was helped by the intervention of **Thomas Murray** and **JR McCulloch**, for whom he edited the *Dictionary of Arts, Sciences and Literature*. Throughout his childhood, PH McKerlie spent his vacations in Galloway. He was attracted to a military career, vividly remembering clambering inside Mons Meg when the gun was restored to Edinburgh Castle. He failed, however, to follow in his brother's footsteps at Woolwich Academy and was offered a partnership in a sugar-planting business in Barbados. After five years there, he suffered a near fatal attack of yellow fever and returned to Britain. In 1845, friends of his father's obtained for him a clerkship in the Accountant General's Department of the Navy. In 1852, he met his wife, Marianne Helena Logan, and settled in Kensington in a house which became a centre for Scottish expatriates. His early military tastes were reflected in *An Account of the Scottish Regiments,* 1862. Work on his magnum opus, the *Lands and their Owners* began when he met James Paterson, author of a work on the history of Ayrshire, who was seeking help for a similar work on Galloway, but ultimately abandoned the whole responsibility to McKerlie. From 1868-1878, McKerlie spent all his leave in Galloway, visiting lost sites, sketching them and obtaining access to charter chests belonging to the great estates. He also corresponded with eminent Norse scholars, such as Professor Vigfusson, and eminent Roman Catholics, such as Sir David Hunter Blair. The whole work was published in five volumes, in 1878. Since he was relentless in pursuing lost links in the descent of estates, a certain number of landowners found that his research into pedigrees did not suit their pretensions to antique or, perhaps, to respectable antecedents. In 1891, however, he expanded on his research into the rise of the great families, this time giving it the form of a continuous narrative in *Galloway in Ancient and Modern Times* and he continued research for a supplementary volume of *Lands and their Owners* for the Wigtownshire estates, which he confessed had given him the greatest trouble. During these years, he held shooting rights at Sheuchan, on land belonging to the Vans Agnews, and when he ultimately became unfit to shoot, rented a house in Stranraer, whence he would go on frequent visits to Wigtown, Whithorn and surrounding areas. He maintained a keen interest in the lands at Cruggleton, near Whithorn, where his ancestors, the Cairrills, had originated, and contributed to the **Marquess of Bute's** restoration of Cruggleton Church after a storm blew down the gable in 1884. His interest in the way family traditions illuminated the history of Scotland continued to the very end of his life, since a proof of a brochure on *Sir William Wallace: the Hero of Scotland* arrived within hours of his death: his ancestor, William McKerlie had been a companion-in-arms of Wallace and died in his defence.

* * *

McKerlie's deeply instilled and informed sense of his own ancestry no doubt gave him insight in to the particular way in which the history of particular, long-resident, leading families settled on ancestral estates could illuminate the complex ebb and flow of peoples and languages in

A Literary Guide

Galloway history. His meticulous investigation of the charters undoubtedly set a new standard, in so far as they directed attention to the investigation of original forms of place names from the sources, and his recording of marriage agreements and sasines give fascinating insight into the complex dynastic alliances which shaped the land ownership of Galloway up to McKerlie's own time. But his account of Galloway ranges more widely than pure family history: he begins both volumes (the second being a supplement to the first) with a lengthy historical account of the dynastic struggles for the control of Galloway, which, while it was controlled by the Lords of Galloway, was effectively an independent kingdom within Scotland. His historical account was ultimately expanded into his *Galloway in Ancient and Modern Times*, and though his views on – for example – the extent of Roman penetration into Galloway and the intervention of the Norsemen may now be questioned, his incidental mentions of monuments and antiquities and his account of the wars of independence in Galloway have not dated. His main work is organised by parish, and the ownership of estates within these are patiently traced from their earliest appearance in legal documents through marriage and descent up to his own day. Not surprisingly, his account of Cruggleton in the parish of Sorbie, ancestral home of the Carrols or Kerlies, is particularly detailed: it includes a description of the re-taking of the Castle by Wallace and his comrade-in-arms, William Kerlie, from the English and their allies, who had usurped it. Another, earlier, story relating to the attempted seizure of Cruggleton by the Norsemen, using an enchanted flag, which McKerlie mentions, had been recorded in a story by **Captain Denniston** in 1825.

BIBLIOGRAPHY: *An Account of the Scottish Regiments* (1862); *History of the Lands and their Owners in Galloway* (1870-1879); *Galloway in Ancient and Modern Times* (1891); *Sir William Wallace: the Hero of Scotland* (1900)

PLACES TO VISIT: Cruggleton Castle may be reached by footpath from Garlieston.

Gordon Fraser
1836-1890
Wigtown

Gordon Fraser, druggist, printer, stationer and entrepreneur in Wigtown, is one of the significant minor writers of the area, thanks to whose industry and amused eye for the eccentricities of small town life, we have a well-documented picture of the characters and institutions of Wigtownshire during the nineteenth century.

Gordon Fraser was son of Bailie Fraser of Wigtown and was apprenticed to a Mr. Walter Malcolm, in a business which combined the trades of druggist, stationer and printer, and which he ultimately purchased and carried on with apparent success. He also taught Pitman's Shorthand and acted as shorthand writer in the law courts, then located in Wigtown. He was local correspondent for several newspapers, including national daily papers, as well as the *Wigtown Free Press* and Kirkcudbright papers. Fraser's *Almanac* appears to have been a yearly publication, to which other local authors, such as **James F Cannon** of Whithorn, contributed. He acted as a sort of poet laureate for Wigtown, publishing poems on local or historic happenings. Most importantly, he published two volumes of stories and historical information, comprising his gleanings from old burgh records and from folk memories of old Wigtown and Whithorn.

* * *

The best of Fraser's verse, most of which tends to the sentimental (as in his two poems published in Harper's *Bards of Galloway*), is *Davy Dumpytail*, his compilation of comic verses, written in various metres and styles, on the saga of the removal by the Town Council of the crows

A Literary Guide

nesting in Wigtown's main square. The verses, often written from a crow's eye view of the controversy, provide the opportunity of providing some gentle correctives to the besetting sins of small town life: "Thus brither, often do we see/ Those clad in brief authority, / Wi' sauls nae bigger than a pea, / An' hearts as sma', / Oppress the puir wi' wanton glee / An' big men claw". He published some short stories, all with local settings, including *The Fairest Flower in Wigtownshire*, in which the action takes place at Culshabbin and Castle Loch in Mochrum, and a romance *Bonnie Phemie , the Wigtown Belle*, set in the days of Edward Bruce and recounting the rout of the Bishop of Whithorn at Brunthouse Brae. Fraser's factual publications, such as his *Penny Guide*, a walking tour to Wigtown, include fascinating information about the multiplicity of professions carried on in the burgh at the time, ranging from mole catcher to photographer. His *Wigtown and Whithorn: Historical and Descriptive Sketches, Stories and Anecdotes, Illustrative of the Racy Wit and Pawky Humour of the District* (1877) derives from the tradition of Scots anecdote established by Dean Ramsay in his popular *Reminiscences of Scottish Life and Character*. Fraser's book consists, however, of much more than a Kailyard-inspired comic view of Scots character. He includes a wide variety of information, anecdote, poems and traditions. His subjects range from antiquarian notes about Wigtown Castle, accounts of the notorious martyrdom of Margaret McLauchlan and Margaret Wilson during the "Killing Times", to information gleaned from old Court and Kirk Session records which reveal the treatment of beggars and sinners. He also includes up to date commercial statistics, such as the tonnage of ships in Wigtown harbour and historical comparisons of the state of roads and transport in his own day and in the previous hundred years. His slightly later publication *Lowland Lore* (1880) consists of further fascinating extracts from Kirk Session and Town Council minute books, and of incidents and stories recorded from old residents of Whithorn and Wigtown, woven together by Fraser into comic narrative. Without Fraser's clanjamphrey of story and fact, we should not have such a rich picture of the peculiar vices and virtues of close-knit life in the self-contained and self-governing burghs in the Machars, prior to the impact of centralisation and economic decline.

BIBLIOGRAPHY:
Wigtown and Whithorn: Historical and Descriptive Sketches, Stories and Anecdotes, Illustrative of the Racy Wit and Pawky Humour of the District (1877); *Lowland Lore: or the Wigtownshire of Long Ago* (1880); *Davy Dumptytail: or the History of the Wigtown Crows* (1887); *Penny Guide to Wigtown and Neighbourhood* (1887); *The Fairest Flower in Wigtownshire* (n.d.); *Bonnie Phemie, the Wigtown Belle* (n.d.)

PLACES TO VISIT: Gordon Fraser is buried at Wigtown Cemetery. The Martyr's Stake is signposted east of the town square.

A Literary Guide

John Lauderdale
1740?–1800?
Kirkinner

John Lauderdale came to live in Kirkinner parish from County Antrim in Ireland in either the 1780's or early 1790's. In 1795, he wrote a reply to **Robert Burns's** *"Address to the Deil", and in 1796, he published, by subscription, a slim volume of "Poems, Chiefly in the Scottish Dialect".*

The biographical information we possess comes entirely from recollections by another Kirkinner author, **Samuel Robinson**, who in 1869 wrote a manuscript biography and also published details of Lauderdale's life in his *Recollections of Wigtonshire* (1872). As a small boy, Robinson remembered Lauderdale as one of the impoverished Irish immigrants who came in numbers to Kirkinner parish in the 1780's and 90's: Lauderdale squatted first in a barn near the farm of Bing, where other Irish families were living. This particular group of immigrants were in effect refugees from the suppression of political unrest in Ireland: they were known as "Croppies" for their short hair, which was cut to show their Jacobin allegiance. Robinson's grandmother, Effie (Elspeth) McGuffog ran the ale-house in Kirkinner and he could recall, listening in to conversations at his grandmother's fireside, Lauderdale's talk of revolutionary politics and anti-clericalism. Lauderdale himself mentions these evening drinking sessions in his *An Alewife to her Clock on Saturday E'en* when the landlady pleads with her impatient clock on behalf of her convivial guests, including "the man that wi' the pen / Maks rackit rhyme". Other poems also give biographical information: he had an early skill for rhyming, which made him unpopular with his schoolmasters; later, he had been in the army and then became a quarryman. Robinson tells us that he also tried to run a small shop in Kirkinner and later to teach at a private school; it seems that most of his endeavours failed, perhaps owing to his drinking habits, and he was largely supported in his old age by the efforts of his devoted wife, Mary Conchie, who kept poultry and collected leeches on the marshes for medical use. His first job in Kirkinner had been rock-cutting for the mill-lade at Milldriggan, an improvement initiated by Lord Daer, who was in process of selling the estate to the Earl of Galloway. The Daer connection was to prove fortunate for Lauderdale, since Daer and his factor, Jeffrey, were Jacobites, and Lauderdale sympathised with their sense of political exclusion: Jeffrey later assisted Lauderdale with the publication of his poems, and possibly with gathering subscribers to finance the printing. Certainly, Lauderdale did not hesitate to pillory in verse those belonging to the political establishment, whether members of the local Wigtown Council, the Church or the nobility, including Sir William Maxwell, for whom he had a particular dislike. Ultimately, it seems that two of his sons who had emigrated to America sent back funds to bring their parents to the new country, and Robinson gives us a final and unforgettable glimpse of Lauderdale, whose revolutionary fervour was undimmed: as he departed from Wigtownshire for the "land of freedom", he made a final gesture of defiance to the magistrates of Wigtown, by taking his stand at the cross of Wigtown and roaring out a favourite Croppie song at the top of his voice, which at the time was an indictable offence.

* * *

Though Lauderdale laid claim only to a modest poetic ambition – "Enough for me, the neibours kens/ What e'er I sing or say or pens" – his first essay into print was nothing less than a challenge to **Burns**, then still living in Dumfries. It was in the form of a reply from the Deil to Burns's *Address*: "Ye ca' me Satan, Nick an' Hornie / And taunts my house wi' gecks and stornie,/ But mock nae mair dear Robin Burnie / Till ye come ben". But though the poem starts promisingly, it loses impetus and suffers in comparison with the polish and technical mastery of Burns. It was a defect of literary training of which Lauderdale was perhaps aware, as he explains in a poem *To a brother poet*: "..as for rules, my honest lad / I never gat, nor sought, nor had". He is at his best in a light satirical vein, using touches of local colour and autobiographical information: "For rather aft I handle glasses, / An' ha'e a liking to the lasses, /Twa fauts that's vera apt to follow, / The pupils o' our Laird Apollo". His poems on convoluted local controversies suffer from our lack of understanding of the contemporary political landscape and sometimes from the vehemency of his vituperation; but at the same time, they give us fascinating glimpses of the condition of Wigtown society at

A Literary Guide

the turn of the eighteenth century and of the frustrations of those on its margins.

BIBLIOGRAPHY:
An Address to the Deil, by Robert Burns, with the Answer, by John Lauderdale, near Wigton (1795); *A Collection of Poems, Chiefly in the Scottish Dialect* (1796); Samuel Robinson, *Reminiscences of Wigtonshire about the Close of Last Century* (1872)

Samuel Robinson
1786-1874
Kirkinner

Samuel Robinson, born at Barglass in the parish of Kirkinner, wrote two autobiographical reminiscences, relating to his boyhood experiences of work aboard a slave ship, and of his early life in Kirkinner parish. Though recollected many years later, Robinson's memories of Wigtownshire constitute a valuable eye-witness account of the farming community before the turn of the nineteenth century.

Samuel Robinson is himself the main authority for the facts which we know relating to his life: he declares in his second book *Reminiscences of Wigtonshire* (1872) that he was born "at a place called 'The Signpost', on a very pleasant piece of tableland, on the farm of Balfern, parish of Kirkinner, Wigtownshire, on the 22nd day of September, 1786". He gives a vivid description of the parish school of Barglass, which he attended, which had a thatched roof, earthen floor, and benches consisting of bog-oaks dug out of the Wigtown mosses. He also declares that his father, a farm-labourer, moved to the farm of Barnhills in the Rhinns of Galloway, to work for John Drew. In 1800, Robinson was given an opportunity through his uncle, to sail on a slave-ship, the "Lady Neilson", from Liverpool. His account of the four years he spent at sea is told in his first book *A Sailor Boy's Experience*, published in 1867. We know little of his subsequent life, except that he did not return to Wigtownshire, and must, from the evidence of his style, have devoted some efforts towards educating himself. His books are written, as he says, "in the evening of a long, laborious and uneventful life", from Pine Cottage, Lesmahagow in Lanarkshire, where he died in 1874.

* * *

A Sailor Boy's Experience, was written in 1867 apparently with the wish to give an eye-witness account of the slave trade, about which, Robinson claims, there had been "many gross mis-statements". Although it claims to be a "plain unvarnished record of simple facts" and despite the narrative's appearing in the form letters written home to a "Schoolfellow", this is clearly a literary fiction, and we can only guess as to what original records, if any, Robinson may have been working from when composing sixty-three years after the event. The fact that a position aboard a slaver was an obvious opening for a boy from the Machars – in this case, one with an uncle who was Captain of a merchant ship and whose mother's cousin was "one of the principal ship owners in Liverpool" – is an interesting reflection on the connections between Liverpool and the coasts of Wigtownshire. Robinson gives a meticulous account of the items which would be bartered on the coast of Africa in exchange for slaves. He also records the loss overboard of another boy from Wigtown. Descriptions of the brutality aboard, including floggings with the "cat", alternate with accounts of ship-board routines and traditions, such as the bizarre customs of "crossing the line", and of wildlife seen while on the voyage. The complement of slaves for the ship was 294, who were acquired by a system of well-understood barter; according to Robinson, there was little cruelty towards the slaves aboard, simply because of their economic value. Robinson's maritime career was ended after an accident to his foot, which prevented him from going to sea again, and the abolition of the slave trade followed shortly thereafter. His second book, *Reminiscences of Wigtonshire* was inspired by the success of the first. Robinson's consciousness of the value of his testimony of eighteenth century Wigtownshire often interferes with its spontaneity, and one could wish for less moral reflection. Nonetheless, his recollections of the invasion of Kirkinner parish by Irish "Croppies", fleeing from retribution after the rebellion in Ireland, is a first-hand account of an undoubted historical and demographic event in Wigtownshire history, and Robinson provides the only biography we have of another Kirkinner poet, himself of "Croppy" origin – **John Lauderdale**. Robinson had clearly revisited Galloway, possibly for the purposes of writing his book, since it consists largely of chapters charting the changes in the roads, diet, educational standards , and climate which had occurred within the eighty years or so of his experience of the area. Through the memories of those he knew in his childhood, including Andrew McCreadie who lived to be 109, his testimony reaches well back into the eighteenth century.

BIBLIOGRAPHY:
A Sailor Boy's Experience aboard a Slave Ship (1867, also 1996 reprint); *Reminiscences of Wigtonshire about the Close of Last Century* (1872, also 1995 reprint)

Andrew Symson
1638-1712
Kirkinner

Andrew Symson was Episcopal minister of Kirkinner parish for about 23 years from 1663, the period of the "Killing Times" when the Covenanters were persecuted. His autobiographical comments, scattered throughout his works, enable us to see this period from the point of view of a humane representative of the Episcopalian party. He is remembered for a manuscript "A Large Description of Galloway", composed for the Royal Geographer, Sir Robert Sibbald, which contains a unique testimony as to the state of Galloway little more than a hundred years after the Reformation.

Symson was descended from a long dynasty of ministers, and both his father and grandfather published works; indeed, when young, Symson acted as amanuensis to his father. He was educated at Edinburgh High School and became a student at Edinburgh University in the late 1650's, becoming acquainted with Alexander, Earl of Galloway. He began his career as a Latin master at Stirling, but, at a point when Presbyterian ministers were leaving their posts as a result of legislation which would have subjected them to Royal control, he soon took advantage of the vacancies arising in the Church. He writes in the preface to his metrical version of the lives of Abraham, Isaac and Jacob (*Tripatriarchicon*) that his presentation to the ministry of Kirkinner took place quietly, that he employed all peaceable methods to regain dissenting parishioners and refused to give names of those not attending his Church to the Commander of government forces in the Stewartry. It is clear, however, that as the religious politics of the late seventeenth century became more polarised, moderates like Symson came under increasing pressure, and ran the risk of pleasing neither Royalists nor Covenanters and of incurring the suspicion of both. From this time, a manuscript list in Symson's hand apparently survives of the "disorderly", including Margaret McLauchlan, later notoriously martyred at Wigtown by drowning at the stake. He records that the "hill-men", those holding illegal conventicles in the hills

A Literary Guide

and moors of Galloway, drew "formerly orderly" parishioners away and that he grew unpopular when he refused to protect those involved in violent rebellion. This threw him on the mercies of the local nobility, including the Earl of Galloway's family, with whom he had remained on good terms, and he was sheltered in their homes when compelled to withdraw into a "quiet lurking place". His friendly contacts at the time with local landowners are reflected in the *Elegies* he composed, most of which are for the gentry and nobility of the Machars. Probably at this time of retirement, he acted as amanuensis to Sir George Mackenzie, who was composing his famous *Law and Customs of Scotland in Matters Criminal*, which he saw through two editions. Despite losing much of his congregation – he comments gratefully in his *Elegy* for Sir David Dunbar of Baldoon that he, with two or three others "never withdrew" – he appears never to have lost his affection for the "very pleasant place" in which his lot was cast, nor his interest in recording life around him. It was in the mid – 1680's that he received a circular from Sir Robert Sibbald, requesting information for a national Atlas and that he began composing his manuscript *A Large Description of Galloway*. In 1686, he appears to have left Galloway for Douglas, Lanarkshire, where he had a brief career as a minister, until leaving the pulpit for good when he was unable to take the oath of allegiance to William of Orange, who became William III, in 1688. Like many ejected Episcopal clergy, he entered the printing, book-selling and publishing business in Edinburgh, and became a recognised printer for the Episcopalian party, which occasionally involved him in controversy. His name often occurs on an imprint with other ousted clergymen, such as Henry Knox and David Freebairn. His printing business, which was at one point joined by his son Matthias, was at the foot of Horse-wynd and in the Cowgate, an area now cleared for a new road. When he died in 1712, he left a collection of several thousand volumes, which were auctioned by his widow, Jane Inglis. He is buried at Greyfriars Church.

* * *

Symson's most valuable work, *A Large Description of Galloway*, which he began in 1684 and revised extensively in 1692, was, for some reason, not published by Sir Robert Sibbald during his lifetime. It finally reached the public only in 1823, when Thomas Maitland, later Lord Dundrennan, discovered the manuscript at the Library of the Faculty of Advocates, an institution with which Symson had a connection during his years as a printer and publisher. It was later incorporated into **Mackenzie's** *History of Galloway* as an appendix, in 1841. The *Description* is in form rather like an early version of the *Statistical Account of Scotland*, conceived over a century later, since it takes the form of a reply to queries about the area, as to its climate, agriculture, customs and antiquities. As a result, we are given tantalising glimpses of the late seventeenth century world of Galloway, of its vanishing superstitious practices, of ancient monuments then still surviving and of current technologies. For example, he describes the new cattle-park belonging to Sir David Dunbar of Baldoon, the making of shell lime on the shores of Wigtown Bay, the dunghills in the centre of Wigtown, and the busy market for the "moor-men" of "Monygaffe". In Symson's day, the tower houses which now dot the landscape as ruins could be described as "good houses": **Lord Stair's** tower at Carscreugh had been lately built "according to the modern architecture", but, as Symson comments with characteristic pithiness, "would have been more pleasant, if it had been in a more pleasant place". Occasionally, the account is frustratingly condensed: in Whithorn, he comments all too briefly on the cathedral ruins surviving one hundred years on from the Reformation, and passes rapidly on to what he sees as the more remarkable matter of an centenarian who was reportedly growing younger by the year. Symson's poetry, like his historical work, might well (and perhaps deservedly) have slipped into obscurity, but for the intervention of others: his *Elegies* were rescued, however, and dramatically so, thanks to Symson's acquaintance with the Dunbar family of Baldoon and to his being, on that account, one of the few contemporary historical witnesses to the real events which formed the basis of the story of the *Bride of Lammermoor* (see entry under **Viscount Stair**). Sir Walter Scott, in his preface to the *Bride of Lammermoor* gave prominence to Symson's *Elegies*, by then very rare, since one was written on the sudden death of the bride, and a later one on the occasion of the death of the groom, by a fall from a horse. Unfortunately for Symson, at the very moment when his verses first reached a nationwide audience in Scott's preface, the great novelist pokes gentle fun at his plodding verses and tame moral: "Then comes the full burst of woe..", Scott writes, in mock-preparation for Symson's poetic climax, which then limps to a close.

A Literary Guide

Perhaps Symson, with his characteristic mildness, would not have objected to fame on these terms: in the preface to the *Tripatriarchicon* he claimed that he would be satisfied if his work were regarded as a "tolerably good trotting poem", and that, if he could not be included among "minores poetas", he would be content to be "inter minimos".

BIBLIOGRAPHY:
Tripatriarchicon (1705); *Elegies* (1705); *A Large Description of Galloway* (1823); William Mackenzie, *The History of Galloway* (1841)

John Ramsay McCulloch
1789-1864
Isle of Whithorn, Whithorn and Glasserton

JR McCulloch was born at the Isle of Whithorn, moved to Glasserton Manse before the age of five, after his father's death, and was educated at Whithorn burgh school; ultimately he married Miss Isabella Stewart from Whithorn. It was an unlikely beginning for one of the chief exponents of the emerging science of political economy, but he emerged with James Mill as the most influential exponents of the doctrines of economics developed by Adam Smith and David Ricardo. He began with articles on economics for the fledgling "Scotsman" newspaper, of which he became one of the first editors; his later "Principles of Political Economy" was received for many years as a crystalline exposition of the principles of classical economics.

John Ramsay McCulloch was born at the Isle of Whithorn on 1st March 1789, the eldest son of (Edward) William McCulloch, laird of Auchengool in the Stewartry of Kirkcudbright, and of Sarah Laing, eldest daughter of the Rev James Laing, minister of Glasserton parish. After his father died, in 1794, the family moved to live with his maternal grandfather at Glasserton Manse, but his mother was deeply unhappy living under the tyrannical regime of her father and, after re-marrying a cousin, a Mr Dempster, she moved to Kinross, leaving her two sons in their grandfather's charge. The boys appear to have been no less ill-treated than their mother, since Dr Laing ultimately entered into a legal dispute over board and lodging for the family. They were fortunate, however, in finding a talented teacher close at hand – a farm servant, Dan Hawkins, who had fled from Ireland after the rebellion of 1798, but who, despite being employed with Dr Laing digging pump wells, was a classical scholar, having been educated for the priesthood. The boys attended the burgh school by day and were

A Literary Guide

taught by Dan Hawkins at night. **Thomas Murray,** in his extended biographical note on McCulloch, states that he had met Hawkins and lent him volumes of Greek poetry, and it was from Hawkins that the boys learnt to recite long passages of Homer in the original. McCulloch, who had succeeded to his paternal grandfather's property at Auchengool, left for Kinross to join his mother. In 1806, he entered the College at Edinburgh, where he developed an interest in history and statistics, finding that the metaphysical classes of **Thomas Brown** were not to his taste. Though he became apprenticed to a writer to the signet, he had no taste for the law, and since he owned houses at the Isle of Whithorn which gave him financial independence, he left the office to study statistics and political economy. In 1811, shortly after he came of age, he re-visited Whithorn, where he rapidly became engaged to and then married to Isabella Stewart, whose mother kept a Whithorn inn. In 1816, he wrote *An Essay on a Reduction of the Interest of the National Debt* on the question of the Corn Laws, a burning issue of the day, and one which was to be shortly brought to the centre of economic thinking by David Ricardo, who published his *Principles of Political Economy and Taxation* in 1817. Between the years of 1817 and 1820, McCulloch edited *The Scotsman* and, after publishing an article on Ricardo's *Principles* in the *Edinburgh Review,* he was asked by the editor, Francis Jeffrey, for regular contributions: the total number of articles he eventually published in the *Review* amounts to 76. By this time, he was lecturing on political economy, and there was some attempt to obtain a chair for him at Edinburgh. In 1822, however, an opportunity to meet the leading thinkers of the day in political economy presented itself when he was invited to London by Ricardo, and met Mill and Malthus. After Ricardo's early death in 1823, the Ricardo Memorial Lectures were founded and McCulloch was invited to give the founding lecture; later, in 1846 he published a *Notice of the Life and Writings of David Ricardo.* His memorial lecture was ultimately expanded into the article on "Political Economy" in *Encyclopaedia Britannica* and an independent work *A Discourse on the Rise, Progress, Peculiar Objects and Importance of Political Economy.* This was further expanded into *The Principles of Political Economy* published in 1825. Perhaps it is an indication of his secure hold in the Edinburgh establishment that he was lampooned for his habit of repeating himself in the *Edinburgh Review,* in a satire by Christopher North (John Wilson) entitled *Some Illustrations of Mr. McCulloch's Principles of Political Economy by Mordecai Mullion,* 1826 and in scattered remarks in *Noctes Ambrosianae.* Shortly after his *Principles* was published, he left Scotland for good, after he was elected to a chair at the new University of London, now University College, in 1828 . He left it, however, possibly amid some disagreement arising from the fact that the chair was unendowed, in 1832. He had, before leaving his appointment, edited the works of Adam Smith, and already commenced work on his *Dictionary of Commerce and Commercial Navigation,* which was the first to collate information relating to trade from consular reports and exact statistics. Other encyclopaedic works, are *A Descriptive and Statistical Account of the British Empire* (1837) including contributions from leading scientists and from **Thomas Murray,** who had made his acquaintance as early as 1817, and *A Dictionary Geographical, Statistical, and Historical, of the Various Countries, Places and Principal Natural Objects in the World,* 1841. He also wrote various treatises on taxation and continued an interest in the historical rise of his own subject, by editing collections of rare treatises on money, economic policy and so on, with biographical sketches of significant economic writers; his own library, on his death, ran to 10,000 volumes. From 1838, he had been appointed Comptroller of the Queen's Stationery Office and lived on the premises, where **Thomas Murray** visited him in 1840. Murray, now a printer and publisher in Edinburgh, not only collaborated on some of McCulloch's encyclopaedic works, but also received frequent Stationery Office printing contracts from him. McCulloch continued his duties at the Stationery Office with exemplary efficiency until his death in 1864, when he was survived by his wife (until 1867) and a dozen children. Despite his lifetime devotion to the "dismal science", McCulloch appears in an appealing light, as described by Murray, who writes: "he retained to the end his broad Scottish accent, his attachment to Whig principles, his native Whithorn, and his native whisky". He was buried at Brompton cemetery. His portrait hangs at the National Portrait Gallery in London.

* * *

McCulloch's *Principles of Political Economy* was not distinguished for its originality, but for its lucid and popular restatement of the classical economic theory of Smith and, more especially, Ricardo, for the triumph

A Literary Guide

of whose theories McCulloch and James Mill vigorously campaigned. By the 1820's and 1830's, as the empire expanded and a prosperous middle class flourished, political economy was a subject in vogue, as demonstrated by the fact that McCulloch gave "conversational classes" in which he tested his audience's grasp of the principles of the subject. Perhaps because of this popular approach, McCulloch is now regarded as guilty of some over-simplification of Ricardo's views; but it was perhaps only late on in the century that the complexities of Ricardo's analyses could be appreciated, and it was Karl Marx who grasped the way in which they might be used to tend towards quite different conclusions. McCulloch's encyclopaedic works are now curiosities for those who wish to gain an insight into the questions relevant to trading at the height of the empire. Almost at the end of the immense bulk of fact accumulated in the *Dictionary, Geographical, Statistical and Historical...*, McCulloch allows himself a brief moment of nostalgia at the end of a long entry for Whithorn and the Isle of Whithorn, which sounds something like a sigh of relief: " It may probably be thought, seeing their limited population and importance, that this notice of Whithorn and its port has been extended to unnecessary length. But not being of the number of those who care nothing for the place to which they belong, we may, perhaps be excused, if, towards the close of this lengthened and laborious survey of so many countries and places, we have lingered for a moment over scenes once familiar and still well remembered. The associations which the mention of this locality calls up are all 'redolent of joy and youth' and are too soothing and pleasing to be instantly dismissed"(1841).

BIBLIOGRAPHY:

An Essay on a Reduction of the Interest of the National Debt (1816); *The Principles of Political Economy* (1825); *A Dictionary, Practical, Theoretical, and Historical, of Commerce and Commercial Navigation* (1832); *A Descriptive and Statistical Account of the British Empire* (1837); *A Dictionary Geographical, Statistical, and Historical, of the Various Countries, Places, and Principal Natural Objects in the World* (1841); *The Works of David Ricardo, Esq., MP; with a Notice of the Life and Writings of the Author* (1846); Thomas Murray, *Autobiographical notes* (1911)

Dumfries and Galloway

PLACES TO VISIT: Glasserton Manse, which is a private house, may be glimpsed along the road between Port William and the Isle of Whithorn; Glasserton Church still functions as part of a joint charge with the Isle of Whithorn and Whithorn Priory Church; it is open on one Sunday every month.

A Literary Guide

Latinus stone and *"Miracula Nyniae Episcopi"*
c. 450 AD and mid-700's AD
Whithorn

It is worth noting that the tradition of literacy in Galloway dates at least to the mid-fifth century, the earliest likely date for the much-discussed "Latinus" stone in Whithorn's Priory Museum. This tradition was flourishing in the mid-700's, when a sophisticated hagiographical poem on the life of St Ninian was composed, possibly at Whithorn. Both works emanated from the Christian church and the later associated pilgrimage centre at Whithorn, which was, according to tradition, founded by Ninian, and later housed his relics.

* * *

The "Latinus" stone has generated much scholarly heat since it was excavated, probably between the front tower of the current Priory Church and the remains of the cathedral nave, in the late 1880's, or early 1890's by William Galloway, architect to the **3rd Marquess of Bute**. On the dating of the "Latinus" stone depend questions about the chronology of the advent of Christianity to North Britain, about the literacy and sophistication of the native Britons, and about the nature of Christian funereal inscriptions and their lettering. Traditionally, the pillar of greywacke was regarded as a tombstone, like other personal memorials from Scotland and England, to the memory of Latinus, a man of 35 and his daughter aged 4 years, erected by the kin of Barrovadus. Recently, however, Professor Charles Thomas has reconsidered the evidence, taking account of the fact that the opening words on the memorial read "We Praise Thee, Lord", a phrase without parallel in the highly stylised world of Christian epigraphy, and of the fact that the Latin word "sinum" may be read as it stands, to mean "refuge" or "church". What was a tombstone becomes, by this transformation, a foundation or dedication stone for a church, perhaps recording the gift of aristocratic donors of the land. The second source indicating a literate Christian society at Whithorn is a Latin poem in heroic hexameters entitled *Miracula Nyniae Episcopi*, or

Miracles of Bishop Ninian. A later life, possibly composed by Ailred of Rievaulx, also survives from the twelfth century. Professor MacQueen has argued for the derivation of both "Lives" from earlier native sources, written in Anglo-Saxon and British-Latin, and for a complex numerological structure in the *Miracula*, which would indicate that it was composed in and for a sophisticated literary community. Interestingly, Charles Thomas has recently also argued for the presence of complex numerological games and Biblical references in the text and design of the "Latinus" stone, and which likewise implies consequences for literary culture and communication in the fifth century : the audience, it is implied, would have understood the sacred significance of certain plays on number and their reference to Biblical texts. The *Miracula*, like the "Life" by Ailred, contains an account of miracles performed by Nynia (the early form of Ninian's name) during his lifetime, and then of those which occurred with the miraculous intervention of his relics after his death. The text is laden with both classical and Biblical allusions, whose juxtaposition now strikes the modern ear as incongruous, but which belonged cheek-by-jowl in the accomplished Latinate culture of the hagiographers of the 8th century. The poem, indeed, is best read as a guide to literary culture and preoccupations of the 8th century, and as an example of the hagiographical genre, than as any accurate historical guide to the foundation of Whithorn or the biography of Ninian. It is interesting to observe the writer emphasising – if not advertising – the effectiveness of cures at Whithorn, by then a cult centre of some magnitude: "This is the house of the Lord which many are eager to visit, for many who have been afflicted with a disease of long-standing hurry there. They eagerly accept the ready gifts of health-bringing healing, and they grow strong in all their limbs by the power of the saint". There are interesting asides about life in a monastic community (one miracle relates to the growing of vegetables in the monastery garden), about diseases and about the nature of cures from physical proximity to the saint's relics: a blind woman "pressed against the earth with her forehead and lay in the hollowed out cave" of the saint's tomb.

A Literary Guide

BIBLIOGRAPHY:
John MacQueen, *St. Nynia: with a Translation of the Miracula Nynie Episcopi and the Vita Niniani* (1990); Charles Thomas, *Whithorn's Christian Beginnings* (1992); Charles Thomas, *Christian Celts* (1998)

PLACES TO VISIT: Whithorn Priory Museum houses the Latinus stone; the Priory nave is all that stands of the cathedral complex.

Jeanie Donnan
1864-1942
Whithorn

Jeanie Donnan, who lived in Whithorn for more than half a century, acquired a substantial reputation locally as the "Galloway Poetess", writing odes on local events, and sentimental verses on childhood and nature.

Jeanie Donnan was born at Gatehouse of Fleet, the fifth child of William Munro and his wife. Her father was a sawyer on the Cally Estate and seems to have encouraged her in her poetic compositions. She was educated at Cally Episcopal School, but was forced to give up classes owing to ill health. It was perhaps at that point, as a solace for her confinement and isolation from other children, that she began to write verses. She married James Donnan when still young, and came to live at 76 George Street, Whithorn. James Donnan was the burgh postman, and later became a town Councillor and Provost. The local minister of the Priory Church, Rev Donald Henry, on hearing her recite a poem at a Literary Church Guild, encouraged her to write and she began to contribute to the "Poet's Corner" of the *Galloway Gazette*, a relationship which lasted forty years. The editor of the *Gazette*, Mr John F Brown, eventually suggested that the works be collected and enlisted the help of another admirer, Dr Michael Macmillan of Birmingham University, who edited the volume, entitled *Hameland* and which appeared in 1906. **SR Crockett** agreed to write the review, commenting that it was the only review he had ever written, but that he recognised the claims of Galloway and of a lady. A later volume, *Heatherbloom*, appeared under the auspices of Mr Thomas Fraser of Dalbeattie, one of the most influential publishers

A Literary Guide

in Dumfries and Galloway, who had seen to the press many works by local authors. In 1930, her *Hills o' Hame* was published, with an introduction by Lord Sands. The proceeds of her publication *War Poems* were dedicated to charities concerned with the war effort. She became an honorary President of the Wigtown Burns Club and was elected a fellow of the Philological Society.

* * *

Though some of Jeanie Donnan's more successful poems are comic works in the vernacular (such as *The Fancy Work Schule*), her theme is more frequently the comforts to be drawn – in a cruel world – from the resilience and beauty of nature, or from the innocence of childhood. Her sensibility to the evils of society, or to the cruelty of fate is counterbalanced by her steadfast faith that these are inflicted upon us with a purpose : "There's seldom a pleasure but's mixed up wi' pain, / Nae dark cloud but has a clear linin' / An' never a loss but somewhere there's a gain - / Content aft follows repinin'". Often her reconciliation of the two will seem too facile for modern taste, but may have reflected her own need to find comfort during her long bouts of ill-health. Occasionally, her descriptive touches are less humdrum, as when she addresses the month of March: "With lenten lilies on your breast / And in your wind-tossed hair". The protests in her war-poetry are sometimes too shrill to have been poetically transmuted and mastered, and sit uneasily with her otherwise patriotic stance.

BIBLIOGRAPHY:
Hameland (1907); *Heatherbloom: Poems and Songs* (1911); *War Poems* (1915, enlarged ed. 1919); *The Hills o' Hame* (1930)

PLACES TO VISIT: A memorial plaque was placed on her house at 76 George Street, Whithorn, by the Editor of the *Galloway Gazette.*

James Fleming Cannon
1844-1915
Whithorn

James Cannon, a native of Whithorn, where he remained through much of his life, published humorous sketches of life and of the eccentricities of the burgh; he also published numerous poems and short stories, which were never collected, in local newspapers and in "The Gallovidian", of which he was one of the promoters.

James Cannon was son of a tailor and clothier in Whithorn, Robert Cannon, who was also tacksman of the salmon fishings at Portyerrock, near the Isle of Whithorn. His mother was Margaret McKie of Garlieston. From both his parents, he heard traditional tales of the area and memories of the days of smuggling. He attended the Parish School under William Kelly and then under Mr Anderson, of Dalbeattie. As a promising student, he also received encouragement and tuition from a Dr Broadfoot, medical practitioner. He became apprenticed to Mr Charles Hawthorn, draper in the town, but even at this time, he was composing verse. He left Whithorn before the age of twenty and took the post of assistant with the firm of Sommerville and Crawford, Miller Street, Glasgow. While in Glasgow, he took lessons in photography from an Italian, Paltroni, and returned to Whithorn, where, for some considerable time, he ran a photography business and married Miss Isabella Rowan, by whom he had ten children, eight of whom survived. He was eventually offered a post as clerk in the office of Gas Commissioners, sold his business in Whithorn to a Mr Ballantine, and left for Edinburgh, where he remained

A Literary Guide

for forty years. Eventually, he became a teller in the Commission office in Waterloo Place. For ten years, he contributed the literary articles to **Gordon Fraser's** *Almanac*, and his articles were republished in the *People's Journal*. He also wrote, frequently under the pseudonym "Mons Meg" or the initials "JFC", for the *Galloway Gazette*, the *Wigtown Free Press*, the *Kirkcudbright Advertiser*, the *People's Friend*, the *Weekly Scotsman* and the *Gallovidian*.

* * *

Cannon's *Droll Recollections of Whithorn and Vicinity*, illustrated by local photographs taken by WT Hawthorn, is less substantial than **Gordon Fraser's** productions in the same vein, but it does contain glimpses of burgh social life, transcriptions of the dialect prevalent at the end of the nineteenth century, as well as anecdotes featuring some of the characters of Whithorn celebrated either locally or nationally, such as **John Ramsay McCulloch**. The reviewer in the *Gallovidian* of 1904 welcomed the work as an account of regional peculiarities, at a time when levelling influences, such as the increase of mobility and communications, were on the advance. The book belongs to a whole genre of literature on the "worthies" of small towns, whose witticisms, use of the vernacular and combination of child-like simplicity and wiliness was regarded as being uniquely Scots. It was against this particular form of pathos and against the reduction of Scots language to the province of comic minor characters, both in real life and in novels (as in Sir Walter Scott's novels and particularly in the Kailyard school of **Barrie** and **Crockett**) that **Hugh MacDiarmid** famously rebelled in his crusade to restore the literary status of Scots. Two of Cannon's poems were published in **Harper's** *Bards of Galloway*, but perhaps his best and longest poem, which, like the others, has a supernatural element, *A Kelpie Tale*, appears in the *Gallovidian*, 1902.

BIBLIOGRAPHY:
Droll Recollections of Whithorn and Vicinity (1904); John Kelso Kelly, *Galloway Men of Mark* (1904)

Sir Herbert Maxwell
1845-1937
Monreith

Sir Herbert Maxwell was 7th Baronet of Monreith, descended from a family prominent in Dumfriesshire history, who later settled estates in the Machars of Wigtownshire. He was a prolific writer, author of sixty works in an extraordinary variety of fields: archaeology, philology, arboriculture and horticulture, fishing and shooting, history and biography. He was probably the most gifted scholarly country gentleman in Scotland for the duration of his long life, and for more than a generation, no scholarly or public endeavour was complete without his participation.

Herbert Eustace Maxwell was born in 1845 in Edinburgh, sole surviving heir to the Maxwell family estate of Monreith; his father was Sir William Maxwell, and his mother, Helenora, youngest daughter of Sir Michael Shaw-Stewart, 5th baronet of Greenock and Blackhall. He was educated at home, by his father and by a governess, then attended schools in the south of England, before going to Eton. His autobiography *Evening Memories* tends to be deprecating about his educational achievements. Certainly, when he went to Christ Church, Oxford, in 1864-5, he failed to pass "reponsions", which would have been the first step towards a commission in the Scots Fusilier Guards. He returned to Monreith, began learning the administration of the estate, and gained an acquaintance with Wigtownshire and its history which was unrivalled in his day. He also became a proficient sportsman, as a horseman, angler and shot, and had

A Literary Guide

already acquired an interest in natural history. He also became an officer in the Ayrshire Militia, in which he served for 21 years. In 1869, he married Mary Fletcher Campbell, of Boquhan, Stirlingshire, and they lived at Airlour House, close to Monreith House. When his father died in 1877, he succeeded to the title; in 1880, he was elected to Parliament for Galloway as a Conservative member. His interests in Parliament were those which were to be reflected in his future writings: the militia, agriculture, game and fisheries. He was active as Lord of the Treasury in 1886-92, and was an assistant whip for nine of the 27 years he spent in Parliament. Probably as a result of financial constraints, he began on a literary career in 1887, with newspaper articles first in local and then in national papers, and from then until 1932, he produced a steady stream of novels, biographies, and works on topography, history, archaeology, horticulture and sport. His first book was *Studies in the Topography of Galloway* (1887), reflecting his knowledge of place-names and geography of his native county, of which he was to become Lord Lieutenant from 1903-35. He was a founding member of the Ayrshire and Galloway Archaeological Association, which was instituted in 1878, and began a series of excavations at St Ninian's Cave in 1883. He was the first Chairman of the Commission on Ancient and Historical Monuments and Constructions of Scotland, having entered Parliament just at the point where Sir John Lubbock was guiding through pioneering legislation for the protection of monuments. Sir Herbert was the first to submit the antiquities on his lands to State care, and the motte at Druchtag, in Mochrum, was one of the earliest monuments to be listed in the country; it was in fact as a result of Sir Herbert's interest and influence that the Wigtownshire *Inventory of Ancient Monuments* is one of the earliest volumes in the series. In 1900, he became President of the Society of Antiquaries of Scotland for thirteen years, and was Rhind Lecturer in Archaeology in 1893 and again in 1912. He was also Chairman of the Trustees of the National Library of Scotland from 1925-32. His Parliamentary career opened the door to the composition of political biographies, and in 1893, he wrote the biography of WH Smith, who became the leader of a Conservative House of Commons. The *Creevey Papers*, which he edited from a mass of manuscript at Whitfield Hall, Northumberland, were an intimate revelation of political gossip of a previous generation: the revelations from the papers of Creevey, who was an MP in the critical period from 1798-1830 and a friend of **Dr Currie**, the biographer of Burns, caused a stir when published in 1903.

Dumfries and Galloway

In pursuit of sport and fishing, Sir Herbert travelled in France and Norway; his son, who was killed in 1914, also published on game and game shooting. After he was forced to withdraw from politics, on financial grounds, he retired to Monreith, where he carried out experiments in grafting and transplanting trees, and kept up a correspondence with the great plantsmen of his day. He was a talented amateur water-colourist, and painted flowers from the Monreith gardens on a daily basis, almost until his death in 1937. His wife died in 1910, and, since his sons predeceased him, he lived on in an isolation which was described by his grandson, **Gavin Maxwell**, in his *House of Elrig*, and was only succeeded by his grandson, Aymer, on his death in 1937. His role in representing the county in many spheres was recognised on his eightieth birthday when a public dinner was held in his honour, chaired by Sir Andrew Agnew, and a presentation was made to him.

* * *

Sir Herbert Maxwell is often compared with his friend Andrew Lang, another prolific and wide-ranging author, who held an equally influential place in Scottish culture and letters. Perhaps because of his comprehensive range, Sir Herbert's talents lay not in the detailed analysis of or original research into a subject, but in his ability to sketch the broad outlines, in an elegant and cultured style. His "causeries" are miscellaneous memories and discussions, often on subjects of natural history or literature : these included *Meridiana, Post-Meridiana, Rainy Days in a Library*, and then his *Memories of the Months* which began with some papers in *Blackwood's Magazine*, and then stretched to seven series, published between 1897 and 1922. His *Memories..* are probably his most characteristic productions, a distillation of the culture of the country gentleman, for whom there was as yet no contradiction between being an expert shot and fisherman, and being devoted to the observation of wildlife. A sample of the entries for the First Series includes "Stonecrops", "The Ruthwell Cross", "Loch Trout-Fishing", and "Capercailzie and Ptarmigan". In his *Scottish Gardens*, one of his more sought-after books, he writes of his own garden at Monreith, and skilfully interweaves remarks on the introduction of the Gregorian calendar with scientific notes on the sub-species of daffodils, and a description of a tapestry embroidered with flowers by an ancestress. *Flowers, a Garden Notebook* is entirely illustrated by Sir Herbert's own paintings. His autobiographical *Evening Memories*, written only five years before his death, is the only

A Literary Guide

work which perhaps permits us to probe behind that well-cultured prose. He includes some interesting discussion of his parents' membership of the Irvingite church (see entry under **Edward Irving**) and of his youthful impatience of the long sermons at Mochrum, which his family attended when in residence at Monreith: "Altogether the services in Mochrum kirk occupied fully three hours. As I was reckoned a delicate boy, I used to be allowed to leave after the first discourse, and walk home. Oh, the unspeakable sense of freedom in escaping from the stuffy kirk into the sunshine (sunshine is chronic over distant memories), and dawdling home among the birds and flowers!" His *Sixty Years a Queen*, published on the occasion of Queen Victoria's Jubilee and first published in serialised parts, achieved the greatest circulation of all amongst his many works. From the point of view of modern research, his *Place Names of Galloway* gives Gaelic more than its due share in originating Galloway names, which are now recognised to have also been influenced by Brythonic, Anglo-Saxon and, occasionally, Norse, languages. His *History of Dumfries and Galloway*, 1896, includes an excellent bibliography of local books under various headings – antiquities, natural history, poetry, novels and so on. Several works were printed as luxury editions and remain collectable: his *Fishing at Home and Abroad*, is dedicated to George V, is illustrated in colour, as is *British Fresh-Water Fishes*.

BIBLIOGRAPHY: *Studies in the Topography of Galloway* (1887); *Meridiana: Noontide Essays* (1892); *Post Meridiana: Afternoon Essays* (1895); *Rainy Days in a Library* (1896); *A History of Dumfries and Galloway* (1896); *Sixty Years a Queen* (1897); *Memories of the Months* (1897-1922); *The Creevey Papers* (1904); *British Fresh-Water Fishes* (1904); *Scottish Gardens* (1908); *Fishing at Home and Abroad* (1913); *Flowers: a Garden Notebook* (1923); *The Place Names of Galloway* (1930); *Evening Memories* (1932)

PLACES TO VISIT: Monreith Gardens are open on a seasonal basis; the House has now been converted into holiday accommodation.

Gavin Maxwell
1914-1969
Elrig

*Gavin Maxwell, grandson of **Sir Herbert Maxwell**, was born at the House of Elrig in Mochrum parish, and, through his "Ring of Bright Water", its sequels, and other books of exploration, became the apostle of the wild to an entire generation. As a record of one man's quest for solitude and for communion with nature, the novel has been ranked with Thoreau's "Walden" or White's "Selborne", although, as his recent biographer, Douglas Botting, comments "never had the simple life been pursued by so complex a character".*

Gavin Maxwell was born in 1914 at the House of Elrig, son of Colonel Aymer Maxwell, the heir to the Monreith estate and a war veteran. His mother was Lady Mary Percy, daughter of the Duke of Northumberland; both his parents were members of the Irvingite church (see entry under **Edward Irving**), a fact which had a considerable impact on Gavin Maxwell's childhood. When Colonel Aymer Maxwell was killed only a few months after his youngest son's birth, leading the Collingwood battalion into action at Antwerp, his widow was at first too overcome by grief to return to Elrig. The family returned to their isolated moorland home only in 1918 and its remoteness served both to cement close ties between Lady Mary and her youngest son, and to give Gavin and his brothers an affinity for the outdoors and a reserve in society which was always to remain with Gavin. Their interests in natural history were strongly encouraged by their aunt, Lady Muriel Percy, who encouraged each of them to specialise in collecting different species of animal, and

A Literary Guide

they set up a laboratory in a gun room. Gavin's gift for taming animals was undoubted at an early age; he also began composing fantastic natural histories, such as his *Book of Birds and Animals*. When he was sent south to a preparatory school in 1924, his early isolation had ill-prepared him for the company of other boys, and the experience was a misery to him. In 1927, he had a respite at home, when he was taught to shoot, a skill for which he was later renowned, by the gamekeeper, Hannam. His later school experiences, at Hurst Court, and then at Stowe, were happier, since the regimes were more relaxed and he was allowed to keep animals. His thoughts, however, were always on the Elrig moors and hills. In 1930, however, he was stricken with a rare blood disorder, which entailed months of convalescence in bed, when he could read and paint in solitude. In 1933, after tuition for college entrance, he entered Hertford College, Oxford, to read Estate Management, but largely ignored his classes, attended some on zoology and medicine, as well as painting, and joining with a country set, which was interested in shooting and hunting. He left in 1937 with a third class degree. He had already published some articles in *The Field* and was looking for a more substantial project of exploration and science, when Peter Scott, the eventual founder of Slimbridge wildfowl sanctuary, suggested that he should explore the northernmost breeding grounds of Steller's Eider. His trip enlarged the collection of wildfowl he had begun on Monreith's White Loch. On the outbreak of war, he volunteered for the Scots Guards and, after completing training courses, he was posted to the Tower of London during the Blitz. After seeing the miseries of a bombing raid, he made a commitment to buy himself an island in the Hebrides, in a bid to provide himself with a fantasy escape from the horrors which surrounded him: "Soay was my Island Valley of Avalon, and Avalon was all the world away". Since his health was too fragile for him to be sent to the front, he volunteered for work with the Special Operations Executive, which had been set up by Churchill to organise sabotage and subversion in enemy territory. In 1942, he became an instructor in a paramilitary training school at Arisaig in the West Highlands, and, despite his reserve and his individualism which made him less than ideal military material, his knowledge of fieldcraft and of weapons made him a valued member of the training team. It was still wartime when he first found leisure to visit the island of Soay by yacht, and, in fulfilment of his pledge, he completed the purchase of it, without, unfortunately, reserving for himself the commercial salmon fishing rights round the island. Towards the end of the war, while he was pondering the question of making Soay a viable investment for himself and a source of income for the inhabitants, he sighted his first basking shark, about which very little was known. The oil, however, could be commercially extracted, and once he had been invalided out of the army with the honorary rank of Major, he obtained finance from family and friends to invest in a commercial shark fishing station on Soay. The account of what turned out to be a financially disastrous venture and of the dramas of his struggles with bureaucracy, harpoons and faulty vessels is given in his *Harpoon at a Venture*. Eventually, he had to face selling off the company and becoming its manager, thereby losing his inheritance in the process. He was now forced to consider a way of making a living, and for some time he attempted to exploit his painting talent by becoming a society portraitist. It was in these unsettled years that he first saw remote Sandaig in the West Highlands, which was to become the world-famous "Camusfearna" of his autobiographical trilogy, and met the poet, Kathleen Raine, who was to become part of the tortured story of his relations with Sandaig and with women. Literary work next presented itself as a way of earning a living, and he had already published poetry in the *New Statesman*; other poetic pieces composed at this time were later to be incorporated into his prose. His book on shark-fishing was published in 1951 to critical acclaim : the *Times* gave the verdict that he was a "man of action who writes like a poet". In 1952, he visited Sicily in search of new material, and discovered the story of Salvatore Giuliano, a bandit-hero, who had been murdered two years previously. In the next two years, he unravelled the truth surrounding the crime: the book which emerged was *God Protect Me from My Friends*. Given that the book penetrated to the murky heart of Sicilian politics, it was inevitable that both Maxwell and his publishers would be implicated in libel actions in the future. Sicilian life was the foundation of another book, on the poverty of the Sicilian tuna fishermen, in *The Ten Pains of Death*. He had already planned a trip to the Arabian marshes with the well-known explorer, Wilfred Thesiger, and finally left for Iraq with Thesiger in 1956. Both men were to write of their experiences in the curiously isolated and unspoilt world of the Marsh Arabs, and Maxwell's *A Reed Shaken by the Wind*, based on his diaries, became a classic of Arabian travel.

Nonetheless, playing second fiddle to Thesiger, who was expedition leader, and being unable to speak Arabic was a frustrating experience for Gavin Maxwell, and his growing depression was only lightened by the prospect of acquiring an otter, a living being on which to lavish some affection. The first otter he was given, Chahala, died before he left Iraq, but he travelled home – a journey which was harrowing both for Maxwell and his otter – with Mijbil, a replacement found for him by the Marsh Arabs. In London, it was discovered that "Mij" belonged to an unknown species, which was named "Lutrogale perspicallata maxwelii", an achievement which Maxwell was to claim as the greatest of his life. Mijbil was first released at Monreith; in 1956, he was taken to Sandaig, where Maxwell had acquired a lease of the isolated cottage in the bay, situated between the burn and the sea – the "ring of bright water" which Kathleen Raine invoked in her poem. The relationship between Kathleen Raine and Maxwell, who was homosexual, was doomed to failure and was punctuated by bitter arguments ; after one of these, Kathleen Raine, in an action which Maxwell was later to see as the ultimate act of betrayal and the cause of the succeeding catalogue of disasters, cursed him, standing under the rowan tree at the burn, and wishing him to suffer "as I am suffering now". In 1957, while Maxwell was working on his Arabian book, he left Kathleen Raine in charge of the household at Sandaig, and she allowed Mijbil to wander towards the village of Glenelg. There, a road-mender, who came to be known as "Big Angus", killed him with a spade. The loss of Mijbil was a crushing blow to Maxwell, but it was also the stimulus to a deeper consideration of a book about his life with his otter, which now required a more serious approach than was suggested by a book he had already proposed to his publishers, entitled *Otter Nonsense*. Meanwhile, another otter, a replacement for Mijbil was acquired from a couple returning to Africa. Maxwell wrote *Ring of Bright Water* at Sandaig, which was still a primitive retreat, without services or the interruptions which later on made it difficult to write there. The very remoteness of the place, however, which made his descriptions attractive as literature and as escapism, caused a tension in Maxwell's life from now on, in that he was committed to maintaining a home for his otter (soon to be joined by Teko, a male) under difficult circumstances, and at the same time, to carry on a full-time career in writing, in order to finance his retreat. Maxwell visited the Atlas mountains in Morocco, where he

Dumfries and Galloway

was investigating the story of the Glaoui brothers, who had deposed two sultans of Morocco and replaced them with puppet governors. When the *Ring of Bright Water* was published in 1960, it was an overnight success, selling over a million copies, and it made Maxwell both rich and famous. He began to receive a huge mailbag of correspondence from those all over the world, in whom the celebration of freedom and of closeness with nature had touched a profound chord. Success brought its own penalties, including the invasion of Sandaig by curious sightseers; there was also the need to keep Edal and Teko apart and to maintain this complex establishment, whose communication with the outside world depended on a thread which was always in danger of breaking. In 1961, under pressure of circumstances, and of his own highly flammable temperament, Maxwell spent the winter in North Africa, largely on the verge of nervous breakdown. His *The Rocks Remain*, one of his darkest books, expresses the mood of that winter. Eventually, he was rescued from the semi-mesmeric state into which he had fallen while living in the medina, by friends and his faithful assistants from Sandaig. There was worse news to come at Sandaig: his otters began to grow aggressive, first to visitors, and then, with quite horrific consequences, to their own keepers. The house was gradually altered to confine the otters to specially designed quarters, and the dream of a prelapsarian relationship with animals seemed to have vanished. Perhaps in a desperate bid to provide himself with an anchor in this tumultuous period, Maxwell married Lavinia Renton in 1962. But the financial strains which were mounting with Sandaig's ever increasing maintenance costs (despite the huge earnings Maxwell derived from the *Ring*), Maxwell's own demanding and often paranoid temperament, his heavy drinking and inability to exist in any loving relationship, meant that the marriage was short-lived. While he was working on *Lords of the Atlas*, he was simultaneously delving into his childhood memories in writing *The House of Elrig*, which was greeted with critical praise when published in 1965. As the Sandaig dream faded and its complex realities mounted, he acquired two lighthouses on Ornsay and Kyleakin and engaged Richard Frere, one of many long-suffering aide-de-camps, to convert them for him. His schemes for the islands included commercial eider duck breeding, which he researched in Iceland, and a zoo-park, but these dreams overlay a deepening financial crisis, which burdened Maxwell's managers and

A Literary Guide

professional advisers. The crisis was at least alleviated for a time by the sale of rights to a film of *Ring of Bright Water*, to be directed by Jack Couffer. The film converted the poetry of the novel into family entertainment, but Maxwell eventually became reconciled to the transformation. He was to attend a showing of the film at Newton Stewart, a pleasant return to his roots, against a backdrop of increasing ill-health and nervous tension. While working on the final novel of the trilogy, *Raven Seek thy Brother*, the final disaster struck Sandaig, when it was burnt to the ground, along with the female otter, Edal, and most of Maxwell's possessions. He planned to move to Kyleakin island, whose heather and rock reminded him of Elrig, "the house that obsessed my childhood". There were already signs that he was extremely ill, and in 1969, it was discovered that he had inoperable cancer. It was a brave man's death. His ashes were interred beneath a rock at Sandaig, and the obituaries of the time recognised his contribution to forming and expressing a particular consciousness of and closeness to the natural world.

* * *

Gavin Maxwell's own extremely complex life was the real material for all his books; indeed, it was never clear whether the extraordinary events which he documented came before the books, or whether the artistic need to create generated a life which was lived at a more than usual pace, and with more than usual drama. What is clear is that the deceptively documentary aspect of many of his works is underlain by deeper meaning, that he was aware of communicating this, and that this is the secret of his appeal; in his lecture on *The Technique of Travel Books* he stated that the travel writer "must have some feeling or thought to communicate, something beyond observable or recordable fact, for him each journey must be to some extent a journey of the spirit, a journey of self-discovery". The saga of his life with the otters charts an almost Biblical line, from the primitive paradise of Camusfearna in the early years, to the intervention of evil through the persona of "Big Angus", and the later disasters brought about – as Gavin Maxwell saw it – through other human agents. Despite the darker mood of the later parts of the trilogy (*The Rocks Remain* and *Raven Seek thy Brother*), Maxwell never broke faith with the idea that "there exists some unritual union with the rest of creation, without which the lives of many are trivial", and that a return to the ideal (perhaps, as his biographer points out, the mental picture he held of his childhood home of Elrig) beyond the trivial, remained possible. The celebrated "herring-fry" scene in the *Ring of Bright Water*, where Maxwell describes his two assistants rushing into the water where some freak of abundance in nature had created showers of silver fish, is something like an epiphany of this union. Maxwell also has an ability to describe nature in tense, economical prose, which sounds more like (and sometimes started its life as) poetry. His description of the waterfall, a significant location in the iconography of Sandaig, in summer, may serve as an example: "In summer, when the water is low, one may pick one's way precariously along the rock at the stream's edge, the almost sheer but wooded sides rising a hundred feet at either hand. Here it is always twilight, for the sun never reaches the bed of the stream, and in summer the sky's light comes down thin and diffused by a stipple of oak and birch leaves whose branches lean out far overhead. Here and there a fallen tree-trunk spans the narrow gorge, its surface worn smooth by the passage of the wildcats' feet. The air is cool, moist, and pungent with the smell of wild garlic and watery things such as ferns and mosses that grow in the damp and the dark. Sometimes the bed of the stream widens to deep pools whose rock flanks afford no foothold, and where it looks as though the black water must be bottomless." In other moods, Maxwell can conjure up the humour of a situation with a few masterly strokes: when Beryl Borders, his secretary, began looking after Sandaig towards the close of its existence, she brought a menagerie of animals with her, which served to complicate its menage, already on the edge of practical and emotional impossibility. Maxwell writes: "the fantastic fertility of the household was crystallised for me by the discovery one day, previously unknown to anyone, of a litter of weaned kittens living in the loft above the lobby". *The House of Elrig* was Maxwell's opportunity to return to the Avalon of his youth: behind the fascinating insights into his aristocratic, isolated family life, into the Irvingite creed of his parents, and his vague perceptions of his distinguished grandfather (see entry under **Sir Herbert Maxwell**), there is always the backdrop of the wild environment of Elrig and its "remembered smells – bog myrtle crushed in the hand, peat-smoke, the sharp acrid tang of hill sheep and sheep-dip from the farm fank beyond the dry stone wall, the almond bitter sweet

A Literary Guide

smell and taste of caterpillar-like bracken fronds". The human environment is always much more threatening and the book is an account of the loss of Elrig, through the medium of school and adulthood; it remains an extraordinarily honest, raw and intimate portrait of an adolescent, confronting the realities of the human society to which he had not been exposed in early life and never found ultimately satisfying.

BIBLIOGRAPHY:
Harpoon at a Venture (1952); *God Protect Me from My Friends* (1956); *A Reed Shaken by the Wind* (1957); *The Ten Pains of Death* (1959); *Ring of Bright Water* (1960); *The Rocks Remain* (1963); *The House of Elrig* (1965); *Lords of the Atlas* (1966); *Raven Seek thy Brother* (1968); Douglas Botting, *Gavin Maxwell - a Life* (1993)

PLACES TO VISIT: An otter sculpture, memorial to Gavin Maxwell, stands at the head of a cliff over Monreith beach. Monreith Gardens, where Mijbil was released into the water of the White Loch of Myrton, are open seasonally to the public.

Dumfries and Galloway

John Patrick, Third Marquess of Bute
1847-1900
Drumwalt, near Mochrum

The Third Marquess of Bute was born to one of the largest fortunes in Europe, and became the greatest private patron of architecture Britain had ever known. His fascination with mediaevalism led to his celebrated conversion to Catholicism, on which Disraeli based the plot of "Lothair". His intervention in Wigtownshire, where he worked on his immense translation of the Breviary, consisted in the restoration of his own seat at Mochrum, and in extensive archaeological investigations at and around Whithorn, the historical site of St Ninian's "Candida Casa".

The Second Marquess, father to John Patrick, had created the family fortune by grasping the critical role the family estates in Scotland and South Wales might play in the onset of industrialisation. He, and the Bute Trustees, created the Cardiff docks, which enabled the vast potential wealth of the South Wales coal field to be unlocked. When he died in 1848, to scenes of mourning usually associated with the death of a monarch, his only son was the richest heir in Britain, and possibly in Europe. He was at first under the charge of his mother, a committed Protestant, but when she died in 1859, she left him to the care of guardians. There was much litigation between the two guardians, Colonel Charles Stuart and Lady Elizabeth Moore, and Bute eventually lived much of his childhood at Galloway House, near Garlieston, where Lord and Lady Galloway had the large family which he lacked. He came under rather different religious influences there than he had experienced from the rigid Presbyterianism of his mother and guardian, and enjoyed discussions with Lord Galloway's family chaplain. His interest in legends and ceremony, which later manifested themselves in his fascination with the mediaeval, with psychic research, astrology, heraldry and with the fine points of liturgy, as well as with architecture, was already apparent. He went on to prep school at May Place, and then to Harrow, where Lord Galloway's sons had already gone before him. He spent holidays either at Galloway House, or at Glentrool, where Lord Galloway had a hunting lodge. **Sir Herbert Maxwell,** his contemporary, recalls: "My only recollection of his room at Harrow, where I once visited him, is of an arrangement whereby bees entered from without into a hive within the room, where their proceedings could be watched". At Harrow, he won two prizes, including a poetry prize for a work on the Black Prince. He visited Palestine in 1865, and then matriculated at Christ Church, Oxford. By this time, his historical sense was leading him towards sympathy with the Roman Catholic Church. By autumn 1866, he had decided to convert and when the decision was announced to his guardians, it caused consternation and even panic. He undertook – reluctantly – not to act until he reached his majority, which was celebrated in 1868. The celebrations in Cardiff, where an ox was roasted, lasted an entire week. It was clear that his conversion, for which he was preparing in late 1868, would not fail to attract public attention. When the news broke, press coverage was extensive, and largely hostile: the *Glasgow Herald* referred to him as "his perverted Lordship" and a West of Scotland provincial paper wrote that it was sure "that the acquisition, except in a pecuniary way, would be of little advantage to those who wheedled him out of his wits and into their snares". The notion of religious factions warring for the soul of this sensitive and idealistic, but immensely powerful and wealthy nobleman set the scene for Disraeli's novel *Lothair*. Disraeli, in fact, was one of those attending Bute's marriage to Hon. Gwendoline FitzAlan Howard in 1872. Bute, however, was not the weak-minded puppet which the press imagined: he was able to learn Hebrew to aid him with the translation of the *Breviary*, wrote a respected article *On the Ancient Language of the Natives of Tenerife*, purchased for himself a working library (ordering three copies of each book, so that he could find them at any seat at which he might be resident), and contributed to, and ultimately bought, the *Scottish Review*, which could be a vehicle for his obscure historical researches. The greatest expression of his mediaeval frenzy was in his architectural patronage, and in archaeological excavations: as a contemporary put it "his hands were never out of the mortar tub". In Wigtownshire, which he had known since childhood, he had inherited, via the Dunbars of Mochrum, the twin-towered fifteenth and sixteenth century fortress at Drumwalt. First, local architect Richard Park, and later Robert Weir Schultz, worked on the conversion of the building, joining the two parts of the building, and creating a walled garden. David Hunter Blair, a friend and biographer, wrote of Mochrum that it was "a queer two-storied tower set in the middle of a Wigtownshire moor, on the edge of a gloomy lake.. in very ugly country.. almost inaccessible by road or rail". When he and Bute stayed there for a fortnight, correcting proofs of the immense Roman *Breviary*, he describes the isolation, of which Bute was completely unaware: "Proofs arrived from the publisher by every post. We used to take long walks, often in pouring rain, through the sodden moors; and in the middle of our walk Bute would extract from his pocket long sheets of proof, and read to me in sonorous tones his admirable translation of collects, lessons or hymns, and invited my criticism, which annoyed him if in the least unfavourable.. An English friend of mine who was staying there became bored almost to frenzy by these strange days and nights, and implored Bute to take him away.." It was almost inevitable that the proximity of his seat to Whithorn, the site of the earliest Scottish church, would attract Bute's attention to the possibilities for excavation and restoration there, particularly when a group of gentlemen amateurs, including **Sir Herbert Maxwell**, had already begun excavation at St Ninian's Cave in the 1880's. In the end, Bute funded excavations at Whithorn for thirteen years, employing William Galloway as his architect, one whom he had also employed on Bute, but who, sadly, did not live to publish his account. Bute's contribution was characteristically generous and thorough-going: he purchased the current Whithorn museum, restored St Ninian's Chapel at the Isle of Whithorn, virtually rebuilt Cruggleton Church, and his architect engaged in other minor archaeological campaigns in the area. The discoveries made during the 1880's form the basis of the museum collection of Christian stones at Whithorn. Bute was also concerned, however, with the souls of the living: he provided several new churches in the area, including an "iron church" at Whithorn at the farm of High Mains, where he installed a group of Premonstratensian canons, the order which originally occupied the Whithorn Priory in the thirteenth century, he was active in promoting annual pilgrimages, and built a Catholic orphanage at Craigeach, near Mochrum. In 1899, after thirty years of the most intense patronage history

A Literary Guide

and the arts had known in Scotland, he died at Dumfries House, Ayrshire. He was buried on the Isle of Bute, but his heart was taken, at his request, and buried in the Holy Land.

* * *

Bute's first composition, the prize poem from Harrow, is undoubtedly an impressive performance for a boy little more than 15 years old, and it is a presage of the tone of life he admired and which he was to adopt: "When the long requiem's assuaging stream / Sounds high and solem through the holy fane, / And loud and frequent in the darkened pale/ The organ's heavy swell is heard the while.." Bute's major work is undoubtedly his massive translation of the *Breviary*, on which he laboured over a ten year period, and which he called his "beloved child". Another translation was from the *Targum*, the commentary by the Jewish Fathers, and he produced a paraphrase of Blind Harry's *William Wallace*. He also contributed over 20 articles to his *Scottish Review* on subjects ranging from St Patrick and *Ancient Celtic Latin Hymns*, to Wagner's Bayreuth, which he had visited. His heraldic interests found outlet in two volumes, including the *Arms of the Royal and Parliamentary Burghs of Scotland* (1897), and his interest in psychical research in *The Alleged Haunting of B... House* (1899). The excavations at Whithorn were never fully published, but the notes of the architect in charge were passed to MacGibbon and Ross, who wrote an account for the "Ayrshire and Galloway Archaeological Association". Perhaps more famous than anything written by Bute was Disraeli's *Lothair*, published during Bute's lifetime, shortly after his conversion, in 1870. Lothair is a wealthy nobleman, left, after his father's death, in the care of two guardians, one of whom is Protestant, another a brilliant Catholic who becomes a cardinal. The resemblance is too pointed to be missed: "Lothair rose, and paced the room with his eyes on the ground. 'I wish I had been born in the middle ages', he exclaimed". If the beginning of Lothair's life sounds familiar, the outcome is different: he becomes involved in the struggle of Garibaldi's patriots in Italy and ends by resisting the blandishments of both political and religious fanatics. The book is laden with the atmosphere of conspiracy, and contains some good portraiture of society life. The critics damned it, but the first edition sold out in two days and there were eight editions in the first year of publication, as "Lothairmania"

Dumfries and Galloway

swept Britain, Europe and America. In 1874, a contemporary, Augustus Hare, who had met Bute for the first time, wrote: "It was like reading *Lothair* in the original, and most interesting at first, but became somewhat monotonous, as he talks incessantly.. of altars, ritual and liturgical differences; and he often almost loses himself and certainly quite lost me, in sentences about 'the unity of the Kosmos'".

BIBLIOGRAPHY:
The Early Days of Sir William Wallace (1876); *The Roman Breviary* (1879); *On the Ancient Language of the Natives of Tenerife* (1891); *The Arms of the Royal and Parliamentary Burghs of Scotland* (1897); *The Alleged Haunting of B— House* (1899); Chapter on Whithorn Priory, in *Archaelogical and Historical Collections Relating to Ayrshire and Galloway, Vol. X* (1899); Benjamin Disraeli, *Lothair* (1870); David Hunter Blair, *John Patrick, 3rd Marquess of Bute* (1921)

PLACES TO VISIT: Whithorn Priory and Museum, Cruggleton Church and St. Ninian's Chapel are all open to the public.

A Literary Guide

Patrick Vaus
?1530-1597
Barnbarroch, near Whauphill

The correspondence of Patrick Waus, laird of Barnbarroch and an important figure in sixteenth century Scottish court circles, gives a fascinating insight into the life and concerns of a Galloway laird in the period of the Reformation, into the rivalries and frequent brutalities of the relationships between the leading families, and into epistolary styles and orthography of the time.

Patrick Vaus was descended from the Norman family of de Vallibus, who acquired lands at Barnbarroch from the late fourteenth century. He was probably born in about 1530; his father was killed at the Battle of Pinkie in 1547. He was sent to school at Musselburgh. He was appointed parson of Wigtown, and later of Douglas; by 1549, he had obtained leave to go abroad to Paris to study; he also seems to have visited Rome. In Paris, he was on the service of the young Queen Mary, at work on clerical affairs, and administering the affairs of a deceased cousin. It seems, however, that he had left the church of Rome in 1560, and married a Protestant, Elizabeth, daughter of Sir Hew Kennedy. His secular career seems rather to have overshadowed his ecclesiastical duties, since he became a knight, privy councillor, and Lord of the Articles, though he did act as commissioner on the subject of the provision of ministers and on their stipends when he represented Wigtownshire in Parliament. Perhaps his most important mission was to negotiate a marriage for James VI with a Danish princess, and later to attend the king when he went to marry the princess, who had been stranded in Norway after a storm. He was rewarded for this mission, and his son received the commendatorship of Crossraguel Abbey for life. His fortunes obviously prospered, since he had purchased lands at Carscreugh, before he inherited Barnbarroch; he also administered the estate of the Earl of Cassilis, whose daughter he married, after the death of his first wife. According to the will he left on his death in 1597, he had three sons and eleven daughters.

* * *

The immense bulk of Vaus' manuscripts were transcribed and published by R Vans Agnew, a descendant. Since they often represent one side of the correspondence – that received by Patrick Vaus – one can only guess at his replies, but the early ones he sent home from his school are fascinating : like many other young men, he writes home giving an account of his expenditure and asking for more funds. He gives us an account of his reading at school, since he has bought "commenteris of ceser", "ane sallust", and "ane silva" (the "Silva" of Buchanan, written against the Franciscans, had led to Buchanan's exile) . He writes to his father: " Ye sall vit I am verie scant of arouis, and ye man send me sum silver for till bay them". What emerges strongly from later letters is the endemic lawlessness in Galloway, and the way in which it could impinge on the life of a well-to-do nobleman like Sir Patrick: the correspondence continually mentions "hornings", the mutual bonds by nobles to defend each other in disputes, both within and outside the law, the use of armed entourages to influence the course of justice, and the abduction of unwilling brides, including Sir Patrick's eleven-year-old niece from Carscreugh. As Gavin Douglas of Baldoon writes of a dispute in 1591, "sa mekill Innosent bluid as is spilt onle throcht the pryde of the twa lordis, and god to forgeif tham that hes the vyit (blame) thairof, and seis na apeirans bot of mair trubill and cumeris". Two of the more spectacular brutalities referred to in the letters are the roasting of the Abbot of Crossraguel by the Earl of Cassilis, in order to force him to sign a lease in his favour for all Abbey lands, and the besieging of the Commendator of Whithorn, also a natural son of James V, in Cruggleton Castle by Robert Fleming. The factionalism was no doubt a consequence of the closely felt blood ties, which is another feature to emerge from the correspondence: every Galloway laird's name appears in Sir Patrick's letters (Ahannay, Garlies, Dunbars, Kennedy, Douglas), and his daughters, whose marriage contracts make interesting reading, were all married to local lairds. The language used is a good guide to the pronunciation of the time and can be revealing when applied to place-names which still exist; the liberal sprinkling of the correspondence with Scots legal and fiscal terms provides an insight into the institutions of the time.

BIBLIOGRAPHY:
Robert Vans Agnew, ed., *Correspondence of Sir Patrick Waus of Barnbarroch, 1540-1597* (1882)

A Literary Guide

James Dalrymple, 1st Viscount Stair
1619-95
Carscreugh, near Glenluce

James Dalrymple, Viscount Stair, acquired the estate of Carscreugh, near Glenluce, and built the tower-house there, whose ruins still stand today. Stair's "Institutions of the Law of Scotland", largely written at Carscreugh and published in 1681, was quite simply the first systematic exposition of the principles of Scottish private law and the first attempt to found Scotland's positive laws on a rational and philosophical basis. Appearing at the time of the negotiations for a Treaty of Union of Parliaments with England, and indeed, written by one of the chief protagonists of the negotiations, it effectively confirmed the independence of a distinctively Scottish jurisprudence and enabled its survival, even after union with a powerful neighbour, possessing a distinctly different legal tradition. The continuing appeal today to Stair in the Scottish Courts, and in the House of Lords, and the daily use of the "Institutions" by practising lawyers, support Stair's claim that "no man did so much, to make the Law of this Kingdom known and constant as I have done, that not only bred lawyers, but generally the nobility and gentry of the nation might know their rights..."

James Dalrymple's origins were in Ayrshire, where he was born at Drummurchie in the parish of Barr in May 1619; his father was the proprietor of the small estate of Stair, which fell to his son in 1624. James Dalrymple's connections with Wigtownshire came through his marriage in 1643 to Margaret Ross, a second cousin, who was a talented and, it seems, strong-minded, heiress to the estate of Balneil, in the upper Luce valley. Eventually, after her father's death, they acquired the lands and

355

estate of Carscreugh, and it is from that point that the Stair family became identified with the area round Glenluce, at the head of Luce Bay. Andrew Symson commented in 1684 that Carscreugh had been erected recently in accordance with "modern architecture", but that, surrounded by bleak moors, it "would have been more pleasant, had it been in a more pleasant place". James Dalrymple was educated at the parish school of Mauchline, and then at Glasgow University. The 1640's were times of growing opposition to the personal government of Charles I and his attempts to impose prelacy on the Church of Scotland. As a convinced Presbyterian, Dalrymple entered the army which had been raised in Scotland by the Covenanters to oppose the king's liturgical innovations, and attained the rank of Captain in the Earl of Glencairn's regiment. At this time, he competed successfully – apparently still wearing his regimental uniform – for the chair of philosophy at Glasgow, which he held for six years and where he must have deepened his knowledge of natural law theory, which was to inform his writing of the "Institutions". Also at this time, he began the private study of civil law, which was not publicly taught at the time in Scotland. By 1647, he became an advocate at the Bar, but rapidly entered political life as one of those commissioned to treat with Charles II for his return to Britain from exile. From this point in his career, the tensions between his moderate Presbyterianism and his convinced monarchism, at a time when the extremes on either side rarely met, involved him in compromises in his public career which gained him many enemies. After the defeat of Charles II's forces by Cromwell at Worcester, Dalrymple had some tentative involvement with the Commonwealth and Protectorate governments, but no doubt the anglicising tendencies of the Cromwell era (Cromwell removed Scottish legal records to the Tower in 1651 and many were subsequently lost) caused him some anxiety and may have turned him more and more towards a systematic exposition of Scottish law. Certainly, after the Restoration of Charles II in 1660, he was received with favour, knighted and appointed to the Court of Session. Once again, however, his Presbyterianism caused him difficulty with the absolutist claims of the new king, and he refused to take the "declaration" which would have made the taking up of arms against the monarch unlawful. He was ultimately permitted to take a modified oath, and began his career in the Court of Session, whose decisions he began recording, and was at work negotiating for a Treaty of Union with England, which probably prompted him to complete his work on the principles and customs of law in Scotland. By the 1670's, he had represented Wigtownshire in Parliament and ultimately oversaw the publication in 1681 of the "Institutions" from his Wigtownshire seat, by now built at Carscreugh, Glenluce. Ultimately, the conditions for holding office under a Stuart king, who was sanctioning the persecution of "conventiclers" (those holding or attending open air religious services, rather than attend churches served by the royally appointed parish ministers) on Dalrymple's estates in South Ayrshire and Wigtownshire, became impossible: the turning point was the passing of the Test Act which required the renunciation of the National Covenant of 1638. Dalrymple did his best to disable the act, by incorporating within it a licence to resist royal tyranny, derived from Knox's Confession of Faith of 1560. After persecution began of those, including himself, who refused to take the oath, he fled in 1682 to Leyden, a flourishing intellectual centre of the time, where he published his *Decisions of the Lords of Council and Session*, and a physical treatise *Physiologia Nova Experimentalis*, which received a favourable review from Pierre Bayle, author of the famous *Dictionary*. While in the Netherlands, he was probably under surveillance from royal spies and, after being indicted for high treason in a plot against Charles II and his brother James, Duke of York, was possibly even subject to attempts at kidnapping. Probably as a result of this persecution, he entered the counsels of William of Orange, who recognised his abilities, and he gradually turned to open rebellion. He sailed with William's flagship, "The Brill" to Torbay in England and was rewarded for his close involvement in the settlement of the crowns on William and Mary by a rapid promotion to the Lord Presidency of the Court of Session, and to the peerage, as Viscount Stair, Lord Glenluce and Stranraer, in 1690. His very capacity for survival in the changing regimes made him subject to accusations of being a time-server in the last years of his life and there were many on both extremes of the political spectrum – both Jacobites and Covenanters – who were ready to find fault with his dominance over the Court of Session. At this time, he felt compelled to publish his *Apology*; but the situation worsened when his son John, also by now a distinguished lawyer, became deeply implicated in the Massacre of Glencoe. Shortly before his death in 1695 he published his philosophical work *A Vindication of the Divine Perfections*. He had established a dynasty, which continued to attain great distinction in Scottish law, in antiquities, and in the military (his grandson, the second Earl, obtained high command under Marlborough, and included references to his military successes in the design of his gardens at Newliston and at Castle Kennedy, Wigtownshire). Perhaps, however, none of his sons, however eminent in the law or the field of battle, ever attained quite the immortality or, indeed, the notoriety of his daughter, Janet Dalrymple, who was the real-life subject of Sir Walter Scott's *Bride of Lammermoor*. It is perhaps the last contradiction in a contradictory career, that the 1st Viscount Stair, who deduced Scots law and custom from rational principle, should obtain mention in the *Introduction* to the most romantic of Scott's novels.

* * *

The name and form of the *Institutions* were inspired by those of Justinian, who codified the laws of the Roman empire in the first half of the sixth century AD: in this context, "institutions", which, in Stair's time, were being published for legal systems all over Europe – in France, Germany and Holland – meant "first principles". Stair's work was in effect bringing Scotland into a general movement of the time to systematise the legal traditions of the emerging nation-states (using the vernacular, rather than Latin) and by appealing to philosophical underpinnings which had origins in Greece, Rome and the mediaeval Scholastics. The deductive form of the work was that employed by many seventeenth century scientific, legal and philosophical writers, who followed a mathematical and syllogistical model deriving ultimately from the Greeks, for rigorous deduction of principles, proceeding from the general to the particular. In this respect, Stair gave Scots law its reliance on principle, which would enable particular cases to be judged according to the general rule under which they fell. The content of the *Institutions* is the private law of Scotland, both civil and commercial, but excludes constitutional and administrative law, taxation, ecclesiastical and particularly criminal law. In his day, the major subject of law was property, particularly land, its transfer and protection. Like his contemporaries on the continent, including Hugo Grotius of the Netherlands by whom he was influenced, Stair drew on a common intellectual inheritance of natural law theory, ultimately derived from the metaphysics of Aristotle, but mediated by Cicero and the Stoics and more recently, the Scholastics, including Thomas Aquinas and the Spanish Jesuit, Suarez. Stair would have been familiar with such philosophical texts as part of his "studium generale" at Glasgow. This was no mere theoretical stance without practical impact, since the theory of natural law held that positive laws, generated by human agencies, were guided by and ultimately could be judged by natural law, which was "written by the finger of God upon man's heart, there to remain forever" and could be known by "right reason". Such general principles, which have been implanted in us by God as fit for our rational nature, were, for example, that promises should be kept, that there should be reparation for injuries, that property should be respected and so on. It implied, however, the possibility of a judgement on the conformity or non-conformity of positive laws to natural law, so enabling civil disobedience as a last resort, if the human authority failed to serve the welfare of the community which it had been instituted to serve. For Stair, the human legislative authority was further curbed by the presence of immemorial customs and institutions, which had a greater antiquity and were more in conformity with "equity" (or natural law) and more fundamental than acts of Parliament. In this latter respect, he emerges as more conservative than other Protestant political theorists of the time, such as Knox, Buchanan, Milton or **Rutherford.** This theoretical amalgam of natural law theory with some of the pragmatism of seventeenth century English constitutional theory allowed him to tread a middle path between the claims of divine right absolutists, who claimed a prescriptive force for the monarch's commands which would have overridden the natural law implanted in each man's conscience, and the radical democrats, who would have claimed supremacy for Parliament. It is interesting to observe how this middle path was followed in his own political career, which fell foul both of the religious intolerance of the Stuart kings, and of the radical claims of the Parliament, suspicious of any monarchical privilege. Stair's own political unpopularity may have contributed to the generation of the macabre legend surrounding his daughter's death, since his enemies may have seized upon rumour and doubts in order to discredit him: if so, they contributed to the genesis of one of the classics of romantic literature. Janet Dalrymple, who had apparently secretly contracted herself to marry the impoverished Lord Rutherfurd, descended from an ancient noble family, was prevailed upon by her parents (and perhaps chiefly her mother) to break the engagement and to marry the son of Sir David Dunbar of Baldoon, in the Machars of Wigtownshire. The facts of the case have been obscured by subsequent versions and controversy: all that is confirmed by the contemporary parish minister of Kirkinner, **Andrew Symson,** who knew both parties, is that the bride died shortly

Dumfries and Galloway

after the marriage and that later the bridegroom died from a riding accident. More lurid versions, however, rapidly circulated: that the bride stabbed her husband on her wedding night and died a grinning maniac (the version embodied by Sir Walter Scott in his novel *The Bride of Lammermoor* and adopted as the basis for Donizetti's opera *Lucia di Lammermoor*), or that the bridegroom stabbed the bride; or, the version favoured by some family members, that the disappointed suitor concealed himself in the wedding chamber and attacked his successful rival. Be that as it may, Sir Walter Scott received the story from a relative, who was in turn related to the Stairs, and who was able to provide details which were incorporated into the novel: the bride's brother remembered long afterwards the marble coldness of his sister's hands as they rode towards the Kirk at Glenluce for the marriage. From the details so gathered, Scott created his most powerful political and sexual drama, dictated while he was apparently fatally ill: though Scott denied that the bride's father was based on the character of the great Lord Stair, with whose work Scott was familiar in his legal capacity, the backdrop of the novel showing the rise to power of the bride's Whiggish family, in contradistinction to the dispossessed and declining old aristocracy of the first suitor's, symbolises much about the Stairs' success at the time.

BIBLIOGRAPHY:
The Institutions of the Law of Scotland (1681); *The Decisions of the Lords of Council and Session* (1683-1687); *Physiologia Nova Experimentalis* (1686); *An Apology for Sir James Dalrymple of Stair* (1690); *A Vindication of the Divine Perfections* ...(1695); Walter Scott, *The Bride of Lammermoor* (1819); AJG Mackay, *Memoir of Sir James Dalrymple* (1873); David M Walker, *Stair Tercentenary Studies* (1981)

PLACES TO VISIT: Castle Kennedy Gardens, Wigtownshire, are open to the public and Castle Kennedy, now ruined, was built by Lord Stair's son and was the ancestral home of the Stair family.

A Literary Guide

Sir John Ross and Sir James Clerk Ross
1777-1856 ; 1800-1862
Stranraer / Inch

Sir John Ross and Sir James Clerk Ross were uncle and nephew from an old Wigtownshire family. John Ross promoted his nephew's career, taking him on his famous journey to discover the North West Passage between the Atlantic and the Pacific. Among their achievements were the mapping of vast areas of the Arctic Circle, the recording of natural history and ethnology of the area and the discovery of the magnetic North Pole, and Sir James Clerk Ross's exploration of the Antarctic, including the Ross Sea and Ice Shelf.

Sir John Ross

Sir James Clerk Ross

Andrew Ross, father to John Ross, was minister at the old Church of Inch, now demolished. He was married to Elizabeth Corsane, member of an old Dumfries family, which had provided many Provosts to the burgh. They had five sons, of whom John Ross was born in 1777. His mother died giving birth to his youngest brother. John Ross entered the Navy, as a First Class Volunteer, at the extraordinarily early age of nine. Until 1789, he served aboard the "Pearl", and was apprenticed at Greenock for four years, during which he went on several voyages to the West Indies and on three to the Baltic. At the age of 17, he entered the East India Company and travelled with the company on three voyages in five years. At this time, he was gaining knowledge in astronomy. In 1799, he became a midshipman, and saw active service aboard two sloops of war and a frigate. In 1803, he joined the flagship of Sir James Saumarez, became a lieutenant in 1805 and showed great bravery when severely wounded at Bilbao, cutting out a Spanish vessel from beneath the batteries. He learnt surveying techniques from Captain William Broughton, who had been himself trained by one of Captain Cook's officers; in 1808-9, he was learning Swedish and serving in the Baltic and at Stockholm. His diplomatic services, negotiating peace in the Baltic, were rewarded with an honour from the king of Sweden, and a promotion in 1812 to the command of the "Briseis", which saw active service during the war. His surveying and astronomical knowledge was developed on board the "Actaeon", which visited the White Sea, where he determined the longitude of Archangel by observing the eclipse of Jupiter's satellites. By 1815, he was in command of the "Driver", operating in the North Sea, and had been at sea for thirty years. At this time, he married Christian Adair, and was planning the building of his Stranraer home, the "North West Castle", whose construction lasted from 1815-1825. By this time, he had a pension and had accumulated prize money from his naval victories. His brother, George, was a merchant and entrepreneur, married to Christian Clark. His third son, James Clark, was born in 1800 and had followed his uncle in joining the Navy, aged 11. His uncle John did everything he could to promote a favourite nephew's career, and James Clark Ross was taken on board the "Briseis" as a First Class Volunteer. It was a close personal and professional relationship which was to last for the rest of John Ross's life, and one which did not always run smoothly. James Clark Ross was given quick promotion to Midshipman and Master's Mate. He moved with his uncle to the "Actaeon" and the "Driver". By 1815, there was a revival of interest in the existence of a "North West passage" between the Atlantic and the Pacific, and much speculation about the existence of a "Polar Sea", which had powerful advocates in the Admiralty. Reports from returning whalers indicated that the conditions were more favourable than they had been for years, in that the ice seemed to be shifting and a passage northwards might be possible. The second Secretary of the Admiralty, Sir John Barrow, was convinced of the existence of an Arctic Sea, which would allow passage for navigation, and through his friendship with Sir Joseph Banks, who was then President of the Royal Society, he was enabled to promote an entire series of Arctic expeditions. Rewards

A Literary Guide

for attaining the furthest northern latitude were offered and the aims of the expedition, which was to be scientific and geographical, were specified: "To endeavour to correct and amend the very defective geography of the Arctic Regions, especially on the side of America. To attempt the circumnavigation of old Greenland, if an island or islands, as there is reason to suppose. To prove the existence or non-existence of Baffin's Bay; and to endeavour to ascertain the practicability of a passage from the Atlantic to the Pacific Ocean, along the Northern Coast of America". John Ross, aboard the "Driver", was serving off the Wigtownshire coast, when the invitation arrived to lead a search for the North West Passage. He selected the "Isabella" as his flagship, and ordered the modifications which would be necessary to withstand the pressure of the ice. Scientific instruments were provided, and special clothing issued for the men. Ross had instructions to head for the Davis Strait, and to look for currents which were believed to hold the clue to the opening of the passage. The Admiralty gave him detailed instructions as to what to do when and if he reached the Pacific. On board was his nephew, James Clark Ross, who joined as a midshipman. As they reached the southern tip of Greenland, they began dropping overboard specially designed copper cylinders, with messages inside in several languages, asking for the place and time of their discovery to be noted, and the whole to be returned to the Admiralty, to enable the course of the cylinders to be logged. As they proceeded north, they made contact both with the native population of Inuit (they met representatives of the Etah Eskimos, hitherto unknown in the West, and Ross called them, somewhat fancifully, "Atlantic Highlanders"), and with friendly whaling ships. Ross assigned his nephew to work with Parry and Sabine, both to become well-known as explorers and naturalists of the Arctic; John Ross himself invented a dredging tool, known as the "deep sea clam", to take samples from the bottom of the sea. Thanks to Ross's leadership and well-stocked provisions, the men were well looked after and suffered no illness, despite the dangers of the ice, storms and near collision with their sister ship. At a critical point, in Lancaster Sound, however, Ross made the decision that there was no passage to be found , because of the obstruction of a range of mountains he claimed to be able to see and which he named "Croker's Mountains". It was a decision which was to haunt Ross for the rest of his life, and later members of both of his own and of the other crew, from the ship

"Alexander", were to claim that they could see, at this point, the prospect of a passage through the ice. Ross turned, and continued to explore the coast of Baffin Bay, baptising capes and coasts liberally after those at home, and, after picking up a polar bear and numerous natural historical samples, returned to the Shetlands. He had successfully mapped Baffin Bay, whose existence had been subject to doubt, extended the whaling grounds, and contributed to knowledge about the native population. His samples included one of "Sabine's Gull" and a "Caput medusae", dredged from the bottom. When, however, Ross announced to the Admiralty that no passage existed, Sir John Barrow was merciless in his treatment of Ross, and there began a vendetta between the two men which lasted for the rest of their lives. The controversy served to jog the memories of officers, including James Clark Ross, who had hitherto remained silent, and who now expressed doubts about what had, or had not, been seen at the bay in Lancaster Sound. When, in 1819, Ross promptly published his account of his *Voyage of Discovery*, Sir John Barrow immediately retaliated in print, and the scientist, Captain Sabine, also took issue with Ross in his *Remarks on the Account of the Late Voyage of Discovery to Baffin's Bay*, to which Ross again replied, point by point. Although Ross might receive promotion from the Admiralty, Barrow was unflinching in his enmity, and prevented him, in the future, from obtaining a ship. Ross retreated to Wigtownshire for ten years, where, after his wife's death in 1833, he was left with a three year old son, Andrew. James Clark Ross, however, continued with Arctic expeditions, and, like many of the officers from the 1818 expedition, went on William Parry's expedition, which, after over-wintering, managed to sail half-way through the passage. Parry believed that there might be a passage closer to the North American mainland, and, in the exploration mounted northwards from Hudson's Bay, James Clark Ross was engaged in the surveying of the inlets, one of which, Ross Bay, was named after him. On this expedition, Ross was the naturalist, and paid particular attention to scientific tests and ornithology, which was rewarded by his discovery of Ross's Gull in 1823. After the expedition returned, having experienced bad damage to one of its vessels, Ross was elected a Fellow of the Linnaean Society. In 1826, an expedition was planned to go to the North Pole over the ice, using two especially designed boats on sledges, of which Parry was to command one and Ross the second, but the

A Literary Guide

headway they made each day was undone by the movement of the ice southwards, so that the attempt was eventually abandoned. Parry and Ross arrived back at the Admiralty just at the moment Franklin and **Richardson** returned from their own land-based Arctic explorations. In 1828, the account of the voyage was published, with Ross contributing the *Appendix* on zoology. His uncle, however, brooding over his earlier failure, was also publishing in this year his reflections on the uses of steam-power, which he proposed to apply to Arctic exploration and which was a notion largely opposed by the Admiralty. His *A Treatise on Navigation by Steam* was published in 1828 and found few supporters, save in Mr Booth, the manufacturer of Booth's Gin. John Ross eventually persuaded Booth to back an expedition and made special adjustments to a steamer, fitting it for Arctic service, and choosing as his second-in-command his nephew, James Clark Ross. The use of a steamer fired the public imagination, and the vessel was the attraction of the fashionable world for the season before it left on its journey northwards. Shortly after leaving port, Ross became aware of the defects in its manufacture and by the time the expedition had reached his native Wigtownshire, it had suffered several engine failures, Ross had had to amputate a man's arm, and his second crew, aboard the "John", had mutinied in Stranraer harbour, almost at Ross's very front door. Given the defects in the "Victory"'s engineering, it was a triumph of determination to reach the Arctic at all, but Ross had later occasion to be thankful that, but for the "Victory"'s inefficiency, he would have gone so far north as never to find his way back through the ice. The expedition returned to the scene of Ross's defeat at Lancaster Sound, and the men were able to plunder the wreck of Parry's vessel for extra stores. Ross named the Boothia peninsula after his patron and managed, despite the ship's being frequently jammed by ice, to penetrate 250 miles further north than any other expedition. They eventually abandoned the machinery on board and used the ship under sail to reach a safe haven for the winter. Thanks to Ross's insight into Arctic conditions, they successfully over-wintered, imitating the Eskimo diet of fat. During these winters, James Clerk Ross made successful contact with the Eskimos, carried out explorations overland to find more about a possible passage, and – most memorably – discovered the magnetic North Pole on 1st June 1831. Their last winter, which set a record for Arctic endurance only surpassed in the twentieth century, was spent using the stores from Parry's wreck and living in an igloo of their own construction. Since the "Victory" had been abandoned, they eventually made their way out in small boats, and were rescued by a whaler, which turned out to be the "Isabella", in which John Ross had first sailed to the Arctic. After four and a half years in the Arctic, Ross was received at Windsor Castle, and was heartened to find that several, including **Richardson**, his brother George, and Captain George Back, had proposed rescue expeditions during their prolonged absence. The results of their expedition were that the exploration and mapping of hundreds of miles of coastline had been made, and a further 500 miles were covered by James Clark Ross on a sledge. The Gulf of Boothia had been discovered and the scientific and zoological discoveries, capped by the discovery of the magnetic pole, were unsurpassed until recent times. Honours came from both home and abroad: Ross was knighted and made Companion of the Bath, and Booth was made a baronet. The Admiralty paid the crew for their long service and all received promotion. Despite the success, there were signs of a split between the two Rosses, as James Clark Ross appeared to dispute whether he had in fact only been a second-in-command, and the elder Ross appeared grudging in the acknowledgement of James Clark Ross's sole credit for the discovery of the magnetic north pole. Nonetheless, the record of the journey was published in 1835, with special reports appended by James Clark Ross. John Ross's publications were never without controversy, however, and in this case, he received, first, a response from the engineer of the "Victory's" engines, and then a further lambasting from Sir John Barrow, whose *Voyages of Discovery and Research within the Arctic Regions, from the Year 1818 to the Present Time* implied, to Ross's outrage, that the expedition had been solely aimed at profit. While the elder Ross was given a consulship at Stockholm from 1839 until 1846, where his old knowledge of Sweden and the Swedes proved useful, James Clark Ross was occupied, until 1838, in conducting the first magnetic survey of the British Isles, with a brief interlude to rescue a whaler stranded in the Davis Straits. His new challenge came when , in that same year, the British Association for the Advancement of Science declared that the greatest geographical and scientific deficiency was in knowledge of the most extreme part of the Southern hemisphere. James Clark Ross, by now the most experienced naval officer in Arctic conditions, as well as a respected

A Literary Guide

authority on science and navigation, was chosen to command the "Erebus". He took with him the young Joseph Dalton Hooker, who was destined to achieve even greater eminence than his father, an eminent naturalist, in the natural sciences. The aims of the expedition were to engage in a series of co-ordinated magnetic observations, to set up magnetic observation stations, and to visit the Falkland Islands. Clearly, both for Ross and the Admiralty, the discovery of the South Magnetic Pole was the principal object. Despite his recent engagement to Ann, daughter of Thomas Coulman of Whitgift Hall, Yorkshire, Ross set off on the immensely long journey. Perhaps his most significant discovery, apart from successful magnetic observations co-ordinated with stations throughout the world, was of the Ross Ice-Shelf, an impenetrable barrier of ice cliffs, which prevented an approach to the Pole. In all, three attempts were made to approach the Pole, each time encountering severe difficulty and, on one occasion, there was near-collision between the two ships and a procession of icebergs. In 1842, after his third trip, the last to be conducted solely under the power of sail, he obtained the gold medal from the Royal Geographical Society, a knighthood and an honorary degree from Oxford. He was happy to settle with his wife, Ann, at Aylesbury, to catch up with writing the account of his voyage, and to be consulted by the Admiralty on scientific matters. Despite a promise to his wife's family not to engage in further exploration, however, this was not to be his last trip. His uncle, Sir John, had been agitating for some time for a rescue expedition to be sent after John Franklin, from whom nothing had been heard by 1847. The Admiralty resisted the notion of a rescue, partly on the strength of John Ross's own record in surviving Arctic winters for over four years; James Clark Ross himself resisted the proposal, but as popular pressure grew, **Sir John Richardson** was dispatched on a route down the Mackenzie river, while, eventually, the choice fell on James Clark Ross to lead an expedition by sea in 1848. In so far as Franklin's rescue was concerned, the expedition was a failure, and the party failed to join his route, returning in 1850; but a further survey of the coast was accomplished. Sir John Ross was still, however, proposing his own scheme, involving smaller boats , which he believed to be the key to success in the Arctic, and eventually received support from the Hudson's Bay Company. By the time of its return in 1851, without news of Franklin, Sir John Ross was 74 years old. Even his personal liability for the financial failure of the expedition did little to dampen his energy, and he took an active interest in the improvement of the connection between Stranraer and Ireland, and the new telegraph service from Ireland to Scotland. When he eventually died in 1856, it was his nephew, who, despite their differences, made the funeral arrangements at Kensal Green Cemetery. James Clark Ross himself lived quietly at Aylesbury, until the death of his beloved wife in 1857, which affected him deeply and may have further contributed to the decline of his health, already somewhat impaired by his tremendous expenditure of energy and strength in the Arctic and Antarctic. He outlived his uncle only by six years, and was buried in Buckinghamshire.

* * *

It is thanks to the meticulous accounts of both Sir John and Sir James Clark Ross that we are able to reconstruct their remarkable voyages. Mostly, they are workmanlike diaries of the facts, but those facts are certainly astounding, and there are occasional hints of the writer's sense of drama, as when John Ross wrote, in his earliest account, that "we are now in a region in which no human being has ever Breathed.." On the occasion, during the second voyage, when they were forced to abandon the erstwhile steam-powered "Victory" and set off in small boats, John Ross reflects on what they were leaving behind, for an uncertain future: "I did not pass the point where she ceased to be visible without stopping to take a sketch of this melancholy desert, rendered more melancholy by the solitary, abandoned and helpless home of our past years, fixed in immoveable ice, till time should perform on her his usual work". The account of the second voyage also includes, along with coloured plates based on the drawings of John Ross, fascinating biographies of the Eskimos, "the narrowest and most insulated tribe of men that has yet been discovered by navigators". James Clark Ross contributed his own account of the discovery of the North Magnetic Pole, somewhat uneasily acknowledged by his uncle in the succeeding chapter, describing how, when they were assured that there was no further deviation possible in the needle from the perpendicular, they erected a cairn and planted the Union Jack. "Had it been a pyramid as large as that of Cheops, I am not quite sure that it would have done more than satisfy our ambition, under the feelings of that exciting day". James Clark Ross's appendix detailing

A Literary Guide

their scientific observations includes a vocabulary of English, Danish and Eskimo words and phrases, and accounts of the fauna, including Ross's Arctic salmon and the *Larus Rossii*, biographies of the crew members, and meticulously recorded observations on meteorology, latitudes and longitudes and geology. His own accounts of the Antarctic voyages include passages demonstrating the dangers to which they were potentially and actually subject: "our ships still rolling and groaning amidst the heavy fragments of crushing bergs, over which the ocean rolled its mountainous waves, throwing huge masses one upon another, and then again burying them deep beneath its foaming waters, dashing and grinding them together with fearful violence."

BIBLIOGRAPHY:
John Ross - *A Voyage of Discovery ... for the Purpose of Exploring Baffin's Bay, and Enquiring in to the Probability of a North-West Passage* (1819); *A Treatise on Navigation by Steam* (1828); *Narrative of a Second Voyage in Search of a North-West Passage ...*(1835) - includes Reports of James Clark Ross; John Barrow, *Voyages of Discovery and Research within the Arctic Regions, from the Year 1818 to the Present Time* (1846); Edward Sabine, *Remarks on the Account of the Late Voyage of Discovery to Baffin's Bay* (1819)

James Clark Ross - *A Voyage of Discovery and Research in the Southern and Antarctic Regions, during the Years 1839-43* (1847)

PLACES TO VISIT: The North West Castle, now extended, has become a hotel in Stranraer; Stranraer Museum has a "Ross Room" display dedicated to the achievement of the Rosses.

Sir Andrew Agnew of Lochnaw 1818-1893
Lochnaw, North Rhins

Sir Andrew Agnew, a member of the family of the Agnews of Lochnaw, which had been established at Lochnaw Castle since 1330, recorded the history of the hereditary sheriffdom held by members of his family. The remarkable continuity of the office, held until 1749, meant that the Agnews witnessed and prominently participated in many of the significant events of Scottish history, such as the Covenanting period and the Jacobite rebellions, and the case material to which Sir Andrew had access gives a unique insight into the social and economic conditions of Wigtownshire over four centuries.

Portrait of Sir Andrew Agnew in the early 1880s. *Courtesy Sir Crispin Agnew.*

Sir Andrew Agnew was born in 1818 and succeeded his father, Sir Andrew, in 1849. His father was remembered for his efforts to legislate on Sabbath observance, and the prominent monument on the hill near Leswalt was erected in his memory. He was educated at Harrow and served with the 93rd Highlanders during the rebellion in Canada in 1838. He retired as captain of the 4th Light Dragoons and was Member of Parliament for the county of Wigtownshire from 1856-1868. He was a member of the Liberal Party, a hard-working back-bencher, but was finally defeated by Lord Garlies, who stood for the Conservatives in 1868. After that date, he spent much time at Lochnaw, being particularly interested in tree-planting on the Lochnaw estate. He was vice-Lieutenant of the County, a Justice of the Peace, and a member of the County Council. Like his father, he was a member of the Free Church of Scotland. In 1845, he married Lady Louisa Noel,

A Literary Guide

daughter of the first Earl of Gainsborough, who predeceased him in 1883, and by whom he had a large family.

* * *

The *Agnews of Lochnaw: a History of the Hereditary Sheriffs of Galloway* appeared in 1864, with a much revised and expanded version, *The Hereditary Sheriffs of Galloway*, appearing posthumously in 1893. Sir Andrew had ready access to his own family papers, and to those of his neighbours, as well as a well-informed "appetite for antiquarian gossip", which enabled him to spice his history with anecdote and family stories. The office of hereditary sheriff was established in 1452, with the principal charge of keeping the peace and executing laws. This included powers of capital punishment for murder or robbery and was rewarded with considerable emoluments, including "the best ox or cow or unridden horse". The Agnews had been established at Lochnaw at least a century prior to their acquiring this office: while in the first volume, he states that the Agnews acquired Lochnaw after one Agneau de l'Isle had been involved with Alexander Bruce in the conquest of Ulster, by the time of writing the second volume he states, with greater probability, that the history of the Agnew family and its relationships with the Baliols and de la Zouches, is an account of how a group of Anglo-Normans, tied by blood in France "and afterwards by those of property in Hertfordshire, gave to Galloway.. six overlords, a justiciary, and a line of hereditary sheriffs, as well as two crowned Scottish kings". Thanks to the continuity of the office until abolition in 1747, the account of the Agnew family provides Sir Andrew with plenty of rich material : the turbulent times of Kennedy ascendancy in Kyle and Galloway (including the incident of the roasting of the Abbot of Crossraguel), the persecution of the Covenanters (during which time the Agnews were deprived of office for refusing to take the Test oath), the stormy reception of the Union in Dumfries and Galloway and the loyal rallying against the Pretender's forces in 1745 are all well described. The second edition is enlivened by accounts of a sixteenth century household, a sheep stealing trial in the seventeenth century, and of the country life of an eighteenth century laird. The cases laid before the sheriff certainly offer fascinating insights into the social and economic conditions of each era: for example, for the sixteenth century, there are accounts of affrays in Edinburgh between

Galloway lairds, all with armed retinues (a social context which forms the background to *The Grey Man* by **SR Crockett**) and of the turbulent relations between baronial neighbours, in which the sheriff was more likely to be participant than impartial judge. In the seventeenth century, we read of the trial of Maggie Osborne as a witch, on the grounds that she was seen to have spat out the holy wafer after communion, and that this was swallowed by a devil in the shape of a toad. Sir Andrew leaves us with a characteristic eighteenth century picture of the last of the sheriffs, a larger than life character, who was mentioned by Sir Walter Scott (*History of Scotland*) and who was remembered riding to court in Wigtown, with a long train of Stranraer lawyers in his retinue, and striking the table with his riding whip when displeased. After the abolition of the hereditary sheriffdom, Lochnaw remained a baron-court, for regulating relations with the estate tenants.

BIBLIOGRAPHY:
The Agnews of Lochnaw: a History of the Hereditary Sheriffs of Galloway (1864); *The Hereditary Sheriffs of Galloway* (1893)

PLACES TO VISIT: The Tor of Craigoch, near Leswalt, was erected to the memory of Sir Andrew Agnew's father, and offers magnificent of the North Rhins peninsula and Loch Ryan.

A Literary Guide

James Barke
1905-1958
Rhins of Galloway

James Barke, the son of farm-workers from Galloway, set his most powerful and epic novel, "The Land of the Leal", in the grinding poverty of farm life in the Rhins of Galloway: the leading characters eventually escape, only to find a different squalor in the industrial landscape of Glasgow. Barke, a Scottish Nationalist with strong socialist leanings, also wrote a series of novels about the life of **Burns** *and produced an edition of the poet's work.*

James Barke

James Barke was born in 1905 in Torwoodlee, Selkirkshire, and moved to Tulliallan in Fife, when he was two. His detailed knowledge of the locations and dairying routines of the Rhins of Galloway came from his parents' experience there. In 1918, they moved to Glasgow; their itinerary from Galloway to the Borders and ultimately to Glasgow is closely paralleled in that of their fictional counterparts in Barke's novel *The Land of the Leal*. Barke entered the employment of the shipbuilders, Barclay Curle, as a cost accountant. In 1933, he embarked on a career of writing, with his first novel *The World His Pillow*, followed by *The Wild MacRaes* (1934) and *Major Operation*, an examination of Glasgow's industrial system from the point of view of a worker and a businessman. The success he achieved encouraged him to give up work at the shipyard and to devote himself to writing: *Gregarach, The End of the High Bridge* and *The Devil in his Kitchen* rapidly appeared. His massive master-work, *The Land of the Leal*, appeared in 1939 and has been compared to Lewis Grassic Gibbon's *A Scots Quair*, whose heroine, Chris Guthrie, also makes the move from a rural scene to industrial poverty in a city. His interest in **Burns** developed during the Second World War, during which he returned to the shipyard, rather than participate in military service. Between 1946 and 1954, five novels (which began as a trilogy) were published describing the life of **Burns**; a posthumous work *Bonnie Jean* appeared in 1959. In 1955, he produced a critical edition of Burns's songs and poems, in which were sixty works published for the first time. Barke collaborated with Sydney Goodsir Smith and DeLancey Ferguson on a definitive edition of the *Merry Muses of Caledonia*. Barke prospered as a result of the sale of the Burns novels, and moved from Glasgow to Daljarrock, Ayrshire, where he and his wife ran a hotel. Unfortunately, Barke began to drink and lost his earnings, and was forced to return to Glasgow. He died there in 1958.

* * *

"The Land of the Leal" is the utopia of which the protagonists of the novel – Jean and David Ramsay – dream, where "all the tears wiped away; all sorrows ended; every discord resolved" and which they in vain seek to grasp, in their progress from the drudgery of farm-work to the new drudgery of the city. It would not be far fetched to regard the novel as a re-assessment of the question of the relationship between the countryside and the city, which exercised the Kailyard school, but without its certainty that rural life was idyllic or that industrial life was wholly without hope. What is impressive in the early part of the book, set in the Rhins of Galloway, is the broad cyclical sweep, the rhythm of the eternal certainties of the land, with its rotation of seasons and duties, which keep the farm-worker bound, and which are echoed on the human level, in the ever-recurring pregnancies, the cycle of life and death. Mingled with the Biblical language, with which the book opens and which belongs to the older generation, whose memories and expectations take us back to the early nineteenth century, is the rich dialect of Galloway and its place-names. At one point in the novel, the land of the Rhins is invoked through a veritable incantation of the harsh and exotic syllables of its remote-sounding Gaelic names: "Ringvinachan, Ringuinea: / Slunkrainey, Slouchnawen, Sandell Bay, Sandhead; / Tarbet, Tandoo, Terally.." The figures in the novel are types , representative of their particular generation and circumstances: Tom Gibson never knew or wished to know anything but work on the land; David and Jean Ramsay, who aspire beyond it,

A Literary Guide

largely fail to make the transition to city life, whereas their son Andy, a thinly disguised representation of Barke himself, becomes a Socialist and joins the fight for the Socialist cause in Spain. The characters are also, however, closely observed individuals, set in an environment described with equally ruthless honesty: there is Jean, with her sharp tongue and extraordinary self-will, and David with his sensitive and intellectual temperament, ultimately highly dependent on Jean. Barke clearly drew on his observation of his parents, who are also described in his autobiography: once again, the lack of sentimentalism in the book belies its apparently pastoral title - *The Green Hills Far Away*. Barke's edition of **Burns'** poetry, which he claimed included twenty poems published for the first time, and another forty not included in collected editions, received short shrift from critics, who claimed that he gave no information on the sources of the new poems, nor distinguished between the songs Burns wrote and those he re-worked from traditional sources. Two of Barke's fictionalised novels of Burns' life refer to the Dumfriesshire period: *The Crest of the Broken Wave* (set at Ellisland) and *The Well of the Silent Harp* (in Dumfries). Barke would have objected to critics who felt that he dwelt unnecessarily on Burns's sexual escapades that, in line with his Marxist-influenced historical relativism, he had "done the best I can for my generation" in interpreting the Bard's life. One cannot help but feel, however, that the combination of novel and accurate history is not always happy.

BIBLIOGRAPHY:
The World His Pillow (1933); *The Wild MacRaes* (1934); *The End of the High Bridge* (1935); *Major Operation* (1936); *The Land of the Leal* (1939); *The Green Hills Far Away* (1940); *The Wind that Shakes the Barley* (1946); *The Song in the Green Thorn Tree* (1947); *The Wonder of All the Gay World* (1949); *The Crest of the Broken Wave* (1953); *The Well of the Silent Harp* (1954); *Poems and Songs of Robert Burns* (1955); *Bonnie Jean* (1959); with Sydney Goodsir Smith, *Merry Muses of Caledonia* (1959)

William Todd
1774-1863
Drummore, Kirkmaiden parish

William Todd was parish schoolmaster of Kirkmaiden for 49 years, having been born in Girthon parish near Gatehouse. He left a slim published "Clerical History of the Parish of Kirkmaiden" and a bulky manuscript history of Kirkmaiden, with invaluable details of its folklore and antiquities, and it was his meticulous recording which enabled later archaeologists to recover the Kirkmadrine Christian stones, some of Scotland's earliest Christian monuments.

Todd's life is known from his own manuscript account, which was written in 1854 at the age of eighty. The writing of it seems to have been partly prompted by the need to write an apologia for himself, after he was deposed from office after 49 years' service by the Kirkmaiden Session, for adhering to the Free Church of Scotland in the "Disruption" of 1843. His autobiography is written with characteristic attention to detail: he was born on the farm at Syllodioch in Girthon parish, where his father worked first as a shoemaker and then took charge of the drove cattle for the Broughton estate, during which time they lived at The Temple at Cally. One of his earliest memories, at three years of age, was of hearing with trepidation of the attack on St Mary's Isle by John Paul Jones. He showed early promise during his education at Gatehouse, writing verses, drawing up a plan of the town, studying Greek and beginning to teach. He continued private teaching of groups of farmers' children, when his family moved to Leswalt, in premises at a farm near Clayhole. When he was selected to draw up the unpopular Militia Lists of young men eligible for military service in 1797, he was subjected to threats by unwilling recruits and deemed it safer to take up a similar teaching post at Kirkmaiden in the Rhins. He eventually succeeded to the parish schoolmaster in 1799 and by 1801 was instrumental in having the school rebuilt in the grounds of the Kirk Covenant near Drummore. Despite cramped conditions even at the new school and his complaints about the

A Literary Guide

popularity of whisky shops in Kirkmaiden, his enthusiasm for learning and recording life around him appears to have continued undimmed throughout his long term of office. He became Session Clerk and Precentor, attempted to found a Temperance Society, visited Edinburgh and studied educational methods there, and by 1815 was corresponding with **Joseph Train**, who was collecting information on Wigtownshire folklore and superstitions for Mr Walter Scott, who was then working on *Tales of My Landlord*. He apparently also designed sundials, made a clock out of wire and wood showing the motions of the heavens, and created a patent bar-frame beehive. By 1841, his hearing was failing and he was seeking to retire on a small pension, but the Disruption of the Church of Scotland over the issue of patronage, in which he took a strong stance for the new Free Kirk, caused a rift with the heritors and Kirk Session, so that he was eventually deposed without pension and lost his house at High Curghie. He retired to a cottage which he built at Drummore, where he had designed the Free Kirk, but even in old age was sought out by Sir Arthur Mitchell for his recollections of antiquities in the parish. He is buried in the churchyard of the Kirk Covenant near Drummore, close to the ruined walls of his old school.

* * *

Todd's sole published work, a slim and now very rare volume on the *Clerical History of the Parish of Kirkmaiden*, 1860, though largely devoted to post-Reformation ministers, contains the sole precious reference to a lost Christian stone discovered close to his own house and schoolroom: "Nigh to the house of Low Curghie, a grave was lately opened up, covered with a flag of slaty stone, on which was a Latin inscription, but so wasted by time that nothing could be gathered from it further than that the person's name was Ventidius and that he was a sub-deacon of the Church". The lost Ventidius stone, showing evidence of an astonishing sophistication in Church organisation in the Rhins in the early 6th Century AD, is one of the group of nationally important Christian gravestones in the Rhins, which may on that account lay claim, along with Whithorn, to be the earliest of Scotland's Christian settlements. In the case of the Kirkmadrine Christian stones too, Todd's observation and minute recording were critical: Sir Arthur Mitchell discovered two

Christian monuments in the churchyard at Kirkmadrine, probably in about 1860, and on asking for information from local residents, was directed to William Todd, by then retired and living in Drummore. From an old drawing, probably made by Todd in about 1810, he was able to discover that the stones had only become gateposts perhaps in the 1840's, but had originally stood in the churchyard itself, and that there had also been a third stone, with a Latin inscription: "Initium et Finis". Todd's drawing and the publicity given to it by Mitchell eventually led to the discovery of the third stone, embedded in the manse gatepost at Sandhead. From these monuments, their apparently Gaulish lettering and names, now on display at Kirkmadrine church, archaeologists have been able to deduce conclusions with significant implications for the Christian mission to Scotland in the fifth and sixth century. Todd's manuscript history of Kirkmaiden parish, conceived along the lines of the *Statistical Account* and including sections on the geography, institutions, religious history and customs of the parish, include tantalising accounts of further monuments, including stone circles, removed or destroyed during his lifetime. Equally important are his records of popular superstitions of the parish, such as the bathing in the wells at St Medan's Cave on "Co' Sunday", in his day already on the decline. He is able to capture glimpses of a vanishing seventeenth century world, in which witches had nearly overrun the parish of Kirkmaiden and the minister was forced to send for a "weird woman from Wigtown", who could help him distinguish the true witches from the false. A spirited vernacular poem by Todd on Meg Elson, a witch who flourished in about 1800, is quoted in full by Innes Macleod in his *Discovering Galloway*. Todd contributed his poems to the *Cheap Magazine*, many letters to local newspapers, and essays on folklore to *The Galloway Register*, which may later have been taken up by **Robert de Bruce Trotter** in his lively account of Rhins life.

BIBLIOGRAPHY:
Statistical, Historical and Miscellaneous Memoranda of Matters Connected with the Parish of Kirkmaiden (1854 - unpublished ms. in Stranraer Public Library); *The Clerical History of the Parish of*

A Literary Guide

Kirkmaiden (1860); Arthur Mitchell, *Inscribed Stones at Kirkmadrine* in - *Proc. of Soc. of Antiquaries of Scotland, Vol. IX* (1870-1872); Innes Macleod, *Discovering Galloway* (1986)

PLACES TO VISIT: Kirk Covenant, Drummore, where Todd is buried, and the Kirkmadrine Stones, Kirkmadrine, near Sandhead, may be visited.

Dumfries and Galloway

A Literary Guide

Index to Authors

Agnew, Sir Andrew	370
Aird, Thomas	102
Anderson, Alexander	168
Barbour, John Gordon	221
Barke, James	373
Barrie, J M	81
Beattie, William	127
Bell, Benjamin	88
Blacklock, Thomas	32
Brown, Thomas	279
Buchan, John	43
Burns, Robert	75
Cannon, J F	334
Carlyle, Thomas	50
Clapperton, Hugh	36
Clark-Kennedy, Captain A W M	235
Crockett, Samuel R	202
Cunningham, Allan	114
Currie, James	137
Dalrymple, James, 1st Viscount Stair	355
Denniston, Captain J M	271
Dick, Rev C H	43
Donnan, Jeanie	332
Douglas, Thomas, 5th Earl Of Selkirk	252
Duncan, Rev Henry	64
Fraser, Gordon	312
Gerrond, John	134
Gillespie, Reverend W	216
Gladstone, Hugh S	149
Grieve, C M	5
Hannay, Patrick	283
Harper, Malcolm M	199
Hawkins, Susannah	70

Dumfries and Galloway

Heron, Robert	211
Heughan, Joseph	183
Hewison, J K	152
Hyslop, James	164
Irving, Edward	28
Jardine, Sir William	48
Kerr, Robert	188
Landsborough, Rev David	224
Latinus Stone	329
Lauderdale, John	315
Lewis, Stewart	58
Lowe, John	219
Macadam, John Loudon	237
McCormick, Andrew	292
McCulloch, J R	324
MacDiarmid, Hugh	See Grieve, C M
McDiarmid, John	105
McDowall, William	98
MacKenna, R W	95
MacKenzie, W	245
McKerlie, P H	309
McNeillie, John	301
MacTaggart, John	260
Malcolm, Sir John	16
Mayne, John	108
Maxwell Gavin	340
Maxwell James Clerk	191
Maxwell Sir Herbert	336
Mickle, W J	12
Miller, Frank	40
Montgomerie, Alexander	258
Morrison, John	131
Muirhead, Dr James	185
Murray, Alexander	295
Murray, Thomas	268
Neill, A S	1

A Literary Guide

Neilson, George	72
Nicholson, John	249
Nicholson, William	264
Paterson, William	122
Patrick, John, 3rd Marquess Of Bute	348
Rae, Peter	172
Reid, Prof H M B	208
Richardson, Sir John	91
Riddell, Maria	84
Robinson, Samuel	318
Ross, Sir James Clerk	361
Ross, Sir John	361
Ruskin, John	306
Rutherford, Samuel	274
Sayers, Dorothy Leigh	242
Service, Robert	119
Sharpe, Charles Kirkpatrick	61
Simpson, Rev Robert	161
Symson, Andrew	320
Telford, Thomas	22
Thomson, Joseph	143
Todd, William	376
Train, Joseph	286
Trotter, Alexander	232
Trotter, Isabella	230
Trotter, Dr James	180
Trotter, Robert de Bruce	176
Trotter, Robert	227
Vaus, Patrick	353
Waugh, Joseph Laing	155
Wilson, John	196
Wilson, Samuel	196
Wilson, Tom	158
Wilson, William	158
Wood, John Maxwell	111

Dumfries and Galloway

A Literary Guide

385

Dumfries and Galloway